BEGINNING
IOS 5 APPLICATION DEVELOPMENT

S0-CCF-084

BEGINNING

iOS 5 Application Development

BEGINNING

iOS 5 Application Development

Wei-Meng Lee

WILEY

John Wiley & Sons, Inc.

Beginning iOS 5 Application Development

Published by
John Wiley & Sons, Inc.
10475 Crosspoint Boulevard
Indianapolis, IN 46256
www.wiley.com

Copyright © 2012 by John Wiley & Sons, Inc., Indianapolis, Indiana

Published simultaneously in Canada

ISBN: 978-1-118-14425-1
ISBN: 978-1-118-22571-4 (ebk)
ISBN: 978-1-118-23584-3 (ebk)
ISBN: 978-1-118-26369-3 (ebk)

Manufactured in the United States of America

10 9 8 7 6 5 4 3 2 1

For general information on our other products and services please contact our Customer Care Department within the United States at (877) 762-2974, outside the United States at (317) 572-3993 or fax (317) 572-4002.

Wiley also publishes its books in a variety of electronic formats and by print-on-demand. Not all content that is available in standard print versions of this book may appear or be packaged in all book formats. If you have purchased a version of this book that did not include media that is referenced by or accompanies a standard print version, you may request this media by visiting http://booksupport.wiley.com. For more information about Wiley products, visit us at www.wiley.com.

Library of Congress Control Number: 2011944672

Dedicated to Steve Jobs, whose vision changed the way we use computers and inspires many to follow his footsteps. Thank you for the inspiration!

ABOUT THE AUTHOR

 **WEI-MENG LEE** is a technologist and founder of Developer Learning Solutions (www
.learn2develop.net), a technology company specializing in hands-on training on
the latest mobile technologies. Wei-Meng has many years of training experience and
his training courses place special emphasis on the learning-by-doing approach. His
hands-on approach to learning programming makes understanding the subject much
easier than reading books, tutorials, and documentation. His name regularly appears in
online and print publications such as DevX.com, MobiForge.com, and *CoDe Magazine*.
Wei-Meng Lee is frequently invited to speak at technological conferences, and recently participated
in Mobile Connections in the United States and DevTeach/DevMobile in Montreal, Canada.
Contact Wei-Meng at weimenglee@learn2develop.net.

ABOUT THE TECHNICAL EDITOR

TRENT SHUMAY is the founder and Chief Architect at Finger Food Studios, Inc., in the Vancouver,
BC, area. After graduating from the UBC Computer Science program, Trent spent 13 years in the
gaming and interactive entertainment space, where handheld gaming devices ignited his passion
for mobile development. Today, Finger Food Studios focuses on developing media-rich, interactive
mobile and web applications. You can reach Trent directly at trent@fingerfoodstudios.com.

CREDITS

ACKNOWLEDGMENTS

OVER THE PAST YEAR OR SO, the development landscape of Apple's iOS has changed greatly. The successful iOS is now in its fifth iteration, and the Xcode IDE has transitioned to a much easier-to-use version 4, with a tight integration of Interface Builder. I have received a lot of feedback from readers of the previous edition of this book, many of whom appreciate the hands-on approach that it takes. I also have received feedback from readers who are stumped by the changes that have occurred between Xcode versions 3 and 4; but such confusion epitomizes the rapid pace of change that all developers experience.

This new edition of the book was revised to cover both new technologies and the various feedback I have received. I had a thorough relook at the exercises readers were having issues with, to ensure that they can be easily followed and achieve the effect I intended. I also took this opportunity to revise all the examples using Xcode 4, which is the IDE included with iOS 5. Of course, this book covers new iOS 5 features — notably, the new iCloud feature that ships with iOS 5. I have also added some topics that would interest most iOS developers, such as how to import and export documents from within your application, programming the various sensors in iOS, and using JSON web services.

Writing a book is always exciting, but along with the excitement are long hours of hard work, straining to get things done accurately and on time. I would like to take this opportunity to thank a number of people who helped to make this book possible.

First, I want to thank my Executive Editor Robert Elliott, who started off as a stranger, but is now my good friend. Robert is not the usual AE, disappearing after the contract is signed. He has been involved throughout the entire writing process and is always ready to help. I can't say enough good things about Robert, so I will just say thank you, Robert!

Next, a huge thanks to Ami Sullivan, my project editor, who is always a pleasure to work with. Ami is the force behind the scenes, who makes the book appear on time on shelves in the bookstores! Thanks, Ami!

I also thank copy editor Luann Rouff and technical editor Trenton Shumay. They have been eagle-eye editing the book, ensuring that every sentence makes sense — both grammatically as well as technically. Thanks, Luann and Trent!

Last, but not least, I want to thank my parents, and my wife, Sze Wa, for all the support they have given me. They have selflessly adjusted their schedules to accommodate my busy schedule when I was working on this book. My wife, as always, has stayed up with me on numerous nights as I furiously worked to meet a deadline, and for this I would like to say to her and my parents: "I love you all!" Finally, to our lovely dog, Ookii, thanks for staying by our side. Now that the book is done, sorry . . . daddy needs to write another book. . .

CONTENTS

INTRODUCTION

APPLE FIRST OFFICIALLY ANNOUNCED the iOS 5 at the Worldwide Developers Conference (WWDC) in June 2011. After 7 betas and with much anticipation, Apple finally rolled out iOS 5 with the vastly improved iPhone 4S. With 200 new features added to the iOS, Apple is set to reign as the king of the mobile platform for the foreseeable future. This means developers also have vast potential for their applications — if you know how to program for the iOS platform. This book will show you how.

When I first started learning about iPhone and iPad development, I went through the same journey that most developers go through: Write a Hello World application, play around with Xcode and Interface Builder, try to understand what the code is doing, and repeat that process. I was also overwhelmed by the concept of a View Controller, and wondered why it was needed if I simply wanted to display a view. My background in developing for Windows Mobile and Android did not help much, and I had to start working with this concept from scratch.

This book was written to help jump-start beginning iPhone and iPad developers. It covers the various topics in a linear manner that enables you to progressively learn without being overwhelmed by the details. I adopt the philosophy that the best way to learn is by doing — hence, the numerous hands-on "Try It Out" sections in each chapter, which first demonstrate how to build something and then explain "How It Works."

Although iPhone and iPad programming is a huge topic, my aim in this book is to get you started with the fundamentals, help you understand the underlying architecture of the SDK, and appreciate why things are done in a certain way. It is beyond the scope of any one book to cover everything under the sun related to iPhone and iPad programming, but I am confident that after reading this book (and doing the exercises), you will be well equipped to tackle your next iPhone or iPad programming challenge.

WHO THIS BOOK IS FOR

This book is for the beginning iPhone and iPad developer who wants to start developing applications using the Apple iOS SDK. To truly benefit from this book, you should have some background in programming and at least be familiar with object-oriented programming concepts. If you are totally new to the Objective-C language, you might want to jump straight to Appendix C, which provides an overview of the language. Alternatively, you can use Appendix C as a quick reference while you tackle the various chapters, checking out the syntax as you try the exercises. Depending on your learning style, one of these approaches should work best for you.

While most of the chapters are geared toward developing for the iPhone, the concepts apply to iPad development as well. In cases where specific features are available only on the iPad, they are pointed out.

NOTE *All the examples discussed in this book were written and tested using the iOS SDK 5.0. While every effort has been made to ensure that the screen shots are as current as possible, the actual screen that you see may differ when the iOS SDK is revised.*

WHAT THIS BOOK COVERS

This book covers the fundamentals of iPhone and iPad programming using the iOS SDK. It is divided into 21 chapters and four appendices.

Chapter 1: Getting Started with iOS 5 Programming covers the various tools found in the iOS SDK and explains their uses in iPhone and iPad development.

Chapter 2: Write Your First Hello World! Application gets you started with Xcode and Interface Builder to build a Hello World application. The focus is on giving you some hands-on practice getting a project up and running quickly. More details on the various project components are covered in subsequent chapters.

Chapter 3: Understanding Views, Outlets, and Actions covers the fundamental concepts of iPhone and iPad programming: outlets and actions. You learn how outlets and actions allow your code to interact with the visual elements in Interface Builder and why they are an integral part of every iPhone and iPad application. You will also learn about the various UI widgets known as *views* that make up the user interface of your application.

Chapter 4: Exploring the Different View Controllers discusses the various View Controllers available in the iOS SDK. You will learn how to develop different types of applications — Single View, Master-Detail, as well as Tabbed applications.

Chapter 5: Enabling Multi-Platform Support for the iPhone and iPad shows how you can port your iPhone applications to the iPad platform. You will also learn how to create universal applications that will run on both the iPhone and the iPad.

Chapter 6: Handling Keyboard Inputs shows you how to deal with the virtual keyboard in your iPhone or iPad. You learn how to hide the keyboard on demand and how to ensure that your views are not blocked by the keyboard when it is displayed.

Chapter 7: Supporting Screen Rotations demonstrates how you can reorient your application's UI when the device is rotated. You learn about the various events that are fired when the device is rotated, and how to force your application to be displayed in a certain orientation.

Chapter 8: Displaying and Persisting Data Using the Table View explores one of the most powerful views in the iOS SDK — the Table View. The Table View is commonly used to display rows of data. In this chapter, you also learn how to implement search capabilities in your Table View.

Chapter 9: Using Application Preferences discusses the use of application settings to persist application preferences. Using application settings, you can access preferences related to your application through the Settings application available on the iPhone and iPad.

Chapter 10: File Handling shows how you can persist your application data by saving the data to files in your application's sandbox directory. You also learn how to access the various folders available in your application sandbox.

Chapter 11: Database Storage Using SQLite covers the use of the embedded SQLite3 database library to store your data.

Chapter 12: Programming iCloud discusses and demonstrates how to store your documents and application-specific data on Apple's new iCloud feature.

Chapter 13: Performing Simple Animations and Video Playback provides an overview of the various techniques you can use to implement basic animations on the iPhone and iPad. You also learn about the various affine transformations supported by the iOS SDK. In addition, you learn how to play back video on the iPhone and iPad.

Chapter 14: Accessing Built-In Applications describes the various ways you can access the iPhone and iPad's built-in applications, such as the Photo Library, Contacts, and others. You also learn how you can invoke built-in applications such as Mail and Safari from within your applications.

Chapter 15: Accessing the Sensors shows how you can access the accelerometer and gyroscope sensors that are included with every iPhone and iPad. You will also learn how to detect shakes to your device.

Chapter 16: Using Web Services teaches you how to consume web services from within your iPhone and iPad application. You will learn the various ways to communicate with four web services — JSON, SOAP, HTTP GET, and HTTP POST. You will also learn how to parse the XML result returned by the web service.

Chapter 17: Bluetooth Programming explores the use of the Game Kit framework for Bluetooth programming. You will learn how to enable two devices to communicate using a Bluetooth connection, and how to implement voice chatting over a Bluetooth connection.

Chapter 18: Bonjour Programming shows how you can publish and find services on the network using the Bonjour protocol.

Chapter 19: Programming Remote Notifications Using Apple Push Notification Services explains how you can implement applications that use push notifications. The APNs enables your applications to continuously receive status updates from a service provider even though the application may not be running.

Chapter 20: Displaying Maps demonstrates how to build a location-based services application using the Map Kit framework. You will also learn how to obtain geographical location data and use it to display a map.

Chapter 21: Programming Background Applications shows how to build applications that can continue to run in the background when the user switches to another application. You will also learn how to use the local notifications feature to schedule notifications that will fire at specific time intervals.

Appendix A: Testing on an Actual Device outlines the steps you need to take to test your application on a real device.

Appendix B: Getting Around in Xcode provides a quick run-through of the many features in Xcode and Interface Builder.

Appendix C: Crash Course in Objective-C offers a brief tutorial in Objective-C. Readers who are new to this language should read this material before getting started.

Appendix D: Answers to Exercises contains the solutions to the end-of-chapter exercises found in every chapter except Chapter 1.

HOW THIS BOOK IS STRUCTURED

This book breaks down the task of learning iPhone and iPad programming into several smaller chunks, enabling you to digest each foundational topic before delving into a more advanced topic. In addition, some chapters cover topics already discussed in a previous chapter. That's because there is usually more than one way of doing things in Xcode and Interface Builder, so this approach enables you to learn the different techniques available for developing iPhone and iPad applications.

If you are a total beginner to iOS programming, start with Chapters 1 and 2. After you are comfortable with the basics, head to the appendices to read more about the tools and language you are using. Once you are ready, you can continue with Chapter 3 and gradually move into more advanced topics.

A useful feature of this book is that all the code samples in each chapter are independent of those discussed in previous chapters. That gives you the flexibility to dive right into the topics that interest you and start working on the Try It Out projects.

WHAT YOU NEED TO USE THIS BOOK

Most of the examples in this book run on the iPhone Simulator (which is included with the iOS SDK). For exercises that access the hardware (such as the accelerometer and gyroscope), you need a real iPhone or iPad. In general, to get the most out of this book, having a real iPhone or iPad device is not necessary (although it is definitely required for testing if you plan to deploy your application on the App Store).

CONVENTIONS

To help you get the most from the text and keep track of what's happening, we've used a number of conventions throughout the book.

TRY IT OUT These Are Exercises or Examples for You to Follow

The Try It Out sections, which appear once or more per chapter, provide hands-on exercises that demonstrate the concept under discussion as you follow the text.

1. They consist of numbered steps.

2. Follow the steps with your copy of the project files.

How It Works

After each Try It Out section, these sections explain the code you've typed in detail.

As for other conventions in the text:

➤ New terms and important words are *highlighted* in italics when first introduced.

➤ Keyboard combinations are treated like this: Control-R.

➤ Filenames, URLs, and code within the text are treated like so: `persistence.properties`.

➤ Code is presented in two different ways:

```
We use a monofont type with no highlighting for most code examples.
```

```
We use bold to emphasize code that is of particular importance in the present
context.
```

 WARNING *Boxes like this one hold important, not-to-be forgotten information that is directly relevant to the surrounding text.*

 NOTE *Notes, tips, hints, tricks, and asides to the current discussion look like this.*

SOURCE CODE AND ANSWERS APPENDIX

As you work through the examples in this book, you may choose either to type in all the code manually or to use the source code files that accompany the book. All the source code used in this book is available for download at www.wrox.com. When at the site, simply locate the book's title (use the Search box or one of the title lists) and click the Download Code link on the book's detail page to obtain all the source code for the book. Code that is included on the website is highlighted by the following icon and/or CodeNote, as shown following the icon:

Available for download on Wrox.com

Listings include the filename in the title. If it is just a code snippet, you'll find the filename in a CodeNote such as this:

Code zip filename available for download at wrox.com

After you download the code, just decompress it with your favorite compression tool. Alternatively, go to the main Wrox code download page at www.wrox.com/dynamic/books/download.aspx to see the code available for this book and all other Wrox books.

Please note that Appendix D, "Answers to the Exercises," is available as a PDF for download.

 NOTE *Because many books have similar titles, you may find it easiest to search by ISBN; this book's ISBN is 978-1-118-14425-1.*

ERRATA

We make every effort to ensure that there are no errors in the text or the code. However, no one is perfect and mistakes do occur. If you find an error in one of our books, such as a spelling mistake or a faulty piece of code, we would be very grateful for your feedback. By sending in errata, you may save another reader hours of frustration and at the same time help us provide even higher-quality information.

To find the errata page for this book, go to www.wrox.com and locate the title using the Search box or one of the title lists. Then, on the book details page, click the Book Errata link. On this page, you can view all errata that has been submitted for this book and posted by Wrox editors. A complete book list, including links to each book's errata, is also available at www.wrox.com/misc-pages/booklist.shtml.

If you don't spot "your" error on the Book Errata page, go to www.wrox.com/contact/techsupport.shtml and complete the form there to send us the error you have found. We'll check the information and, if appropriate, post a message to the book's errata page and fix the problem in subsequent editions of the book.

P2P.WROX.COM

For author and peer discussion, join the P2P forums at p2p.wrox.com. The forums are a web-based system for you to post messages relating to Wrox books and related technologies and interact with other readers and technology users. The forums offer a subscription feature to email you topics of interest of your choosing when new posts are made to the forums. Wrox authors, editors, other industry experts, and your fellow readers are present on these forums.

At p2p.wrox.com, you will find a number of different forums that will help you not only as you read this book, but also as you develop your own applications. To join the forums, just follow these steps:

1. Go to p2p.wrox.com and click the Register link.

2. Read the terms of use and click Agree.

3. Complete the required information to join as well as any optional information you want to provide and click Submit.

4. You will receive an email with information describing how to verify your account and complete the joining process.

After you join, you can post new messages and respond to messages that other users post. You can read messages at any time on the web. If you want to have new messages from a particular forum emailed to you, click the Subscribe to This Forum icon by the forum name in the forum listing.

For more information about how to use the Wrox P2P, be sure to read the P2P FAQs for answers to questions about how the forum software works as well as for many common questions specific to P2P and Wrox books. To read the FAQs, click the FAQ link on any P2P page.

1

Getting Started with iOS 5 Programming

WHAT YOU WILL LEARN IN THIS CHAPTER

- ➤ How to obtain the iOS SDK - Software Development Kit

- ➤ Components included in the iOS SDK

- ➤ Features of the development tools — Xcode, Interface Builder, and iOS Simulator

- ➤ Capabilities of the iOS Simulator

- ➤ Architecture of iOS

- ➤ Characteristics of the iPhone and iPad

Welcome to the world of iOS programming! That you are now holding this book shows that you are fascinated with the idea of developing your own iPhone and iPad applications and want to join the ranks of the tens of thousands of developers whose applications are already deployed in the App Store.

As the Chinese adage says, "To accomplish your mission, first sharpen your tools." Successful programming requires that you first know your tools well. Indeed, this couldn't be truer for iOS programming — you need to be familiar with quite a few tools before you can even get started. Hence, this chapter describes the various relevant tools and information you need to jump on the iOS development bandwagon.

Without further ado, it's time to get down to work.

OBTAINING THE TOOLS AND SDK

To develop for iOS, you need to download the iOS SDK. The iOS SDK comes with free Xcode from the Mac App Store (see Figure 1-1).

FIGURE 1-1

Before you download and install Xcode, make sure you satisfy the following system requirements:

➤ Only Intel Macs are supported, so if you have another processor type (such as the older G4 or G5 Macs), you're out of luck.

➤ Your system is updated with the latest Mac OS X Lion release.

An actual iPhone/iPod touch/iPad is highly recommended, although not strictly necessary. To test your application, you can use the included iOS Simulator (which enables you to simulate an iPhone or an iPad). However, to test certain hardware features like the accelerometer and gyroscope, you need to use a real device.

When Xcode is downloaded, proceed with installing it. Accept a few licensing agreements and then select the destination folder in which to install the SDK.

If you select the default settings during the installation phase, the various tools will be installed in the /Developer/Applications folder (see Figure 1-2).

FIGURE 1-2

COMPONENTS OF XCODE

The Xcode package includes a suite of development tools to help you create applications for your iPhone, iPod touch, and iPad. It includes the following:

➤ **Xcode IDE** — Integrated development environment (IDE) that enables you to manage, edit, and debug your projects

➤ **Dashcode** — Integrated development environment (IDE) that enables you to develop web-based iPhone and iPad applications and Dashboard widgets. Dashcode is beyond the scope of this book.

➤ **iOS Simulator** — Provides a software simulator to simulate an iPhone or an iPad on your Mac

➤ **Interface Builder** — Visual editor for designing user interfaces for your iPhone and iPad applications

➤ **Instruments** — Analysis tool to help you both optimize your application and monitor for memory leaks in real time

The following sections discuss each tool (except Dashcode) in more detail.

Xcode

To launch Xcode, double-click the Xcode icon located in the /Developer/Applications folder (refer to Figure 1-2). Alternatively, go the quicker route and use Spotlight: Simply type **Xcode** into the search box and Xcode should be in the Top Hit position.

Figure 1-3 shows the Xcode Welcome screen.

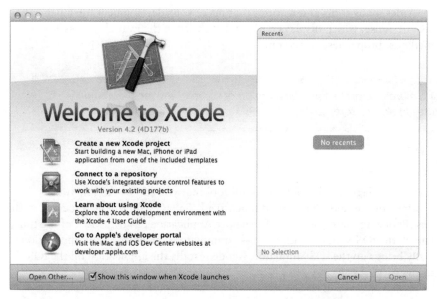

FIGURE 1-3

Using Xcode, you can develop different types of iPhone, iPad, and Mac OS X applications using the various project templates shown in Figure 1-4.

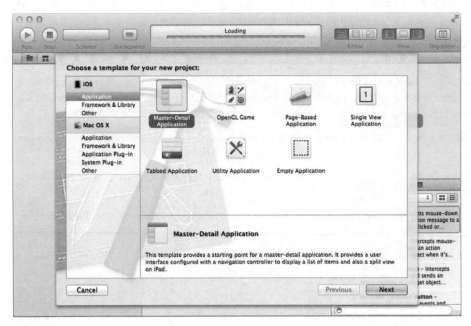

FIGURE 1-4

For iOS applications, each template gives you the option to select the platform you are targeting — iPhone, iPad, or Universal (runs on both iPhone and iPad).

The IDE in Xcode provides many tools and features that make your development life much easier. One such feature is Code Sense, which displays a popup list showing the available classes and members, such as methods, properties, and so on.

 NOTE *For a more comprehensive description of some of the most commonly used features in Xcode, refer to Appendix B.*

iOS Simulator

The iOS Simulator, shown in Figure 1-5, is a very useful tool that you can use to test your application without using your actual iPhone/iPod touch/iPad. The iOS Simulator is located in the /Developer/Platforms/iPhoneSimulator.platform/Developer/Applications folder. Most of the time, you don't need to launch the iOS Simulator directly — running (or debugging) your application in Xcode automatically brings up the iOS Simulator. Xcode installs the application on the iOS Simulator automatically.

FIGURE 1-5

THE IOS SIMULATOR IS NOT AN EMULATOR

To understand the difference between a simulator and an emulator, keep in mind that a simulator tries to mimic the behavior of a real device. In the case of the iOS Simulator, it simulates the real behavior of an actual iPhone/iPad device. However, the Simulator itself uses the various libraries installed on the Mac (such as QuickTime) to perform its rendering so that the effect looks the same as an actual iPhone. In addition, applications tested on the Simulator are compiled into x86 code, which is the byte-code understood by the Simulator. A real iPhone device, conversely, uses ARM-based code.

In contrast, an emulator emulates the working of a real device. Applications tested on an emulator are compiled into the actual byte-code used by the real device. The emulator executes the application by translating the byte-code into a form that can be executed by the host computer running the emulator.

To understand the subtle difference between simulation and emulation, imagine you are trying to convince a child that playing with knives is dangerous. To *simulate* this, you pretend to cut yourself with a knife and groan in pain. To *emulate* this, you actually cut yourself.

The iOS Simulator can simulate different versions of the iOS (see Figure 1-6. To support older versions of the SDK, you need to install the previous versions of the SDKs). This capability is useful if you need to support older versions of the platform, as well as test and debug errors reported in the application on specific versions of the OS.

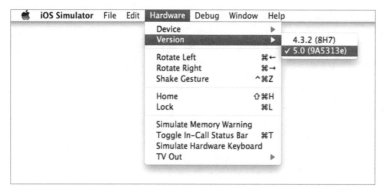

FIGURE 1-6

In addition, the iOS Simulator can simulate different devices — iPad (see Figure 1-7), iPhone (3G and 3GS), and iPhone 4 with Retina display (see Figure 1-8).

FIGURE 1-7

FIGURE 1-8

Features of the iOS Simulator

The iOS Simulator simulates various features of a real iPhone, iPod touch, or iPad device. Features you can test on the iOS Simulator include the following:

➤ Screen rotation — left, right, top, and upside down

➤ Support for gestures:

  ➤ Tap

  ➤ Touch and Hold

  ➤ Double-tap

  ➤ Swipe

  ➤ Rotate

  ➤ Drag

  ➤ Pinch

➤ Low-memory warning simulations

However, the iOS Simulator, being a software simulator for the real device, does have its limitations. The following features are not available on the iOS Simulator:

➤ Making phone calls

➤ Accessing the accelerometer

➤ Sending and receiving SMS messages

➤ Installing applications from the App Store

➤ Camera

➤ Microphone

➤ Several features of OpenGL ES

 NOTE *In the latest release of the SDK (5.0), the iOS Simulator enables you to simulate different locations as well as movements. Chapter 20 discusses this in more detail.*

Note also that the speed of the iOS Simulator is more tightly coupled to the performance of your Mac than the actual device. Therefore, it is important that you test your application on a real device, rather than rely exclusively on the iOS Simulator for testing.

Despite the iOS Simulator's limitations, it is definitely a useful tool for testing your applications. That said, testing your application on a real device is imperative before you deploy it on the App Store.

Uninstalling Applications from the iOS Simulator

The user domain of the iOS file system for the iOS Simulator is stored in the ~/Library/ Application Support/iPhone Simulator/ folder.

 NOTE *The ~/Library/Application Support/iPhone Simulator/ folder is also known as <iPhoneUserDomain>.*

All third-party applications are stored in the <iPhoneUserDomain>/<version_no>/Applications/ folder. When an application is deployed onto the iOS Simulator, an icon is created on the Home screen and a file and a few folders are created within the Applications folder (see Figure 1-9).

FIGURE 1-9

To uninstall (delete) an application, execute the following steps:

1. Click and hold the icon of the application on the Home screen until all the icons start wriggling. Note that all the icons now have an X button displayed on their top-left corner.

2. Click the X button next to the icon of the application you want to uninstall (see Figure 1-10).

3. An alert window appears asking if you are sure you want to delete the icon. Click Delete to confirm the deletion.

FIGURE 1-10

WARNING *When an application is uninstalled, the corresponding file and folder in the Applications folder are deleted automatically.*

The easiest way to reset the iOS Simulator to its original state is to select iOS Simulator ⇨ Reset Content and Settings . . . .

Interface Builder

Interface Builder is a visual tool that enables you to design the user interfaces for your iPhone/iPad applications. Using Interface Builder, you drag and drop views onto windows and then connect the various views with outlets and actions so that they can programmatically interact with your code.

 NOTE *Outlets and actions are discussed in more detail in Chapter 3, and Appendix B discusses Interface Builder in more detail.*

Figure 1-11 shows the various windows in Interface Builder.

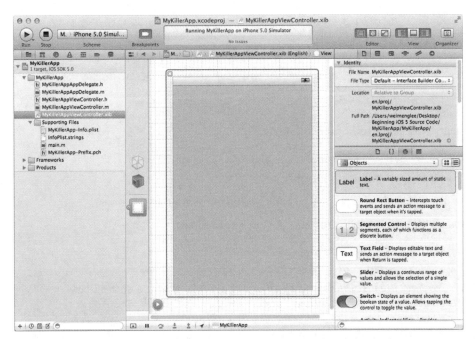

FIGURE 1-11

Instruments

The Instruments application (see Figure 1-12) enables you to dynamically trace and profile the performance of your Mac OS X, iPhone, and iPad applications.

FIGURE 1-12

Using Instruments, you can do all of the following:

➤ Stress test your applications.

➤ Monitor your applications for memory leaks.

➤ Gain a deep understanding of the executing behavior of your applications.

➤ Track difficult-to-reproduce problems in your applications.

> **NOTE** *Covering the Instruments application is beyond the scope of this book. For more information, refer to Apple's documentation, at* `http://developer` `.apple.com/mac/library/documentation/DeveloperTools/Conceptual/` `InstrumentsUserGuide/Introduction/Introduction.html`.

ARCHITECTURE OF THE IOS

Although this book doesn't explore the innards of iOS, understanding some of its important characteristics is useful. Figure 1-13 shows the different abstraction layers that make up the Mac OS X and iOS (which is used by the iPhone, iPod touch, and iPad).

 NOTE *The iOS is architecturally very similar to the Mac OS X except that the topmost layer is Cocoa Touch for the iPhone, rather than the Cocoa Framework.*

FIGURE 1-13

The bottom layer is the Core OS, which is the foundation of the operating system. It is in charge of memory management, the file system, networking, and other OS tasks, and it interacts directly with the hardware. The Core OS layer consists of components such as the following:

➤ OS X Kernel

➤ Mach 3.0

➤ BSD

➤ Sockets

➤ Security

➤ Power Management

➤ Keychain

➤ Certificates

➤ File System

➤ Bonjour

The Core Services layer provides an abstraction over the services provided in the Core OS layer. It provides fundamental access to iOS services and consists of the following components:

➤ Collections

➤ Address Book

➤ Networking

➤ File Access

➤ SQLite

➤ Core Location

➤ Net Services

➤ Threading

➤ Preferences

➤ URL Utilities

The Media layer provides multimedia services that you can use in your iPhone and iPad applications. It consists of the following components:

➤ Core Audio

➤ OpenGL

➤ Audio Mixing

➤ Audio Recording

➤ Video Playback

➤ JPG, PNG, TIFF

➤ PDF

➤ Quartz

➤ Core Animation

➤ OpenGL ES

The Cocoa Touch layer provides an abstraction layer to expose the various libraries for programming the iPhone and iPad, such as the following:

➤ Multi-Touch events

➤ Multi-Touch controls

➤ Accelerometer

➤ View Hierarchy

➤ Localization

➤ Alerts

➤ Web Views

➤ People Picker

➤ Image Picker

➤ Controllers

In iOS programming, all the functionalities in each layer are exposed through various frameworks that you will use in your project. Subsequent chapters in this book demonstrate how to use these frameworks in your projects.

NOTE *A framework is a software library that provides specific functionalities. Refer to Apple's documentation at* `http://developer.apple.com/ iphone/library/documentation/Miscellaneous/Conceptual/ iPhoneOSTechOverview/iPhoneOSFrameworks/iPhoneOSFrameworks.html` *for a list of frameworks included in the SDK.*

SOME USEFUL INFORMATION BEFORE YOU GET STARTED

You now have a good idea of the tools involved in iPhone and iPad application development. Before you go ahead and take the plunge, the following sections discuss some useful information that can make your journey more pleasant.

Versions of iOS

At the time of writing, iOS is in its fifth revision — that is, version 5.0. Its major versions are as follows:

➤ **1.0** — Initial release of the iPhone

➤ **1.1** — Additional features and bug fixes for 1.0

➤ **2.0** — Released with iPhone 3G; comes with App Store

➤ **2.1** — Additional features and bug fixes for 2.0

➤ **2.2** — Additional features and bug fixes for 2.1

➤ **3.0** — Third major release of the iPhone OS

➤ **3.1** — Additional features and bug fixes for 3.0

➤ **3.2** — This version release is for the iPad only.

➤ **4.0** — Fourth major release of the iPhone OS. Renamed as iOS. This version is designed for the new iPhone 4 and it also supports older devices, such as the iPod touch and iPhones.

➤ **5.0** — Fifth major release of the iOS. Supports new features like iCloud, iMessage, Twitter integration, Notification Center, etc.

For a detailed description of the features in each release, see `http://en.wikipedia.org/wiki/ IPhone_OS_version_history`.

Testing on Real Devices

One of the most common complaints about developing applications for the iPhone and iPad is how difficult Apple makes it to test a new application on an actual device. Nonetheless, for security reasons, Apple requires all applications to be signed with a valid certificate; and for testing purposes, a developer certificate is required.

To test your applications on a device, you must sign up for the iOS Developer Program and request that a developer certificate be installed onto your device. Appendix A outlines these steps in detail.

Screen Resolutions

The iPhone 4S is a beautiful device with a high-resolution screen. At 3.5 inches (diagonally), the iPhone screen supports multi-touch operation and allows a pixel resolution of 960 × 640 at 326 ppi (see Figure 1-14). When designing your application, note that because of the status bar, the actual resolution is generally limited to 920 × 640 pixels. Of course, you can turn off the status bar programmatically to gain access to the full 960 × 640 resolution.

Also, be mindful that users may rotate the device to display your application in landscape mode. You need to make provisions to your user interface so that applications can still work properly in landscape mode.

 NOTE *Chapter 7 discusses how to handle screen rotations.*

The older iPhones (iPhone 3G/3GS) and the iPod touch have lower resolutions compared to the iPhone 4/4S. They have a resolution of 480 × 320 pixels, one quarter of the resolution of the iPhone 4.

When programming for the iPhones, it is important to note the difference between points and pixels. For example, the following statement specifies a frame that starts from the point (20,10) with a width of 280 points and a height of 50 points:

```
CGRect frame = CGRectMake(20, 10, 280, 50);
```

On the older iPhones, a point corresponds to a pixel. Thus, the preceding statement translates directly to the pixel (20,10), with a width of 280 pixels and a height of 50 pixels. However, if the statement is executed within the iPhone 4/4S, a point translates to *two* pixels. Thus, the preceding statement translates into the pixel (40,20), with a width of 560 pixels and a height of 100 pixels. The translation is performed automatically

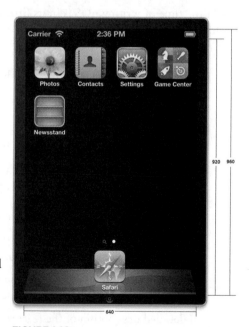

FIGURE 1-14

by the OS, which is very useful because it enables older applications to run and scale correctly without modifications on the iPhone 4/4S.

The iPad has a pixel resolution of 1,024 × 768 at 132 ppi.

Table 1-1 summarizes the screen resolutions for the various platforms.

TABLE 1-1: Platform Resolutions

PLATFORM	RESOLUTION (PIXELS)	VISIBLE REAL ESTATE WITHOUT THE STATUS BAR (PIXELS) — LANDSCAPE MODE	VISIBLE REAL ESTATE WITHOUT THE STATUS BAR (PIXELS) — PORTRAIT MODE
iPhone 4/4S	960 × 640	960 × 600	920 × 640
iPhone 3G/3GS, iPod touch	480 × 320	480 × 300	460 × 320
iPad	1024 × 768	1024 × 748	1004 × 768

SUMMARY

This chapter offered a quick tour of the available tools used for iPhone and iPad application development. You had a look at the iOS Simulator, which you will use to test your applications without using a real device. The Simulator is a very powerful tool that you will use very often in your iPhone development journey.

You also learned some of the characteristics of the iPhone and iPad, such as screen resolutions, as well as characteristics of the operating systems. In the next chapter, you will develop your first iOS application, and soon be on your way to iOS nirvana!

▶ **WHAT YOU LEARNED IN THIS CHAPTER**

TOPIC	KEY CONCEPTS
Obtaining the iOS SDK	Download Xcode 4 from the Mac App Store.
iOS Simulator	Most of the testing can be done on the iOS Simulator. However, it is strongly recommended that you have a real device for actual testing.
Limitations of the iOS Simulator	Access to hardware is generally not supported by the Simulator. For example, the camera, accelerometer, voice recording, and so on are not supported.
Frameworks in the iOS SDK	The iOS SDK provides several frameworks that perform specific functionalities on the iPhone. You program your iOS applications using all these frameworks.

2

Writing Your First Hello World! Application

WHAT YOU WILL LEARN IN THIS CHAPTER

- ➤ How to create a new iPhone project
- ➤ Building your first iPhone application using Xcode
- ➤ Designing the user interface (UI) of your iPhone application with Interface Builder
- ➤ How to add an icon to your iPhone application
- ➤ How to display launch images for your iPhone application

Now that you have installed the iOS SDK, you are ready to start developing for the iPhone! Programming books customarily start by demonstrating how to develop a "Hello World!" application. This approach enables you to use the various tools quickly without getting bogged down with the details. It also provides you with instant gratification: You see for yourself that things really work, which can be a morale booster that inspires you to learn more.

GETTING STARTED WITH XCODE

Power up Xcode and you should see the Welcome screen, shown in Figure 2-1.

 NOTE The easiest way to start Xcode is to type **Xcode** in Spotlight and then press the Enter key to launch it.

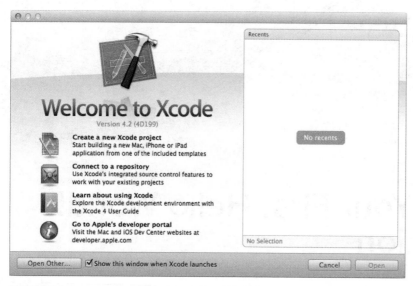

FIGURE 2-1

To create a new iPhone project, click the Create a new Xcode project button (or choose File ➪ New ➪ New Project). Figure 2-2 shows the different types of projects you can create using Xcode. The left panel shows the two primary categories — iPhone OS and Mac OS X. The iPhone uses the iOS, so click the Application item listed under iOS to view the different templates available for developing your iPhone application.

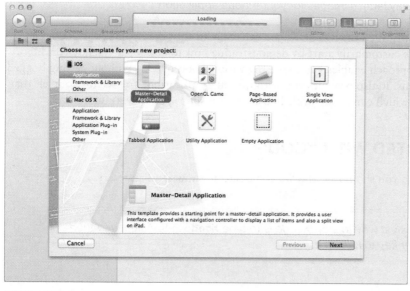

FIGURE 2-2

Although you can create quite a few types of iPhone applications, for this chapter select the Single View Application template and then click Next.

 NOTE *Subsequent chapters show you how to develop some of the other types of iOS applications, such as Tabbed applications and Master-Detail applications.*

Name the project `HelloWorld` and provide a company identifier for your application (you typically use your company's domain name in reverse order, such as net.learn2develop for my `www.learn2develop.net` domain). Name the Class Prefix to be the same as the project name and select iPhone as the Device Family. Finally, ensure that all the options are unchecked and then click Next (see Figure 2-3). You will be asked to select a folder in which to save your project. Xcode then proceeds to create the project for the template you have selected. Figure 2-4 shows the various files and folders automatically created for your project.

The left panel of Xcode shows the groups in the project. You can expand each group or folder to reveal the files contained in it. To edit a particular file, select it from the list, and the editor on the right panel opens the file for editing. If you want a separate window for editing, simply double-click the file to edit it in a new window.

FIGURE 2-3

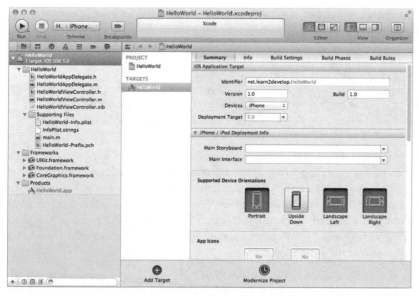

FIGURE 2-4

Using Interface Builder

At this point, the project has no UI. To prove this, simply press Command-R (or select Product ⇨ Run), and your application is deployed to the included iPhone Simulator. Figure 2-5 shows the blank screen displayed on the iPhone Simulator. Note how it looks now, because as you go through the chapter you will see changes occur based on your actions.

FIGURE 2-5

NOTE *By default, the iPhone Simulator that is launched shows the image of the iPhone 4. However, the screen resolution for this simulator is still 320x480 pixels, simulating the older iPhone 3GS's screen resolution. If you want to simulate the Retina display of an iPhone 4 or iPhone 4S, you need to select Hardware ⇨ Device ⇨ iPhone (Retina).*

Obviously, a blank screen is not very useful. Therefore, it's time to try adding some views to your application's UI. In the list of files in your project, you'll notice a file with the .xib extension — HelloWorldViewController.xib. Files with .xib extensions are basically XML files containing the UI definitions of an application. You can edit .xib files by either modifying their XML content or, more easily (and more sanely), using Interface Builder.

Interface Builder, integrated into Xcode (prior to Xcode 4, Interface Builder is a separate application that ships with the iOS SDK), enables you to build the UI of iPhone (and Mac) applications by using drag and drop.

Select the HelloWorldViewController.xib file to edit it using Interface Builder. Figure 2-6 shows Interface Builder displaying the content of HelloWorldViewController.xib.

 NOTE *Refer to Appendix B for a crash course on Interface Builder if you are not familiar with it.*

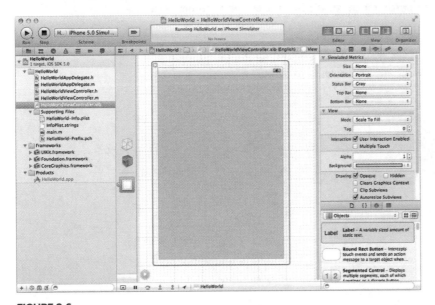

FIGURE 2-6

In the Utilities area on the right, go to the Object Library section and scroll down to the Label view and drag and drop a Label onto the View window (see Figure 2-7).

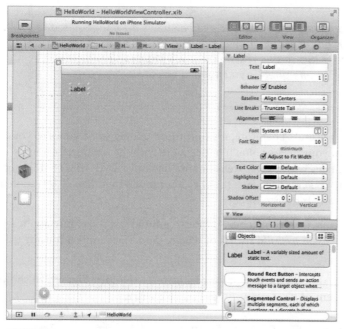

FIGURE 2-7

After the Label is added, select it and go to the Attributes Inspector window (you can view this by choosing View ➪ Utilities ➪ Show Attributes Inspector). Enter **Hello World!** in the Text field (see Figure 2-8). Then, in the Alignment field, click the center alignment button.

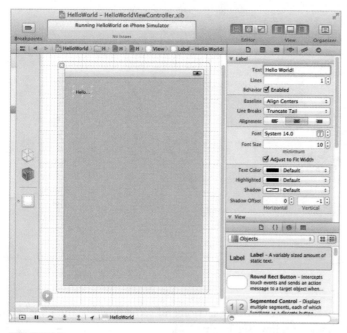

FIGURE 2-8

With the Label still selected, click on the "T" icon displayed next to the Font field and select the Helvetica Custom font (see Figure 2-9). Set the font size to 36.

Resize the Label so that it now looks like Figure 2-10.

Next, from the Library window, drag and drop a Text Field to the View window, followed by a Round Rect Button. Modify the attribute of the Round Rect Button by entering **Click Me!** in the Title field of its Attributes Inspector window. Figure 2-11 shows how the View window looks now.

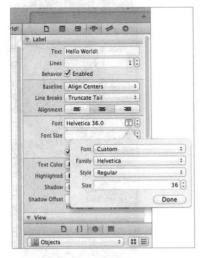

FIGURE 2-9

FIGURE 2-10

FIGURE 2-11

NOTE *Rather than specify the* Text *or* Title *property of a view to make the text display in the view (for example, the Label and the Round Rect Button), you can simply double-click the view itself and type the text directly. After doing this, you can rearrange the views and resize them to suit your needs. Interface Builder provides you with alignment guidelines to help you arrange your controls in a visually pleasing layout.*

Run the application again by pressing Command-R. The iPhone Simulator now displays the modified UI (see Figure 2-12).

Click the Text Field and watch the keyboard automatically appear (see Figure 2-13).

Click the Home button on the iPhone Simulator, and you will see that your application has been installed on the Simulator. To go back to the application, simply click the HelloWorld icon (see Figure 2-14).

FIGURE 2-12

FIGURE 2-13

FIGURE 2-14

 NOTE *By default, starting with iOS 4, all applications built using the iOS SDK support multitasking. Hence, when you press the Home button on your iPhone, your application is not terminated; it is sent to the background and suspended. Tapping an application icon resumes the application. Chapter 21 contains more details about background execution of your iOS applications.*

Writing Some Code

By now you should be comfortable enough with Xcode and Interface Builder to write some code. This section will give you a taste of programming the iPhone.

In the `HelloWorldViewController.h` file, add a declaration for the `btnClicked:` action:

```
#import <UIKit/UIKit.h>

@interface HelloWorldViewController : UIViewController

-(IBAction) btnClicked:(id) sender;

@end
```

The bold statement creates an action (commonly known as an *event handler*) named `btnClicked:`. With the action declared, save the file and return to Interface Builder by clicking the `HelloWorldViewController.xib` file.

Earlier in this chapter, when you edited the `HelloWorldViewController.xib` file, you saw three icons displayed in Interface Builder (see Figure 2-15) These three icons, from top to bottom, are File's Owner, First Responder, and View.

FIGURE 2-15

Control-click the Round Rect Button in the View window and drag it to the File's Owner item (see Figure 2-16). A small popup containing the `btnClicked:` action appears. Select the `btnClicked:` action. Basically, what you are doing here is linking the Round Rect Button with the action (`btnClicked:`) so that when the user clicks the button, the action is invoked.

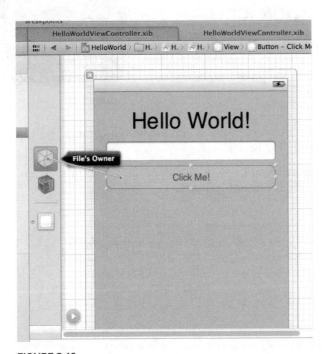

FIGURE 2-16

In the `HelloWorldViewController.m` file, add the code that provides the implementation for the `btnClicked:` action:

```
#import "HelloWorldViewController.h"

@implementation HelloWorldViewController

-(IBAction) btnClicked:(id) sender {
    //---display an alert view---
    UIAlertView *alert =
        [[UIAlertView alloc] initWithTitle:@"Hello World!"
                                    message:@"iPhone, here I come!"
                                   delegate:self
```

```
                              cancelButtonTitle:@"OK"
                              otherButtonTitles:nil];

        [alert show];
        [alert release];
    }
```

The preceding code displays an alert containing the sentence "iPhone, here I come!"

That's it! Run the application again. This time, when you click the Round Rect Button, an Alert view displays (see Figure 2-17).

CUSTOMIZING YOUR APPLICATION ICON

As shown earlier, the application installed on your iPhone Simulator uses a default white image as an icon. You can, however, customize this icon. When designing icons for your iPhone and iPad applications, bear the following in mind:

FIGURE 2-17

➤ Design your icon to be 57× 57 pixels (for iPhone), 114×114 pixels (for iPhone high resolution), or 72×72 pixels (for iPad). For distribution through the App Store, you also need to prepare a 512×512 pixel image.

➤ Use square corners for your icon image because iPhone automatically rounds them. It also adds a glossy surface (you can turn off this feature, though).

NOTE *Apple has published a description of the various images that you can use in your iPhone application. For details, see* `http://developer.apple.com/library/ios/#documentation/userexperience/conceptual/mobilehig/IconsImages/IconsImages.html`*.*

The following Try It Out demonstrates how to add an icon to your application so that the iPhone will use it instead of the default white image.

TRY IT OUT Adding an Icon to the Application

1. To add an icon to your application, drag and drop an image (named as icon.png in this example) onto the Supporting Files folder of your project. You will be asked if you want to make a copy of the image you are dropping. Check this option so that a copy of the image will be stored in your project folder (see Figure 2-18).

2. Select the `HelloWorld-Info.plist` item (also located under the Supporting Files folder, the `HelloWorld-Info.plist` file is commonly referred to as the `info.plist` file). Expand the `Icon files` array item and add an item to it by clicking the + button displayed next to it. Set its value to the name of the icon, `icon.png` (see Figure 2-19). This specifies the name of the image to be used as the application icon.

3. Press Command-R to run the application and test it on the iPhone Simulator. Click the Home button to return to the main screen of the iPhone. You should see the newly added icon (see Figure 2-20). Observe that iOS automatically applies a glossy effect to your icon. It also rounds the four corners of the image.

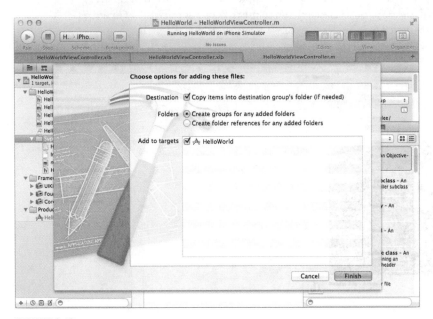

FIGURE 2-18

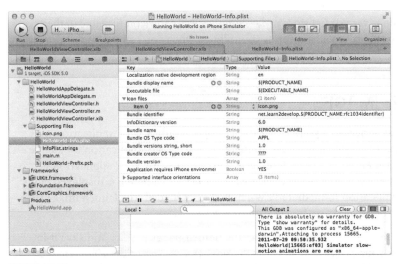

FIGURE 2-19

FIGURE 2-20

HOW TO TURN OFF THE GLOSSY SURFACE ON YOUR ICON

To turn off the glossy effect applied to your icon, you need to add the
`UIPrerenderedIcon` key (the friendly name for this key is "Icon already includes
gloss effects") to the `HelloWorld-Info.plist` file in your Xcode project and then
set it to `YES` (see Figure 2-21). For more details on the various keys that you can set
in your `HelloWorld-Info.plist` file, refer to Apple's documentation at `http://
developer.apple.com/iphone/library/documentation/General/Reference/
InfoPlistKeyReference/Articles/iPhoneOSKeys.html`.

FIGURE 2-21

How It Works

Setting an icon for your application is very straightforward — simply specify the icon filename in the `Icon
files` array item's first array element and it will appear in your iPhone when you run the application again.

DISPLAYING LAUNCH IMAGES

In order to enhance the user experience of your application, Apple requires your application to
include a *launch image*. Basically, a launch image is an image of what your application looks like
when it is loaded for the first time. Using a launch image ensures that while your application is
being loaded, the user is not staring at a blank screen. Instead, the launch image is displayed. This
engages the user with your application immediately. When it is fully loaded, the launch image then
disappears, and your application displays its first screen, ready to use.

Creating a launch image is simple — you merely create a file named `Default.png` and save it in
the application bundle (i.e., in your project, such as the `Supporting Files` folder). This image
needs to have a resolution of 480×320 pixels (or 960×640 for iPhone's Retina display). When your

application is loaded, the system will automatically display this image and then hide it when the first View window of your application is ready to be shown. If you want to display different launch images depending on the resolution of the device, you can do the following:

➤ Create an image named `Default.png` with a resolution of 320×480. This launch image will be loaded when your application is loaded on an iOS device with a screen resolution of 320×480 (e.g., the iPhone 3GS).

➤ Create an image named `Default@2x.png` with a resolution of 640×960. This launch image will be loaded when your application is loaded on an iOS device with a screen resolution of 640×960 (e.g., the iPhone 4 or iPhone 4S).

You can create the launch image from scratch using a photo-editing application, or easily capture one using the Organizer tool that is part of Xcode — all you need to do is view and capture the image you want to use as the launch image on your iPhone. The following Try It Out describes how to add a launch image using the Organizer.

TRY IT OUT   Adding a Launch Image to the Application

1. With the iPhone connected to your Mac, launch Xcode and select Window ➪ Organizer.

2. You should now be able to see the name of the device attached to your Mac. Click the Use for Development button and then click the Screenshots tab (see Figure 2-22).

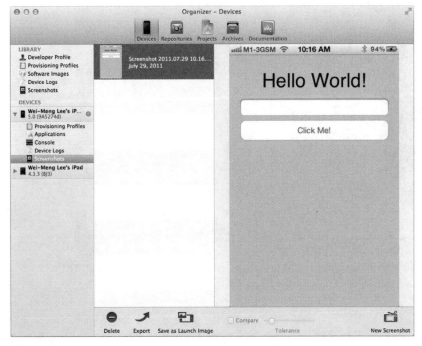

FIGURE 2-22

3. View the desired image on your iPhone. In this example, I have deployed the application onto my iPhone (Appendix A shows you how to deploy an application onto a real iOS device) and then launched it. I will capture the first View window that appears so that I can use it as a launch image. Click the New Screenshot button located on the bottom, right corner of the window to capture the screenshot.

4. All the captured images are shown in the middle of the Organizer window. Select the image that you want to use and click the Save As Launch Image . . . button.

5. You will be prompted to select the project that you want to use for the launch image (see Figure 2-23). You will also be asked to name the image. If you are capturing an image from a Retina display device (such as the iPhone 4 or iPhone 4S), name it `Default@2x`. If not, name it `Default`.

6. The file will be copied to the `HelloWorld` Xcode project (see Figure 2-24).

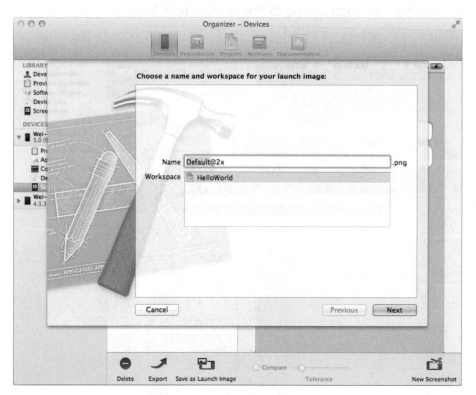

FIGURE 2-23

FIGURE 2-24

7. Observe that the captured image contains the status bar. You should erase the status bar using a graphics editor tool, as the status bar should not be displayed to users (see Figure 2-25). Interestingly, this area is automatically hidden by the status bar on the device when it is loaded.

8. Press Command-R to test the application on the iPhone Simulator. Notice that the application loads as usual, but if you try to click the Text Field or Round Rect Button in the initial couple of seconds, they will not be responsive, as the actual `HelloWorldViewController` View window has not been loaded yet (you are still seeing the launch image). After a few seconds, the actual `HelloWorldViewController` View window is loaded and you can click the Text Field or Round Rect buttons.

How It Works

When you include an image named `Default@2x.png` (or `Default.png`) in your project, it will be displayed when your application is first being loaded. This improves the user experience by creating the impression that your application loads immediately.

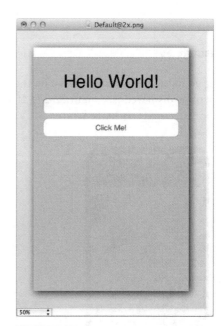

FIGURE 2-25

Pay attention to the dimension of the image; it will not be displayed during loading if it is the wrong size. If your application has only a single launch image (either `Default.png` or `Default@2x.png`), the launch image will be displayed regardless of device screen resolution. If you have multiple launch images, then a different launch image will be loaded for different devices. To prove this, add another image with a resolution of 320x480 (see Figure 2-26) and name it `Default.png`.

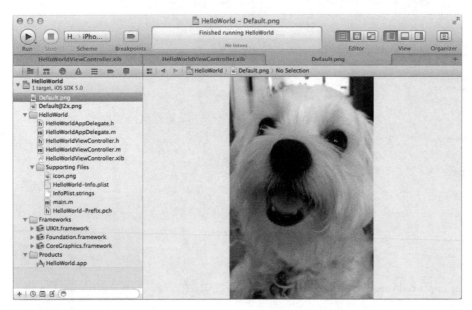

FIGURE 2-26

If you now run the application on the iPhone Simulator, you will notice that the `Default.png` will be displayed (see Figure 2-27). If you run it on the iPhone (Retina) Simulator, you will see the `Default@2x.png` loaded.

FIGURE 2-27

While Apple has explicitly stated that the launch image is meant to improve the user experience of your application, not to display a "splash screen" for it (like the example just shown), a lot of developers are making use of this feature to display splash screens for their applications.

SUMMARY

This chapter provided a brief introduction to developing your first iPhone application. You have created a simple iPhone application, designed its user interface using some of the built-in views, and then test it on the iPhone Simulator. You have also learned how to write a simple action for your Button so that it can display a message when the user clicks on it. Finally, you saw how to assign an image to be used as the icon for your application and how to set a launch image for your application.

Although you likely still have many questions, the aim of this chapter was to get you started. The next few chapters dive deeper into the details of iPhone programming, gradually revealing the secrets of how all those components that seem so mysterious at first work together to create your application.

EXERCISES

1. You want to add an icon to an iPhone project in Xcode. What is the size of the image that you should provide?

2. What is the easiest way to add a launch image to an iPhone application?

3. When adding an image to the Supporting Files folder in your Xcode project, why do you need to check the "Copy items into destination group's folder (If needed)" option?

Answers to the exercises can be found in Appendix D.

▶ **WHAT YOU LEARNED IN THIS CHAPTER**

TOPIC	KEY CONCEPTS
Xcode	Create your iPhone Application project and write code that manipulates your application.
Interface Builder	Build your iPhone UI using the various views located in the Library.
Adding an application icon	Add an image to the project and then specify the image name in the Icon files item of the `info.plist` file.
Adding a launch image	Add an image named `Default.png` or (`Default@2x.png`) to the Supporting Files folder of your project.
Creating icons for your iPhone applications	Icon size is 57×57 pixels and 114×114 pixels (high resolution). For App Store hosting, the size is 512×512 pixels.

3

Understanding Views, Outlets, and Actions

WHAT YOU WILL LEARN IN THIS CHAPTER

- ➤ How to declare and define outlets
- ➤ How to declare and define actions
- ➤ Connecting outlets and actions to the views in your View window
- ➤ How to use the UIAlertView to display an alert view to the user
- ➤ How to use the UIActionSheet to display some options to the user
- ➤ Using the UIPageControl to control paging
- ➤ How to use the UIImageView to display images
- ➤ How to use the UIWebView to display web content in your application
- ➤ Dynamically adding views to your application during runtime

In the previous chapter, you built a simple Hello World! iPhone application without understanding much about the underlying details of how things work together. In fact, one of the greatest hurdles in gaining proficiency with iOS programming is the large number of details you need to learn before you can get an application up and running. Hence, this chapter starts with the basics of creating the user interface (UI) of an iPhone application, and describes how your code connects with the various graphical widgets.

OUTLETS AND ACTIONS

As you begin to program iOS applications, you need to first understand the concept of outlets and actions. In iOS programming, you use actions and outlets to connect your code to the various views in your UI. Think of actions as event handlers in the traditional object-oriented programming world, and outlets as object references. If you are familiar with traditional programming languages such as Java or C#, this is a concept that requires some time to get used to — not because it is difficult, but because it is a different way of doing things. At the end of this section, you will have a solid understanding of what outlets and actions are in iOS and how to create them, and be on your way to creating great iOS applications.

TRY IT OUT Creating Outlets and Actions

codefile OutletsAndActions.zip available for download at Wrox.com

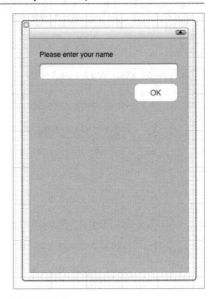

1. Using Xcode, create a Single View Application (iPhone) project and name it **OutletsAndActions**. You will also use the project name as the Class Prefix and ensure that you have the Use Automatic Reference Counting option unchecked.

2. Select the `OutletsAndActionsViewController.xib` file in order to edit it using Interface Builder. Populate the View window with three views: Label, Text Field, and Round Rect Button. Set the Label with the text "Please enter your name" by double-clicking on it. Set the Round Rect Button with the "OK" string (see Figure 3-1).

3. In Xcode, modify the `OutletsAndActionsViewController.h` file with the following statements shown in bold:

```
#import <UIKit/UIKit.h>
```

FIGURE 3-1

```
@interface OutletsAndActionsViewController : UIViewController
{
    //---declaring the outlet---
    IBOutlet UITextField *txtName;
}

//---expose the outlet as a property---
@property (nonatomic, retain) UITextField *txtName;

//---declaring the action---
-(IBAction) btnClicked:(id) sender;

@end
```

4. In the `OutletsAndActionsViewController.m` file, define the following statements in bold:

```objc
#import "OutletsAndActionsViewController.h"

@implementation OutletsAndActionsViewController

//---synthesize the property---
@synthesize txtName;

//---displays an alert view when the button is clicked---
-(IBAction) btnClicked:(id) sender {
    NSString *str =
        [[NSString alloc] initWithFormat:@"Hello, %@", txtName.text];
    UIAlertView *alert =
        [[UIAlertView alloc] initWithTitle:@"Hello!"
                                   message:str
                                  delegate:self
                         cancelButtonTitle:@"Done"
                         otherButtonTitles:nil];
    [alert show];
    [str release];
    [alert release];
}

- (void)dealloc {
    //---release the outlet---
    [txtName release];
    [super dealloc];
}
```

5. In the `OutletsAndActionsViewController.xib` window, Control-click and drag the File's Owner item to the Text Field (see Figure 3-2). A popup will appear; select the outlet named `txtName`.

6. Control-click and drag the OK Round Rect Button to the File's Owner item (see Figure 3-3). Select the action named `btnClicked:`.

7. Right-click the OK Round Rect Button to display its events (see Figure 3-4). Notice that the Round Rect Button has several events, but one particular event — Touch Up Inside — is now connected to the action you specified (`btnClicked:`). Because the Touch Up Inside event is so commonly used, it is automatically connected to the action when you Control-click and drag it to the File's Owner item. To connect other events to the action, simply click the circle displayed next to each event and then drag it to the File's Owner item.

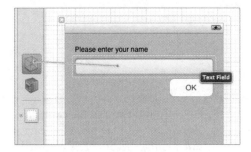

FIGURE 3-2

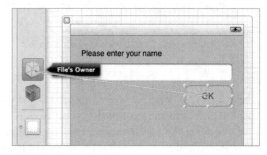

FIGURE 3-3

8. That's it! Press Command-R to test the application on the iPhone Simulator. Enter a name in the Text Field and click the OK button. An alert view displays a welcome message (see Figure 3-5).

FIGURE 3-4

FIGURE 3-5

How It Works

As mentioned earlier, you use actions and outlets to connect your code to the various views in your UI. Actions are represented using the IBAction keyword, whereas outlets use the IBOutlet keyword:

```
#import <UIKit/UIKit.h>

@interface OutletsAndActionsViewController : UIViewController
{
    //---declaring the outlet---
    IBOutlet UITextField *txtName;
}

//---expose the outlet as a property---
@property (nonatomic, retain) UITextField *txtName;

//---declaring the action---
-(IBAction) btnClicked:(id) sender;

@end
```

The IBOutlet identifier is used to prefix variables so that Interface Builder can synchronize the display and connection of outlets with Xcode. The @property keyword indicates to the compiler that you want the txtName outlet to be exposed as a property. The nonatomic keyword indicates that there is no need to ensure that the property is used in a thread-safe manner because it is not used in multiple threads. The default behavior is `atomic`; specifying `nonatomic` actually improves your application's performance.

> **NOTE** *The* `IBOutlet` *tag can also be added to the* `@property` *identifier. This syntax is common in the Apple documentation:*
>
>   @property (nonatomic, retain) **IBOutlet** UITextField *txtName;

> **NOTE** *For information about using the* `nonatomic` *and* `retain` *identifiers, refer to Appendix C, where you can find an introduction to Objective-C, the language used for iOS programming. The* `@synthesize` *keyword, discussed shortly, is also explained in more detail there.*

The `IBAction` identifier is used to synchronize action methods. An *action* is a method that can handle events raised by views (for example, when a button is clicked) in the View window. An *outlet*, on the other hand, is an object that enables your code to programmatically reference a view on the View window.

Once your actions and outlets are added to the header (`.h`) file of the View controller, you need to connect them to your views in Interface Builder.

When you Control-click and drag the File's Owner item to the Text Field and select `txtName`, you essentially connect the outlet you have created (`txtName`) with the Text Field on the View window. In general, to connect outlets you Control-click and drag the File's Owner item to the view on the View window.

CONNECTING OUTLETS AND ACTIONS TO VIEWS

To connect outlets to views, Control-click and drag the File's Owner item onto the required view in the View window. Note that you need to ensure that the type of the outlet is declared correctly; otherwise, you will not be able to connect it to the view. For example, if you declare `txtName` as `UITextView` (another type of view similar to the Text Field) and try to connect it to a Text Field on the View window, Interface Builder will not be able to connect it for you.

To connect an action to a view, Control-click and drag a view to the File's Owner item. Hence, for the OK Round Rect Button, you Control-click and drag the button to the File's Owner item and then select the action named `btnClicked:`. Alternatively, you can right-click on a view and drag and drop the event you want to connect over the File's Owner item.

In the implementation file (.m), you use the @synthesize keyword to indicate to the compiler that it should create the getter and setter for the specified property:

 WARNING *Forgetting to add the @synthesize keyword is one of the most common mistakes that developers make. If you don't remember to add this statement, you will encounter a runtime error when the application is executed. Appendix C covers getter and setter methods in more detail.*

```
#import "OutletsAndActionsViewController.h"

@implementation OutletsAndActionsViewController

//---synthesize the property---
@synthesize txtName;

//---displays an alert view when the button is clicked---
-(IBAction) btnClicked:(id) sender {
    NSString *str =
        [[NSString alloc] initWithFormat:@"Hello, %@", txtName.text];
    UIAlertView *alert =
        [[UIAlertView alloc] initWithTitle:@"Hello!"
                                   message:str
                                  delegate:self
                         cancelButtonTitle:@"Done"
                         otherButtonTitles:nil];
    [alert show];
    [str release];
    [alert release];
}

- (void)dealloc {
    //---release the outlet---
    [txtName release];
    [super dealloc];
}
```

The btnClicked: action simply displays an alert view with a message containing the user's name. Note that it has a parameter sender of type id. The sender parameter enables you to programmatically determine who actually invokes this action. This is useful when you have multiple views connected to one single action. For such cases, you often need to know which view invokes this method, and the sender parameter will contain a reference to the calling view.

USING VIEWS

So far, you have seen quite a number of views in action: Round Rect Button, Text Field, and Label. All these views are quite straightforward, but they provide a good opportunity for learning how to apply the concepts behind outlets and actions.

To use more views, you can locate them in the Object Library window in the Utilities panel (see Figure 3-6).

The Library is broadly divided into the following sections:

➤ **Objects & Controllers** — Contains views that control other views, such as the View Controller, Tab Bar Controller, Navigation Controller, and so on

➤ **Data Views** — Contains views that display data, such as the Image View, Table View, Data Picker, Picker View, and so on

➤ **Controls** — Contains views that accept input from users as well as display values, such as the Label, Round Rect Button, Text Field, and so on

➤ **Windows & Bars** — Contains views that display other miscellaneous views, such as View, Search Bar, Toolbar, and so on

➤ **Gesture Recognizers** — Contains classes that perform gesture recognition. Gestures include the tap, the pinch, rotation, and so on

In the following sections, you learn how to use some of the views available in the Library. Although it is beyond the scope of this book to show the use of every view, you will see a number of views in action throughout the book. By learning some of the fundamental view concepts in this chapter, you can use other views later without problems.

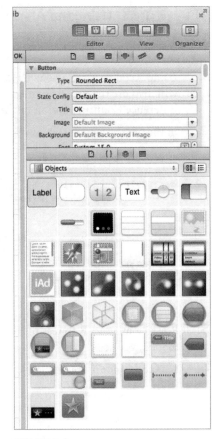

FIGURE 3-6

Using the Alert View

One of the views not listed in the Library is the `UIAlertView`. The `UIAlertView` displays an alert view to the user and is usually created during runtime. Hence, you have to create it using code.

 NOTE *You actually saw the* `UIAlertView` *in the previous section. In this section, you will learn how it actually works.*

The `UIAlertView` is useful for cases in which you have to display a message to the user. In addition, it can serve as a quick debugging tool when you want to observe the value of a variable during runtime.

The following Try It Out explores the `UIAlertView` in more detail.

TRY IT OUT | **Using the Alert View**

codefile UsingViews.zip available for download at Wrox.com

1. Using Xcode, create a new Single View Application (iPhone) project and name it **UsingViews**. You will also use the project name as the Class Prefix and ensure that you have the Use Automatic Reference Counting option unchecked.

2. In the `UsingViewsViewController.m` file, add the following bold code to the `viewDidLoad` method:

```
- (void)viewDidLoad
{
    UIAlertView *alert =
        [[UIAlertView alloc] initWithTitle:@"Hello"
                                   message:@"This is an alert view"
                                  delegate:self
                         cancelButtonTitle:@"OK"
                         otherButtonTitles:nil];
    [alert show];
    [alert release];
    [super viewDidLoad];
}
```

3. Press Command-R to test the application on the iPhone Simulator. When the application is loaded, you see the alert view shown in Figure 3-7. Clicking the OK button dismisses the alert.

4. In Xcode, modify the `otherButtonTitles` parameter by setting it with the value shown in bold:

```
- (void)viewDidLoad
{
    UIAlertView *alert =
        [[UIAlertView alloc] initWithTitle:@"Hello"
                                   message:@"This is an alert view"
                                  delegate:self
                         cancelButtonTitle:@"OK"
                         otherButtonTitles:@"Option 1", nil];
    [alert show];
    [alert release];
    [super viewDidLoad];
}
```

5. In the `UsingViewsViewController.h` file, add the following line that appears in bold:

```
#import <UIKit/UIKit.h>

@interface UsingViewsViewController : UIViewController
<UIAlertViewDelegate>

@end
```

6. In the `UsingViewsViewController.m` file, add the following method:

```
- (void)   alertView:(UIAlertView *)alertView
clickedButtonAtIndex:(NSInteger)buttonIndex {
```

FIGURE 3-7

```
        NSLog(@"%d", buttonIndex);
}
```

7. Press Command-R to test the application on the iPhone Simulator. Notice that there is now one more button in addition to the OK button (see Figure 3-8). Clicking either the OK button or the Option 1 button dismisses the alert.

8. Back in Xcode, modify the `otherButtonTitles` parameter by setting it with the value shown in bold:

FIGURE 3-8

```
- (void)viewDidLoad
{
    UIAlertView *alert =
        [[UIAlertView alloc] initWithTitle:@"Hello"
                            message:@"This is an alert view"
                            delegate:self
                 cancelButtonTitle:@"OK"
                 otherButtonTitles:@"Option 1", @"Option 2", nil];
    [alert show];
    [alert release];
    [super viewDidLoad];
}
```

9. Press Command-R to test the application in the iPhone Simulator again. Observe the placement of the three buttons (see Figure 3-9). Clicking any of the buttons dismisses the alert.

10. Click any one of the buttons — Option 1, Option 2, or OK.

FIGURE 3-9

11. In Xcode, press Command-Shift-C to view the Output window (you can also select View ⇨ Debug Area ⇨ Activate Console from the menu). Observe the values printed. You can rerun the application a number of times, clicking the different buttons to observe the values printed. The values printed for each button clicked are as follows:

➤ OK button — 0

➤ Option 1 — 1

➤ Option 2 — 2

How It Works

To use `UIAlertView`, you first instantiate it and initialize it with the various arguments:

```
        UIAlertView *alert =
            [[UIAlertView alloc] initWithTitle:@"Hello"
                                message:@"This is an alert view"
                                delegate:self
                     cancelButtonTitle:@"OK"
                     otherButtonTitles:nil];
```

The first parameter is the title of the alert view, which you set to `"Hello"`. The second is the message, which you set to `"This is an alert view"`. The third is the delegate, which you need to set to an object that will handle the events fired by the `UIAlertView` object. In this case, you set it to `self`, which means that the event handler will be implemented in the current class — that is, the View Controller. The `cancelButtonTitle` parameter displays a button to dismiss your alert view. Last, the `otherButtonTitles` parameter enables you to display additional buttons if needed. If no additional buttons are needed, simply set this to `nil`.

To show the alert view modally, use the `show` method:

```
[alert show];
```

 WARNING *Note that showing the alert view modally using the* `show` *method does not cause the program to stall execution at this statement. The subsequent statements after this line continue to execute even though the user may not have dismissed the alert.*

For simple use of the alert view, you don't really need to handle the events fired by it. Tapping the OK button (as set in the `cancelButtonTitle` parameter) simply dismisses the alert view.

If you want more than one button, you need to set the `otherButtonTitles` parameter, like this:

```
UIAlertView *alert =
    [[UIAlertView alloc] initWithTitle:@"Hello"
                        message:@"This is an alert view"
                        delegate:self
                  cancelButtonTitle:@"OK"
                  otherButtonTitles:@"Option 1", @"Option 2",
                                    nil];
```

Note that you need to end the `otherButtonTitles` parameter with a `nil` or a runtime error will occur.

 NOTE *There is no limit to how many buttons you can display in a* `UIAlertView`, *but I don't advise using more than two buttons. If you try to use more buttons than you have screen space for, the buttons will overflow the screen, which can look very messy.*

Now that you have more than one button, you need to be able to determine which button the user pressed — in particular, whether Option 1 or Option 2 was pressed. To do so, you need to handle the event raised by the `UIAlertView` class. You do so by ensuring that your View Controller implements the `UIAlertViewDelegate` protocol:

```
@interface UsingViewsViewController : UIViewController
<UIAlertViewDelegate>

@end
```

The `UIAlertViewDelegate` protocol contains several methods associated with the alert view. To know which button the user tapped, you need to implement the `alertView:clickedButtonAtIndex:` method:

```
- (void)   alertView:(UIAlertView *)alertView
clickedButtonAtIndex:(NSInteger)buttonIndex {
    NSLog(@"%d", buttonIndex);
}
```

The index of the button clicked is passed in via the `buttonIndex` parameter.

 NOTE *Refer to Appendix C for a discussion of the concept of protocols in Objective-C.*

Using the Action Sheet

Although the alert view can display multiple buttons, its primary use is still as a mechanism to alert users when something happens. If you need to display a message to the user with multiple options, you should use an action sheet, rather than the alert view. An *action sheet* displays a collection of buttons from which the user can select one.

To include an action sheet, use the following code snippet:

```
UIActionSheet *action =
    [[UIActionSheet alloc] initWithTitle:@"Title of Action Sheet"
                              delegate:self
                     cancelButtonTitle:@"OK"
                destructiveButtonTitle:@"Delete Message"
                     otherButtonTitles:@"Option 1", @"Option 2", nil];
[action showInView:self.view];
[action release];
```

To handle the event fired by the action sheet when one of the buttons is tapped, implement the `UIActionSheetDelegate` protocol in your View Controller, like this:

```
#import <UIKit/UIKit.h>

@interface UsingViewsViewController : UIViewController
<UIActionSheetDelegate>

@end
```

When a button is tapped, the `actionSheet:clickedButtonAtIndex:` event will be fired:

```
- (void) actionSheet:(UIActionSheet *)actionSheet
clickedButtonAtIndex:(NSInteger)buttonIndex{
    NSLog(@"%d", buttonIndex);
}
```

Figure 3-10 shows the action sheet when it is displayed on the iPhone Simulator. Observe that the action sheet pops up from the bottom of the View window.

One important aspect of the action sheet is that when it is used on the iPad, you should not display an action sheet in the `viewDidLoad` method — doing so causes an exception to be raised during runtime. Instead, you can display it in, say, an `IBAction` method.

Figure 3-11 shows the action sheet when displayed on the iPad. Interestingly, on the iPad the OK button (set by the `cancelButtonTitle:` parameter) is not displayed.

FIGURE 3-10

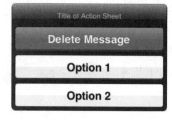

FIGURE 3-11

The value (`buttonIndex`) of each button when clicked is as follows:

➤ Delete Message — 0

➤ Option 1 — 1

➤ Option 2 — 2

➤ OK — 3

On the iPad, when the user taps on an area outside of the action sheet, the action sheet is dismissed and the value of `buttonIndex` becomes 3. Interestingly, if you specified `nil` for the `cancelButtonTitle:` part, the value of `buttonIndex` would be –1 when the action sheet is dismissed.

Page Control and Image View

Near the bottom of the iPhone's Home screen is a series of dots (see Figure 3-12). A lighted dot represents the currently selected page. As you swipe the page to the next page, the next dot lights, and the first one

FIGURE 3-12

dims. In the figure, the dots indicate that the first page is the active page. In the iOS SDK, the series of dots is represented by the `UIPageControl` class.

In the following Try It Out, you learn to use the Page Control within your own application to switch between images displayed in the Image View.

TRY IT OUT   **Using the Page Control and the Image View**

1. Using the `UsingViews` project created in the previous section, add five images to the Supporting Files folder by dragging and dropping them from the Finder. Figure 3-13 shows the five images added to the project.

2. Select the `UsingViewsViewController.xib` file to edit it using Interface Builder.

3. Drag and drop two Image Views onto the View window (see Figure 3-14). At this point, overlap them (but not entirely) as shown in the figure.

4. With the first Image View selected, open the Attributes Inspector window and set the `Tag` property to 0. Select the second Image View and set the `Tag` property to **1** (see Figure 3-15).

5. Drag and drop the Page Control onto the View window and set its number of pages to **5** (see Figure 3-16). Ensure that you increase the width of the Page Control so that all the dots are now visible.

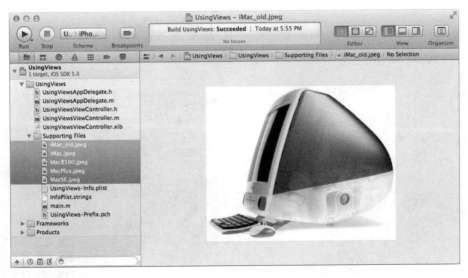

FIGURE 3-13

6. Set the Background color of the View window to black so that the dots inside the Page Control are clearly visible (see Figure 3-17).

7. In Xcode, declare three outlets two `UIImageView` objects, and a variable in the `UsingViewsViewController.h` file:

```
#import <UIKit/UIKit.h>

@interface UsingViewsViewController : UIViewController
    <UIAlertViewDelegate, UIActionSheetDelegate>
{
    IBOutlet UIPageControl *pageControl;
    IBOutlet UIImageView *imageView1;
    IBOutlet UIImageView *imageView2;
    UIImageView *tempImageView, *bgImageView;
    int prevPage;
}

@property (nonatomic, retain) UIPageControl *pageControl;
@property (nonatomic, retain) UIImageView *imageView1;
@property (nonatomic, retain) UIImageView *imageView2;

@end
```

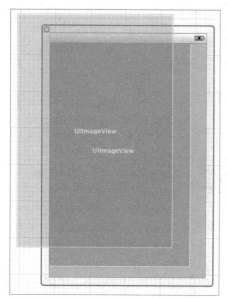

FIGURE 3-14

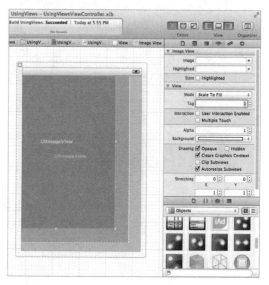

FIGURE 3-15

8. In Interface Builder, connect the three outlets to the views on the View window. Figure 3-18 shows the connections made for the `imageView1`, `imageView2`, and `pageControl` outlets.

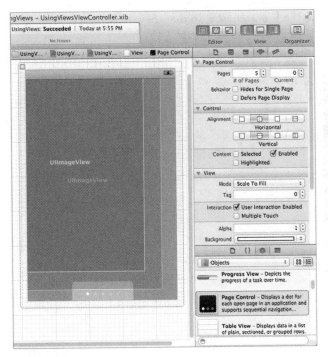

FIGURE 3-16

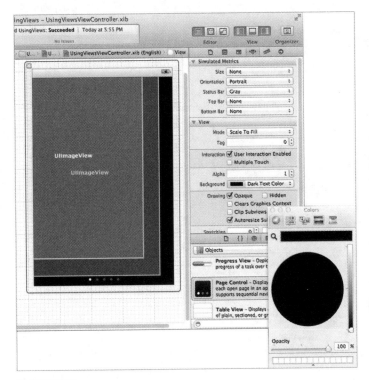

FIGURE 3-17

9. You can now rearrange the Image Views on the View window so that they overlap each other. In particular, set the size of the Image View to be 320x420 (see Figure 3-19).

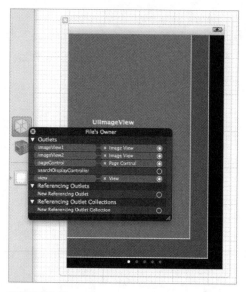

FIGURE 3-18

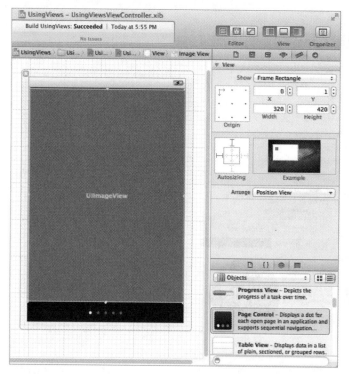

FIGURE 3-19

10. In Xcode, add the following statements in bold to the `UsingViewsViewController.m` file:

```objc
#import "UsingViewsViewController.h"

@implementation UsingViewsViewController

@synthesize pageControl;
@synthesize imageView1, imageView2;

- (void)viewDidLoad
{
    //---initialize the first imageview to display an image---
    [imageView1 setImage:[UIImage imageNamed:@"iMac_old.jpeg"]];
    tempImageView = imageView2;

    //---make the first imageview visible and hide the second---
    [imageView1 setHidden:NO];
    [imageView2 setHidden:YES];

    //---add the event handler for the page control---
    [pageControl addTarget:self
                    action:@selector(pageTurning:)
          forControlEvents:UIControlEventValueChanged];

    prevPage = 0;

    [super viewDidLoad];
}

//---when the page control's value is changed---
- (void) pageTurning: (UIPageControl *) pageController {
    //---get the page number you can turning to---
    NSInteger nextPage = [pageController currentPage];
    switch (nextPage) {
        case 0:
            [tempImageView setImage:
             [UIImage imageNamed:@"iMac_old.jpeg"]];
            break;
        case 1:
            [tempImageView setImage:
             [UIImage imageNamed:@"iMac.jpeg"]];
            break;
        case 2:
            [tempImageView setImage:
             [UIImage imageNamed:@"Mac8100.jpeg"]];
            break;
        case 3:
            [tempImageView setImage:
             [UIImage imageNamed:@"MacPlus.jpeg"]];
            break;
        case 4:
            [tempImageView setImage:
             [UIImage imageNamed:@"MacSE.jpeg"]];
            break;
```

```
        default:
            break;
    }

    //---switch the two imageview views---
    if (tempImageView.tag == 0) { //---imageView1---
        tempImageView = imageView2;
        bgImageView = imageView1;
    }
    else {                              //---imageView2---
        tempImageView = imageView1;
        bgImageView = imageView2;
    }

    UIViewAnimationOptions transitionOption;

    if (nextPage > prevPage)
        //---if moving from left to right---
        transitionOption = UIViewAnimationOptionTransitionFlipFromLeft;
    else
        //---if moving from right to left---
        transitionOption = UIViewAnimationOptionTransitionFlipFromRight;

    //---animate by flipping the images---
    [UIView transitionWithView:tempImageView
                  duration:2.5
                    options:transitionOption
                animations:^{
                        [tempImageView setHidden:YES];
                }
                completion:NULL];

    [UIView transitionWithView:bgImageView
                  duration:2.5
                    options:transitionOption
                animations:^{
                        [bgImageView setHidden:NO];
                }
                completion:NULL];

    prevPage = nextPage;
}

- (void)dealloc {
    [pageControl release];
    [imageView1 release];
    [imageView2 release];
    [super dealloc];
}
```

11. Press Command-R to test the application on the iPhone Simulator. When you tap the Page Control located at the bottom of the screen, the Image View flips to display the next one. Figure 3-20 shows the transitioning of two images.

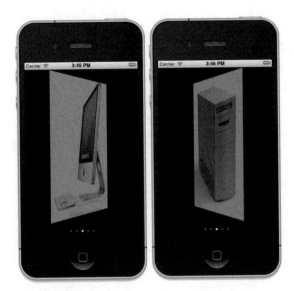

FIGURE 3-20

How It Works

When the View window is first loaded, you get one of the Image Views to display an image and then hide the other:

```
//---initialize the first imageview to display an image---
[imageView1 setImage:[UIImage imageNamed:@"iMac_old.jpeg"]];
tempImageView = imageView2;

//---make the first imageview visible and hide the second---
[imageView1 setHidden:NO];
[imageView2 setHidden:YES];
```

You then wire the Page Control so that when the user taps it, an event is fired and triggers a method. In this case, the pageTurning: method is called:

```
//---add the event handler for the page control---
[pageControl addTarget:self
            action:@selector(pageTurning:)
    forControlEvents:UIControlEventValueChanged];
```

In the pageTurning: method, you determine which image you should load based on the value of the Page Control:

```
//---when the page control's value is changed---
- (void) pageTurning: (UIPageControl *) pageController {

    //---get the page number you can turning to---
    NSInteger nextPage = [pageController currentPage];
    switch (nextPage) {
```

```
        case 0:
            [tempImageView setImage:
             [UIImage imageNamed:@"iMac_old.jpeg"]];
            break;
        case 1:
            [tempImageView setImage:
             [UIImage imageNamed:@"iMac.jpeg"]];
            break;
        case 2:
            [tempImageView setImage:
             [UIImage imageNamed:@"Mac8100.jpeg"]];
            break;
        case 3:
            [tempImageView setImage:
             [UIImage imageNamed:@"MacPlus.jpeg"]];
            break;
        case 4:
            [tempImageView setImage:
             [UIImage imageNamed:@"MacSE.jpeg"]];
            break;
        default:
            break;
    }
    //...
}
```

You then switch the two Image Views and animate them by using the various methods in the `UIView` class:

```
//---switch the two imageview views---
if (tempImageView.tag == 0) { //---imageView1---
    tempImageView = imageView2;
    bgImageView = imageView1;
}
else {                        //---imageView2---
    tempImageView = imageView1;
    bgImageView = imageView2;
}

UIViewAnimationOptions transitionOption;

if (nextPage > prevPage)
    //---if moving from left to right---
    transitionOption = UIViewAnimationOptionTransitionFlipFromLeft;
else
    //---if moving from right to left---
    transitionOption = UIViewAnimationOptionTransitionFlipFromRight;

//---animate by flipping the images---
[UIView transitionWithView:tempImageView
                  duration:2.5
                   options:transitionOption
                animations:^{
                    [tempImageView setHidden:YES];
                }
```

```
                       completion:NULL];

[UIView transitionWithView:bgImageView
                  duration:2.5
                   options:transitionOption
                animations:^{
                     [bgImageView setHidden:NO];
                }
                completion:NULL];

prevPage = nextPage;
```

Specifically, you apply the flipping transitions to the Image Views using the transitionWithView:duration:options:animations:completion: method:

```
//---animate by flipping the images---
[UIView transitionWithView:tempImageView
                  duration:2.5
                   options:transitionOption
                animations:^{
                     [tempImageView setHidden:YES];
                }
                completion:NULL];
```

This method enables you to specify the animation that you want to perform on a specified view (transitionWithView:), the duration of the animation (duration:), the transition options (options:), the code that makes the changes to the view (animations:), and the code to execute when the animation ends. In this example, if the user is flipping the images from left to right, you will flip the images from left to right, and vice versa.

Using the Web View

To load web pages from within your application, you can embed a web browser in your application through the use of a Web View (UIWebView). Using the Web View, you can send a request to load web content, which is very useful if you want to convert an existing web application into a native application (such as those written using Dashcode). All you need to do is embed all the HTML pages into your Supporting Files folder in your Xcode project and load the HTML pages into the Web View during runtime.

 NOTE Depending on how complex your web application is, you may have to do some additional work to port it to a native application if it involves server-side technologies such as CGI, PHP, or others.

The following Try It Out shows how to use the Web View to load a web page.

TRY IT OUT Loading a Web Page Using the Web View

codefile UsingViews2.zip available for download at Wrox.com

1. Using Xcode, create a new Single View Application (iPhone) project and name it UsingViews2. You will also use the project name as the Class Prefix and ensure that you have the Use Automatic Reference Counting option unchecked.

2. Select the UsingViews2ViewController.xib file to edit it using Interface Builder.

3. From the Library, add a Web View to the View window (see Figure 3-21). In the Attributes Inspector window for the Web View, check the Scales Page to Fit property.

4. In the UsingViews2ViewController.h file, declare an outlet for the Web View:

```
#import <UIKit/UIKit.h>

@interface UsingViews2ViewController : UIViewController
{
    IBOutlet UIWebView *webView;
}

@property (nonatomic, retain) UIWebView *webView;

@end
```

5. In Interface Builder, connect the webView outlet to the Web View.

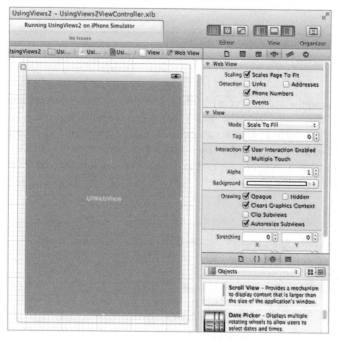

FIGURE 3-21

6. In the `UsingViews2ViewController.m` file, add the following statements that appear in bold:

```
#import "UsingViews2ViewController.h"

@implementation UsingViews2ViewController

@synthesize webView;

- (void)viewDidLoad {
    NSURL *url = [NSURL URLWithString:@"http://www.apple.com"];
    NSURLRequest *req = [NSURLRequest requestWithURL:url];
    [webView loadRequest:req];
    [super viewDidLoad];
}

- (void)dealloc {
    [webView release];
    [super dealloc];
}
```

7. Press Command-R to test the application on the iPhone Simulator. You should see the application loading the page from Apple.com (see Figure 3-22).

How It Works

To load the Web View with a URL, you first instantiate an NSURL object with a URL via the URLWithString method:

```
NSURL *url = [NSURL URLWithString:@"http://www.apple.com"];
```

FIGURE 3-22

You then create an NSURLRequest object by passing the NSURL object to its requestWithURL: method:

```
NSURLRequest *req = [NSURLRequest requestWithURL:url];
```

Finally, you load the Web View with the NSURLRequest object via the loadRequest: method:

```
[webView loadRequest:req];
```

ADDING VIEWS DYNAMICALLY USING CODE

Up to this point, all the UIs of your application have been created visually using Interface Builder. Although Interface Builder makes it relatively easy to build a UI using drag-and-drop, sometimes you are better off using code to create it. One such instance is when you need a dynamic UI, such as for games.

> **NOTE** *Interface Builder may be easy to use, but it can be confusing to some people. Because you often have more than one way of doing things in Interface Builder, it can create unnecessary complications. I know of developers who swear by creating their UIs using code.*

In the following Try It Out, you learn how to create views dynamically from code, which will help you understand how views are constructed and manipulated.

TRY IT OUT Creating Views from Code

codefile DynamicViews.zip available for download at Wrox.com

1. Using Xcode, create a Single View Application (iPhone) project and name it `DynamicViews`. You will also use the project name as the Class Prefix and ensure that you have the Use Automatic Reference Counting option unchecked.

2. In the `DynamicViewsViewController.m` file, add the following statements that appear in bold:

```
#import "DynamicViewsViewController.h"

@implementation DynamicViewsViewController

- (void)loadView {
    //---create a UIView object---
    UIView *view =
        [[UIView alloc] initWithFrame:[UIScreen mainScreen].applicationFrame];

    //---set the background color to light gray---
    view.backgroundColor = [UIColor lightGrayColor];

    //---create a Label view---
    CGRect frame = CGRectMake(10, 15, 300, 20);
    UILabel *label = [[UILabel alloc] initWithFrame:frame];
    label.textAlignment = UITextAlignmentCenter;
    label.backgroundColor = [UIColor clearColor];
    label.font = [UIFont fontWithName:@"Verdana" size:20];
    label.text = @"This is a label";
    label.tag = 1000;

    //---create a Button view---
    frame = CGRectMake(10, 70, 300, 50);
    UIButton *button = [UIButton buttonWithType:UIButtonTypeRoundedRect];
    button.frame = frame;
    [button setTitle:@"Click Me, Please!" forState:UIControlStateNormal];
    button.backgroundColor = [UIColor clearColor];
    button.tag = 2000;
    [button addTarget:self
            action:@selector(buttonClicked:)
```

```
           forControlEvents:UIControlEventTouchUpInside];

    [view addSubview:label];
    [view addSubview:button];

    self.view = view;

    [label release];
    [view release];
}

-(IBAction) buttonClicked: (id) sender{
    UIAlertView *alert =
        [[UIAlertView alloc] initWithTitle:@"Action invoked!"
                            message:@"Button clicked!"
                            delegate:self
                      cancelButtonTitle:@"OK"
                      otherButtonTitles:nil];
    [alert show];
    [alert release];
}
```

3. Press Command-R to test the application on the iPhone Simulator. Figure 3-23 shows that the Label and Round Rect Button are displayed on the View window. Click the button to see an alert view displaying a message.

How It Works

You implemented the `loadView` method defined in your View Controller to programmatically create your views. You should implement this method

FIGURE 3-23

only if you are generating your UI during runtime. The method is automatically called when the `view` property of your View Controller is called but its current value is `nil`.

NOTE *Chapter 4 discusses some of the commonly used methods in a View Controller.*

The first view you create is the `UIView` object, which enables you to use it as a container for more views:

```
//---create a UIView object---
UIView *view =
    [[UIView alloc] initWithFrame:
        [UIScreen mainScreen].applicationFrame];

//---set the background color to light gray---
view.backgroundColor = [UIColor lightGrayColor];
```

Next, you create a Label and set it to display a string:

```
//---create a Label view---
CGRect frame = CGRectMake(10, 15, 300, 20);
UILabel *label = [[UILabel alloc] initWithFrame:frame];
label.textAlignment = UITextAlignmentCenter;
label.backgroundColor = [UIColor clearColor];
label.font = [UIFont fontWithName:@"Verdana" size:20];
label.text = @"This is a label";
label.tag = 1000;
```

Notice that you have also set the `tag` property, which is very useful for enabling you to search for particular views during runtime.

You also create a Round Rect Button by calling the `buttonWithType:` method with the `UIButtonTypeRoundedRect` constant. This method returns a `UIRoundedRectButton` object (which is a subclass of `UIButton`):

```
//---create a Button view---
frame = CGRectMake(10, 70, 300, 50);
UIButton *button = [UIButton buttonWithType:
                         UIButtonTypeRoundedRect];
button.frame = frame;
[button setTitle:@"Click Me, Please!"
        forState:UIControlStateNormal];
button.backgroundColor = [UIColor clearColor];
button.tag = 2000;
```

You then wire an event handler for its `Touch Up Inside` event so that when the button is tapped, the `buttonClicked:` method is called:

```
[button addTarget:self
         action:@selector(buttonClicked:)
    forControlEvents:UIControlEventTouchUpInside];
```

Next, you add the `label` and `button` views to the `view` you created earlier:

```
[view addSubview:label];
[view addSubview:button];
```

Finally, you assign the `view` object to the `view` property of the current View controller:

```
self.view = view;
```

 NOTE *Within the* `loadView` *method, you should not get the value of the* `view` *property (setting it is alright), like this:*

```
[self.view addSubview:label];  //---this is not OK---
self.view = view;              //---this is OK---
```

Trying to get the value of the view property in this method will result in a circular reference and cause memory overflow.

UNDERSTANDING VIEW HIERARCHY

As views are created and added, they are added to a tree data structure. Views are displayed in the order that they are added. To verify this, modify the location of the UIButton object you created earlier by changing its location to CGRectMake(10, 30, 300, 50), as in the following:

```
//---create a Button view---
//frame = CGRectMake(10, 70, 300, 50);
frame = CGRectMake(10, 30, 300, 50);
```

When you now run the application again, you will notice that the Round Rect Button overlaps the Label (see Figure 3-24) because the button was added last:

FIGURE 3-24

```
[view addSubview:label];
[view addSubview:button];
```

To switch the order in which the views are displayed after they have been added, use the exchangeS ubviewAtIndex:withSubviewAtIndex: method:

```
[view addSubview:label];
[view addSubview:button];
[view exchangeSubviewAtIndex:1 withSubviewAtIndex:0];

self.view = view;
[label release];
[view release];
```

The preceding statement in bold swaps the order of the Label and Round Rect Button. When the application is run again, the Label will now appear on top of the Round Rect Button (see Figure 3-25).

FIGURE 3-25

To learn the order of the various views already added, you can use the following code segment to print the value of the tag property for each view:

```
[view addSubview:label];
[view addSubview:button];
[view exchangeSubviewAtIndex:1 withSubviewAtIndex:0];

for (int i=0; i<[view.subviews count]; ++i) {
    UIView *v = [view.subviews objectAtIndex:i];
    NSLog(@"%d", v.tag);
}
```

If you run the preceding code, you will see the following printed in the Output window:

```
2011-07-30 00:57:18.461 DynamicViews[2652:ef03] 2000
2011-07-30 00:57:18.463 DynamicViews[2652:ef03] 1000
```

The following method recursively prints out all the views contained in a `UIView` object:

```
-(void) printViews:(UIView *) view {
    if ([view.subviews count] > 0){
        for (int i=0; i<[view.subviews count]; ++i) {
            UIView *v = [view.subviews objectAtIndex:i];
            NSLog(@"View index: %d Tag: %d",i, v.tag);
            [self printViews:v];
        }
    } else
        return;
}
```

You can call the preceding method from the `viewDidLoad` method:

```
- (void)viewDidLoad
{
    [self printViews:self.view];
    [super viewDidLoad];
}
```

The preceding code snippet will print out the following output:

```
2011-07-30 00:57:18.463 DynamicViews[2652:ef03] View index: 0 Tag: 2000
2011-07-30 00:57:18.464 DynamicViews[2652:ef03] View index: 0 Tag: 0
2011-07-30 00:57:18.464 DynamicViews[2652:ef03] View index: 1 Tag: 1000
```

To remove a view from the current view hierarchy, use the `removeFromSuperview` method of the view you want to remove. For example, the following statement removes the `label` view:

```
[label removeFromSuperview];
```

SUMMARY

This chapter explored the roles played by outlets and actions in an iPhone application. Outlets and actions are the cornerstone of iOS development, so understanding their use is extremely important. Throughout this book, you will come across them frequently. You have also seen the use of some of the commonly used views in the Library.

In the next chapter, you learn about the various types of View controllers supported by the iOS SDK, and how you can use them to build different types of iPhone and iPad applications.

EXERCISES

1. Declare and define an outlet for a `UITextField` view using code.

2. Declare and define an action using code.

3. When do you use an alert view and when do you use an action sheet?

4. Create a `UIButton` from code and wire its `Touch Up Inside` event to an event handler.

Answers to the exercises can be found in Appendix D.

▶ WHAT YOU LEARNED IN THIS CHAPTER

TOPIC	KEY CONCEPTS
Action	An action is a method that can handle events raised by views (for example, when a button is clicked, etc.) in the View window.
Outlet	An outlet allows your code to programmatically reference a view on the View window.
Adding outlet using code	Use the `IBOutlet` keyword: `IBOutlet UITextField *txtName;`
Adding action using code	Use the `IBAction` keyword: `-(IBAction) btnClicked:(id) sender;`
Connecting actions	To link actions, you commonly drag from the view in the View window onto the File's Owner item.
Connection outlets	To link outlets, you commonly drag from the File's Owner item onto the required view in the View window.

Using the `UIAlertView`	`UIAlertView *alert =`
	`[[UIAlertView alloc]`
	`        initWithTitle:@"Hello!"`
	`            message:@"Hello, world!"`
	`            delegate:self`
	`   cancelButtonTitle:@"Done"`
	`   otherButtonTitles:nil];`
	`[alert show];`
	`[alert release];`

Handling events fired by `UIAlertView`	Ensure that your View Controller conforms to the `UIAlertViewDelegate` protocol.

Using the `UIActionSheet`	`UIActionSheet *action =`
	`[[UIActionSheet alloc]`
	`        initWithTitle:@"Title of Action Sheet"`
	`            delegate:self`
	`   cancelButtonTitle:@"OK"`
	`destructiveButtonTitle:@"Delete Message"`
	`   otherButtonTitles:@"Option 1", @"Option 2",`
	`            nil];`
	
	`[action showInView:self.view];`
	`[action release];`

Handling events fired by `UIActionSheet`	Ensure that your View Controller conforms to the `UIActionSheetDelegate` protocol.

TOPIC	KEY CONCEPTS
Wiring up the events for the UIPageControl	```[pageControl addTarget:self action:@selector(pageTurning:) forControlEvents:UIControlEventValueChanged];```
Using the UIImageView	```[imageView1 setImage: [UIImage imageNamed:@"iMac_old.jpeg"]];```
Using the UIWebView	```NSURL *url = [NSURL URLWithString:@"http://www.apple.com"]; NSURLRequest *req = [NSURLRequest requestWithURL:url]; [webView loadRequest:req];```

4

Exploring the Different View Controllers

WHAT YOU WILL LEARN IN THIS CHAPTER

➤ Understanding the structure of a Single View Application project

➤ How to create an Empty Application project and manually add a View controller and a View window to it

➤ Creating views dynamically during runtime

➤ Wiring up events of views with event handlers via code

➤ How to switch to another View window during runtime

➤ How to animate the switching of views

➤ How to create a Master-Detail application

➤ How to create a Tabbed application

So far you've dealt only with single-view applications — that is, applications with a single View controller for controlling the View window. The previous chapters all use the Single View Application template available in the iOS SDK because it is the simplest way to get started with iOS programming. When you create a Single View Application project, there is one View controller (named `<Class_Prefix>`ViewController by the iOS SDK) by default.

In real-life applications, you often need more than one View controller, with each controlling a different View windows displaying different information. This chapter explains the various types of projects you can create for your iPhone and iPad and how each utilizes a different type of View controller. You will also learn how to create multiple View windows in your application and then programmatically switch among them during runtime. In addition, you learn how to animate the switching of View windows using the built-in animation methods available in the iOS SDK.

THE SINGLE VIEW APPLICATION TEMPLATE

When you create a Single View Application project using Xcode, you automatically have a single view in your application. Until now, you have been using it without understanding much about how it works under the hood. In the following Try It Out, you will dive into the details and unravel all the magic that makes your application work.

TRY IT OUT Creating a Single View Application Project

codefile SingleViewBasedApp.zip available for download at Wrox.com

1. Using Xcode, create a Single View Application (iPhone) project (see Figure 4-1) and click Next.

FIGURE 4-1

2. Name the project **SingleViewBasedApp**. Set the Class Prefix to be `SingleViewBasedApp` and ensure that you have the Use Automatic Reference Counting option unchecked. Click Next and then Create.

3. Press Command-R to test the application on the iPhone Simulator. The application displays an empty screen, as shown in Figure 4-2.

How It Works

What you have just created is a Single View Application project. By default, the Single View Application template includes a single View window, controlled by a View controller class.

First, take a look at the files and folders created for your project in Xcode. In particular, note the folders and files listed under the project name (see Figure 4-3).

FIGURE 4-2   FIGURE 4-3

As you can see, many files are created for you by default when you create a new project. The iOS SDK tries to make your life simpler by creating some of the items that you will use most often when you develop an iOS application. Table 4-1 describes the various files created in the project by default.

NOTE *The types and number of files created vary according to the type of project you have selected. The Single View Application template is a good starting point for understanding the various files involved.*

TABLE 4-1: Project Files Created by Default

FILE	DESCRIPTION
SingleViewBasedApp.app	The application bundle (executable), which contains the executable as well as the data that is bundled with the application
SingleViewBasedApp_Prefix.pch	Contains the prefix header for all files in the project. The prefix header is included by default in the other files in the project.
SingleViewBasedAppAppDelegate.h	Header file for the application delegate
SingleViewBasedAppAppDelegate.m	Implementation file for the application delegate
SingleViewBasedAppViewController.h	Header file for a View controller
SingleViewBasedAppViewController.m	Implementation file for a View controller
SingleViewBasedAppViewController.xib	XIB file containing the user interface of a View window
CoreGraphics.framework	C-based as for low-level 2D rendering
Foundation.framework	APIs for foundational system services such as data types, XML ,URL, and so on
UIKit.framework	Provides fundamental objects for constructing and managing your application's user interface
SingleViewBasedApp-Info.plist	A dictionary file that contains information about your project, such as icon, application name, and more; information is stored in key/value pairs.
main.m	The main file that bootstraps your iOS application

The `main.m` file contains code that bootstraps your application, and you rarely need to modify it:

```
#import <UIKit/UIKit.h>

#import "SingleViewBasedAppAppDelegate.h"

int main(int argc, char *argv[])
{
    @autoreleasepool {
        return UIApplicationMain(argc, argv, nil,
        NSStringFromClass([SingleViewBasedAppAppDelegate class]));
    }
}
```

Most of the hard work is done by the `UIApplicationMain()` function, which loads the `SingleViewBasedAppAppDelegate` class to obtain more information about the project. In particular, it looks at the main XIB file you will use for your project.

THE XIB AND NIB EXTENSIONS

iOS application development always includes files with the `.xib` extension (sometimes also known as NIB files), so it is useful to know what these extensions stand for. The current Mac OS X was built upon an operating system called NeXTSTEP, from a company known as NeXT (founded by Apple's cofounder, Steve Jobs, in 1985). The N in NIB stands for NeXTSTEP. As for .xib, the X presumably stands for XML because its content is saved as an XML file. The IB stands for Interface Builder, the design tool that enables you to visually construct the UI for your application.

Application Delegate

The `SingleViewBasedAppAppDelegate.m` file contains code that is typically executed after the application has finished loading, or just before it is terminated. For this example, its content is as follows:

> **NOTE** When creating your project using Xcode, the filename of your application delegate will always be appended with the string `AppDelegate`. For example, if the project name (and Class Prefix) is `SingleViewBasedApp`, then the application delegate will be called `SingleViewBasedAppAppDelegate`.

```objc
#import "SingleViewBasedAppAppDelegate.h"

#import "SingleViewBasedAppViewController.h"

@implementation SingleViewBasedAppAppDelegate

@synthesize window = _window;
@synthesize viewController = _viewController;

- (void)dealloc
{
    [_window release];
    [_viewController release];
    [super dealloc];
}

- (BOOL)application:(UIApplication *)application
didFinishLaunchingWithOptions:(NSDictionary *)launchOptions
{
```

```objc
    self.window = [[[UIWindow alloc] initWithFrame:[[UIScreen mainScreen]
    bounds]] autorelease];
    // Override point for customization after application launch.
    self.viewController = [[[SingleViewBasedAppViewController alloc]
initWithNibName:@"SingleViewBasedAppViewController" bundle:nil] autorelease];
    self.window.rootViewController = self.viewController;
    [self.window makeKeyAndVisible];
    return YES;
}

- (void)applicationWillResignActive:(UIApplication *)application
{
    /*
    Sent when the application is about to move from active to inactive state.
This can occur for certain types of temporary interruptions (such as an incoming
phone call or SMS message) or when the user quits the application and it begins
the transition to the background state.
    Use this method to pause ongoing tasks, disable timers, and throttle down
OpenGL ES frame rates. Games should use this method to pause the game.
    */
}

- (void)applicationDidEnterBackground:(UIApplication *)application
{
    /*
    Use this method to release shared resources, save user data, invalidate
timers, and store enough application state information to restore your application
to its current state in case it is terminated later.
    If your application supports background execution, this method is called
instead of applicationWillTerminate: when the user quits.
    */
}

- (void)applicationWillEnterForeground:(UIApplication *)application
{
    /*
    Called as part of the transition from the background to the inactive state;
here you can undo many of the changes made on entering the background.
    */
}

- (void)applicationDidBecomeActive:(UIApplication *)application
{
    /*
    Restart any tasks that were paused (or not yet started) while the application
was inactive. If the application was previously in the background, optionally
refresh the user interface.
    */
}

- (void)applicationWillTerminate:(UIApplication *)application
{
    /*
    Called when the application is about to terminate.
    Save data if appropriate.
```

```
            See also applicationDidEnterBackground:.
            */
    }

    @end
```

When the application has finished launching, it sends its delegate the
`application:DidFinishLaunchingWithOptions:` message. In the preceding
case, it creates a `UIWindow` object based on the current screen size, and then creates
an instance of the `SingleViewBasedAppViewController` class together with the
`SingleViewBasedAppViewController.xib` file. Once the View controller is instantiated, it is
assigned to the root View controller of the `UIWindow` object:

```
    self.window = [[[UIWindow alloc] initWithFrame:[[UIScreen mainScreen]
    bounds]] autorelease];
    // Override point for customization after application launch.
    self.viewController = [[[SingleViewBasedAppViewController alloc]
initWithNibName:@"SingleViewBasedAppViewController" bundle:nil] autorelease];
    self.window.rootViewController = self.viewController;
    [self.window makeKeyAndVisible];
```

The `SingleViewBasedAppAppDelegate.h` file contains the declaration of the members of the
`SingleViewBasedAppAppDelegate` class:

```
    #import <UIKit/UIKit.h>

    @class SingleViewBasedAppViewController;

    @interface SingleViewBasedAppAppDelegate : UIResponder <UIApplicationDelegate>

    @property (strong, nonatomic) UIWindow *window;

    @property (strong, nonatomic) SingleViewBasedAppViewController *viewController;

    @end
```

Of particular interest is this line:

```
    @interface SingleViewBasedAppAppDelegate : UIResponder <UIApplicationDelegate>
```

The `<UIApplicationDelegate>` statement specifies that the delegate class should implement the
`UIApplicationDelegate` protocol. Put simply, it means that the delegate class will handle
events (or messages) defined in the `UIApplicationDelegate` protocol. Examples of events in the
`UIApplicationDelegate` protocol include the following (you saw some of these implemented in
the `SingleViewBasedAppAppDelegate.m` file.):

➤ `Application:DidFinishLaunchingWithOptions:`

➤ `applicationWillTerminate:`

➤ `applicationDidDidReceiveMemoryWarning:`

➤ Other methods that inform you if the application is receding into the background or coming
back into the foreground. You will learn more about these methods in Chapter 21.

The application delegate class is also a good place to put your global objects and methods, as they are accessible from all the other classes in your project.

 NOTE *Protocols are discussed in more detail in Appendix C.*

Controlling Your UI Using View Controllers

In iOS programming, you typically use a View controller to manage a View window, as well as to perform navigation and memory management. In the Single View Application project template, Xcode automatically uses a View controller to help you manage your *View window*. Think of a View window as a screen (or window) you see on your iOS device.

Earlier in this chapter, you saw that the `SingleViewBasedAppAppDelegate.m` file creates an instance of the `SingleViewBasedAppViewController` class together with the `SingleViewBasedAppViewController.xib` file.

Select the `SingleViewBasedAppViewController.xib` file from Xcode, and you should see three icons: File's Owner, First Responder, and View (see Figure 4-4). Select the File's Owner item and view the Identity Inspector window (View ➪ Utilities ➪ Show Identity Inspector). Observe that the Class is set to `SingleViewBasedAppViewController`. This means that the View window is being controlled by the `SingleViewBasedAppViewController` class.

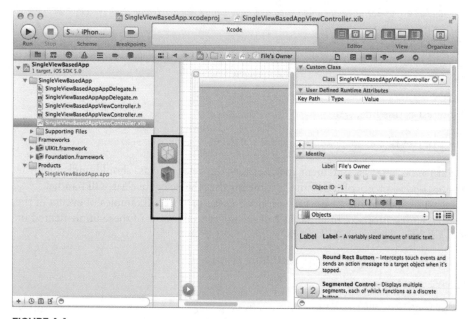

FIGURE 4-4

NOTE When creating your project using Xcode, the filename of your View controller will always be `<Class_Prefix>ViewController`. For example, if the project name is `SingleViewBasedApp`, and you name the class prefix to be the same as your project name, then the View Controller will be called `SingleViewBasedAppViewController`.

You can right-click (or Control-click) the File's Owner item to view its properties (see Figure 4-5). Note that the `view` outlet is connected to the `View` item.

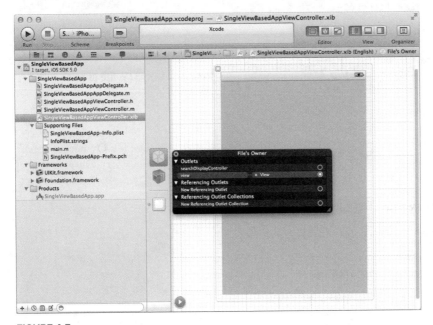

FIGURE 4-5

The `View` item represents the screen that appears on your application. Double-click View to display it.

The `SingleViewBasedAppViewController` class is represented by two files: `SingleViewBasedAppViewController.h` and `SingleViewBasedAppViewController.m`. The `SingleViewBasedAppViewController` class is where you write the code to interact with the views of your application.

The content of the `SingleViewBasedAppViewController.h` file looks like this:

```
#import <UIKit/UIKit.h>

@interface SingleViewBasedAppViewController : UIViewController

@end
```

Note that the `SingleViewBasedAppViewController` class inherits from the `UIViewController` base class, which provides most of the functionality available on a View window.

The content of the `SingleViewBasedAppViewController.m` file looks like this:

```
#import "SingleViewBasedAppViewController.h"

@implementation SingleViewBasedAppViewController

- (void)didReceiveMemoryWarning
{
    [super didReceiveMemoryWarning];
    // Release any cached data, images, etc that aren't in use.
}

#pragma mark - View lifecycle

- (void)viewDidLoad
{
    [super viewDidLoad];
    // Do any additional setup after loading the view, typically from a nib.
}

- (void)viewDidUnload
{
    [super viewDidUnload];
    // Release any retained subviews of the main view.
    // e.g. self.myOutlet = nil;
}

- (void)viewWillAppear:(BOOL)animated
{
    [super viewWillAppear:animated];
}

- (void)viewDidAppear:(BOOL)animated
{
    [super viewDidAppear:animated];
}

- (void)viewWillDisappear:(BOOL)animated
{
    [super viewWillDisappear:animated];
}

- (void)viewDidDisappear:(BOOL)animated
{
    [super viewDidDisappear:animated];
}

- (BOOL)shouldAutorotateToInterfaceOrientation:
   (UIInterfaceOrientation)interfaceOrientation
{
    // Return YES for supported orientations
    return (interfaceOrientation != UIInterfaceOrientationPortraitUpsideDown);
}

@end
```

The `SingleViewBasedAppViewController.m` file contains a number of methods commonly used by most developers. This is where you populate your View controllers with code to make it do interesting things.

THE EMPTY APPLICATION TEMPLATE

In this section, you discover another type of application template you can create using the iOS SDK: the *Empty Application* template. Unlike the Single View Application template, the Empty Application template does not include a View controller by default. Instead, it provides only the skeleton of an iOS application — you need to add your own views and their respective View controllers. Therefore, an Empty Application project presents a good opportunity for you to learn how View controllers work and appreciate all the work needed to connect the View controllers and XIB files. When you understand how View controllers work, you will be on your way to creating more sophisticated applications.

To put first things first, execute the following Try It Out to create an Empty Application project and then progressively add a View controller to it.

TRY IT OUT Creating an Empty Application Project

codefile EmptyApp.zip available for download on Wrox.com

1. Using Xcode, create an Empty Application (iPhone) project (see Figure 4-6) and name it **EmptyApp.** You must also use the project name as the Class Prefix. Ensure that you have the Use Automatic Reference Counting option unchecked. Observe the files created for this project type (see Figure 4-7). Apart from the usual supporting files, note that there are only two delegate files (`EmptyAppAppDelegate.h` and `EmptyAppAppDelegate.m`).

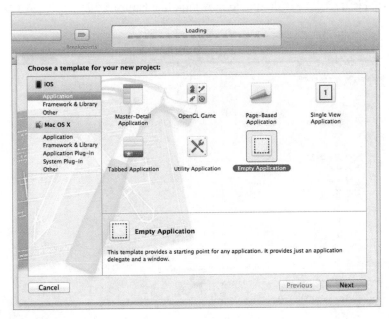

FIGURE 4-6

2. Press Command-R to test the application. An empty screen is displayed on the iPhone Simulator. This is because the Empty Application template provides only the skeleton structure for a simple iOS application — just a window and the application delegate.

3. Right-click the project name and add a new file. In the New File window, click the Cocoa Touch item and select the UIViewController subclass template (see Figure 4-8). Click Next.

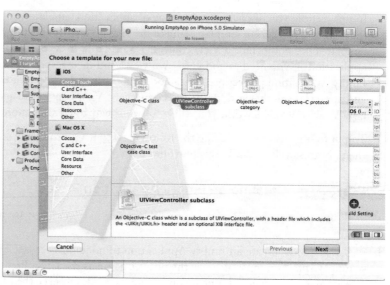

FIGURE 4-7   **FIGURE 4-8**

4. Name the item `HelloWorldViewController.m`. Ensure that the "With XIB for user interface" check box is checked (see Figure 4-9). Xcode should now look like Figure 4-10.

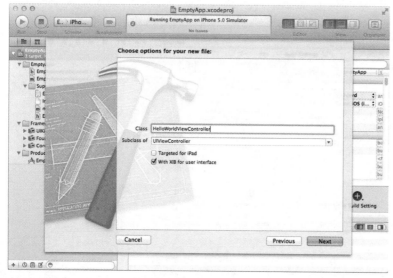

FIGURE 4-9

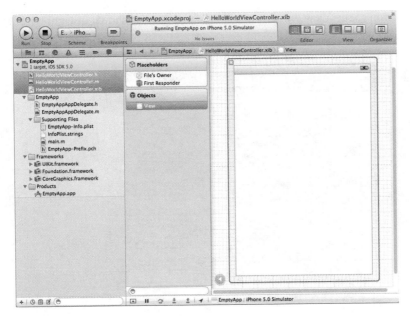

FIGURE 4-10

5. Select the `HelloWorldViewController.xib` file to edit it in Interface Builder.

6. Set the background color of the View window to Light Gray Color (see Figure 4-11).

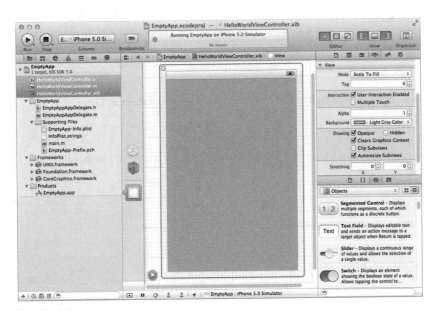

FIGURE 4-11

7. Add a Round Rect Button to the View window and label the button as shown in Figure 4-12.

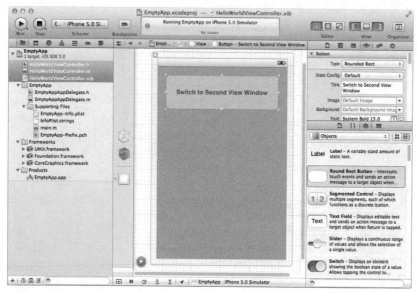

FIGURE 4-12

8. Back in Xcode, insert the bold lines in the following code into the `EmptyAppAppDelegate.h` file:

```
#import <UIKit/UIKit.h>

@class HelloWorldViewController;

@interface EmptyAppAppDelegate : UIResponder <UIApplicationDelegate>

@property (strong, nonatomic) UIWindow *window;

@property (strong, nonatomic) HelloWorldViewController *viewController;

@end
```

9. In the `EmptyAppAppDelegate.m` file, insert the following code that appears in bold:

```
#import "EmptyAppAppDelegate.h"
#import "HelloWorldViewController.h"

@implementation EmptyAppAppDelegate

@synthesize window = _window;
@synthesize viewController = _viewController;

- (void)dealloc
{
    [_window release];
```

```
        [_viewController release];
        [super dealloc];
    }

    - (BOOL)application:(UIApplication *)application didFinishLaunchingWithOptions:
        (NSDictionary *)launchOptions
    {
        self.window = [[[UIWindow alloc] initWithFrame:[[UIScreen mainScreen] bounds]]
            autorelease];
        // Override point for customization after application launch.
        self.window.backgroundColor = [UIColor whiteColor];

        self.viewController = [[[HelloWorldViewController alloc]
          initWithNibName:@"HelloWorldViewController" bundle:nil] autorelease];
        self.window.rootViewController = self.viewController;

        [self.window makeKeyAndVisible];
        return YES;
    }
```

10. That's it! Press Command-R to test the application on the iPhone Simulator. The button should appear on the main screen of the application as shown in Figure 4-13.

How It Works

When you create an iPhone project using the Empty Application template, Xcode provides you with only the bare minimum number of items in your project — some supporting files and the application delegate. You need to add your own View controller(s) and view(s).

In the preceding exercise, you added a View Controller class and an accompanying XIB file to the project. When the application has finished launching, you add the View window represented by the `HelloWorldViewController` object to the window so that it is visible:

FIGURE 4-13

```
        self.viewController = [[[HelloWorldViewController alloc]
            initWithNibName:@"HelloWorldViewController" bundle:nil] autorelease];
        self.window.rootViewController = self.viewController;
```

Adding a View Controller and Views Programmatically

Another commonly used technique to create the UI of your application is to programmatically create the views during runtime without using Interface Builder. This provides a lot of flexibility, especially when you are writing games for which the application's UI is constantly changing.

In the following Try It Out, you learn how to create a View window using an instance of the `UIViewController` class and then programmatically add views to it.

TRY IT OUT Adding a View Controller and Views Programmatically

1. Using the EmptyApp project, right-click the project name in Xcode and add a new file. Select the UIViewController subclass item and name it **SecondViewController**. Ensure that the "With XIB for user interface" check box is unchecked. Xcode should now look like Figure 4-14.

FIGURE 4-14

2. Add the following bold code to SecondViewController.h:

```
#import <UIKit/UIKit.h>

@interface SecondViewController : UIViewController
{
    //---create two outlets - label and button---
    UILabel *label;
    UIButton *button;
}

//---expose the outlets as properties---
@property (nonatomic, retain) UILabel *label;
@property (nonatomic, retain) UIButton *button;

//---declaring the IBAction---
-(IBAction) buttonClicked: (id) sender;

@end
```

3. Add the following bold code to SecondViewController.m:

```
- (void)viewDidLoad
{
    //---create a CGRect for the positioning---
    CGRect frame = CGRectMake(20, 10, 280, 50);

    //---create a Label view---
    label = [[UILabel alloc] initWithFrame:frame];
    label.textAlignment = UITextAlignmentCenter;
    label.font = [UIFont fontWithName:@"Verdana" size:20];
    label.text = @"This is a label";
    label.backgroundColor = [UIColor lightGrayColor];

    //---create a Button view---
    frame = CGRectMake(20, 60, 280, 50);
    button = [UIButton buttonWithType:UIButtonTypeRoundedRect];
    button.frame = frame;
    [button setTitle:@"OK" forState:UIControlStateNormal];
    button.backgroundColor = [UIColor clearColor];

    //---add the action handler and set current class as target---
    [button addTarget:self
            action:@selector(buttonClicked:)
```

```
            forControlEvents:UIControlEventTouchUpInside];

    self.view.backgroundColor = [UIColor lightGrayColor];

    //---add the views to the View window---
    [self.view addSubview:label];
    [self.view addSubview:button];
    [super viewDidLoad];
}

-(IBAction) buttonClicked: (id) sender{
    UIAlertView *alert =
    [[UIAlertView alloc] initWithTitle:@"Action invoked!"
                               message:@"Button clicked!"
                              delegate:self
                     cancelButtonTitle:@"OK"
                     otherButtonTitles:nil];
    [alert show];
    [alert release];
}

- (void)dealloc {
    [label release];
    [button release];
    [super dealloc];
}
```

4. Add the following bold code to `HelloWorldViewController.h`:

```
#import <UIKit/UIKit.h>
#import "SecondViewController.h"

@interface HelloWorldViewController : UIViewController
{
    //---create an instance of the view controller---
    SecondViewController *secondViewController;
}

-(IBAction) btnClicked:(id) sender;

@end
```

5. Add the following bold code to `HelloWorldViewController.m`:

```
#import "HelloWorldViewController.h"

@implementation HelloWorldViewController

-(IBAction) btnClicked:(id) sender
{
    //---add the view of the view controller to the current View---
    if (secondViewController==nil) {
        secondViewController =
        [[SecondViewController alloc] initWithNibName:@"SecondViewController"
```

```
                                                      bundle:nil];
      }
      [self.view addSubview:secondViewController.view];
}

- (void)dealloc {
      [secondViewController release];
      [super dealloc];
}
```

6. Select `HelloWorldViewController.xib` to edit it in Interface Builder. Control-click the Round Rect Button and drag it over the File's Owner item. Select `btnClicked:`. Right-clicking on the File's Owner item will reveal the connections as shown in Figure 4-15.

7. Press Command-R to test the application on the iPhone Simulator. Clicking the button will reveal the second View window (see Figure 4-16). Clicking the OK button reveals the alert view.

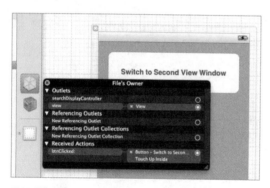

FIGURE 4-15

FIGURE 4-16

8. Back in Xcode, add the following bold code to `SecondViewController.m`:

```
-(IBAction) buttonClicked: (id) sender{
     /*
     UIAlertView *alert =
     [[UIAlertView alloc] initWithTitle:@"Action invoked!"
                                message:@"Button clicked!"
                               delegate:self
                      cancelButtonTitle:@"OK"
                      otherButtonTitles:nil];
     [alert show];
     [alert release];
```

```
*/
//---remove the current view; essentially hiding the view---
[self.view removeFromSuperview];
}
```

9. Press Command-R to test the application on the iPhone Simulator again. As usual, clicking the button will reveal the second View window. Clicking the OK button will now hide the second View window and show the first View window.

How It Works

In this Try It Out, you created a new View controller and its accompanying XIB file. Instead of populating the View windows with the Label and Round Rect Button in Interface Builder, you have added them using code, through the viewDidLoad method:

```
- (void)viewDidLoad
{
    //---create a CGRect for the positioning---
    CGRect frame = CGRectMake(20, 10, 280, 50);

    //---create a Label view---
    label = [[UILabel alloc] initWithFrame:frame];
    label.textAlignment = UITextAlignmentCenter;
    label.font = [UIFont fontWithName:@"Verdana" size:20];
    label.text = @"This is a label";
    label.backgroundColor = [UIColor lightGrayColor];

    //---create a Button view---
    frame = CGRectMake(20, 60, 280, 50);
    button = [UIButton buttonWithType:UIButtonTypeRoundedRect];
    button.frame = frame;
    [button setTitle:@"OK" forState:UIControlStateNormal];
    button.backgroundColor = [UIColor clearColor];

    //---add the action handler and set current class as target---
    [button addTarget:self
               action:@selector(buttonClicked:)
     forControlEvents:UIControlEventTouchUpInside];

    self.view.backgroundColor = [UIColor lightGrayColor];

    //---add the views to the View window---
    [self.view addSubview:label];
    [self.view addSubview:button];
    [super viewDidLoad];
}
```

Observe that you also added an action for the Round Rect Button so that when it is clicked, an action can be performed. To connect an action to a view, you use the addTarget:action:forControlEvents: method of a view. In this case, it is wired to the buttonClicked: method:

```
-(IBAction) buttonClicked: (id) sender{
    UIAlertView *alert =
    [[UIAlertView alloc] initWithTitle:@"Action invoked!"
```

```
                            message:@"Button clicked!"
                           delegate:self
                  cancelButtonTitle:@"OK"
                  otherButtonTitles:nil];
    [alert show];
    [alert release];
}
```

In the `HelloWorldViewController` class, the Round Rect Button is wired to the `btnClicked:` action:

```
-(IBAction) btnClicked:(id) sender
{
    //---add the view of the view controller to the current View---
    if (secondViewController==nil) {
        secondViewController =
        [[SecondViewController alloc] initWithNibName:@"SecondViewController"
                                               bundle:nil];
    }
    [self.view addSubview:secondViewController.view];
}
```

In this case, when a user clicks this button, you create a new instance of the `SecondViewController` class and then add its View window over the current View window. As a result, the `SecondViewController`'s View window covers the entire current window, giving the impression that the current window has transitioned to the next window.

To return to the first View window, you have to hide the current View window using the `removeFromSuperview` method of the `view` object:

```
    //---remove the current view; essentially hiding the view---
    [self.view removeFromSuperview];
```

CONTROL EVENTS

Users typically interact with views on a View window. A very good example is the Round Rect Button, which allows the user to tap on it so that it can perform an action. In this case, the Round Rect Button needs to support a series of events (known as Control Events) so that it knows how the user is interacting with it. For example, if you want to perform an action when the user touches a button (with the finger still touching the button), you need to handle the `UIControlEventTouchDown` event. If you want to perform another action when the finger is lifted, you need to handle the `UIControlEventTouchUpInside` event.

You can use the following list of events for views:

➤   `UIControlEventTouchDown`

➤   `UIControlEventTouchDownRepeat`

➤   `UIControlEventTouchDragInside`

➤ UIControlEventTouchDragOutside

➤ UIControlEventTouchDragEnter

➤ UIControlEventTouchDragExit

➤ UIControlEventTouchUpInside

➤ UIControlEventTouchUpOutside

➤ UIControlEventTouchCancel

➤ UIControlEventValueChanged

➤ UIControlEventEditingDidBegin

➤ UIControlEventEditingChanged

➤ UIControlEventEditingDidEnd

➤ UIControlEventEditingDidEndOnExit

➤ UIControlEventAllTouchEvents

➤ UIControlEventAllEditingEvents

➤ UIControlEventApplicationReserved

➤ UIControlEventSystemReserved

➤ UIControlEventAllEvents

The use of each event is detailed at `http://developer.apple.com/library/ios/#documentation/UIKit/Reference/UIControl_Class/Reference/Reference.html`.

Animating the Switching of Views

The switching of View windows that you have just seen in the previous section happens instantaneously — the two View windows change immediately without any visual cues. One of the key selling points of iOS is its animation capabilities. Therefore, for the switching of views, you can make the display a little more interesting by performing some simple animations, such as flipping one View window to reveal another. The following Try It Out shows you how.

TRY IT OUT Animating View Transitions

1. Using the same project, add the following bold code to the `HelloWorldViewController.m` file:

```
-(IBAction) btnClicked:(id) sender
{
    //---add the view of the view controller to the current View---
    if (secondViewController==nil) {
        secondViewController =
            [[SecondViewController alloc] initWithNibName:@"SecondViewController"
                                                   bundle:nil];
```

```
    }
    [UIView transitionWithView:self.view
                      duration:0.5
                       options:UIViewAnimationOptionTransitionFlipFromRight |
                               UIViewAnimationOptionLayoutSubviews |
                               UIViewAnimationOptionAllowAnimatedContent
                    animations:^{
                        [self.view addSubview:secondViewController.view];
                    }
                    completion:NULL];
}
```

2. In the `SecondViewController.m` file, add the following code that appears in bold:

```
-(IBAction) buttonClicked: (id) sender{
    /*
    UIAlertView *alert =
    [[UIAlertView alloc] initWithTitle:@"Action invoked!"
                               message:@"Button clicked!"
                              delegate:self
                     cancelButtonTitle:@"OK"
                     otherButtonTitles:nil];
    [alert show];
    [alert release];
    */
    [UIView transitionWithView:self.view.superview
                      duration:0.5
                       options:UIViewAnimationOptionTransitionFlipFromLeft |
                               UIViewAnimationOptionLayoutSubviews |
                               UIViewAnimationOptionAllowAnimatedContent
                    animations:^{
                        //---remove the current view; essentially hiding the view---
                        [self.view removeFromSuperview];
                    }
                    completion:NULL];
}
```

3. Press Command-R to test the application on the iPhone Simulator. Click the buttons on both View windows and notice the direction in which the two Views flip to one another (see Figure 4-17).

How It Works

First, examine the animation that is applied to the `HelloWorldViewController`. You perform the animation by calling the `transitionWithView:duration:options:animations:` method of the `UIView` class to start the animation:

```
[UIView transitionWithView:self.view
                  duration:0.5
```

FIGURE 4-17

```
            options:UIViewAnimationOptionTransitionFlipFromRight |
                          UIViewAnimationOptionLayoutSubviews |
                          UIViewAnimationOptionAllowAnimatedContent
    animations:^{
        [self.view addSubview:secondViewController.view];
    }
    completion:NULL];
```

The `transitionWithView:` label specifies the view that you are animating. The `duration:` label specifies the duration of the animation, in seconds. Here, you set it to half a second. The `options:` method sets the types of animation you want to perform, in particular the `UIViewAnimationOptionTransitionFlipFromRight` option flips the view object around a vertical axis from right to left. The `animations:` label specifies the block object that contains the changes you want to make to the specified view.

The animation performed on the `SecondViewController` is similar to that of the `HelloWorldViewController`, except that the view to animate must be set to `self.view.superview` (which is actually the `HelloWorldViewController`):

```
[UIView transitionWithView:self.view.superview
            duration:0.5
              options:UIViewAnimationOptionTransitionFlipFromLeft |
                        UIViewAnimationOptionLayoutSubviews |
                        UIViewAnimationOptionAllowAnimatedContent
    animations:^{
        //---remove the current view; essentially hiding the view---
        [self.view removeFromSuperview];
    }
    completion:NULL];
```

THE MASTER-DETAIL APPLICATION TEMPLATE

Beginning with the iOS SDK 3.2, a new application template exclusive to the iPad became available: Split View–based Application. It enables you to create a split-view interface for your iPad application, which is essentially a master-detail interface. The left side of the screen displays a list of selectable items, while the right-side displays details about the item selected. In iOS 5, Apple has merged the Split View-based Application template with the existing Navigation-based Application template, calling it the *Master-Detail Application template*. In essence, when your Master-Detail Universal application is run on the iPhone, it will behave just like a Navigation-based application. When it is run on the iPad, it will behave like a Split View-based application.

To see how the Master-Detail Application template works, take a look at the following Try It Out.

TRY IT OUT   **Creating a Master-Detail Application**

codefile MasterDetail.zip available for download at Wrox.com

1.   Using Xcode, select the new Master-Detail Application template (see Figure 4-18). Click Next.

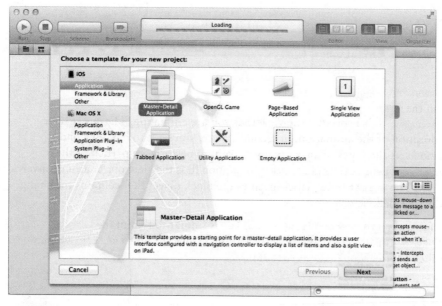

FIGURE 4-18

2. Name the project **MasterDetail** and select the `Universal` device family (see Figure 4-19). Recall that you also use the project name as the Class Prefix and must ensure that you have the Use Automatic Reference Counting option unchecked. Click Next.

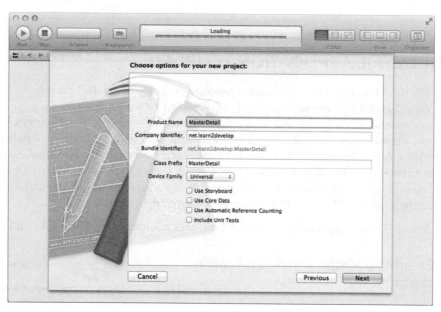

FIGURE 4-19

3. Observe the files created (see Figure 4-20). Notice that there is one delegate class (`MasterDetailAppDelegate`), and two View controller classes (`MasterDetailMasterViewController` and `MasterDetailDetailViewController`), as well as four XIB files (two for iPhone and two for iPad).

4. Select the iPhone 5.0 Simulator scheme (see Figure 4-21) and press Command-R to debug the application on the iPhone Simulator.

FIGURE 4-20

FIGURE 4-21

5. Figure 4-22 shows the application displaying a table view containing a single item named Detail. Clicking the Detail item causes the application to navigate to the next Detail window.

FIGURE 4-22

6. Back in Xcode, select the iPad 5.0 Simulator scheme and press Command-R to debug the application on the iPad Simulator.

7. Figure 4-23 shows the iPad Simulator in Portrait mode. Clicking the Master button displays a PopoverView containing a table view with the Detail item.

8. Press Command-→ to switch the iPad Simulator to landscape mode. Figure 4-24 shows the application with two panes: One containing the Master pane and another containing the Detail pane.

FIGURE 4-23

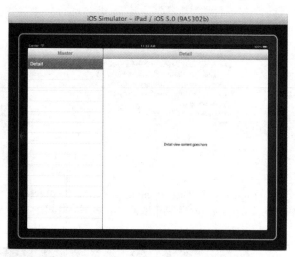

FIGURE 4-24

How It Works

The Master-Detail application is very versatile. When it is run as an iPhone application, it functions as a Navigation-based application. When it is run as an iPad application, it functions as a Split-View-based application. To understand how it works, first, note the content of the `MasterDetailAppDelegate.h` file:

```
#import <UIKit/UIKit.h>

@interface MasterDetailAppDelegate : UIResponder <UIApplicationDelegate>

@property (strong, nonatomic) UIWindow *window;

@property (strong, nonatomic) UINavigationController *navigationController;

@property (strong, nonatomic) UISplitViewController *splitViewController;

@end
```

Notice that it contains two View controller objects of type
UISplitViewController (splitViewController) and
UINavigationController (navigationController).

The UISplitViewController is a container View controller that contains two View controllers, allowing you to implement a master-detail interface. The UINavigationController is a controller that manages the navigation of View controllers.

Next, look at the content of the MasterDetailAppDelegate.m file:

```objc
#import "MasterDetailAppDelegate.h"

#import "MasterDetailMasterViewController.h"

#import "MasterDetailDetailViewController.h"

@implementation MasterDetailAppDelegate

@synthesize window = _window;
@synthesize navigationController = _navigationController;
@synthesize splitViewController = _splitViewController;

- (void)dealloc
{
    [_window release];
    [_navigationController release];
    [_splitViewController release];
    [super dealloc];
}

- (BOOL)application:(UIApplication *)application didFinishLaunchingWithOptions:
        (NSDictionary *)launchOptions
{
    self.window = [[[UIWindow alloc] initWithFrame:[[UIScreen mainScreen] bounds]]
        autorelease];
    // Override point for customization after application launch.
    if ([[UIDevice currentDevice] userInterfaceIdiom] ==
UIUserInterfaceIdiomPhone) {
        MasterDetailMasterViewController *masterViewController =
        [[[MasterDetailMasterViewController alloc]
        initWithNibName:@"MasterDetailMasterViewController_iPhone" bundle:nil]
autorelease];
        self.navigationController = [[[UINavigationController alloc]
        initWithRootViewController:masterViewController] autorelease];
        self.window.rootViewController = self.navigationController;
    } else {
        MasterDetailMasterViewController *masterViewController =
        [[[MasterDetailMasterViewController alloc]
        initWithNibName:@"MasterDetailMasterViewController_iPad" bundle:nil]
autorelease];
        UINavigationController *masterNavigationController =
            [[[UINavigationController alloc] initWithRootViewController:masterViewContr
oller] autorelease];

        MasterDetailDetailViewController *detailViewController =
[[[MasterDetailDetailViewController alloc]
```

```
            initWithNibName:@"MasterDetailDetailViewController_iPad" bundle:nil]
    autorelease];
            UINavigationController *detailNavigationController =
             [[[UINavigationController alloc] initWithRootViewController:detailViewControl
    ler] autorelease];

            self.splitViewController = [[[UISplitViewController alloc] init]
    autorelease];
            self.splitViewController.delegate = detailViewController;
            self.splitViewController.viewControllers = [NSArray
            arrayWithObjects:masterNavigationController, detailNavigationController, nil];

            self.window.rootViewController = self.splitViewController;
        }
        [self.window makeKeyAndVisible];
        return YES;
    }
```

Observe that when the application has been loaded, it first checks to see if it is running
as an iPhone application. If it is, it loads `navigationController` with an instance of the
`MasterDetailMasterViewController` class, using the `MasterDetailMasterViewController_`
`iPhone.xib` file:

```
    MasterDetailMasterViewController *masterViewController =
    [[[MasterDetailMasterViewController alloc]
        initWithNibName:@"MasterDetailMasterViewController_iPhone" bundle:nil]
    autorelease];
            self.navigationController = [[[UINavigationController alloc]
        initWithRootViewController:masterViewController] autorelease];
            self.window.rootViewController = self.navigationController;
```

Figure 4-25 summarizes the actions performed.

If it is running as an iPad application, it will do the following:

➤ Instantiate `masterViewController` using the
`MasterDetailMasterViewController` class, using
the `MasterDetailMasterViewController_iPad.xib` file

➤ Load `masterNavigationController` with
`masterViewController`

➤ Instantiate `detailViewController` with the
`MasterDetailDetailViewController` class, using
the `MasterDetailDetailViewController_iPad.xib` file

➤ Load `detailNavigationController` with
`detailViewController`

➤ Load `splitViewController` with `masterViewController`
and `detailNavigationController`

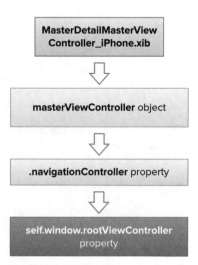

FIGURE 4-25

```
        MasterDetailMasterViewController *masterViewController =
    [[[MasterDetailMasterViewController alloc]
    initWithNibName:@"MasterDetailMasterViewController_iPad" bundle:nil]
autorelease];
        UINavigationController *masterNavigationController =
    [[[UINavigationController alloc]
    initWithRootViewController:masterViewController] autorelease];

        MasterDetailDetailViewController *detailViewController =
    [[[MasterDetailDetailViewController alloc] initWithNibName:@"MasterDetailDetailViewCon
    troller_iPad" bundle:nil] autorelease];
        UINavigationController *detailNavigationController =
    [[[UINavigationController alloc]
    initWithRootViewController:detailViewController] autorelease];

        self.splitViewController = [[[UISplitViewController alloc] init]
    autorelease];
        self.splitViewController.delegate = detailViewController;
        self.splitViewController.viewControllers = [NSArray
    arrayWithObjects:masterNavigationController, detailNavigationController, nil];

        self.window.rootViewController = self.splitViewController;
```

Figure 4-26 summarizes the actions performed.

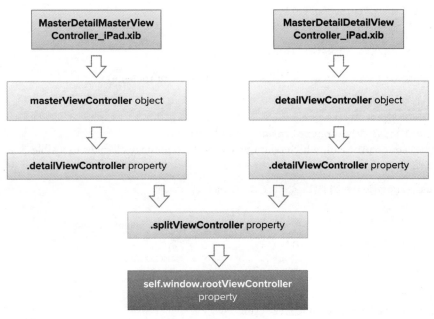

FIGURE 4-26

In short, for each View controller (`MasterDetailMasterViewController` and `MasterDetailDetailViewController`), you have two XIB files: one for iPhone and one for iPad.

At this point, it would be useful to take a look at each View controller to examine its contents. Here is the `MasterDetailMasterViewController.h` file:

```
#import <UIKit/UIKit.h>

@class MasterDetailDetailViewController;

@interface MasterDetailMasterViewController : UITableViewController

@property (strong, nonatomic) MasterDetailDetailViewController *detailViewController;

@end
```

Notice that this class inherits from the `UITableViewController` base class, not the `UIViewController` class. In a master-detail application, the master usually contains a list of items for selection, hence this class contains a Table View. The `UITableViewController` class is a subclass of the `UIViewController` class, providing the capability to display a table containing rows of data. (Chapter 8 discusses the Table View in more detail.)

Here is the content of the `MasterDetailDetailViewController.h` file:

```
#import <UIKit/UIKit.h>

@interface MasterDetailDetailViewController
    : UIViewController <UISplitViewControllerDelegate>

@property (strong, nonatomic) id detailItem;

@property (strong, nonatomic) IBOutlet UILabel *detailDescriptionLabel;

@end
```

Notice that the `MasterDetailDetailViewController` class implements the `UISplitViewControllerDelegate` protocol, which contains methods to manage changes to visible View controllers.

Now take a look at the `MasterDetailDetailViewController.m` file:

```
#import "MasterDetailDetailViewController.h"

@interface MasterDetailDetailViewController ()
@property (strong, nonatomic) UIPopoverController *masterPopoverController;
- (void)configureView;
@end

@implementation MasterDetailDetailViewController

@synthesize detailItem = _detailItem;
@synthesize detailDescriptionLabel = _detailDescriptionLabel;
```

```objc
@synthesize masterPopoverController = _masterPopoverController;

- (void)setDetailItem:(id)newDetailItem
{
    if (_detailItem != newDetailItem) {
        [_detailItem release];
        _detailItem = [newDetailItem retain];

        // Update the view.
        [self configureView];
    }

    if (self.masterPopoverController != nil) {
        [self.masterPopoverController dismissPopoverAnimated:YES];
    }
}

- (void)configureView
{
    // Update the user interface for the detail item.

    if (self.detailItem) {
        self.detailDescriptionLabel.text = [self.detailItem description];
    }
}

- (void)splitViewController:(UISplitViewController *)splitController
    willHideViewController:(UIViewController *)viewController
    withBarButtonItem:(UIBarButtonItem *)barButtonItem
    forPopoverController:(UIPopoverController *)popoverController
{
    barButtonItem.title = NSLocalizedString(@"Master", @"Master");
    [self.navigationItem setLeftBarButtonItem:barButtonItem animated:YES];
    self.masterPopoverController = popoverController;
}

- (void)splitViewController:(UISplitViewController *)splitController
    willShowViewController:(UIViewController *)viewController
    invalidatingBarButtonItem:(UIBarButtonItem *)barButtonItem
{
    // Called when the view is shown again in the split view, invalidating the
button and popover controller.
    [self.navigationItem setLeftBarButtonItem:nil animated:YES];
    self.masterPopoverController = nil;
}

//...
//...
//...
@end
```

The setDetailItem method (it is actually also a property) allows outside classes to pass in a value to this class so that it can display it in the Label through the configureView method.

You also need to handle two important events in this View Controller (both are defined in the `UISplitViewControllerDelegate` protocol):

➤ `splitViewController:willHideViewController:withBarButtonItem:` `forPopover-Controller:` — Fired when the iPad switches to portrait mode (where the Popover View is shown and the TableView is hidden)

➤ `splitViewController:willShowViewController:invalidatingBarButtonItem:` — Fired when the iPad switches to landscape mode (where the Popover View is hidden and the Table View is shown)

Displaying Some Items in the Master-Detail Application

Now that you have seen a Master-Detail application in action, it is time to make some changes to it and see how useful it is. The following Try It Out displays a list of movie names; and when a movie is selected, the name appears in the details View window.

TRY IT OUT Displaying Some Items

1. Using the `MasterDetail` project, add the following bold statements to the `MasterDetailMasterViewController.h` file:

```
#import <UIKit/UIKit.h>

@class MasterDetailDetailViewController;

@interface MasterDetailMasterViewController : UITableViewController
{
    NSMutableArray *listOfMovies;
}

@property (strong, nonatomic) MasterDetailDetailViewController *detailViewController;

@end
```

2. Add the following bold statements to the `MasterDetailMasterViewController.m` file:

```
- (void)viewDidLoad
{
    //---initialize the array---
    listOfMovies = [[NSMutableArray alloc] init];
    [listOfMovies addObject:@"Training Day"];
    [listOfMovies addObject:@"Remember the Titans"];
    [listOfMovies addObject:@"John Q."];
    [listOfMovies addObject:@"The Bone Collector"];
    [listOfMovies addObject:@"Ricochet"];
    [listOfMovies addObject:@"The Siege"];
    [listOfMovies addObject:@"Malcolm X"];
    [listOfMovies addObject:@"Antwone Fisher"];
    [listOfMovies addObject:@"Courage Under Fire"];
```

```objc
    [listOfMovies addObject:@"He Got Game"];
    [listOfMovies addObject:@"The Pelican Brief"];
    [listOfMovies addObject:@"Glory"];
    [listOfMovies addObject:@"The Preacher's Wife"];

    //---set the title---
    self.navigationItem.title = NSLocalizedString(@"Movies", @"Movies");
    [super viewDidLoad];

    // Do any additional setup after loading the view, typically from a nib.
    if ([[UIDevice currentDevice] userInterfaceIdiom] == UIUserInterfaceIdiomPad)
    {
        [self.tableView selectRowAtIndexPath:[NSIndexPath indexPathForRow:0
    inSection:0] animated:NO scrollPosition:UITableViewScrollPositionMiddle];
        self.detailViewController =
    (MasterDetailDetailViewController *) [[self.splitViewController.viewControllers
        lastObject] topViewController];
    }
}

- (NSInteger)tableView:(UITableView *)tableView
    numberOfRowsInSection:(NSInteger)section
{
    //return 1;
    return [listOfMovies count];
}

// Customize the appearance of table view cells.
- (UITableViewCell *)tableView:(UITableView *)tableView
    cellForRowAtIndexPath:(NSIndexPath *)indexPath
{
    static NSString *CellIdentifier = @"Cell";

    UITableViewCell *cell = [tableView
    dequeueReusableCellWithIdentifier:CellIdentifier];
    if (cell == nil) {
        cell = [[[UITableViewCell alloc]
    initWithStyle:UITableViewCellStyleDefault reuseIdentifier:CellIdentifier]
    autorelease];
        if ([[UIDevice currentDevice] userInterfaceIdiom] ==
    UIUserInterfaceIdiomPhone) {
            cell.accessoryType = UITableViewCellAccessoryDisclosureIndicator;
        }
    }

    // Configure the cell.
    //cell.textLabel.text = NSLocalizedString(@"Detail", @"Detail");
    cell.textLabel.text = [listOfMovies objectAtIndex:indexPath.row];

    return cell;
}

- (void)tableView:(UITableView *)tableView didSelectRowAtIndexPath:(NSIndexPath
    *)indexPath
```

```
{
    if ([[UIDevice currentDevice] userInterfaceIdiom] ==
    UIUserInterfaceIdiomPhone) {
        if (!self.detailViewController) {
            self.detailViewController = [[[MasterDetailDetailViewController alloc]
    initWithNibName:@"MasterDetailDetailViewController_iPhone" bundle:nil]
autorelease];
        }
    self.detailViewController.detailItem =
    [NSString stringWithFormat:@"%@", [listOfMovies objectAtIndex:indexPath.row]];

        [self.navigationController pushViewController:self.detailViewController
    animated:YES];
    }
    else
    {
        self.detailViewController.detailItem =
        [NSString stringWithFormat:@"%@", [listOfMovies objectAtIndex:indexPath.row]];
    }
}
```

3. Press Command-R to test the application on the iPhone Simulator. Figure 4-27 shows the list of movies names shown in the master View controller. Clicking on a movie name will cause the application to navigate to the detail View controller.

FIGURE 4-27

4. Press Command-R to test the application on the iPad Simulator. When the Simulator is in portrait mode, the application shows a list of movies within the PopoverView (see Figure 4-28). Selecting a movie displays the movie name on the detail View controller. You can also switch to landscape mode and select the movies from the TableView (see Figure 4-29).

FIGURE 4-28

FIGURE 4-29

How It Works

First, you initialized a mutable array with a list of movie names and set the title of the navigation controller to Movies:

```
//---initialize the array---
listOfMovies = [[NSMutableArray alloc] init];
[listOfMovies addObject:@"Training Day"];
[listOfMovies addObject:@"Remember the Titans"];
[listOfMovies addObject:@"John Q."];
[listOfMovies addObject:@"The Bone Collector"];
[listOfMovies addObject:@"Ricochet"];
[listOfMovies addObject:@"The Siege"];
[listOfMovies addObject:@"Malcolm X"];
[listOfMovies addObject:@"Antwone Fisher"];
[listOfMovies addObject:@"Courage Under Fire"];
[listOfMovies addObject:@"He Got Game"];
[listOfMovies addObject:@"The Pelican Brief"];
[listOfMovies addObject:@"Glory"];
[listOfMovies addObject:@"The Preacher's Wife"];

//---set the title---
self.navigationItem.title = NSLocalizedString(@"Movies", @"Movies");
```

For an iPad application, you need to set the `detailViewController` property to the last View Controller stored in the `SplitViewController`:

```
if ([[UIDevice currentDevice] userInterfaceIdiom] == UIUserInterfaceIdiomPad)
{
    [self.tableView selectRowAtIndexPath:[NSIndexPath indexPathForRow:0
inSection:0] animated:NO scrollPosition:UITableViewScrollPositionMiddle];
    self.detailViewController =
    (MasterDetailDetailViewController *)
[[self.splitViewController.viewControllers lastObject] topViewController];
}
}
```

The value returned by the `tableView:numberOfRowsInSection:` method sets the number of rows to be displayed, which in this case is the size of the mutable array:

```
- (NSInteger)tableView:(UITableView *)tableView numberOfRowsInSection:
  (NSInteger)section
{
    //return 1;
    return [listOfMovies count];
}
```

The `tableView:cellForRowAtIndexPath:` method is fired for each item in the mutable array, thereby populating the TableView:

```
// Customize the appearance of table view cells.
- (UITableViewCell *)tableView:(UITableView *)tableView
  cellForRowAtIndexPath:(NSIndexPath *)indexPath
{
    static NSString *CellIdentifier = @"Cell";

    UITableViewCell *cell = [tableView
    dequeueReusableCellWithIdentifier:CellIdentifier];
    if (cell == nil) {
        cell = [[[UITableViewCell alloc]
    initWithStyle:UITableViewCellStyleDefault reuseIdentifier:CellIdentifier]
    autorelease];
        if ([[UIDevice currentDevice] userInterfaceIdiom] ==
    UIUserInterfaceIdiomPhone) {
            cell.accessoryType = UITableViewCellAccessoryDisclosureIndicator;
        }
    }

    // Configure the cell.
    //cell.textLabel.text = NSLocalizedString(@"Detail", @"Detail");
    cell.textLabel.text = [listOfMovies objectAtIndex:indexPath.row];

    return cell;
}
```

When an item is selected in the TableView, you pass the movie name selected to the `MasterDetailDetailViewController` object via its `detailItem` property:

```
- (void)tableView:(UITableView *)tableView didSelectRowAtIndexPath:(NSIndexPath *)
  indexPath
{
    if ([[UIDevice currentDevice] userInterfaceIdiom] ==
    UIUserInterfaceIdiomPhone) {
        if (!self.detailViewController) {
            self.detailViewController = [[[MasterDetailDetailViewController alloc]
    initWithNibName:@"MasterDetailDetailViewController_iPhone" bundle:nil]
autorelease];
        }
        self.detailViewController.detailItem =
        [NSString stringWithFormat:@"%@", [listOfMovies objectAtIndex:
indexPath.row]];

        [self.navigationController pushViewController:self.detailViewController
    animated:YES];
    }
    else
    {
        self.detailViewController.detailItem =
        [NSString stringWithFormat:@"%@", [listOfMovies objectAtIndex:indexPath.row]];
    }
}
```

THE TABBED APPLICATION TEMPLATE

So far, you have seen the use of three types of application template provided by the iOS SDK: Single View Application, Empty Application, and Master-Detail Application. A fourth type of application template exists: The Tabbed Application template. The following Try It Out uses the Tabbed Application template to create a project and shows what a Tabbed application looks like. Download the necessary project files as indicated.

TRY IT OUT   Creating a Tabbed Application

codefile TabbedApp.zip available for download at Wrox.com

---

1. Using Xcode, select the Tabbed Application project (iPhone) (see Figure 4-30) and click Next.

2. Name the project **TabbedApp** (see Figure 4-31), use the project name as the Class Prefix, and ensure that you have the Use Automatic Reference Counting option unchecked. Click Next.

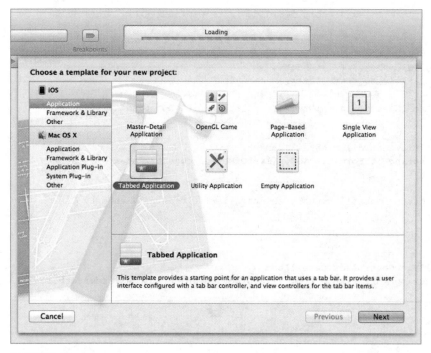

FIGURE 4-30

FIGURE 4-31

3. Examine the content of the project (see Figure 4-32). In addition to the usual application delegate files, it also contains two View controllers (`TabbedAppFirstViewController` and `TabbedAppSecondViewController`) and two XIB files: `TabbedAppFirstViewController.xib` and `TabbedAppSecondViewController.xib`.

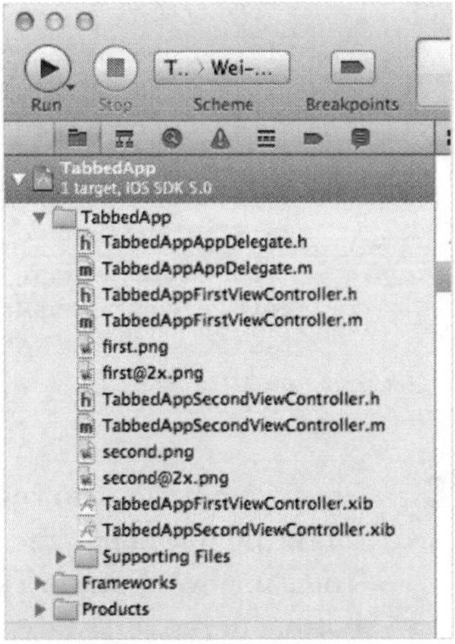

4. Examine the content of the `TabbedAppAppDelegate.h` file, which is as follows:

```
#import <UIKit/UIKit.h>

@interface TabbedAppAppDelegate : UIResponder
<UIApplicationDelegate, UITabBarControllerDelegate>

@property (strong, nonatomic) UIWindow *window;

@property (strong, nonatomic) UITabBarController *tabBarController;

@end
```

FIGURE 4-32

Instead of the usual `UIViewController` class, you are now using the `UITabBarController` class, which inherits from the `UIViewController` class. A `TabBarController` is a specialized `UIViewController` class that contains a collection of View controllers.

5. When the application has finished loading, it creates two instances of the two View controllers and then assigns them to the `tabBarController` property, as evident in the `TabbedAppAppDelegate.m` file:

```
#import "TabbedAppAppDelegate.h"

#import "TabbedAppFirstViewController.h"

#import "TabbedAppSecondViewController.h"

@implementation TabbedAppAppDelegate

@synthesize window = _window;
@synthesize tabBarController = _tabBarController;

- (void)dealloc
{
    [_window release];
    [_tabBarController release];
    [super dealloc];
}

- (BOOL)application:(UIApplication *)application didFinishLaunchingWithOptions:
  (NSDictionary *)launchOptions
{
    self.window = [[[UIWindow alloc] initWithFrame:[[UIScreen mainScreen] bounds]]
      autorelease];
```

```
// Override point for customization after application launch.
UIViewController *viewController1 = [[[TabbedAppFirstViewController alloc]
  initWithNibName:@"TabbedAppFirstViewController" bundle:nil] autorelease];
UIViewController *viewController2 = [[[TabbedAppSecondViewController alloc]
  initWithNibName:@"TabbedAppSecondViewController" bundle:nil] autorelease];
self.tabBarController = [[[UITabBarController alloc] init] autorelease];
self.tabBarController.viewControllers = [NSArray arrayWithObjects:
  viewController1, viewController2, nil];
self.window.rootViewController = self.tabBarController;
[self.window makeKeyAndVisible];
return YES;
}
```

6. Press Command-R to run the application on the iPhone Simulator (see Figure 4-33). You can now click the Tab Bar Items at the bottom of the screen to switch between the two views.

How It Works

Basically, the magic of a Tabbed application is in the use of the UITabBarController class. The Tab Bar Controller contains a collection of View Controllers. In this case, it has two View controllers. The first View controller inside the UITabBarController instance is always displayed when it is added to the current view:

FIGURE 4-33

```
self.tabBarController.viewControllers = [NSArray arrayWithObjects:
  viewController1, viewController2, nil];
```

When the user touches the Tab Bar Items, each corresponding View controller is loaded to display its View window.

If you look at the content of the TabbedAppFirstViewController.m file, you will see that in the initWithNibName:bundle: method, you create the title and image to be displayed on the Tab Bar:

```
#import "TabbedAppFirstViewController.h"

@implementation TabbedAppFirstViewController

- (id)initWithNibName:(NSString *)nibNameOrNil bundle:(NSBundle *)nibBundleOrNil
{
    self = [super initWithNibName:nibNameOrNil bundle:nibBundleOrNil];
    if (self) {
        self.title = NSLocalizedString(@"First", @"First");
        self.tabBarItem.image = [UIImage imageNamed:@"first"];
    }
    return self;
}
```

The image in this case is referring to two images in your project: `first.png` (loaded when the application is run on a non-retina display device) and `first@2x.png` (loaded when the application is run on a retina display device).

SUMMARY

This chapter provided a detailed look at the various application templates provided by the iOS SDK: Single View Application, Empty Application, Master-Detail Application, and Tabbed Application. Each one uses a different type of View controller. It is important to have a good understanding of how the various pieces of an iOS project are put together — knowing that enables you to build applications with sophisticated user interfaces.

EXERCISES

1. Write the code snippet that enables you to create a View controller programmatically.

2. Write the code snippet that creates a view dynamically during runtime.

3. Write the code snippet that wires an event of a view to an event handler.

4. In the `EmptyApp` project created earlier in this chapter, create an action to display an alert view when the button in the `HelloWorldViewController` class is pressed.

Answers to the exercises can be found in Appendix D.

▶ **WHAT YOU LEARNED IN THIS CHAPTER**

TOPIC	KEY CONCEPTS
Types of iPhone/iPad Applications	Single View application, Empty application, Master-Detail application, and Tabbed Application

Coding a Label view	```label = [[UILabel alloc] initWithFrame:frame];```
	```label.textAlignment = UITextAlignmentCenter;```
	```label.font = [UIFont fontWithName:@"Verdana" size:20];```
	```label.text = @"This is a label";```

Coding a Button view	```frame = CGRectMake(20, 60, 280, 50);```
	```button = [UIButton buttonWithType:UIButtonTypeRoundedRect];```
	```button.frame = frame;```
	```[button setTitle:@"OK" forState:UIControlStateNormal];```
	```button.backgroundColor = [UIColor clearColor];```

Wiring up an event to an event handler	```[button addTarget:self```
	```action:@selector(buttonClicked:)```
	```forControlEvents:UIControlEventTouchUpInside]```

Switching to another view	```//---instantiate the second view controller---```
	```mySecondViewController = [[MySecondViewController alloc]```
	```initWithNibName:nil```
	```bundle:nil];```
	```//---add the view from the second view controller---```
	```[window addSubview:mySecondViewController.view];```

Animating the view transition	```[UIView transitionWithView:self.view```
	```duration:0.5 options:UIViewAnimationOptionTransitionFlipFromRight```
	```animations:^{```
	```[self.view addSubview:secondViewController.view];```
	```}```
	```completion:NULL];```

5

Enabling Multi-Platform Support for the iPhone and iPad

WHAT YOU WILL LEARN IN THIS CHAPTER

➤ Modifying a project's Targeted Device Family setting to support both the iPhone and the iPad

➤ How to programmatically detect the device being run

➤ How to create a Universal application

Besides the iPhone and iPod touch, another device using the iOS is the iPad. Out of the box, the iPad will run your existing iPhone applications using the same screen size that is available on the iPhone and iPod touch — 320 × 480 pixels. Therefore, your applications will utilize only a portion of the screen. However, applications running in this default mode do not do justice to the much bigger screen real estate afforded by the iPad. Clearly, this was merely an interim size that can be used until developers port their application's UI to the much bigger iPad screen. In order to support the different devices, you need to modify your applications so that they can take advantage of the capabilities of each device type.

Though the iPad is also running the iOS, you should be aware of some subtle differences when porting your applications over to the new device. This chapter examines two techniques you can use to port your existing iPhone apps to support both the iPhone and the iPad.

TECHNIQUE 1 — MODIFYING THE DEVICE TARGET SETTING

The easiest way to ensure that your iPhone application runs as an iPad application (that is, full screen) is to modify the Targeted Device Family setting in your Xcode project. The following Try It Out shows you how to achieve this.

> **TRY IT OUT** **Modifying the Device Target Setting**
>
> *codefile MyiPhoneApp.zip available for download at Wrox.com*

1. Using Xcode, create a new Single View Application (iPhone) project and name it **MyiPhoneApp**. (You will also use the project name as the Class Prefix.) Ensure that you have the Use Automatic Reference Counting option unchecked.

2. Select the `MyiPhoneAppViewController.xib` file to edit it in Interface Builder.

3. Populate the View window with the following views (see Figure 5-1):

➤ Label (set it to display "Please enter your name")

➤ Text field

➤ Round Rect button (set it to display "OK")

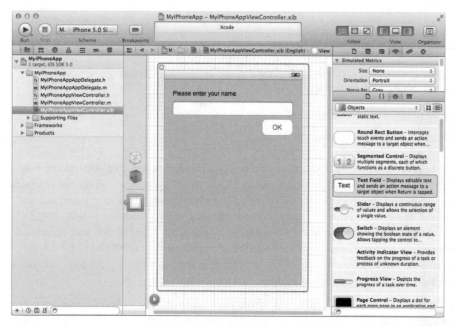

FIGURE 5-1

4. Back in Xcode, press Command-R to test the application on the iPhone Simulator. You should see the screen shown in Figure 5-2.

5. At the top-left corner of the Xcode window, select the iPad 5.0 Simulator scheme (see Figure 5-3).

FIGURE 5-2

FIGURE 5-3

6. Press Command-R again. This time, the application will be shown running in the iPhone Simulator (simulating the iPad), running as an iPhone application (see Figure 5-4). This is the default behavior of iPhone applications running on the iPad.

FIGURE 5-4

7. In Xcode, select the `MyiPhoneApp` project name. In the Summary tab, change the Devices option to Universal (see Figure 5-5). If you click the Build Settings tab now, you will see that the Targeted Device Family setting is now set to iPhone/iPad (see Figure 5-6).

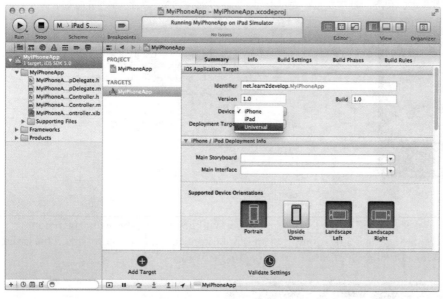

FIGURE 5-5

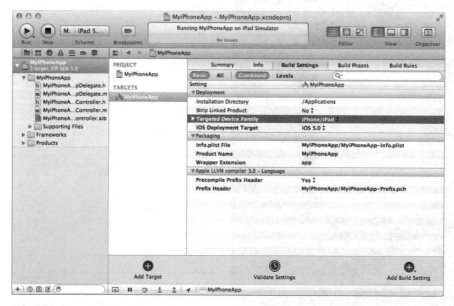

FIGURE 5-6

8. Press Command-R to test the application on the iPhone Simulator (with the iPad 5.0 Simulator scheme selected) again. This time, your application will run natively as an iPad application — that is, full screen (see Figure 5-7).

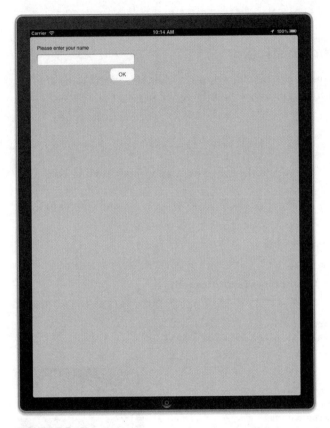

FIGURE 5-7

How It Works

In this example, you first created an iPhone application that you then tested on the iPhone Simulator, simulating both the iPhone and the iPad. By default, all iPhone applications run in their original screen size — 320 x 480 pixels. If you want your iPhone application to run full screen on the iPad, you have to modify the Targeted Device Family setting in your project.

The Targeted Device Family setting provides three different values: iPhone, iPad, or iPhone/iPad. Setting it to iPhone/iPad ensures that your application can automatically detect the device on which it is running, and runs your application full screen.

Notice that the UI of the application is exactly the same as that on the iPhone. It is your responsibility to re-layout your UI when the application is running on the iPad. One way would be to programmatically reposition your views when your application detects that it is running on an iPad. Another way would be to use the Size Inspector window to set the Autosize property of each view on the View window to anchor the view to the edges of the screen. The next section describes how to detect the device on which an application is currently running.

Detecting the Platform Programmatically

In order to re-layout your UI according to the device on which it is running, it is useful to be able to programmatically detect if your application is running on an iPhone/iPod touch or an iPad. The following Try It Out shows you how.

TRY IT OUT Detecting the Device

1. Using the project created in the previous section, add the following statements shown in bold to the MyiPhoneAppViewController.m file:

```
- (void)viewDidLoad
{
#if (__IPHONE_OS_VERSION_MAX_ALLOWED >= 30200)

    NSString *str;
    if (UI_USER_INTERFACE_IDIOM() == UIUserInterfaceIdiomPad) {
        str = [NSString stringWithString:@"Running as an iPad application"];
    } else {
        str = [NSString stringWithString:
                @"Running as an iPhone/iPod touch application"];
    }

    UIAlertView *alert =
        [[UIAlertView alloc] initWithTitle:@"Platform"
                                   message:str
                                  delegate:nil
                         cancelButtonTitle:@"OK"
                         otherButtonTitles:nil];
    [alert show];
    [alert release];

#endif

    [super viewDidLoad];
}
```

2. In Xcode, choose the iPhone 5.0 Simulator scheme and press Command-R to test the application on the iPhone Simulator. You will see the message displayed in Figure 5-8.

3. In Xcode, choose the iPad 5.0 Simulator scheme and press Command-R to test the application on the iPhone Simulator. You will see the message displayed in Figure 5-9.

FIGURE 5-8

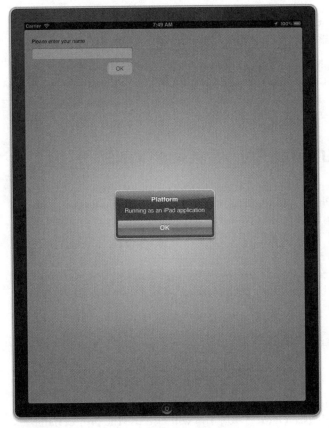

FIGURE 5-9

How It Works

The preceding code includes a conditional compilation directive to indicate that if the application is compiled against the minimum iOS version of 3.2, then it will include a block of code to programmatically detect the type of application it is currently running as:

```
#if (__IPHONE_OS_VERSION_MAX_ALLOWED >= 30200)

//---code within this block will be compiled if application is compiled
// for iPhone OS 3.2 and above---

#endif
```

To detect if the application is running on an iPad, you check the result of the UI_USER_INTERFACE_IDIOM() function. This function returns the interface idiom supported by the current device. If it is an iPad, then the result of this function will be UIUserInterfaceIdiomPad:

```
NSString *str;
if (UI_USER_INTERFACE_IDIOM() == UIUserInterfaceIdiomPad) {
    str = [NSString stringWithString:@"Running as an iPad application"];
```

```
    } else {
        str = [NSString stringWithString:
                @"Running as an iPhone/iPod touch application"];
```

If the application is running as an iPhone application (that is, not full screen) on the iPad, the `UI_USER_INTERFACE_IDIOM()` function will return `UIUserInterfaceIdiomPhone`.

TECHNIQUE 2 — CREATING UNIVERSAL APPLICATIONS

The previous technique shows how you can modify the Targeted Device Family setting to create a single application that runs on both the iPhone and the iPad, called a *Universal* application. The challenge is adapting the UI of the application for each platform — you have to programmatically detect the type of device the application is running on and then modify the layout of the UI dynamically.

Apple recommends that you create a Universal application, one that targets both the iPhone and the iPad, with separate XIB files representing the UI for each platform. The following Try It Out demonstrates how you can create a Universal application.

TRY IT OUT   Creating a Universal Application

codefile Universal.zip available for download at Wrox.com

1.   Using Xcode, create a Single View Application project and name it **MyUniversalApp**. Ensure that you select Universal for the Device Family (see Figure 5-10). You will also use the project name as the Class Prefix. Ensure that the Use Automatic Reference Counting option is unchecked.

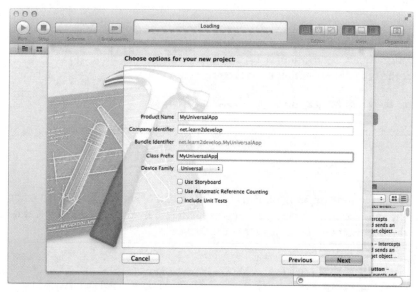

FIGURE 5-10

2. Observe that you now have two XIB files (see Figure 5-11) in your project.

FIGURE 5-11

3 Select the `MyUniversalAppViewController_iPhone.xib` file to edit it in Interface Builder. 3. Add a Label view to the View window and label it as shown in Figure 5-12.

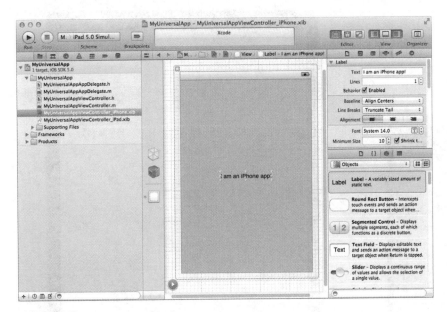

FIGURE 5-12

4. Select the `MyUniversalAppViewController_iPad.xib` file to edit it in Interface Builder. Add a Label view to the middle of the View window and label it as shown in Figure 5-13.

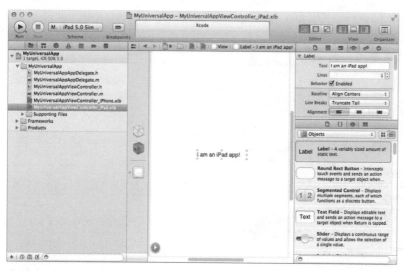

FIGURE 5-13

5. Press Command-R to test the application on the iPhone Simulator, first using the iPhone 5.0 Simulator scheme, followed by the iPad 5.0 Simulator scheme. You will see the application running on the iPhone Simulator as an iPhone app (see Figure 5-14) and as an iPad app (see Figure 5-15).

FIGURE 5-14   **FIGURE 5-15**

How It Works

This has been a very straightforward exercise. First, you created a Universal application using Xcode. When you create a Universal application project, Xcode automatically creates two XIB files for you – one for iPhone and one for iPad. When the application is loaded, it automatically detects the platform on which it is running. This is evident in the application delegate:

```
- (BOOL)              application:(UIApplication *)application
didFinishLaunchingWithOptions:(NSDictionary *)launchOptions
{
    self.window = [[[UIWindow alloc] initWithFrame:[[UIScreen mainScreen] bounds]]
    autorelease];
    // Override point for customization after application launch.
    if ([[UIDevice currentDevice] userInterfaceIdiom] ==
UIUserInterfaceIdiomPhone)
                              {
        self.viewController =
            [[[MyUniversalAppViewController alloc]
                initWithNibName:@"MyUniversalAppViewController_iPhone"
                        bundle:nil] autorelease];
    } else {
        self.viewController =
            [[[MyUniversalAppViewController alloc]
                initWithNibName:@"MyUniversalAppViewController_iPad"
                        bundle:nil] autorelease];
    }
    self.window.rootViewController = self.viewController;
    [self.window makeKeyAndVisible];
    return YES;
}
```

If the application is running on the iPhone, the MyUniversalAppViewController will be loaded using the MyUniversalAppViewController_iPhone.xib file. If it is running on the iPad, then the same View Controller will load the MyUniversalAppViewController_iPad.xib file. Note that in this case, you have two different XIB files, and only one View Controller for the two XIB files. The important thing to keep in mind about a Universal application is that you need to create separate XIB files for the different platforms — one for the iPhone and one for the iPad. Once you do that, you can then load the appropriate XIB files during runtime. Using this approach, you have only one executable for your application.

It is worth pointing out that the MyUniversalApp-Info.plist file now has one additional key: Supported interface orientations (iPad). The project will use this key (see Figure 5-16) to set the supported interface orientation for the application when it is run as an iPad app.

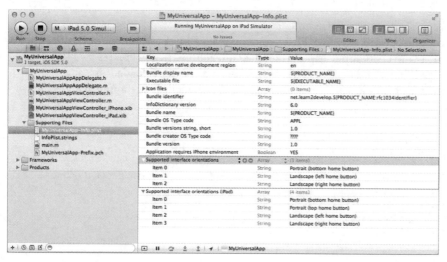

FIGURE 5-16

CHOOSING A PORTING TECHNIQUE

Now that you have seen the two techniques for porting your iPhone application to support the iPad, which technique should you adopt?

If your application does not have many UI changes when running on either the iPhone or the iPad, using the first technique (modifying the device target setting) is the easiest way to support two platforms without changing much code, and it uses a single set of XIB files. All you need to do is ensure that when the application runs on the iPad, the UI is rearranged correctly — this can be done programmatically in your View Controller or set in Interface Builder. Most developers should benefit from creating Universal applications. When you have an application that supports two different platforms, creating a Universal application enables you to have one code base with several XIB files designed specifically for the iPhone and the iPad. This technique saves you the trouble of uploading two different editions of your application to the AppStore. You need to upload just one version of your application and it will automatically support both platforms.

SUMMARY

In this chapter, you have seen how to port an existing iPhone application to support both the iPhone and the iPad. In general, the Universal application approach is the recommended one, as it enables you to maintain just one code base that can target multiple platforms.

EXERCISES

1. What function enables you to determine the device platform on which your application is currently running?

2. What are the different values available for the Targeted Device Family setting in your Xcode project?

Answers to the exercises can be found in Appendix D.

▶ **WHAT YOU LEARNED IN THIS CHAPTER**

TOPIC	KEY CONCEPTS
Supporting an application natively on the iPhone and iPad	Change the Devices item in the Summary tab of your project to Universal. Alternatively, modify the Targeted Device Family Setting of the project in Xcode, setting it to iPhone/iPad.
Detecting the device programmatically	Use the `UI_USER_INTERFACE_IDIOM()` function.
Creating a Universal application	Choose the Universal option in the Targeted Device Family setting when creating your new Xcode project.

Handling Keyboard Inputs

➤ How to customize the keyboard for different types of inputs

➤ How to hide the keyboard when you are done typing

➤ Detecting whether a keyboard is visible

➤ Using ScrollView to contain other views

➤ How to shift views to make way for the keyboard

One of the controversial aspects of the iPhone is the multi-touch keyboard that enables users to input data into their iPhone. Critics of the iPhone have pointed out its lack of a physical keyboard for data entry, whereas ardent supporters of virtual keyboards swear by its ease of use.

What makes the iPhone keyboard so powerful is its intelligence in tracking what you type, followed by suggestions for the word you are typing, and automatically correcting the spelling and inserting punctuation for you. In addition, the keyboard knows when to appear at the right time — it appears when you tap a Text Field or Text View, and it goes away automatically when you tap a non-input view. You can also input data in different languages.

For iPhone application programmers, the key concern is how to integrate the keyboard into the application. How do you make the keyboard go away naturally when it is no longer needed? And how do you ensure that the view with which the user is currently interacting is not blocked by the keyboard? In this chapter, you learn various ways to deal with the keyboard programmatically.

USING THE KEYBOARD

In iPhone programming, the views most commonly associated with the keyboard are the Text Field and the Text View. When a Text Field is tapped (or clicked, if you are using the Simulator), the keyboard is automatically displayed. The data that the user taps on the keyboard is then inserted into the Text Field. The following Try It Out demonstrates this.

TRY IT OUT | Using a Text Field for Inputs

codefile KeyboardInputs.zip available for download at Wrox.com

1. Using Xcode, create a new Single View Application (iPhone) project and name it **KeyboardInputs**. You will also use the project name as the Class Prefix and ensure that you have the Use Automatic Reference Counting option unchecked.

2. Select the `KeyboardInputsViewController.xib` file to edit it using Interface Builder.

3. Populate the View window with the Label and Text Field views (see Figure 6-1). Set the Label to display the text "Alphanumeric Input."

4. Press Command-R in Xcode to run the application on the iPhone Simulator. When the application is loaded, the keyboard is initially hidden; and when the user clicks the Text Field, the keyboard automatically appears (see Figure 6-2).

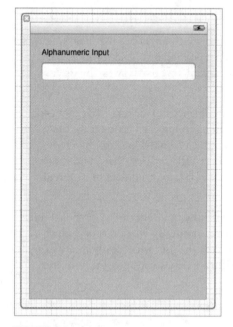

FIGURE 6-1

FIGURE 6-2

How It Works

The beauty of the iPhone user interface is that when the system detects that the current active view is a Text Field, the keyboard automatically appears; you don't need to do anything to bring up the keyboard. Using the keyboard, you can enter alphanumeric data as well as numbers and special characters (such as symbols). The keyboard in the iPhone also supports characters of languages other than English, such as Chinese and Hebrew.

CUSTOMIZING THE TYPE OF INPUTS

To learn more about the input behaviors, go to Interface Builder, select the Text Field, and view its Attributes Inspector window (choose View ➪ Utilities ➪ Show Attributes Inspector). Figure 6-3 shows that window. In particular, pay attention to the section at the bottom that contains items named Capitalization, Correction, Keyboard, and so on.

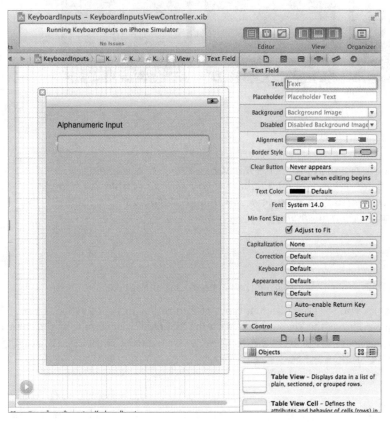

FIGURE 6-3

This section contains several items you can configure to determine how the keyboard handles the text entered:

➤ **Capitalization** — Enables you to capitalize the words, the sentences, or all the characters of the data entered via the keyboard.

➤ **Correction** — Enables you to indicate whether you want the keyboard to provide suggestions for words that are not spelled correctly. You can also choose the Default option, which defaults to the user's global text correction settings.

➤ **Keyboard** — Enables you to choose the different types of keyboard for entering different types of data. Figure 6-4 shows (from left to right) the keyboard configured with the following Keyboard types: Email Address, Phone Pad, and Number Pad.

FIGURE 6-4

 NOTE *If the keyboard is configured using the Number Pad type, then no period (".") is provided to enter decimal-point numbers. If you need to enable users to enter a decimal number (such as currency), you should configure the keyboard using the Numbers and Punctuation type.*

➤ **Appearance** — Enables you to choose how the keyboard should appear

➤ **Return Key** — Enables you to show different types of Return key in your keyboard (see Figure 6-5). Figure 6-6 shows the keyboard set with the "Google" key serving as the Return key (the Return key appears as "Search"). Alternatively, setting the Return key as "Search" will also show the Return key as "Search."

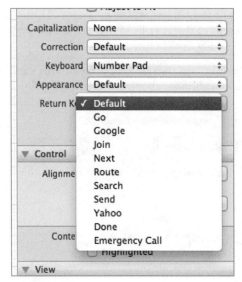

FIGURE 6-5

FIGURE 6-6

➤ **Auto-Enable Return Key check box** — Indicates that if no input is entered for a field, the Return key will be disabled (grayed out). It is enabled again if at least one character is entered.

➤ **Secure check box** — Indicates whether the input will be masked, or hidden from view (see Figure 6-7). This is usually used for password input.

Dismissing the Keyboard

You know that the keyboard in the iPhone automatically appears when a Text Field is selected. What about making it go away when you are done typing? You have two ways to dismiss the keyboard.

FIGURE 6-7

 NOTE *On the iPad, you can make the keyboard go away without any programming effort on your part — simply tapping the bottom right key on the keyboard dismisses it.*

First, you can dismiss the keyboard by tapping the Return key on the keyboard. This method requires you to handle the `Did End On Exit` event of the Text Field that caused the keyboard to appear. This method is demonstrated in the following Try It Out.

Second, you can dismiss the keyboard when the user taps outside a Text Field. This method, which requires some additional coding, makes your application much more user-friendly. The subsequent Try It Out illustrates this method.

TRY IT OUT   Dismissing the Keyboard (Technique 1)

1. Using the `KeyboardInputs` project, edit the `KeyboardInputsViewController.h` file by adding the following bold statements:

   ```
   #import <UIKit/UIKit.h>

   @interface KeyboardInputsViewController : UIViewController

   -(IBAction) doneEditing:(id) sender;

   @end
   ```

2. Select the `KeyboardInputsViewController.xib` file to edit it in Interface Builder. Right-click the Text Field in the View window and then click the circle next to the `Did End On Exit` event and drag it to the File's Owner item. The `doneEditing:` action you have just created should appear. Select it. Figure 6-8 shows the event connected to the File's Owner item.

3. In the `KeyboardInputsViewController.m` file, provide the implementation for the `doneEditing:` action:

   ```
   #import "KeyboardInputsViewController.h"

   @implementation KeyboardInputsViewController

   -(IBAction) doneEditing:(id) sender {
       [sender resignFirstResponder];
   }
   ```

4. Press Command-R to run the application on the iPhone Simulator.

FIGURE 6-8

5. When the application appears on the iPhone Simulator, tap the Text Field. The keyboard should appear. Using the keyboard, type some text into the view and click the Return key when you are done. The keyboard now goes away.

How It Works

What you have just done is connect the `Did End On Exit` event of the Text Field with the `doneEditing:` action you have created. When you are editing the content of a Text Field using the keyboard, clicking the Return key on the keyboard fires the `Did End On Exit` event of the Text Field. In this case, it invokes the `doneEditing:` action, which contains the following statement:

```
[sender resignFirstResponder];
```

The `sender` in this case refers to the Text Field, and `resignFirstResponder` asks the Text Field to resign its First-Responder status. Essentially, it means that you do not want to interact with the Text Field anymore and that the keyboard is no longer needed. Hence, the keyboard should hide itself.

NOTE *The First Responder in a view always refers to the current view with which the user is interacting. In this example, when you click the Text Field, it becomes the First Responder and activates the keyboard automatically.*

An alternative way to hide the keyboard is when the user taps an area outside of the Text Field. This method is more natural and does not require the user to manually tap the Return key on the keyboard to hide it. The following Try It Out shows how this method can be implemented.

TRY IT OUT Dismissing the Keyboard (Technique 2)

1. Using the `KeyboardInputs` project, select the `KeyboardInputsViewController.xib` file to edit it using Interface Builder.

2. Add a Round Rect Button to the View window (see Figure 6-9).

3. With the Round Rect Button selected, choose Editor ➪ Arrange ➪ Send to Back. This makes the button appear behind the other views.

4. Resize the Round Rect Button so that it now covers the entire screen (see Figure 6-10).

5. In the Attributes Inspector window, set the Type of the Round Rect Button to Custom (see Figure 6-11).

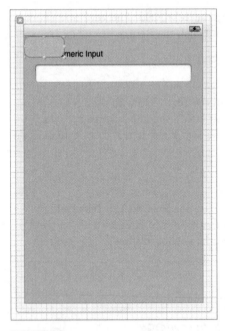

FIGURE 6-9

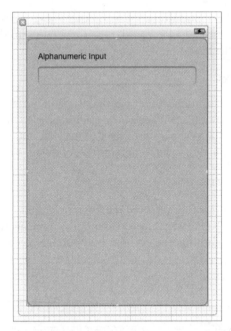

FIGURE 6-10

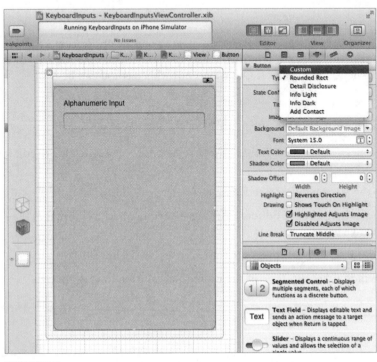

FIGURE 6-11

6. In Xcode, edit the `KeyboardInputsViewController.h` file by adding the following bold statements:

```
#import <UIKit/UIKit.h>

@interface KeyboardInputsViewController : UIViewController
{
    IBOutlet UITextField *textField;
}

@property (nonatomic, retain) UITextField *textField;

-(IBAction) doneEditing:(id) sender;
-(IBAction) bgTouched:(id) sender;

@end
```

7. In Interface Builder, Control-click and drag the File's Owner item onto the Text Field. The `textField` outlet should appear. Select it.

8. Control-click and drag the Round Rect Button view onto the File's Owner item in the `KeyboardInputsViewController.xib` window. Select the `bgTouched:` action (see Figure 6-12).

> **NOTE** The `Touch Up Inside` *event of the Round Rect Button is wired to the* `bgTouched:` *action.*

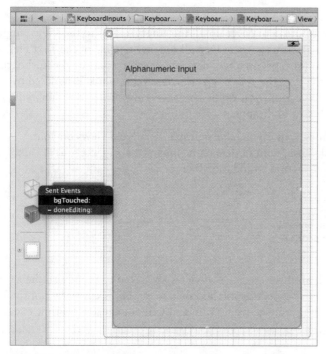

FIGURE 6-12

9. In the `KeyboardInputsViewController.m` file, add the following statements highlighted in bold:

```
#import "KeyboardInputsViewController.h"

@implementation KeyboardInputsViewController

@synthesize textField;

-(IBAction) bgTouched:(id) sender {
    [textField resignFirstResponder];
}

-(IBAction) doneEditing:(id) sender {
    [sender resignFirstResponder];
}

-(void) dealloc {
    [textField release];
    [super dealloc];
}
```

10. That's it. Press Command-R in Xcode to deploy the application onto the iPhone Simulator. Then, try the following:

➤ Click the Text Field to bring up the keyboard.

➤ When you are done, click the Return key on the keyboard to dismiss it. Alternatively, click any of the empty spaces outside the Text Field to dismiss the keyboard.

How It Works

In this example, you added a Round Rect Button to cover up all the empty spaces in the View window of your application. Essentially, the button acts as a net to trap all touches outside of the Text Field on the View window, so when the user clicks (or taps, on a real device) the screen outside the keyboard and the Text Field, the Round Rect Button fires the `Touch Up Inside` event, which is handled by the `bgTouched:` action. In the `bgTouched:` action, you explicitly asked `textField` to resign its First-Responder status, which causes the keyboard to disappear.

The technique used in this example applies even if you have multiple Text Field views on your view. Suppose you have three Text Field views, with outlets named `textField`, `textField2`, and `textField3`. In that case, the `bgTouched:` action would look like this:

```
-(IBAction) bgTouched:(id) sender {
    [textField resignFirstResponder];
    [textField2 resignFirstResponder];
    [textField3 resignFirstResponder];
}
```

When the `bgTouched:` action is invoked, all three `TextField` views are asked to relinquish their First-Responder status. Calling the `resignFirstResponder` method on a view that is currently not the First Responder is harmless; hence, the preceding statements are safe and will not cause a runtime exception.

UNDERSTANDING THE RESPONDER CHAIN

The prior Try It Out is a good example of the responder chain in action. In the iPhone, events are passed through a series of event handlers known as the *responder chain*. As you touch the screen of your iPhone, the iPhone generates events that are passed up the responder chain. Each object in the responder chain checks whether it can handle the event. In the preceding example, when the user taps on the Label, the Label checks whether it can handle the event. Because the Label does not handle the Touch event, it is passed up the responder chain. The large background button that you have added is now next in line to examine the event. Because it handles the Touch Up Inside event, the event is consumed by the button.

In summary, objects higher up in the responder chain examine the event first and handle it if it is applicable. Any object can then stop the propagation of the event up the responder chain, or pass the event up the responder chain if it only partially handles the event.

Automatically Displaying the Keyboard When the View Window Is Loaded

Sometimes you might want to straightaway set a Text Field as the active view and display the keyboard without waiting for the user to do so. In such cases, you can use the becomeFirstResponder method of the view. The following code shows that the Text Field will be the First Responder as soon as the View window is loaded:

```
- (void)viewDidLoad {
    [textField becomeFirstResponder];
    [super viewDidLoad];
}
```

DETECTING THE PRESENCE OF THE KEYBOARD

Up to this point, you have seen the various ways to hide the keyboard after you are done using it. However, note one problem: When the keyboard appears, it takes up a significant portion of the screen. If your Text Field is located at the bottom of the screen, it would be covered by the keyboard. As a programmer, it is your duty to ensure that the view is relocated to a visible portion of the screen. Surprisingly, this is not taken care of by the SDK; you have to do the hard work yourself.

 NOTE *The keyboard in the iPhone (3G and 3GS) takes up 216 pixels (432 pixels for iPhone 4 and iPhone 4S) in height when in portrait mode, and 162 pixels (324 pixels for iPhone 4 and iPhone 4S) when in landscape mode. For the iPad, the keyboard takes up 264 pixels in height when in portrait mode, and 352 pixels when in landscape mode.*

First, though, it is important that you understand a few key concepts related to the keyboard:

➤ You need to be able to programmatically know when a keyboard is visible or hidden. To do so, your application needs to register for the `UIKeyboardDidShowNotification` and `UIKeyboardDidHideNotification` notifications.

➤ You also need to know when and which Text Field is currently being edited so that you can relocate it to a visible portion of the screen. You can determine this information through the `textFieldDidBeginEditing:` method declared in the `UITextFieldDelegate` protocol.

Confused? Worry not; the following sections make it all clear.

Using the Scroll View

The key to relocating the view that is currently being hidden by the keyboard is to use a Scroll View to contain all the views on the View window. When a view (such as the Text Field) is hidden by the keyboard when the user taps on it, you can scroll all the views contained within the Scroll View upwards so that the view currently responding to the tap is visible. Before you learn how to do that, however, you need to first understand how the Scroll View works. The following Try It Out shows you that.

TRY IT OUT **Understanding the Scroll View**

codefile Scroller.zip available for download at Wrox.com

1. Using Xcode, create a new Single View Application (iPhone) project and name it `Scroller`. You will also use the project name as the Class Prefix and ensure that you have the Use Automatic Reference Counting option unchecked.

2. Select the `ScrollerViewController.xib` file to edit it in Interface Builder.

3. Populate the View window with a Scroll View (see Figure 6-13).

4. Add two Round Rect Buttons to the Scroll View (see Figure 6-14).

5. To add more views to the Scroll View so that the user can view more than what the View window typically displays at one time, perform the following steps:

a. Click the Scroll View to select it. If you cannot select it, click on the title bar of the View window first and then click the Scroll View again.

b. Shift the Scroll View upwards (see the left of Figure 6-15).

c. Expand the height of the Scroll View by clicking and dragging the center dot of the Scroll View downwards. The Scroll View should now look like what is shown on the right in Figure 6-15.

6. Add a Text Field to the bottom of the Scroll View (see Figure 6-16).

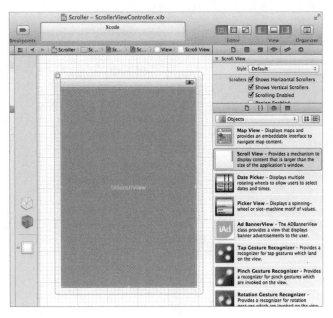

FIGURE 6-13

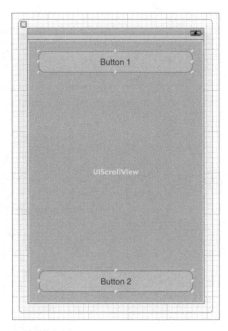

FIGURE 6-14

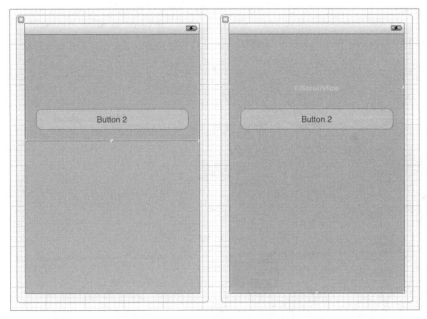

FIGURE 6-15

FIGURE 6-16

7. Select the Scroll View and view its Size Inspector window (View ⇨ Utilities ⇨ Show Size Inspector; see Figure 6-17). Observe that its size is 320 × 713 points (in my case). If you do not see the same size as what I have, this is a good time to adjust the size so that it is the same as mine. You will need to use this value in your code, which you do next.

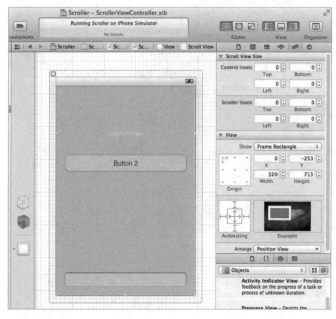

FIGURE 6-17

NOTE *The unit of measurement used in Interface Builder is* points. *For the iPhone 3G/3GS, a point corresponds to a pixel. For the iPhone 4 and iPhone 4S, a point is equal to two pixels. Specifying the size in points enables your application to work correctly on both the older and newer iPhones. The conversion between points and pixels is done automatically by the iOS.*

8. Back in Xcode, add the following code in bold to the `ScrollViewController.h` file:

```
#import <UIKit/UIKit.h>

@interface ScrollerViewController : UIViewController
{
    IBOutlet UIScrollView *scrollView;
}

@property (nonatomic, retain) UIScrollView *scrollView;

@end
```

9. In Interface Builder, Control-click and drag the File's Owner item over to the Scroll View. Select `scrollView`.

10. Insert the following bold code in the `ScrollerViewController.m` file:

```
#import "ScrollerViewController.h"

@implementation ScrollerViewController

@synthesize scrollView;

- (void)viewDidLoad {
    scrollView.frame = CGRectMake(0, 0, 320, 460);
    [scrollView setContentSize:CGSizeMake(320, 713)];
    [super viewDidLoad];
}

- (void)dealloc {
    [scrollView release];
    [super dealloc];
}
```

11. To test the application on the iPhone Simulator, press Command-R. You can now flick the Scroll View up and down to reveal all the views contained in it (see Figure 6-18)!

12. Tap on the Text Field located at the bottom. The keyboard will automatically appear. However, observe that the Text Field is now covered by the keyboard (see Figure 6-19). You need to ensure that the current view is not hidden by the keyboard; the next section shows you how.

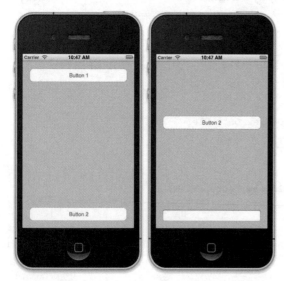

FIGURE 6-18

FIGURE 6-19

How It Works

This example is pretty straightforward. You use the Scroll View as a container for other views. If you have more views than what you can display on the screen, you can expand the Scroll View and put all your views in it. The important point to remember is that you need to set the content size and the frame size of the Scroll View. The frame size determines the visible area of the Scroll View. The content size sets the overall size of the Scroll View. As long as the content size is larger than the frame size, the Scroll View will be scrollable.

Scrolling Views When the Keyboard Appears

Now that you understand how the Scroll View works, the following activity explains how you can scroll all the views contained within it when the keyboard appears.

TRY IT OUT **Shifting Views**

1. Using the same project created in the previous section, add a few more Labels and Text Fields to the bottom of the Scroll View (see Figure 6-20) in Interface Builder.

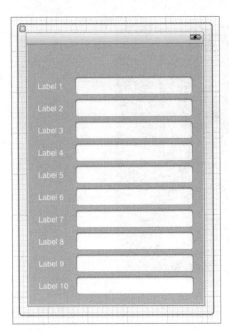

FIGURE 6-20

2. In the `ScrollerViewController.h` file, add the following code in bold:

```
#import <UIKit/UIKit.h>

@interface ScrollerViewController : UIViewController
{
    IBOutlet UIScrollView *scrollView;

    UITextField *currentTextField;
    BOOL keyboardIsShown;
}

@property (nonatomic, retain) UIScrollView *scrollView;

@end
```

3. In Interface Builder, right-click each Text Field and connect the `delegate` outlet to the File's Owner item (see Figure 6-21).

FIGURE 6-21

> **NOTE** Step 3 is important because it enables the various events
> (textFieldDidBeginEditing:, textFieldDidEndEditing:, and
> textFieldShouldReturn:) to be handled by your View Controller.

4. Change the content size of the Scroll View to match its new size:

```
- (void)viewDidLoad {
    scrollView.frame = CGRectMake(0, 0, 320, 460);
    [scrollView setContentSize:CGSizeMake(320, 1040)];
    [super viewDidLoad];
}
```

> **NOTE** You can confirm the new content size of the Scroll View by looking at its
> Size Inspector window.

5. Add the following methods to the `ScrollerViewController.m` file:

```objc
//--before the View window appears--
-(void) viewWillAppear:(BOOL)animated {
    //--registers the notifications for keyboard--
    [[NSNotificationCenter defaultCenter]
        addObserver:self
            selector:@selector(keyboardDidShow:)
                name:UIKeyboardDidShowNotification
            object:self.view.window];

    [[NSNotificationCenter defaultCenter]
        addObserver:self
            selector:@selector(keyboardDidHide:)
                name:UIKeyboardDidHideNotification
                object:nil];
    [super viewWillAppear:animated];
}

//--when a Text Field begins editing--
-(void) textFieldDidBeginEditing:(UITextField *)textFieldView {
    currentTextField = textFieldView;
}

//--when the user taps on the return key on the keyboard--
-(BOOL) textFieldShouldReturn:(UITextField *) textFieldView {
    [textFieldView resignFirstResponder];
    return NO;
}

//--when a TextField view is done editing--
-(void) textFieldDidEndEditing:(UITextField *) textFieldView {
    currentTextField = nil;
}

//--when the keyboard appears--
-(void) keyboardDidShow:(NSNotification *) notification {
    if (keyboardIsShown) return;

    NSDictionary* info = [notification userInfo];

    //--obtain the size of the keyboard--
    NSValue *aValue =
        [info objectForKey:UIKeyboardFrameEndUserInfoKey];
    CGRect keyboardRect =
        [self.view convertRect:[aValue CGRectValue] fromView:nil];

    NSLog(@"%f", keyboardRect.size.height);

    //--resize the scroll view (with keyboard)--
    CGRect viewFrame = [scrollView frame];
    viewFrame.size.height -= keyboardRect.size.height;
```

```
    scrollView.frame = viewFrame;

    //--scroll to the current text field--
    CGRect textFieldRect = [currentTextField frame];
    [scrollView scrollRectToVisible:textFieldRect animated:YES];

    keyboardIsShown = YES;
}

//--when the keyboard disappears--
-(void) keyboardDidHide:(NSNotification *) notification {
    NSDictionary* info = [notification userInfo];

    //--obtain the size of the keyboard--
    NSValue* aValue =
        [info objectForKey:UIKeyboardFrameEndUserInfoKey];
    CGRect keyboardRect =
        [self.view convertRect:[aValue CGRectValue] fromView:nil];

    //--resize the scroll view back to the original size
    // (without keyboard)--
    CGRect viewFrame = [scrollView frame];
    viewFrame.size.height += keyboardRect.size.height;
    scrollView.frame = viewFrame;

    keyboardIsShown = NO;
}

//--before the View window disappear--
-(void) viewWillDisappear:(BOOL)animated {
    //--removes the notifications for keyboard--
    [[NSNotificationCenter defaultCenter]
        removeObserver:self
                name:UIKeyboardDidShowNotification
              object:nil];

    [[NSNotificationCenter defaultCenter]
        removeObserver:self
                name:UIKeyboardDidHideNotification
              object:nil];
    [super viewWillDisappear:animated];
}
```

6. Press Command-R to test the application on the iPhone Simulator. Tap on the various Text Fields and observe the different views scrolling into position (see Figure 6-22).

How It Works

The first thing you did was connect the delegate outlet of each Text Field to the File's Owner item. This step is important, as it ensures that when any of the Text Fields are tapped, the following three events will be handled:

FIGURE 6-22

➤ `textFieldDidBeginEditing:`

➤ `textFieldDidEndEditing:`

➤ `textFieldShouldReturn:`

Because the Scroll View contained more views than it could display at one time, you needed to change its content size:

```
- (void)viewDidLoad {
    scrollView.frame = CGRectMake(0, 0, 320, 460);
    [scrollView setContentSize:CGSizeMake(320, 1040)];
    [super viewDidLoad];
}
```

Next, before the View window appeared, you registered two notifications: `UIKeyboardDidShowNotification` and `UIKeyboardDidHideNotification`. These two notifications enable you to know when the keyboard has either appeared or disappeared. You registered the notifications via the `viewWillAppear:` method:

```
//--before the View window appears--
-(void) viewWillAppear:(BOOL)animated {
    //--registers the notifications for keyboard--
    [[NSNotificationCenter defaultCenter]
        addObserver:self
            selector:@selector(keyboardDidShow:)
                name:UIKeyboardDidShowNotification
            object:self.view.window];

    [[NSNotificationCenter defaultCenter]
        addObserver:self
            selector:@selector(keyboardDidHide:)
                name:UIKeyboardDidHideNotification
            object:nil];
    [super viewWillAppear:animated];
}
```

When any of the Text Fields are tapped, the `textFieldDidBeginEditing:` method will be called:

```
//--when a Text Field begins editing--
-(void) textFieldDidBeginEditing:(UITextField *)textFieldView {
    currentTextField = textFieldView;
}
```

Here, you saved a copy of the Text Field currently being tapped. When the user taps the Return key on the keyboard, the `textFieldShouldReturn:` method will be called:

```
//--when the user taps on the return key on the keyboard--
-(BOOL) textFieldShouldReturn:(UITextField *) textFieldView {
    [textFieldView resignFirstResponder];
    return NO;
}
```

Next, you hid the keyboard by calling the `resignFirstResponder` method of the Text Field, which then triggers another event, `textFieldDidEndEditing:`. Here, you set the `currentTextField` to nil:

```
//—-when a TextField view is done editing—-
-(void) textFieldDidEndEditing:(UITextField *) textFieldView {
    currentTextField = nil;
}
```

When the keyboard appears, it calls the `keyboardDidShow:` method (which is set via the notification):

```
//—-when the keyboard appears—-
-(void) keyboardDidShow:(NSNotification *) notification {
    if (keyboardIsShown) return;

    NSDictionary* info = [notification userInfo];

    //—-obtain the size of the keyboard—-
    NSValue *aValue =
        [info objectForKey:UIKeyboardFrameEndUserInfoKey];
    CGRect keyboardRect =
        [self.view convertRect:[aValue CGRectValue] fromView:nil];

    NSLog(@"%f", keyboardRect.size.height);

    //—-resize the scroll view (with keyboard)—-
    CGRect viewFrame = [scrollView frame];
    viewFrame.size.height -= keyboardRect.size.height;
    scrollView.frame = viewFrame;

    //—-scroll to the current text field—-
    CGRect textFieldRect = [currentTextField frame];
    [scrollView scrollRectToVisible:textFieldRect animated:YES];

    keyboardIsShown = YES;
}
```

This obtains the size of the keyboard — in particular, its height. This is important, as the keyboard has different heights depending on whether it is in landscape mode or portrait mode. You then resize the view frame of the Scroll View and scroll the Text Field until it is visible.

What happens when the keyboard is visible and the user taps on another Text Field? In this case, the `keyboardDidShow:` method will be called again, but because the `keyboardIsShown` method is set to YES, the method immediately exits. If the Text Field that is tapped is partially hidden, it will automatically be scrolled to a visible region on the View window.

When the keyboard disappears, the `keyboardDidHide:` method is called:

```
//—-when the keyboard disappears—-
-(void) keyboardDidHide:(NSNotification *) notification {
    NSDictionary* info = [notification userInfo];

    //—-obtain the size of the keyboard—-
    NSValue* aValue =
```

```
        [info objectForKey:UIKeyboardFrameEndUserInfoKey];
    CGRect keyboardRect =
        [self.view convertRect:[aValue CGRectValue] fromView:nil];

    //--resize the scroll view back to the original size
    // (without keyboard)--
    CGRect viewFrame = [scrollView frame];
    viewFrame.size.height += keyboardRect.size.height;
    scrollView.frame = viewFrame;

    keyboardIsShown = NO;
}
```

This restores the size of the view frame of the Scroll View to the one without the keyboard.

Finally, before the View window disappears, you remove the notifications that you set earlier:

```
//--before the View window disappear--
-(void) viewWillDisappear:(BOOL)animated {
    //--removes the notifications for keyboard--
    [[NSNotificationCenter defaultCenter]
        removeObserver:self
                name:UIKeyboardDidShowNotification
            object:nil];

    [[NSNotificationCenter defaultCenter]
        removeObserver:self
                name:UIKeyboardDidHideNotification
            object:nil];
    [super viewWillDisappear:animated];
}
```

SUMMARY

In this chapter, you learned various techniques for dealing with the keyboard in your iPhone application. In particular, this chapter showed you how to hide the keyboard when you are done entering data, how to detect the presence or absence of the keyboard, and how to ensure that views are not blocked by the keyboard.

EXERCISES

1. How do you hide the keyboard for a `UITextField` object?

2. How do you detect whether the keyboard is visible or not?

3. How do you get the size of the keyboard?

4. How do you display more views than the View window can display at any one time?

Answers to the exercises can be found in Appendix D.

▶ **WHAT YOU LEARNED IN THIS CHAPTER**

TOPIC	KEY CONCEPTS
Making the keyboard go away	Use the `resignFirstResponder` method on a `UITextField` object to resign its First-Responder status.
Displaying the different types of keyboard displayed	Modify the keyboard type by changing the text input traits of a `UITextField` object in the Attributes Inspector window.
Handling the Return key of the keyboard	Either handle the `Did End On Exit` event of a `UITextField` object or implement the `textFieldShouldReturn:` method in your View Controller (remember to ensure that your View Controller class is the delegate for the `UITextField` object).
Making a Scroll View scrollable	Set its frame size and content size. As long as the content size is larger than the frame size, the Scroll View is scrollable.
Detecting when the keyboard appears or hides	Register for two notifications: `UIKeyboardDidShowNotification` and `UIKeyboardDidHideNotification`.
Detecting which `UITextField` object has started editing	Implement the `textFieldDidBeginEditing:` method in your View Controller.
Detecting which `UITextField` object has ended editing	Implement the `textFieldDidEndEditing:` method in your View Controller.

7
Supporting Screen Rotations

WHAT YOU WILL LEARN IN THIS CHAPTER

➤ How to support the four different types of screen orientation

➤ Events that are fired when a device rotates

➤ How to reposition the views in a View window when the orientation of a device changes

➤ How to change the screen rotation dynamically during runtime

➤ How to fix the orientation of your application before it is loaded

The Hello World! application in Chapter 2 showed you how your iPhone application supports viewing in either the portrait or landscape mode. This chapter dives deeper into the topic of screen orientation. In particular, it demonstrates how to manage the orientation of your application when the device is rotated. You will also learn how to reposition your views when the device is rotated so that your application can take advantage of the change in screen dimensions.

RESPONDING TO DEVICE ROTATIONS

One of the features that modern mobile devices support is the capability to detect the current orientation — portrait or landscape — of the device. An application can take advantage of this to re-adjust the device's screen to maximize use of the new orientation. A good example is Safari on the iPhone. When you rotate the device to landscape orientation, Safari automatically rotates its view so that you have a wider screen to view the content of the page (see Figure 7-1).

The iOS SDK contains several events that you can handle to ensure that your application is aware of changes in orientation. Check them out in the following Try It Out.

FIGURE 7-1

TRY IT OUT Supporting Different Screen Orientations

codefile ScreenRotations.zip available for download at Wrox.com

1. Using Xcode, create a new Single View Application (iPhone) project and name it ScreenRotations. You will also use the project name as the Class Prefix and ensure that you have the Use Automatic Reference Counting option unchecked.

2. Press Command-R to test the application on the iPhone 4 Simulator.

3. Change the iPhone Simulator orientation by pressing either Command-→ (rotate it to the right) or Command-← (rotate it to the left) key combination. Observe that the application stays upright when the Simulator is either in portrait (upright) mode or in landscape mode (see Figure 7-2). However, if the Simulator is in the portrait upside down mode, the application's orientation stays in its previous orientation (before it was rotated).

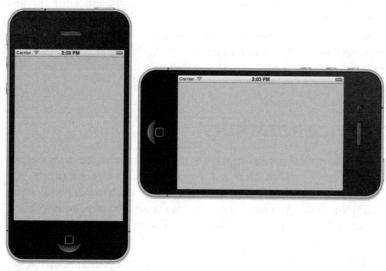

FIGURE 7-2

How It Works

By default, the iPhone Application project you created using Xcode supports three screen orientations: portrait and the two landscape modes (landscape left and landscape right). This is evident in the `shouldAutorotateToInterfaceOrientation:` method defined in the View controller:

```
(BOOL)shouldAutorotateToInterfaceOrientation:(UIInterfaceOrientation)
 interfaceOrientation
{
    // Return YES for supported orientations
    return (interfaceOrientation != UIInterfaceOrientationPortraitUpsideDown);
}
```

The `shouldAutorotateToInterfaceOrientation:` method is called when the View window is loaded and whenever orientation of the device changes. This method passes in a single parameter — the orientation to which the device has been changed. The returning value of this method determines whether the current orientation is supported. For a particular orientation to be supported, this method must return YES. In other words, the preceding states that the application should stay upright for all orientation modes, except when the device is in the portrait upside-down mode (see Figure 7-3).

FIGURE 7-3

> **NOTE** On the iPad, the default behavior of an application supports all orientations — portrait as well as landscape modes. While you can specify the specific orientations supported by your application, based on the UI guidelines provided by Apple, iPad applications should support all screen orientations.

NOTE *On the iPhone and iPad, screen rotation is automatically handled by the OS. When the OS detects a change in screen orientation, it fires the* shouldAutorotateToInterfaceOrientation: *event; it is up to the developer to decide how the application should display in the target orientation.*

To support all orientations, simply return a YES to allow your application to display upright for all orientations:

```
- (BOOL)shouldAutorotateToInterfaceOrientation:
(UIInterfaceOrientation)interfaceOrientation
{
    // Return YES for supported orientations
    //return (interfaceOrientation !=
      UIInterfaceOrientationPortraitUpsideDown);
    return YES;
}
```

 NOTE *To easily differentiate between* UIInterfaceOrientationLandscapeLeft *and* UIInterfaceOrientationLandscapeRight, *just remember that* UIInterfaceOrientationLandscapeLeft *refers to the Home button positioned on the left, and* UIInterfaceOrientationLandscapeRight *refers to the Home button positioned on the right.*

Rotating to a Different Screen Orientation

You have a total of four constants to use for specifying screen orientations:

➤ UIInterfaceOrientationPortrait — Displays the screen in portrait mode

➤ UIInterfaceOrientationPortraitUpsideDown — Displays the screen in portrait mode but with the Home button at the top of the screen

➤ UIInterfaceOrientationLandscapeLeft — Displays the screen in landscape mode with the Home button on the left

➤ UIInterfaceOrientationLandscapeRight — Displays the screen in landscape mode with the Home button on the right

If you want your application to support specific screen orientations, override the shouldAutorotateTo-InterfaceOrientation: method and then use the || (logical OR) operator to specify all the orientations it supports, like this:

```
- (BOOL)shouldAutorotateToInterfaceOrientation:
(UIInterfaceOrientation)interfaceOrientation {
    // Return YES for supported orientations
```

```
    return (interfaceOrientation == UIInterfaceOrientationPortrait ||
            interfaceOrientation == UIInterfaceOrientationLandscapeLeft);
}
```

The preceding code snippet enables your application to support both the portrait and the landscape left modes.

Handling Rotations

The View Controller declares several methods that you can implement to handle the rotation of the screen. The ability to implement these methods is important because it enables you to reposition the views on the View window, or you can stop media playback while the screen is rotating. You can implement the following methods:

➤ `willAnimateFirstHalfOfRotationToInterfaceOrientation:`

➤ `willAnimateSecondHalfOfRotationFromInterfaceOrientation:`

➤ `willRotateToInterfaceOrientation:`

➤ `willAnimateRotationToInterfaceOrientation:`

The `willAnimateFirstHalfOfRotationToInterfaceOrientation:` method is called just before the rotation of the View window starts, whereas the `willAnimateSecondHalfOfRotationFrom Interfaceorientation:` method is fired when the rotation is halfway through. In iOS 5, these two methods have been deprecated in favor of the smoother, single-stage animation using either the `willRotateToInterfaceOrientation:` or the `willAnimateRotationToInterfaceOrientation:` methods.

The next two sections take a more detailed look at the last two methods.

willRotateToInterfaceOrientation:

The first two methods mentioned in the previous section are called consecutively — first `willAnimateFirstHalfOfRotationTo-InterfaceOrientation:`, followed by `willAnimateSecondHalfOfRotationFromInterface-Orientation`. If you don't need two separate methods for handling rotation, you can use the simpler `willRotateToInterfaceOrientation:` method (recommended in iOS 5).

The `willRotateToInterfaceOrientation:` method is invoked before the orientation starts. In contrast to the previous two events, this is a one-stage process. Note that if you implement this method, the `willAnimateFirstHalfOfRotationToInterfaceOrientation:` and `willAnimateSecondHalfOfRotationFromInterfaceOrientation:` methods will still be called (if you implemented them).

The method looks like this:

```
- (void)willRotateToInterfaceOrientation:
(UIInterfaceOrientation) toInterfaceOrientation
    duration:(NSTimeInterval) duration {

}
```

The `toInterfaceOrientation` parameter indicates the orientation to which it is changing, and the `duration` parameter indicates the duration of the rotation, in seconds.

willAnimateRotationToInterfaceOrientation:

The `willAnimateRotationToInterfaceOrientation:` event is called before the animation of the rotation starts.

> **NOTE** If you handle both the `willRotateToInterfaceOrientation:` and the `willAnimateRotationToInterfaceOrientation:` methods, the former will be called first, followed by the latter.

The method looks like this:

```
- (void)willAnimateRotationToInterfaceOrientation:
(UIInterfaceOrientation)interfaceOrientation
    duration:(NSTimeInterval)duration {

}
```

The `interfaceOrientation` parameter specifies the target orientation to which it is rotating.

> **NOTE** If you implement this method, the `willAnimateFirstHalfOfRotationTo-InterfaceOrientation:` and `willAnimateSecondHalfOfRotationFrom-InterfaceOrientation:` events will not be called anymore (if you implemented them).

In the following Try It Out, you will reposition the views on your user interface (UI) when the device changes orientation.

TRY IT OUT **Repositioning Views during Orientation Change**

1. Using the project created earlier, select the `ScreenRotationsViewController.xib` file and add a Round Rect Button to the View window (see Figure 7-4).

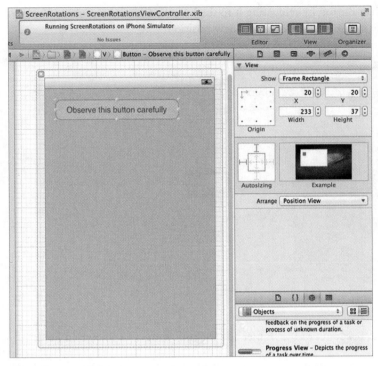

FIGURE 7-4

2. Observe its size and positioning by viewing the Size Inspector window. Here, its position is (20,20) and its size is 233 by 37 points.

3. Rotate the orientation of the View window from portrait to landscape mode by changing its Orientation attribute to Landscape in the Attributes Inspector window (see Figure 7-5).

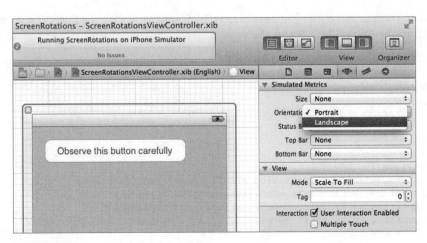

FIGURE 7-5

4. Reposition the Round Rect Button by relocating it to the bottom-right corner of the View window (see Figure 7-6). Also observe and take note of its new position.

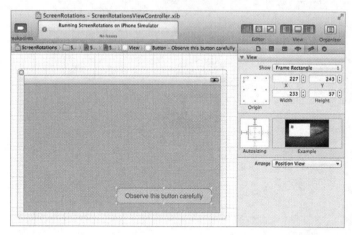

FIGURE 7-6

5. In the `ScreenRotationsViewController.h` file, add the following code shown in bold:

```
#import <UIKit/UIKit.h>

@interface ScreenRotationsViewController : UIViewController
{
    IBOutlet UIButton *btn;
}

@property (nonatomic, retain) UIButton *btn;

@end
```

6. In Interface Builder, connect the outlet you have created by Control-clicking the File's Owner item and dragging over to the Round Rect Button. Select `btn`.

7. In the `ScreenRotationsViewController.m` file, add the following bold code:

```
#import "ScreenRotationsViewController.h"

@implementation ScreenRotationsViewController

@synthesize btn;

-(void) positionViews {
    UIInterfaceOrientation destOrientation = self.interfaceOrientation;
    if (destOrientation == UIInterfaceOrientationPortrait ||
        destOrientation == UIInterfaceOrientationPortraitUpsideDown) {
        //--if rotating to portrait mode--
        btn.frame = CGRectMake(20, 20, 233, 37);
    } else {
```

```
            //--if rotating to landscape mode--
            btn.frame = CGRectMake(227, 243, 233, 37);
    }
}

- (void)willRotateToInterfaceOrientation:
(UIInterfaceOrientation) toInterfaceOrientation
    duration:(NSTimeInterval) duration {
    [self positionViews];
}

- (BOOL)shouldAutorotateToInterfaceOrientation:
(UIInterfaceOrientation)interfaceOrientation
{
    // Return YES for supported orientations
    return YES;
}

- (void)viewDidLoad {
    [self positionViews];
    [super viewDidLoad];
}

- (void)dealloc {
    [btn release];
    [super dealloc];
}
```

8. Press Command-R in Xcode to deploy the application onto the iPhone Simulator.

9. Observe that when the iPhone Simulator is in portrait mode, the Round Rect Button is displayed in the top-left corner; but when you change the orientation to landscape mode, it is repositioned to the bottom-right corner (see Figure 7-7).

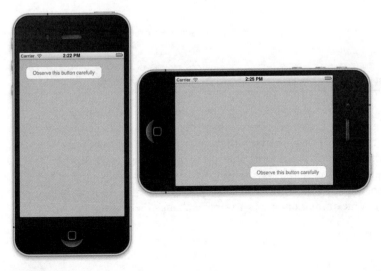

FIGURE 7-7

How It Works

This project illustrated how you can reposition the views on your application when the device changes orientation. You first created an outlet and connected it to the Round Rect Button on the View window.

When the device is being rotated, the `willRotateToInterfaceOrientation:` method that you implemented is called so that you can reposition the Round Rect Button. When this method is called, you can obtain the destination orientation using the `interfaceOrientation` property of the current View window (`self`), like this:

```
UIInterfaceOrientation destOrientation = self.interfaceOrientation;
```

Using this information, you position the Round Rect Button according to the destination orientation by altering its `frame` property via the `positionViews` method, which you have defined:

```
-(void) positionViews {
    UIInterfaceOrientation destOrientation = self.interfaceOrientation;
    if (destOrientation == UIInterfaceOrientationPortrait ||
        destOrientation == UIInterfaceOrientationPortraitUpsideDown) {
        //—-if rotating to portrait mode—-
        btn.frame = CGRectMake(20, 20, 233, 37);
    } else {
        //—-if rotating to landscape mode—-
        btn.frame = CGRectMake(227, 243, 233, 37);
    }
}
```

You should also call the `positionViews` method in the `viewDidLoad` method so that the Round Rect Button can be displayed correctly when the View window is loaded:

```
- (void)viewDidLoad {
    [self positionViews];
    [super viewDidLoad];
}
```

PROPERTIES FOR DEALING WITH THE POSITIONING OF VIEWS

In the previous example, you used the `frame` property to change the position of a view during runtime. The `frame` property defines the rectangle occupied by the view, with respect to its superview (the view that contains it). Using the `frame` property enables you to set the positioning and size of a view. Besides using the `frame` property, you can also use the `center` property, which sets the center of the view, also with respect to its superview. You usually use the `center` property when you are performing some animation and just want to change the position of a view.

PROGRAMMATICALLY ROTATING THE SCREEN

You've seen how your application can handle changes in device orientation when the user rotates the device. Sometimes (such as when you are developing a game), however, you want to force the application to display in a certain orientation independently of the device's orientation.

There are two scenarios to consider:

➤ Rotating the screen orientation during runtime when your application is running

➤ Displaying the screen in a fixed orientation when the View window has been loaded

Rotating during Runtime

During runtime, you can programmatically rotate the screen by using the setOrientation: method on an instance of the UIDevice class. Suppose you want to let users change the screen orientation: They press the Round Rect Button. Using the project created earlier, you can code it as follows (you need to connect the Touch Up Inside event of the button to this IBAction):

```
-(IBAction) btnClicked: (id) sender{
    [[UIDevice currentDevice]
        setOrientation:UIInterfaceOrientationLandscapeLeft];
}
```

The setOrientation: method takes a single parameter specifying the orientation to which you want to change.

 NOTE *After you have programmatically switched the orientation of your application, your application's rotation can still be changed when the device is physically rotated. The orientation that it can be changed to is dependent on what you set in the* shouldAutorotateToInterfaceOrientation: *method.*

Fixing the View Window to a Specific Orientation

When a View window is loaded, by default it is always displayed in portrait mode. If your application requires that you fix the View window in a particular orientation when it has been loaded, you can do so by modifying a particular key (Initial Supported interface orientations) in the info.plist file located in the Supporting Files folder of your Xcode project.

For example, if you want to force your View window to display in the landscape left mode, set the first array item of the Initial Supported interface orientations key to Landscape (left home button), as shown in Figure 7-8).

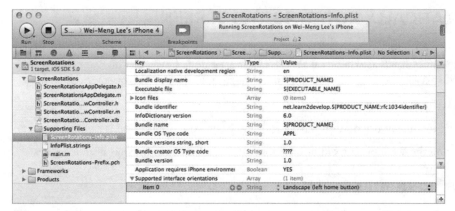

FIGURE 7-8

Then, modify the `shouldAutorotateToInterfaceOrientation:` method as follows:

```
- (BOOL) shouldAutorotateToInterfaceOrientation:
(UIInterfaceOrientation)interfaceOrientation {
    // Return YES for supported orientations
    return (interfaceOrientation == UIInterfaceOrientationLandscapeLeft);
}
```

The application will now load in landscape mode and will be fixed in this orientation even if you rotate the device.

 NOTE *Remember to set the orientation to which you are changing to in the* `shouldAutorotateToInterfaceOrientation:` *method.*

SUMMARY

This chapter explained how changes in screen orientation are handled by the various methods in the View Controller class. Proper handling of screen orientations will make your application more useable and improve the user experience.

EXERCISES

1. Suppose you want your application to support only the landscape right and landscape left orientations. How should you modify your code?

2. What is the difference between the `frame` and `center` property of a view?

Answers to the exercises can be found in Appendix D.

▶ WHAT YOU LEARNED IN THIS CHAPTER

TOPIC	KEY CONCEPTS
Handling device rotations	Implement the `willRotateToInterfaceOrientation:` and `willAnimateRotationToInterfaceOrientation:` methods.
Four orientations supported	`UIInterfaceOrientationPortrait` `UIInterfaceOrientationLandscapeLeft` `UIInterfaceOrientationLandscapeRight` `UIInterfaceOrientationPortraitUpsideDown`
Events fired when device is rotated	`willAnimateFirstHalfOfRotationToInterfaceOrientation:`
Properties for changing the position of a view	Use the `frame` property for changing the positioning and size of a view. Use the `center` property for changing the positioning of a view.

8

Creating and Persisting Data Using the Table View

WHAT YOU WILL LEARN IN THIS CHAPTER

➤ Manually adding a Table view to a view, and wiring the data source and delegate to your View Controller

➤ Handling the various Table view events to populate it with items

➤ Enabling users to select Table view items

➤ Displaying text and images in the rows of the Table view

➤ Displaying the items from a property list in a Table view

➤ Grouping the items in a Table view into sections

➤ Adding indexing to the Table view

➤ Adding search capabilities to the Table view

➤ Adding disclosures and checkmarks to rows in the Table view

➤ Navigating to another View window

One of the most commonly used views in iOS applications is the Table view. The Table view is used to display lists of items from which users can select, or users can tap an item to display more information about it. Figure 8-1 shows a Table view in action in the Safari application.

The Table view is such an important topic that it deserves a chapter of its own. Hence, in this chapter, you examine the Table view in detail, and learn about the various building blocks that make it such a versatile view.

FIGURE 8-1

CREATING A SIMPLE TABLE VIEW

The best way to understand how to use a Table view in your application is to create a new Single View Application project and then manually add a Table view to the View window and wire it to a View Controller. That way, you can understand the various building blocks of the Table view.

Without further ado, use the following Try It Out to create a new project and see how to put a Table view together!

TRY IT OUT   Using a Table View

Codefile [TableViewExample.zip] available for download at Wrox.com

1. Create a new Single View Application (iPhone) project and name it **TableViewExample**. You will also use the project name as the Class Prefix and ensure that you have the Use Automatic Reference Counting option unchecked.

2. Select the `TableViewExampleViewController.xib` file to edit it in Interface Builder.

3. Drag the `Table View` from the Object Library and drop it onto the View window (see Figure 8-2).

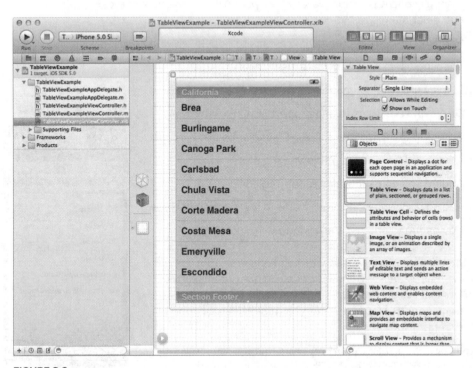

FIGURE 8-2

4. Right-click the Table view and connect the `dataSource` outlet to the File's Owner item (see Figure 8-3). Do the same for the `delegate` outlet.

FIGURE 8-3

5. In the `TableViewExampleViewController.h` file, add the following statement that appears in bold:

```
#import <UIKit/UIKit.h>

@interface TableViewExampleViewController : UIViewController
<UITableViewDataSource>

@end
```

6. In the `TableViewExampleViewController.m` file, add the following statements that appear in bold:

```
#import "TableViewExampleViewController.h"

@implementation TableViewExampleViewController

NSMutableArray *listOfMovies;

//---insert individual row into the table view---
- (UITableViewCell *)tableView:(UITableView *)tableView
        cellForRowAtIndexPath:(NSIndexPath *)indexPath {

    static NSString *CellIdentifier = @"Cell";

    //--try to get a reusable cell--
    UITableViewCell *cell =
```

```
    [tableView dequeueReusableCellWithIdentifier:CellIdentifier];

    //---create new cell if no reusable cell is available---
    if (cell == nil) {
        cell = [[[UITableViewCell alloc] initWithStyle:UITableViewCellStyleDefault
                                    reuseIdentifier:CellIdentifier]
                autorelease];
    }

    //---set the text to display for the cell---
    NSString *cellValue = [listOfMovies objectAtIndex:indexPath.row];
    cell.textLabel.text = cellValue;

    return cell;
}

//---set the number of rows in the table view---
- (NSInteger)tableView:(UITableView *)tableView
 numberOfRowsInSection:(NSInteger)section {
    return [listOfMovies count];
}

- (void)viewDidLoad
{
    //---initialize the array---
    listOfMovies = [[NSMutableArray alloc] init];

    //---add items---
    [listOfMovies addObject:@"Training Day"];
    [listOfMovies addObject:@"Remember the Titans"];
    [listOfMovies addObject:@"John Q."];
    [listOfMovies addObject:@"The Bone Collector"];
    [listOfMovies addObject:@"Ricochet"];
    [listOfMovies addObject:@"The Siege"];
    [listOfMovies addObject:@"Malcolm X"];
    [listOfMovies addObject:@"Antwone Fisher"];
    [listOfMovies addObject:@"Courage Under Fire"];
    [listOfMovies addObject:@"He Got Game"];
    [listOfMovies addObject:@"The Pelican Brief"];
    [listOfMovies addObject:@"Glory"];
    [listOfMovies addObject:@"The Preacher's Wife"];
    [super viewDidLoad];
}
```

7. Press Command-R to test the application on the iPhone Simulator. Figure 8-4 shows the Table view displaying a list of movies.

How It Works

You start the application by creating an NSMutableArray object called listOfMovies containing a list of movie names. The items stored in this array will be displayed by the Table view.

FIGURE 8-4

```
- (void)viewDidLoad
{
    //---initialize the array---
    listOfMovies = [[NSMutableArray alloc] init];

    //---add items---
    [listOfMovies addObject:@"Training Day"];
    [listOfMovies addObject:@"Remember the Titans"];
    [listOfMovies addObject:@"John Q."];
    [listOfMovies addObject:@"The Bone Collector"];
    [listOfMovies addObject:@"Ricochet"];
    [listOfMovies addObject:@"The Siege"];
    [listOfMovies addObject:@"Malcolm X"];
    [listOfMovies addObject:@"Antwone Fisher"];
    [listOfMovies addObject:@"Courage Under Fire"];
    [listOfMovies addObject:@"He Got Game"];
    [listOfMovies addObject:@"The Pelican Brief"];
    [listOfMovies addObject:@"Glory"];
    [listOfMovies addObject:@"The Preacher's Wife"];
    [super viewDidLoad];
}
```

To populate the Table view with items, you need to handle several events contained in the `UITableViewDataSource` protocol. Hence, you need to ensure that your View Controller conforms to this protocol:

```
#import <UIKit/UIKit.h>

@interface TableViewExampleViewController : UIViewController
<UITableViewDataSource>
@end
```

The `UITableViewDataSource` protocol contains several events that you can implement to supply data to the Table view. Two events that you have handled (and they are mandatory in this protocol) in this example are as follows:

➤ `tableView:numberOfRowsInSection:`

➤ `tableView:cellForRowAtIndexPath:`

The `tableView:numberOfRowsInSection:` event indicates how many rows you want the Table view to display. In this case, you set it to the number of items in the `listOfMovies` array:

```
//---set the number of rows in the table view---
- (NSInteger)tableView:(UITableView *)tableView
 numberOfRowsInSection:(NSInteger)section {
    return [listOfMovies count];
}
```

The `tableView:cellForRowAtIndexPath:` event inserts a cell in a particular location of the Table view. This event is fired once for each row of the Table view that is visible.

One of the parameters contained in the `tableView:didSelectRowAtIndexPath:` event is of the type `NSIndexPath`. The `NSIndexPath` class represents the path of a specific item in a nested array collection. To determine which row is currently being populated, you simply call the `row` property of the `NSIndexPath` object (`indexPath`) and then use the row number to reference against the `listOfMovies` array. The value is then used to set the text value of the row in the Table view:

```
//---insert individual row into the table view---
- (UITableViewCell *)tableView:(UITableView *)tableView
        cellForRowAtIndexPath:(NSIndexPath *)indexPath {

    static NSString *CellIdentifier = @"Cell";

    //---try to get a reusable cell---
    UITableViewCell *cell =
    [tableView dequeueReusableCellWithIdentifier:CellIdentifier];

    //---create new cell if no reusable cell is available---
    if (cell == nil) {
        cell = [[[UITableViewCell alloc]
    initWithStyle:UITableViewCellStyleDefault
                                  reuseIdentifier:CellIdentifier]
               autorelease];
    }

    //---set the text to display for the cell---
    NSString *cellValue = [listOfMovies objectAtIndex:indexPath.
        row];
    cell.textLabel.text = cellValue;

    return cell;
}
```

Each row in the Table View is represented by a `UITableViewCell` object. Specifically, you use the `dequeueReusableCellWithIdentifier:` method of the `UITableView` class to obtain an instance of the `UITableViewCell` class. The `dequeueReusableCellWithIdentifier:` method returns a reusable Table view cell object. This is important because if you have a large table (say, with 10,000 rows) and you create a single `UITableViewCell` object for each row, you would generate a large performance and memory hit. In addition, because a Table view displays only a fixed number of rows at any one time, reusing the cells that have been scrolled out of view makes sense. This is exactly what the `dequeueReusableCellWithIdentifier:` method does. Therefore, for example, if 10 rows are visible in the Table view, only 10 `UITableViewCell` objects are ever created — they are always reused when the user scrolls through the Table view.

As the user flicks the Table view to review more rows (that are hidden), the `tableView:cellForRowAtIndexPath:` event is continually fired, enabling you to populate the newly visible rows with data.

 NOTE *The* `tableView:cellForRowAtIndexPath:` *event is not fired continuously from start to finish. For example, if the Table view has 100 rows to display, the event is fired continuously for the first, say, 10 rows that are visible. When the user scrolls down the Table view, the* `tableView:cellForRowAtIndexPath:` *event is fired for the next few visible rows.*

Adding a Header and Footer

You can display a header and footer for the Table view by simply implementing either of the following two methods in your View Controller:

```
- (NSString *)tableView:(UITableView *)tableView
titleForHeaderInSection:(NSInteger)section{
    //--display "Movie List" as the header--
    return @"Movie List";
}

- (NSString *)tableView:(UITableView *)tableView
titleForFooterInSection:(NSInteger)section {
    //--display "by Denzel Washington" as the footer--
    return @"by Denzel Washington";
}
```

If you insert the preceding statements in the `TableViewExampleViewController.m` file and rerun the application, you see the header and footer of the Table view, as shown in Figure 8-5.

Adding an Image

In addition to text, you can display an image next to the text of a cell in a Table view. Suppose you have an image named `apple.jpeg` in the Supporting Files folder of your project (see Figure 8-6).

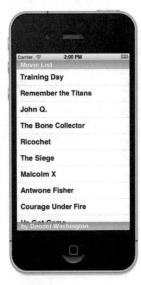

FIGURE 8-5

NOTE *You can simply drag and drop an image to the Supporting Files folder of Xcode. When prompted, ensure that you save a copy of the image in your project.*

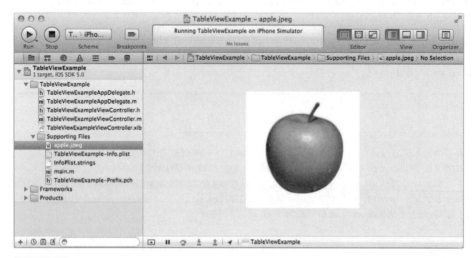

FIGURE 8-6

To display an image next to the text of a cell, insert the following statements that appear in bold into the `tableView:cellForRowAtIndexPath:` method:

```
//---insert individual row into the table view---
- (UITableViewCell *)tableView:(UITableView *)tableView
        cellForRowAtIndexPath:(NSIndexPath *)indexPath {

    static NSString *CellIdentifier = @"Cell";

    //---try to get a reusable cell---
    UITableViewCell *cell =
    [tableView dequeueReusableCellWithIdentifier:CellIdentifier];

    //---create new cell if no reusable cell is available---
    if (cell == nil) {
        cell = [[[UITableViewCell alloc] initWithStyle:UITableViewCellStyleDefault
                                    reuseIdentifier:CellIdentifier]
                autorelease];
    }

    //---set the text to display for the cell---
    NSString *cellValue = [listOfMovies objectAtIndex:indexPath.row];
```

```
    cell.textLabel.text = cellValue;

    //---display an image---
    UIImage *image = [UIImage imageNamed:@"apple.jpeg"];
    cell.imageView.image = image;

    return cell;
}
```

Press Command-R to test the application. The image is now displayed next to each row (see Figure 8-7).

Notice that the `UITableViewCell` object already has the `imageView` property. All you need to do is create an instance of the `UIImage` class and then load the image from the Supporting Files folder of your project.

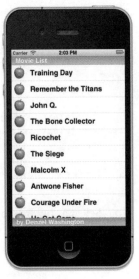

FIGURE 8-7

Displaying the Item Selected

So far, you have seen how to populate the Table view with items by ensuring that your View Controller conforms to the `UITableViewDataSource` protocol. This protocol takes care of populating the Table view, but if you want to select the items in a Table view, you need to conform to another protocol — `UITableViewDelegate`.

The `UITableViewDelegate` protocol contains events that enable you to manage selections, edit and delete rows, and display a header and footer for each section of a Table view.

To use the `UITableViewDelegate` protocol, modify the `TableViewExampleViewController.h` file by adding the statement in bold as follows:

```
#import <UIKit/UIKit.h>

@interface TableViewExampleViewController : UIViewController
<UITableViewDataSource, UITableViewDelegate>

@end
```

Again, if you have connected the `delegate` outlet to the File's Owner item previously (refer to Figure 8-3), you don't need to add the preceding statement (`UITableViewDelegate`). However, doing both doesn't hurt.

The following Try It Out shows how you can enable users to make selections in a Table view.

TRY IT OUT   Making a Selection in a Table View

1. Using the same project created earlier, add the following method to the `TableViewExampleViewController.m` file:

```
- (void)       tableView:(UITableView *)tableView
didSelectRowAtIndexPath:(NSIndexPath *)indexPath {
    NSString *movieSelected = [listOfMovies objectAtIndex:indexPath.row];
```

```
    NSString *msg = [NSString stringWithFormat:@"You have selected %@",
                    movieSelected];
    UIAlertView *alert =
        [[UIAlertView alloc] initWithTitle:@"Movie selected"
                                message:msg
                                delegate:self
                          cancelButtonTitle:@"OK"
                          otherButtonTitles:nil];
    [alert show];
    [alert release];
}
```

2. Press Command-R to test the application on the iPhone Simulator.

3. Select a row by tapping it. When a row is selected, an Alert view displays the row you have selected (see Figure 8-8).

How It Works

One of the methods declared in the `UITableViewDelegate` protocol is `tableView:didSelectRowAtIndexPath:`, which is calls when the user selects a row in the Table view.

FIGURE 8-8

As usual, to determine which row has been selected, you simply call the `row` property of the `NSIndexPath` object (`indexPath`) and then use the row number to reference against the `listOfMovies` array:

```
    NSString *movieSelected = [listOfMovies objectAtIndex:indexPath.row];
```

After the selected movie is retrieved, you simply display it using the `UIAlertView` class:

```
    UIAlertView *alert =
        [[UIAlertView alloc] initWithTitle:@"Movie selected"
                                message:msg
                                delegate:self
                          cancelButtonTitle:@"OK"
                          otherButtonTitles:nil];
    [alert show];
    [alert release];
```

NOTE The `row` property of the `NSIndexPath` class is one of the additions made by the `UIKit` framework to enable the identification of rows and sections in a Table view, so be aware that the original class definition of the `NSIndexPath` class does not contain the `row` property.

Indenting

Another event in the `UITableViewDelegate` protocol is `tableView:indentationLevelForRowAtIndexPath:`. When you handle this event, it is fired for every row that is visible on the screen. To set an indentation for a particular row, simply return an integer indicating the level of indentation:

```
- (NSInteger)                tableView:(UITableView *)tableView
indentationLevelForRowAtIndexPath:(NSIndexPath *)indexPath {
    return [indexPath row] % 2;
}
```

In the preceding example, the indentation alternates between 0 and 1, depending on the current row number. Figure 8-9 shows how the Table view looks if you insert the preceding code in the `TableViewExampleViewController.m` file.

Modifying the Height of Each Row

Another method defined in the `UITableViewDelegate` protocol is `tableView:heightForRowAtIndexPath:`. This method enables you to modify the height of each row. The following method specifies that each row now takes up 70 points (see Figure 8-10):

```
- (CGFloat)   tableView:(UITableView *)tableView
heightForRowAtIndexPath:(NSIndexPath *)indexPath {
    return 70;
}
```

The key advantage of using this method is that you can set the height of each individual row based on the `indexPath` parameter.

USING THE TABLE VIEW IN A MASTER-DETAIL APPLICATION

In the previous sections, you created a Single View Application project, manually added a Table view to the View window, connected the data source, and delegated to the File's Owner item. You then handled all the relevant events defined in the two protocols — `UITableViewDelegate` and `UITableViewDataSource`, so that you could populate the Table view with items and make them selectable.

In real life, the Table view is often used with a Master-Detail (previously known as the Navigation-based Application) project because users often need to select an item from a Table view and then

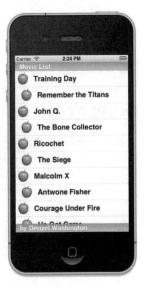

FIGURE 8-9

FIGURE 8-10

navigate to another window showing details about the item selected. For this reason, the Master-Detail Application template in the iOS SDK by default uses the UITableView class instead of the UIView class. This section demonstrates how to use a Table view from within a Master-Detail Application project.

DISPLAYING SECTIONS

In addition to displaying a series of rows in a Table view, you can group items into sections and then create a header for the related items in each section. In the following Try It Out, you learn how to use the Table view from within a Master-Detail Application project and group the items into sections. At the same time, you learn how to display items stored in a property list, as opposed to an array.

TRY IT OUT Displaying Sections in a Table View

Codefile [TableView.zip] available for download at Wrox.com

1. Using Xcode, create a new project and select the Master-Detail Application project template and click Next (see Figure 8-11).

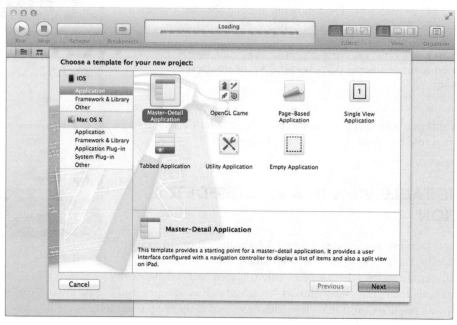

FIGURE 8-11

2. Name the project **TableView** and click Next and then Finish (see Figure 8-12). Leave the Class Prefix empty and ensure that you have the Use Automatic Reference Counting option unchecked.

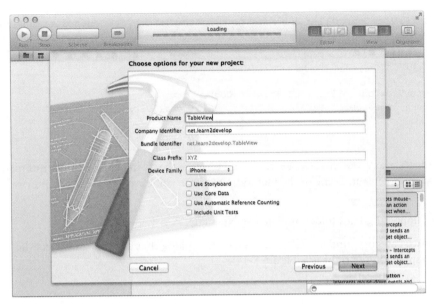

FIGURE 8-12

3. Select the `MasterViewController.xib` file to edit in Interface Builder. This file represents the first View window that will be loaded when your application starts.

4. Notice that in the `MasterViewController.xib` window you now have a `TableView` item instead of the usual `View` item (see Figure 8-13).

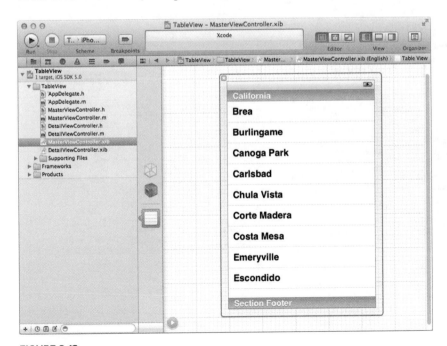

FIGURE 8-13

5. Examine the `MasterViewController.h` file and note that the `MasterViewController` class now extends the `UITableViewController` base class:

```
#import <UIKit/UIKit.h>
@class DetailViewController;
@interface MasterViewController : UITableViewController
@property (strong, nonatomic) DetailViewController *detailViewController;

@end
```

6. Also examine the `MasterViewController.m` file and observe that it includes a number of method stubs that you can implement. Some of the methods are those you have defined in the previous Try It Out.

7. Right-click the Supporting Files folder and choose New File. . . .

8. Select the Resource category (under iOS) on the left of the dialog that appears and select the Property List template on the right (see Figure 8-14).

FIGURE 8-14

9. Name the property list `Movies.plist`. The property list is now saved in the Supporting Files folder of your project. Select it and create the list of items, as shown in Figure 8-15.

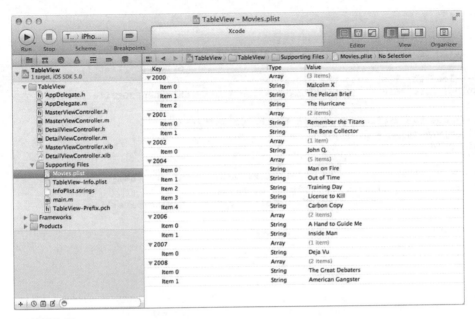

FIGURE 8-15

10. In the `MasterViewController.h` file, add the following statements that appear in bold:

```
#import <UIKit/UIKit.h>
@class DetailViewController;
@interface MasterViewController : UITableViewController
{
    NSDictionary *movieTitles;
    NSArray *years;
}
@property (strong, nonatomic) DetailViewController *detailViewController;

@property (nonatomic, retain) NSDictionary *movieTitles;
@property (nonatomic, retain) NSArray *years;

@end
```

11. In the `MasterViewController.m` file, add the following statements that appear in bold:

```
#import "MasterViewController.h"

#import "DetailViewController.h"

@implementation MasterViewController
```

```objc
@synthesize detailViewController = _detailViewController;
@synthesize movieTitles;
@synthesize years;

- (void)viewDidLoad
{
    //---path to the property list file---
    NSString *path = [[NSBundle mainBundle] pathForResource:@"Movies"
                                                     ofType:@"plist"];

    //---load the list into the dictionary---
    NSDictionary *dic = [[NSDictionary alloc] initWithContentsOfFile:path];

    //---save the dictionary object to the property---
    self.movieTitles = dic;
    [dic release];

    //---get all the keys in the dictionary object and sort them---
    NSArray *array = [[self.movieTitles allKeys]
                        sortedArrayUsingSelector:@selector(compare:)];

    //---save the keys in the years property---
    self.years = array;
    [super viewDidLoad];
}

// Customize the number of sections in the table view.
- (NSInteger)numberOfSectionsInTableView:(UITableView *)tableView
{
    //return 1;
    return [self.years count];
}

- (NSInteger)tableView:(UITableView *)tableView
 numberOfRowsInSection:(NSInteger)section
{
    //return 1;
    //---check the current year based on the section index---
    NSString *year = [self.years objectAtIndex:section];

    //---returns the movies in that year as an array---
    NSArray *movieSection = [self.movieTitles objectForKey:year];

    //---return the number of movies for that year as the number of rows in that
    // section ---
    return [movieSection count];
}

// Customize the appearance of table view cells.
- (UITableViewCell *)tableView:(UITableView *)tableView
```

```
    cellForRowAtIndexPath:(NSIndexPath *)indexPath
{
    static NSString *CellIdentifier = @"Cell";

    UITableViewCell *cell = [tableView
    dequeueReusableCellWithIdentifier:CellIdentifier];
    if (cell == nil) {
        cell = [[[UITableViewCell alloc] initWithStyle:UITableViewCellStyleDefault
    reuseIdentifier:CellIdentifier] autorelease];
        cell.accessoryType = UITableViewCellAccessoryDisclosureIndicator;
    }
        // Configure the cell.
    //---get the year---
    NSString *year = [self.years objectAtIndex:[indexPath section]];

    //---get the list of movies for that year---
    NSArray *movieSection = [self.movieTitles objectForKey:year];

    //---get the particular movie based on that row---
    cell.textLabel.text = [movieSection objectAtIndex:[indexPath row]];

    // cell.textLabel.text = NSLocalizedString(@"Detail", @"Detail");
    return cell;
}

- (NSString *)tableView:(UITableView *)tableView
titleForHeaderInSection:(NSInteger)section {
    //---get the year as the section header---
    NSString *year = [self.years objectAtIndex:section];
    return year;
}

- (void)dealloc {
    [movieTitles release];
    [years release];
    [super dealloc];
}
```

FIGURE 8-16

12. Press Command-R to test the application on the iPhone Simulator. As shown in Figure 8-16, the movies are now grouped into sections organized by year.

13. You can also change the style of the Table view by selecting the TableView item in Interface Builder and then changing the Style attribute in the Attributes Inspector window to Grouped (see Figure 8-17).

14. If you rerun the application, the appearance of the Table view is now different (see Figure 8-18).

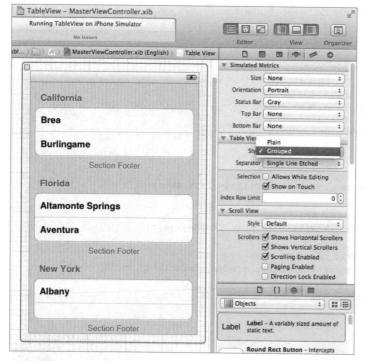

FIGURE 8-17

FIGURE 8-18

How It Works

This exercise covered quite a number of concepts, and you may need some time to absorb them all. First, you create a property list in your project. You populate the property list with several key/value pairs. Essentially, you can visualize the key/value pairs stored in the property list as shown in Figure 8-19.

Key	Value
2000	"Malcolm x", "The Pelican Brief", "The Hurricane"
2001	"Remember the Titans", "The Bone Collector"
2002	"John Q."
2004	"Man on Fire", "Out of Time", "Training Day", "License to Kill", "Carbon Copy"
2006	"A Hand to Guide Me", "Inside Man"
2007	"Deja Vu"
2008	"The Great Debaters", "American Gangster"

FIGURE 8-19

Each key represents a year, and the value for each key represents the movies released in that particular year. You use the values stored in the property list to display them in the Table view.

Within the `MasterViewController` class, you create two properties: `movieTitles` (an `NSDictionary` object) and `years` (an `NSArray` object).

When the View window is loaded, you first locate the property list and load the list into the `NSDictionary` object, followed by retrieving all the years into the `NSArray` object:

```
- (void)viewDidLoad
{
    //---path to the property list file---
    NSString *path = [[NSBundle mainBundle] pathForResource:@"Movies"
                                                     ofType:@"plist"];

    //---load the list into the dictionary---
    NSDictionary *dic = [[NSDictionary alloc] initWithContentsOfFile:path];

    //---save the dictionary object to the property---
    self.movieTitles = dic;
    [dic release];

    //---get all the keys in the dictionary object and sort them---
    NSArray *array = [[self.movieTitles allKeys]
                        sortedArrayUsingSelector:@selector(compare:)];

    //---save the keys in the years property---
    self.years = array;
    [super viewDidLoad];
}
```

Because the Table view now displays the list of movies in sections with each section representing a year, you need to tell the Table view how many sections there are. You do so by implementing the `numberOfSectionsInTableView:` method:

```
- (NSInteger)numberOfSectionsInTableView:(UITableView *)tableView
{
    //return 1;
    return [self.years count];
}
```

After the Table view knows how many sections to display, it must also know how many rows to display in each section. You provide that information by implementing the `tableView:numberOfRowsInSection:` method:

```
- (NSInteger)tableView:(UITableView *)tableView
  numberOfRowsInSection:(NSInteger)section
{
    //return 1;
    //---check the current year based on the section index---
```

```
        NSString *year = [self.years objectAtIndex:section];

        //---returns the movies in that year as an array---
        NSArray *movieSection = [self.movieTitles objectForKey:year];

        //---return the number of movies for that year as the number of rows in that
        // section ---
        return [movieSection count];
    }
```

To display the movies for each section, you implement the `tableView:cellForRowAtIndexPath:` method and extract the relevant movie titles from the `NSDictionary` object:

```
- (UITableViewCell *)tableView:(UITableView *)tableView
    cellForRowAtIndexPath:(NSIndexPath *)indexPath
{
    static NSString *CellIdentifier = @"Cell";

    UITableViewCell *cell = [tableView
    dequeueReusableCellWithIdentifier:CellIdentifier];
    if (cell == nil) {
        cell = [[[UITableViewCell alloc]
    initWithStyle:UITableViewCellStyleDefault reuseIdentifier:CellIdentifier]
autorelease];
        cell.accessoryType = UITableViewCellAccessoryDisclosureIndicator;
    }

    // Configure the cell.
    //---get the year---
    NSString *year = [self.years objectAtIndex:[indexPath section]];

    //---get the list of movies for that year---
    NSArray *movieSection = [self.movieTitles objectForKey:year];

    //---get the particular movie based on that row---
    cell.textLabel.text = [movieSection objectAtIndex:[indexPath row]];

    // cell.textLabel.text = NSLocalizedString(@"Detail", @"Detail");
    return cell;
}

- (NSString *)tableView:(UITableView *)tableView
titleForHeaderInSection:(NSInteger)section {
    //---get the year as the section header---
    NSString *year = [self.years objectAtIndex:section];
    return year;
}
```

Finally, you implement the `tableView:titleForHeaderInSection:` method to retrieve the year as the header for each section:

```
- (NSString *)tableView:(UITableView *)tableView
titleForHeaderInSection:(NSInteger)section {
    //---get the year as the section header---
    NSString *year = [self.years objectAtIndex:section];
    return year;
}
```

Adding Indexing

The list of movies is pretty short, so scrolling through the list is not too much of a hassle. However, imagine a movie list containing 10,000 titles spanning 100 years. In this case, scrolling from the top of the list to the bottom can take a long time. A useful feature of the Table view is the capability to display an index on the right side of the view. An example is the A–Z index list available in your Contacts list. To add an index list to your Table view, you just need to implement the `sectionIndexTitlesForTableView:` method and return the array containing the section headers, which is the `years` array in this case:

```
- (NSArray *)sectionIndexTitlesForTableView:(UITableView *)tableView {
    return self.years;
}
```

 NOTE If the Table view's style is set to `Grouped`, the index will overlap with the layout of the Table view.

Figure 8-20 shows the index displayed on the right side of the Table view.

Adding Search Capability

A common function associated with the Table view is the capability to search the items contained within it. For example, the Contacts application provides the search bar at the top for easy searching of contacts.

The following Try It Out demonstrates how to add search functionality to the Table view.

FIGURE 8-20

TRY IT OUT Adding a Search Bar to the Table View

1. Using the same project created in the previous section, in Interface Builder drag a Search Bar from the Library and drop it onto the Table view (see Figure 8-21).

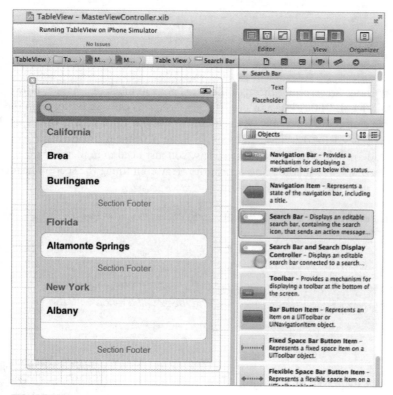

FIGURE 8-21

2. In the `MasterViewController.h` file, add the following statements that appear in bold:

```
#import <UIKit/UIKit.h>
@class DetailViewController;
@interface MasterViewController : UITableViewController
<UISearchBarDelegate>
{
    NSDictionary *movieTitles;
    NSArray *years;
    IBOutlet UISearchBar *searchBar;
}
@property (strong, nonatomic) DetailViewController *detailViewController;

@property (nonatomic, retain) NSDictionary *movieTitles;
@property (nonatomic, retain) NSArray *years;
@property (nonatomic, retain) UISearchBar *searchBar;

@end
```

3. In Interface Builder, Control-click and drag the File's Owner item to the Search Bar and select `searchBar`.

4. Right-click the Search Bar and connect the `delegate` to the File's Owner item (see Figure 8-22).

5. In the `MasterViewController.m` file, add the following statements that appear in bold:

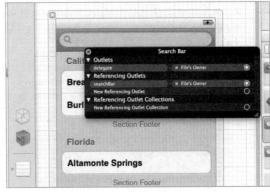

FIGURE 8-22

```objc
#import "MasterViewController.h"

#import "DetailViewController.h"

@implementation MasterViewController
@synthesize detailViewController = _detailViewController;
@synthesize movieTitles;
@synthesize years;

@synthesize searchBar;

- (void)viewDidLoad
{
    //---path to the property list file---
    NSString *path = [[NSBundle mainBundle] pathForResource:@"Movies"
                                         ofType:@"plist"];
    //---load the list into the dictionary---
    NSDictionary *dic = [[NSDictionary alloc] initWithContentsOfFile:path];

    //---save the dictionary object to the property---
    self.movieTitles = dic;
    [dic release];

    //---get all the keys in the dictionary object and sort them---
    NSArray *array = [[self.movieTitles allKeys]
                    sortedArrayUsingSelector:@selector(compare:)];

    //---save the keys in the years property---
    self.years = array;

    //---Search---
    self.tableView.tableHeaderView = searchBar;
    self.searchBar.autocorrectionType = UITextAutocorrectionTypeYes;

    [super viewDidLoad];
}

- (void)dealloc {
    [searchBar release];
    [movieTitles release];
    [years release];
    [super dealloc];
}
```

6. Press Command-R to test the application on the iPhone Simulator. Figure 8-23 shows the Search Bar displayed at the top of the Table view.

7. Back in Xcode, edit the `MasterViewController.h` file by adding the following statements that appear in bold:

```
#import <UIKit/UIKit.h>
@class DetailViewController;
@interface MasterViewController : UITableViewController
<UISearchBarDelegate>
{
    NSDictionary *movieTitles;
    NSArray *years;
    IBOutlet UISearchBar *searchBar;

    BOOL isSearchOn;
    BOOL canSelectRow;
    NSMutableArray *listOfMovies;
    NSMutableArray *searchResult;
}
@property (strong, nonatomic) DetailViewController *detailViewController;
@property (nonatomic, retain) NSDictionary *movieTitles;
@property (nonatomic, retain) NSArray *years;
@property (nonatomic, retain) UISearchBar *searchBar;

- (void) doneSearching:(id)sender;
- (void) searchMoviesTableView;
@end
```

FIGURE 8-23

8. In the `MasterViewController.m` file, add the following methods:

```
//---fired when the user taps on the searchbar---
- (void)searchBarTextDidBeginEditing:(UISearchBar *)searchBar {
    isSearchOn = YES;
    if (searchBar.text.length>0){
        canSelectRow = YES;
        self.tableView.scrollEnabled = YES;
    } else {
        canSelectRow = NO;
        self.tableView.scrollEnabled = NO;
    }

    //---add the Done button at the top---
    self.navigationItem.rightBarButtonItem =
    [[[UIBarButtonItem alloc]
      initWithBarButtonSystemItem:UIBarButtonSystemItemDone
      target:self
      action:@selector(doneSearching:)]
     autorelease];
}

//---done with the searching---
- (void) doneSearching:(id)sender {
```

```objc
        isSearchOn = NO;
        canSelectRow = YES;
        self.tableView.scrollEnabled = YES;
        self.navigationItem.rightBarButtonItem = nil;

        //---hides the keyboard---
        [searchBar resignFirstResponder];

        //---refresh the TableView---
        [self.tableView reloadData];
}

//---fired when the user types something into the searchbar---
- (void)searchBar:(UISearchBar *)searchBar
    textDidChange:(NSString *)searchText {

        //---if there is something to search for---
        if ([searchText length] > 0) {
            canSelectRow = YES;
            self.tableView.scrollEnabled = YES;
            [self searchMoviesTableView];
        }
        else {
            //---nothing to search---
            canSelectRow = NO;
            self.tableView.scrollEnabled = NO;
        }
        [self.tableView reloadData];
}

//---performs the searching using the array of movies---
- (void) searchMoviesTableView {
        //---clears the search result---
        [searchResult removeAllObjects];

        for (NSString *str in listOfMovies) {
            NSRange titleResultsRange = [str rangeOfString:searchBar.text
                                                   options:NSCaseInsensitiveSearch];
            if (titleResultsRange.length > 0)
                [searchResult addObject:str];
        }
}

//---fired when the user taps the Search button on the keyboard---
- (void)searchBarSearchButtonClicked:(UISearchBar *)searchBar {
        [self searchMoviesTableView];
}

- (NSIndexPath *)tableView:(UITableView *)tableView
  willSelectRowAtIndexPath:(NSIndexPath *)indexPath {
        if (canSelectRow)
            return indexPath;
        else
            return nil;
}
```

9. Modify the following methods in bold in the `MasterViewController.m` file:

```objc
- (void)viewDidLoad
{
    //---path to the property list file---
    NSString *path = [[NSBundle mainBundle] pathForResource:@"Movies"
                                                     ofType:@"plist"];
    //---load the list into the dictionary---
    NSDictionary *dic = [[NSDictionary alloc] initWithContentsOfFile:path];

    //---save the dictionary object to the property---
    self.movieTitles = dic;
    [dic release];

    //---get all the keys in the dictionary object and sort them---
    NSArray *array = [[self.movieTitles allKeys]
                      sortedArrayUsingSelector:@selector(compare:)];

    //---save the keys in the years property---
    self.years = array;

    //---Search---
    self.tableView.tableHeaderView = searchBar;
    self.searchBar.autocorrectionType = UITextAutocorrectionTypeYes;

    //---copy all the movie titles in the dictionary into
    // the listOfMovies array---
    listOfMovies = [[NSMutableArray alloc] init];
    for (NSString *year in array) {    //---get all the years---
        //---get all the movies for a particular year---
        NSArray *movies = [movieTitles objectForKey:year];
        for (NSString *title in movies) {
            [listOfMovies addObject:title];
        }
    }

    //---used for storing the search result---
    searchResult = [[NSMutableArray alloc] init];
    isSearchOn = NO;
    canSelectRow = YES;

    [super viewDidLoad];
}

// Customize the number of sections in the table view.
- (NSInteger)numberOfSectionsInTableView:(UITableView *)tableView
{
    //return 1;
    if (isSearchOn)
        return 1;
    else
        return [self.years count];
```

```objc
}

- (NSInteger)tableView:(UITableView *)tableView
 numberOfRowsInSection:(NSInteger)section
{
    //return 1;
    if (isSearchOn) {
        return [searchResult count];
    } else {
        //---check the current year based on the section index---
        NSString *year = [self.years objectAtIndex:section];

        //---returns the movies in that year as an array---
        NSArray *movieSection = [self.movieTitles objectForKey:year];

        //---return the number of movies for that year as the number of rows in that
        // section---
        return [movieSection count];
    }
}

// Customize the appearance of table view cells.
- (UITableViewCell *)tableView:(UITableView *)tableView
    cellForRowAtIndexPath:(NSIndexPath *)indexPath
{
    static NSString *CellIdentifier = @"Cell";

    UITableViewCell *cell = [tableView
    dequeueReusableCellWithIdentifier:CellIdentifier];
    if (cell == nil) {
        cell = [[[UITableViewCell alloc]
    initWithStyle:UITableViewCellStyleDefault reuseIdentifier:CellIdentifier]
autorelease];
        cell.accessoryType = UITableViewCellAccessoryDisclosureIndicator;
    }

    // Configure the cell.
    if (isSearchOn) {
        NSString *cellValue = [searchResult objectAtIndex:indexPath.row];
        cell.textLabel.text = cellValue;
    } else {
        //---get the year---
        NSString *year = [self.years objectAtIndex:[indexPath section]];

        //---get the list of movies for that year---
        NSArray *movieSection = [self.movieTitles objectForKey:year];

        //---get the particular movie based on that row---
        cell.textLabel.text = [movieSection objectAtIndex:[indexPath row]];
        // cell.textLabel.text = NSLocalizedString(@"Detail", @"Detail");
    }
    return cell;
}

- (NSString *)tableView:(UITableView *)tableView
titleForHeaderInSection:(NSInteger)section {
```

```
    //---get the year as the section header---
    NSString *year = [self.years objectAtIndex:section];
    if (isSearchOn)
        return nil;
    else
        return year;
}

- (NSArray *)sectionIndexTitlesForTableView:(UITableView *)tableView {
    if (isSearchOn)
        return nil;
    else
        return self.years;
}

- (void)dealloc {
    [listOfMovies release];
    [searchResult release];

    [searchBar release];
    [movieTitles release];
    [years release];
    [super dealloc];
```

10. Press Command-R to test the application on the iPhone Simulator.

11. Tap the Search Bar and the keyboard will appear. Observe the following:

➤ When the keyboard appears and the Search Bar has no text in it, the Table view contains the original list and the items are not selectable.

➤ As you type, the Table view displays the movies whose title contains the characters you are typing, as demonstrated in Figure 8-24, wherein "on" was typed into the search bar of the right-most image and movie titles containing "on" are now displayed. You can select a search result by tapping it. Observe that your application will navigate to another View window. You will learn more about this in the next section.

➤ When you tap the Done button, the keyboard disappears and the original list appears.

FIGURE 8-24

How It Works

This is quite a bit of work, but it is actually quite easy to follow the details. First, you add an outlet to connect to the Search Bar:

```
IBOutlet UISearchBar *searchBar;
```

You then define two Boolean variables so that you can track whether the search process is ongoing and specify whether the user can select the rows in the Table view:

```
BOOL isSearchOn;
BOOL canSelectRow;
```

You then define two NSMutableArray objects so that you can use one to store the list of movies and another to temporarily store the result of the search:

```
NSMutableArray *listOfMovies;
NSMutableArray *searchResult;
```

When the View window is first loaded, you first associate the Search Bar with the Table view and then copy the entire list of movie titles from the NSDictionary object into the NSMutableArray:

```
//---Search---
self.tableView.tableHeaderView = searchBar;
self.searchBar.autocorrectionType = UITextAutocorrectionTypeYes;

//---copy all the movie titles in the dictionary into
// the listOfMovies array---
listOfMovies = [[NSMutableArray alloc] init];
for (NSString *year in array) {    //---get all the years---
    //---get all the movies for a particular year---
    NSArray *movies = [movieTitles objectForKey:year];
    for (NSString *title in movies) {
        [listOfMovies addObject:title];
    }
}

//---used for storing the search result---
searchResult = [[NSMutableArray alloc] init];
isSearchOn = NO;
canSelectRow = YES;
```

When the user taps the Search Bar, the searchBarTextDidBeginEditing: event (one of the methods defined in the UISearchBarDelegate protocol) fires. In this method, you add a Done button to the top-right corner of the screen. When the Done button is tapped, the doneSearching: method is called (which you define next):

```
//---fired when the user taps on the searchbar---
- (void)searchBarTextDidBeginEditing:(UISearchBar *)searchBar {
    isSearchOn = YES;

    if (searchBar.text.length>0){
```

```
        canSelectRow = YES;
        self.tableView.scrollEnabled = YES;
    } else {
        canSelectRow = NO;
        self.tableView.scrollEnabled = NO;
    }

    //---add the Done button at the top---
    self.navigationItem.rightBarButtonItem =
    [[[UIBarButtonItem alloc]
      initWithBarButtonSystemItem:UIBarButtonSystemItemDone
      target:self
      action:@selector(doneSearching:)]
     autorelease];
}
```

The `doneSearching:` method makes the Search Bar resign its First Responder status (thereby hiding the keyboard). At the same time, you reload the Table view by calling the `reloadData` method of the Table view. This causes the various events associated with the Table view to be fired again:

```
//---done with the searching---
- (void) doneSearching:(id)sender {
    isSearchOn = NO;
    canSelectRow = YES;
    self.tableView.scrollEnabled = YES;
    self.navigationItem.rightBarButtonItem = nil;

    //---hides the keyboard---
    [searchBar resignFirstResponder];

    //---refresh the TableView---
    [self.tableView reloadData];
}
```

As the user types into the Search Bar, the `searchBar:textDidChange:` event is fired for each character entered. In this case, if the Search Bar has at least one character, the `searchMoviesTableView` method (which you define next) is called:

```
//---fired when the user types something into the searchbar---
- (void)searchBar:(UISearchBar *)searchBar
    textDidChange:(NSString *)searchText {

    //---if there is something to search for---
    if ([searchText length] > 0) {
        canSelectRow = YES;
        self.tableView.scrollEnabled = YES;
        [self searchMoviesTableView];
    }
    else {
        //---nothing to search---
```

```
            canSelectRow = NO;
            self.tableView.scrollEnabled = NO;
        }
        [self.tableView reloadData];
    }
```

The `searchMoviesTableView` method performs the searching on the `listOfMovies` array. You
use the `rangeOfString:options:` method of the `NSString` class to perform a case-insensitive search
of each movie title using the specified string. The returned result is an `NSRange` object, which contains
the location and length of the search string being searched. If the length is more than zero, then a
match has been found, and hence you add it to the `searchResult` array:

```
    //---performs the searching using the array of movies---
    - (void) searchMoviesTableView {
        //---clears the search result---
        [searchResult removeAllObjects];

        for (NSString *str in listOfMovies) {
            NSRange titleResultsRange = [str rangeOfString:searchBar.text
                                           options:NSCaseInsensitiveSearch];
            if (titleResultsRange.length > 0)
                [searchResult addObject:str];
        }
    }
```

When the user taps the Search button (on the keyboard), you make a call to the
`searchMoviesTableView` method:

```
    //---fired when the user taps the Search button on the keyboard---
    - (void)searchBarSearchButtonClicked:(UISearchBar *)searchBar {
        [self searchMoviesTableView];
    }
```

You also implement the `tableView:willSelectRowAtIndexPath:` method to check whether or not
rows are selectable:

```
    - (NSIndexPath *)tableView:(UITableView *)tableView
      willSelectRowAtIndexPath:(NSIndexPath *)indexPath {
        if (canSelectRow)
            return indexPath;
        else
            return nil;
    }
```

The rest of the methods are straightforward. If the search is currently active (as determined by the
`isSearchOn` variable), then you display the list of titles contained in the `searchResult` array. If not,
then you display the entire list of movies.

Disclosures and Checkmarks

Because users often select rows in a Table view to view more detailed information, rows in a Table view often sport images such as an arrow or a checkmark (these images are known as *accessories*). There are three types of accessories that you can display:

➤ Checkmark

➤ Disclosure indicator

➤ Detail Disclosure button

To display a disclosure or a checkmark accessory, you use the accessoryType property of the UITableViewCell object, as shown by default in the tableView:cellForRowAtIndexPath: event:

```objc
- (UITableViewCell *)tableView:(UITableView *)tableView
cellForRowAtIndexPath:(NSIndexPath *)indexPath
{
    static NSString *CellIdentifier = @"Cell";

    UITableViewCell *cell = [tableView
dequeueReusableCellWithIdentifier:CellIdentifier];
    if (cell == nil) {
        cell = [[[UITableViewCell alloc] initWithStyle:UITableViewCellStyleDefault
reuseIdentifier:CellIdentifier] autorelease];
        cell.accessoryType = UITableViewCellAccessoryDisclosureIndicator;
    }

    // Configure the cell.
    if (isSearchOn) {
        NSString *cellValue = [searchResult objectAtIndex:indexPath.row];
        cell.textLabel.text = cellValue;
    } else {
        //---get the year---
        NSString *year = [self.years objectAtIndex:[indexPath section]];

        //---get the list of movies for that year---
        NSArray *movieSection = [self.movieTitles objectForKey:year];

        //---get the particular movie based on that row---
        cell.textLabel.text = [movieSection objectAtIndex:[indexPath row]];
        // cell.textLabel.text = NSLocalizedString(@"Detail", @"Detail");
    }
    return cell;
}
```

You can use the following constants for the accessoryType property:

➤ UITableViewCellAccessoryCheckmark

➤ UITableViewCellAccessoryDisclosureIndicator

➤ UITableViewCellAccessoryDetailDisclosureButton

Figure 8-25 shows the Detail Disclosure button and Checkmark accessories.

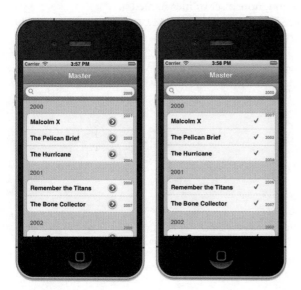

FIGURE 8-25

Of the three accessory types, only the `UITableViewCellAccessoryDetailDisclosureButton` can handle one additional tap event of the user. To handle the additional event when the user taps the Detail Disclosure button, you need to implement the `tableView:accessoryButtonTappedForRowWithIndexPath:` method:

```
- (void)tableView:(UITableView *)tableView
accessoryButtonTappedForRowWithIndexPath:(NSIndexPath *)indexPath {
    //---insert code here---
    // e.g. navigate to another view to display detailed information, etc
}
```

Figure 8-26 shows the two different events fired when a user taps the content of the cell, as well as the Detail Disclosure button.

Commonly, you use the Detail Disclosure button to display detailed information about the selected row.

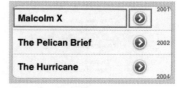

FIGURE 8-26

Navigating to Another View

One of the features of a Master-Detail Application project is the capability to navigate from one View window to another. For example, the user can select an item from the Table view and the application will navigate to another View window showing the details about the item selected. By default, Xcode creates a second View window so that your application can navigate to it. In the following Try It Out, you modify the application you have been building so that when the user selects a movie, the application displays the name of the movie selected in the second View window.

TRY IT OUT Displaying the Movie Selected in a Second View Window

1. Using the project created in the previous section, note a set of files named
   `DetailViewController.xib`, `DetailViewController.h`, and `DetailViewController.m`. The
   `DetailViewController.m` file contains the following methods:

```
- (void)setDetailItem:(id)newDetailItem
{
    if (_detailItem != newDetailItem) {
        _detailItem = newDetailItem;

        // Update the view.
        [self configureView];
    }
}

- (void)configureView
{
    // Update the user interface for the detail item.

    if (self.detailItem) {
        self.detailDescriptionLabel.text = [self.detailItem description];
    }
}
```

2. Select the `DetailViewController.xib` file to edit it in Interface Builder. Right-click on the File's
   Owner item to view its connections. Note that the `detailDescriptionLabel` outlet is connected
   to the `Label` (see Figure 8-27).

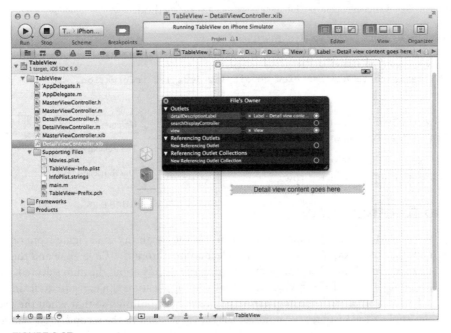

FIGURE 8-27

3. Add the following bold code to the `tableView:didSelectRowAtIndexPath:` method located in the `MasterViewController.m` file:

```objc
- (void)tableView:(UITableView *)tableView didSelectRowAtIndexPath:
(NSIndexPath *
    )indexPath
{
    NSString *message;
    if (!isSearchOn) {
        NSString *year = [self.years objectAtIndex:[indexPath section]];
        NSArray *movieSection = [self.movieTitles objectForKey:year];
        NSString *movieTitle = [movieSection objectAtIndex:[indexPath row]];
        message = [NSString stringWithFormat:@"You have selected %@", movieTitle];
    } else {
        if ([searchResult count]==0) return;
        message =
            [NSString stringWithFormat:@"You have selected %@",
                [searchResult objectAtIndex:indexPath.row]];
    }

    if (!self.detailViewController) {
        self.detailViewController = [[[DetailViewController alloc]
initWithNibName:@"DetailViewController" bundle:nil] autorelease];
    }

    self.detailViewController.detailItem = message;

    [self.navigationController
        pushViewController:self.detailViewController
                animated:YES];
}
```

4. Press Command-R to test the application on the iPhone Simulator. As shown in Figure 8-28, when you click on one of the movies in the Table view, the application navigates to another View window, showing the name of the movie selected.

How It Works

In order to enable navigation to another View window, you need to create an instance of its corresponding View controller. Fortunately, Xcode does this for you automatically.

In the `DetailViewController` class, there is a property named `detailItem` (which is defined as follows) as well as a method named `configureView`:

FIGURE 8-28

```objc
- (void)setDetailItem:(id)newDetailItem
{
    if (_detailItem != newDetailItem) {
```

```
        _detailItem = newDetailItem;

        // Update the view.
        [self configureView];
    }
}

- (void)configureView
{
    // Update the user interface for the detail item.

    if (self.detailItem) {
        self.detailDescriptionLabel.text = [self.detailItem description];
    }
}
```

You use this property to pass the name of the movie selected. Once this property is set, it will call the configureView method to update the Label on the View window.

When the user selects an item in the Table view, you first determine the name of the movie (in the tableView:didSelectRowAtIndexPath: method) selected:

```
NSString *message;
if (!isSearchOn) {
    NSString *year = [self.years objectAtIndex:[indexPath section]];
    NSArray *movieSection = [self.movieTitles objectForKey:year];
    NSString *movieTitle = [movieSection objectAtIndex:[indexPath row]];
    message = [NSString stringWithFormat:@"You have selected %@", movieTitle];
} else {
    if ([searchResult count]==0) return;
    message =
        [NSString stringWithFormat:@"You have selected %@",
            [searchResult objectAtIndex:indexPath.row]];
}
```

You then navigate to the DetailViewController class by instantiating a copy of it and then set the detailItem property to the name of the movie selected:

```
if (!self.detailViewController) {
    self.detailViewController = [[[DetailViewController alloc]
initWithNibName:@"DetailViewController" bundle:nil] autorelease];
}

self.detailViewController.detailItem = message;
```

Finally, to navigate to the new View window, you use the pushViewController: method of the Navigation Controller:

```
[self.navigationController
    pushViewController:self.detailViewController
            animated:YES];
```

SUMMARY

In this chapter, you had a good look at the Table view and learned how to customize it to display items in various formats. You also learned how to implement search functionality in the Table view, which is an essential function in real-world applications. In addition, you learned how to move between View windows in a Navigation-based application.

EXERCISES

1. Name the two protocols to which your View Controller must conform when using the Table view in your view. Briefly describe their uses.

2. Which method should be implemented if you want to add an index to a Table view?

3. Name the three disclosure and checkmark accessories that you can use. Which one handles user taps?

Answers to the exercises can be found in Appendix D.

▶ **WHAT YOU LEARNED IN THIS CHAPTER**

TOPIC	KEY CONCEPTS
Adding items to a Table view	Handle the various events in the `UITableViewDataSource` protocol.
Allowing users to select rows in a Table view	Handle the various events in the `UITableViewDelegate` protocol.
Adding images to rows in a Table view	Use the `image` property of the `UITableViewCell` class and set it to an instance of the `UIImage` class containing an image.
Using a property list with a Table view	Use the following code snippet to locate the property list: **NSString *path = [[NSBundle mainBundle]** **pathForResource:@"Movies"** **ofType:@"plist"];** Then use a combination of `NSDictionary` and `NSArray` objects to retrieve the key/value pairs stored in the property list.
Grouping items in a Table view in sections	Implement the following methods: `numberOfSectionsInTableView:tableView:numberOfRowsInSection:tableView:titleForHeaderInSection:`.
Adding an index to a Table view	Implement the `sectionIndexTitlesForTableView:` method.
Adding disclosure and checkmark images to a row in a Table view	Set the `accessoryType` property of an `UITableViewCell` object to one of the following: * `UITableViewCellAccessoryDetailDisclosureButton` * `UITableViewCellAccessoryCheckmark` * `UITableViewCellAccessoryDisclosureIndicator`.
Implementing a search in a Table view	Use the Search Bar view and handle the various events in the `UISearchBarDelegate` protocol.
Navigating to another View window	Use the `pushViewController:` method of the Navigation Controller.

9

Using Application Preferences

WHAT YOU WILL LEARN IN THIS CHAPTER

➤ How to add application preferences to your application

➤ How to programmatically access the Settings values

➤ How to reset your application's preferences settings

If you are a relatively seasoned Mac OS X user, you're familiar with the concept of application preferences. Almost every Mac OS X application has application-specific settings that are used to configure the application's appearance and behavior. These settings are known as the *application preferences*.

In iOS, applications also have application preferences. In contrast to Mac OS X applications, however, whose application preferences are an integral part of the application, iPhone preferences are centrally managed by an application called Settings (see Figure 9-1).

The Settings application displays the preferences of system applications as well as third-party applications. Tapping any setting displays the details, where you can configure the preferences of an application.

In this chapter, you learn how to incorporate application preferences into your application and modify them programmatically during runtime.

FIGURE 9-1

CREATING APPLICATION PREFERENCES

Creating application preferences for your iOS application is a relatively straightforward process. It involves adding a resource called the Settings Bundle to your project, configuring a property list file, and then deploying your application. When your application is deployed, the application preferences are automatically created for you in the Settings application.

The following Try It Out shows how to add application preferences to your iPhone application project in Xcode.

TRY IT OUT Adding Application Preferences

1. Using Xcode, create a new Single View Application (iPhone) project and name it `ApplicationSettings`. You will also use the project name as the Class Prefix. Ensure that you have unchecked the Use Automatic Reference Counting option.

2. Right-click the project name in Xcode and add a new file. Click the Resource template category and select Settings Bundle (see Figure 9-2). Click Next.

FIGURE 9-2

3. When asked to name the file, use the default name of `Settings.bundle` and click Save.

4. The `Settings.bundle` item should now be part of your project (see Figure 9-3). Expand it and click the `Root.plist` item to view its content using the default Property List editor (see Figure 9-4).

5. Press Command-R to test the application on the iPhone Simulator. When the application is loaded on the Simulator, press the Home key to return to the main screen of the iPhone. Click the Settings application. You can now see a new Settings entry, ApplicationSettings (see Figure 9-5). Click the ApplicationSettings entry to see the default settings created for you.

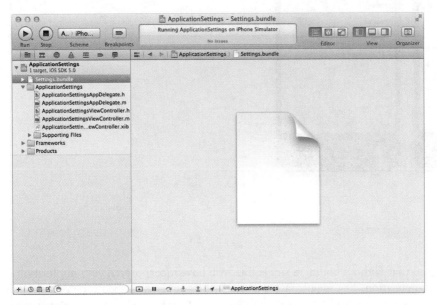

FIGURE 9-3

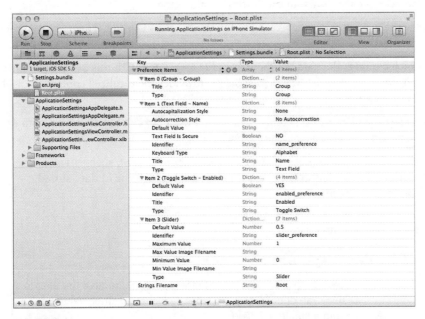

FIGURE 9-4

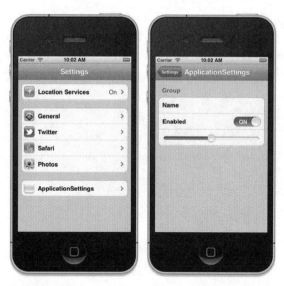

FIGURE 9-5

How It Works

It seems almost magical that without coding a single line, you have incorporated your application preferences into your application. The magic part is actually the `Settings.bundle` file that you have added to your project. It contains two files: `Root.plist` and `Root.strings`. The `Root.plist` file is an XML file that contains a collection of dictionary objects (key/value pairs). These key/value pairs are translated into the preferences entries shown in the Settings application.

Take a moment to review the use of the various keys used in the `Root.plist` file. There are two root-level keys in the `Root.plist` file:

➤ `StringsTable`, which contains the name of the strings file associated with this `Settings.bundle` file. In this case, it is pointing to `Root.strings`. This file provides the localized content to display to the user for each of your preferences.

➤ `PreferenceSpecifiers`, which is of type `Array` and contains an array of dictionaries, with each item containing the information for a single preference.

Each preference is represented by an item (known as `PreferenceSpecifiers`), such as `Item 0`, `Item 1`, `Item 2`, and so on. Each item has a `Type` key, which indicates the type of data stored. Table 9-1 describes the preference specifiers.

TABLE 9-1: List of Preference Specifiers and Usage

ELEMENT TYPE	DESCRIPTION	USE FOR
PSTextFieldSpecifier	A text field preference. Displays an optional title and an editable text field.	Preferences that require the user to specify a custom string value

ELEMENT TYPE	DESCRIPTION	USE FOR
PSTitleValueSpecifier	A read-only string preference	Displaying preference values as formatted strings
PSToggleSwitchSpecifier	A toggle switch preference	Configuring a preference that can have only one of two values
PSSliderSpecifier	A slider preference	Preferences that represent a range of values. The value for this type is a real number whose minimum and maximum you specify.
PSMultiValueSpecifier	A multivalue preference	Preferences that support a set of mutually exclusive values
PSGroupSpecifier	A group item preference	Organizing groups of preferences on a single page
PSChildPaneSpecifier	A child pane preference	Linking to a new page of preferences

By default, the various items inside the `Root.plist` file are represented using their user-friendly names, such as Default Value, Text Field Is Secure, and so on. However, for editing purposes (such as adding new keys into the file), it is always easier to display the keys in their raw format. To do so, right-click on another item inside the `.plist` file and select Show Raw Keys/Values (see Figure 9-6). Doing so makes the editor toggle between displaying the names in user-friendly format and displaying them in raw form.

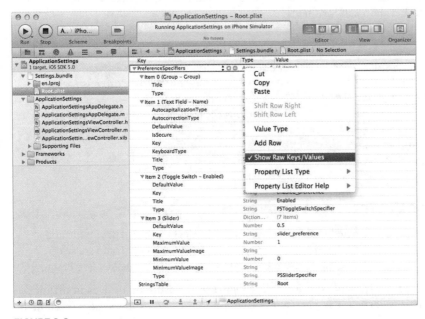

FIGURE 9-6

Each `PreferenceSpecifiers` key contains a list of subkeys that you can use. For example, the `PSTextFieldSpecifier` key provides `Type`, `Title`, `Key`, `DefaultValue`, `IsSecure`, `KeyBoardType`, `AutocapitalizationType`, and `AutocorrectionType` keys. You then set each key with its appropriate values.

Examine the `Root.plist` file in more detail. Note, for example, that `Item 2` has four keys under it: `Type`, `Title`, `Key`, and `DefaultValue`. The `Type` key specifies the type of information it is going to store. In this case, it is a `PSToggleSwitchSpecifier`, which means it will be represented visually as an On/Off switch. The `Title` key specifies the text that will be shown for this item (Item 2). The `Key` key is the identifier that uniquely identifies this key so that you can programmatically retrieve the value of this item in your application. Finally, the `DefaultValue` key specifies the default value of this item. In this case, it is checked, indicating that the value is On.

> **NOTE** The key/value pair in the `Root.plist` file is case sensitive, so you need to be careful when modifying the entries. A single typo can result in a nonfunctional application.

In the next Try It Out, you modify the `Root.plist` file so that you can use it to store a user's credentials. This is very useful when you are writing an application that requires users to log in to a server. When users access your application for the first time, they supply their login credentials, such as username and password. Your application can then store the credentials in the application preferences so that the next time the users access your application, the application can automatically retrieve the credentials, rather than ask for them.

> **NOTE** For more information on the use of each key, refer to Apple's "Settings Application Schema Reference" documentation. The easiest way to locate it is to do a web search for the title. The full URL is `http://developer.apple` `.com/library/ios/documentation/PreferenceSettings/Conceptual/` `SettingsApplicationSchemaReference/` `SettingsApplicationSchemaReference.pdf`.

TRY IT OUT Modifying the Application Preferences

1. In Xcode (using the same project created in the previous section), select the `Root.plist` file and remove all four items (Item 0 to Item 3) under the `PreferenceSpecifiers` key. To do so, select individual items under the `PreferenceSpecifiers` key and then press the Delete key (see Figure 9-7).

2. Modify the entire `Root.plist` file so that it looks like Figure 9-8. Ensure that the capitalization of each key and value pair is correct. Pay particular attention to the `Type` and `Value` of each item.

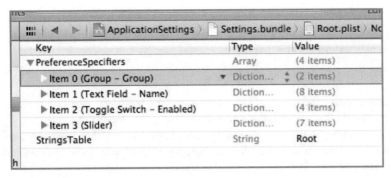

FIGURE 9-7

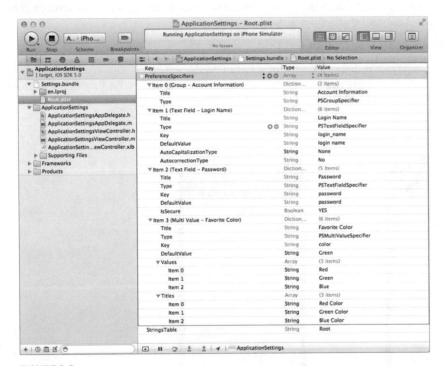

FIGURE 9-8

3. Save the project and press Command-R to test the application on the iPhone Simulator. Click the Home button and launch the Settings application again. Select the ApplicationSettings settings and observe the preferences shown (see Figure 9-9). Clicking the Favorite Color setting will display a page for choosing your favorite color (see Figure 9-10).

4. Make some changes to the settings values and then press the Home button to return to the Home screen. The changes in the settings are automatically saved to the device. When you return to the Settings page again, the new values will be displayed.

How It Works

What you have done is basically modify the `Root.plist` file to store three preferences: Login Name, Password, and Favorite Color. For the Password field, you use the `IsSecure` key to indicate that the value must be masked when displaying it to the user. Of particular interest is the Favorite Color preference, for which you use the `Titles` and `Values` keys to display a list of selectable options and their corresponding values to store on the iPhone.

The following preference specifiers are used in this example:

➤ `PSGroupSpecifier` — Used to display a group for the settings. In this case, all the settings are grouped under the Account Information group.

➤ `PSTextFieldSpecifier` — Specifies a text field

➤ `PSMultiValueSpecifier` — Specifies a list of selectable values. The `Titles` item contains a list of visible text from which users can select. The `Values` item is the corresponding value for the text selected by the user. For example, if a user selects Blue Color as the favorite color, the value `Blue` will be stored on the iPhone.

FIGURE 9-9

FIGURE 9-10

PROGRAMMATICALLY ACCESSING THE SETTINGS VALUES

Of course, the preferences settings are of little use if you can't programmatically access them from within your application. In the following sections, you modify the application so that you can load the preferences settings as well as make changes to them programmatically.

First, use the following Try It Out to prepare the UI by connecting the necessary outlets and actions.

TRY IT OUT   Preparing the UI

1. Using the project created in the previous section, select the `ApplicationSettingsViewController.xib` file to edit it in Interface Builder.

2. Populate the View window with the following views (see Figure 9-11):

   ➤ Round Rect Button

   ➤ Label

   ➤ Text Field

   ➤ Picker View

3. In Xcode, insert the following code that appears in bold into the `ApplicationSettingsViewController.h` file:

```objc
#import <UIKit/UIKit.h>

@interface ApplicationSettingsViewController : UIViewController
    <UIPickerViewDataSource, UIPickerViewDelegate> {
        IBOutlet UITextField *loginName;
        IBOutlet UITextField *password;
        IBOutlet UIPickerView *favoriteColor;
    }

@property (nonatomic, retain) UITextField *loginName;
@property (nonatomic, retain) UITextField *password;
@property (nonatomic, retain) UIPickerView *favoriteColor;

-(IBAction) loadSettings: (id) sender;
-(IBAction) saveSettings: (id) sender;
-(IBAction) doneEditing: (id) sender;

@end
```

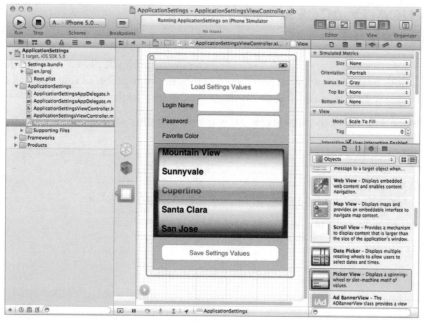

FIGURE 9-11

4. In Interface Builder, connect the outlets and action to the various views. In the
    ApplicationSettingsViewController.xib window, do the following:

    ➤ Control-click and drag the File's Owner item to the first Text Field and select loginName.

    ➤ Control-click and drag the File's Owner item to the second Text Field and select password.

    ➤ Control-click and drag the File's Owner item to the Picker View and select favoriteColor.

    ➤ Control-click and drag the Picker View to the File's Owner item and select dataSource.

    ➤ Control-click and drag the Picker View to the File's Owner item and select delegate.

    ➤ Control-click and drag the Load Settings Value button to the File's Owner item and select
    loadSettings:.

    ➤ Control-click and drag the Save Settings Value button to the File's Owner item and select
    saveSettings:.

    ➤ Right-click the Load Settings Value button and connect the Did End on Exit event to the
    File's Owner item. Select doneEditing:.

    ➤ Right-click the Save Settings Value button and connect the Did End on Exit event to the
    File's Owner item. Select doneEditing:.

5. Right-click the File's Owner item to verify that all the connections are connected properly (see Figure 9-12).

FIGURE 9-12

6. In Xcode, add the following bold code to the `ApplicationSettingsViewController.m` file:

```
#import "ApplicationSettingsViewController.h"

@implementation ApplicationSettingsViewController

@synthesize loginName;
@synthesize password;
@synthesize favoriteColor;
NSMutableArray *colors;
NSString *favoriteColorSelected;

-(IBAction) doneEditing:(id) sender {
    [sender resignFirstResponder];
}

- (void)viewDidLoad {
    //---create an array containing the colors values---
    colors = [[NSMutableArray alloc] init];
```

```
        [colors addObject:@"Red"];
        [colors addObject:@"Green"];
        [colors addObject:@"Blue"];
        [super viewDidLoad];
}


//---number of components in the Picker View---
- (NSInteger)numberOfComponentsInPickerView:(UIPickerView *)thePickerView {
    return 1;
}


//---number of items(rows) in the Picker View---
- (NSInteger)pickerView:(UIPickerView *)thePickerView
numberOfRowsInComponent:(NSInteger)component {
    return [colors count];
}


//---populating the Picker view---
- (NSString *)pickerView:(UIPickerView *)thePickerView
            titleForRow:(NSInteger)row
          forComponent:(NSInteger)component {
    return [colors objectAtIndex:row];
}


//---the item selected by the user---
- (void)pickerView:(UIPickerView *)thePickerView
        didSelectRow:(NSInteger)row
        inComponent:(NSInteger)component {
    favoriteColorSelected = [colors objectAtIndex:row];
}


- (void)dealloc {
    [colors release];
    [favoriteColorSelected release];
    [loginName release];
    [password release];
    [favoriteColor release];
    [super dealloc];
}
```

7. That's it! Press Command-R to test the application on the iPhone Simulator. Figure 9-13 shows the Picker View loaded with the three colors.

FIGURE 9-13

How It Works

So far, all the work that has been done prepares the UI for displaying the values retrieved from the preferences settings. In particular, you needed to prepare the Picker View to display a list of colors from which the user can choose.

To load the Picker View with the three colors, you ensure that the `ApplicationSettingsViewController` class conforms to the `UIPickerViewDataSource` and `UIPickerViewDelegate` protocols:

```
@interface ApplicationSettingsViewController : UIViewController
    <UIPickerViewDataSource, UIPickerViewDelegate> {
```

The `UIPickerViewDataSource` protocol defines the methods to populate the Picker View with items, while the `UIPickerViewDelegate` protocol defines the methods to enable users to select an item from the Picker View.

In the `ApplicationSettingsViewController.m` file, you first created an `NSMutableArray` object to store the list of colors available for selection, in the `viewDidLoad` method:

```
- (void)viewDidLoad {
    //---create an array containing the colors values---
    colors = [[NSMutableArray alloc] init];
    [colors addObject:@"Red"];
    [colors addObject:@"Green"];
    [colors addObject:@"Blue"];
    [super viewDidLoad];
}
```

To set the number of components (columns) in the Picker View, you implemented the `numberOfComponentsInPickerView:` method:

```
//---number of components in the Picker View---
- (NSInteger)numberOfComponentsInPickerView:(UIPickerView *)thePickerView {
    return 1;
}
```

To set the number of items (rows) you want to display in the Picker View, you implemented the `pickerView:numberOfRowsInComponent:` method:

```
//---number of items(rows) in the Picker View---
- (NSInteger)pickerView:(UIPickerView *)thePickerView
numberOfRowsInComponent:(NSInteger)component {
    return [colors count];
}
```

To populate the Picker View with the three colors, you implemented the `pickerView:titleForRow:forComponent:` method:

```
//---populating the Picker view---
- (NSString *)pickerView:(UIPickerView *)thePickerView
            titleForRow:(NSInteger)row
            forComponent:(NSInteger)component {
    return [colors objectAtIndex:row];
}
```

To save the color selected by the user in the Picker View, you implemented the `pickerView:didSelectRow:inComponent:` method:

```
//---the item selected by the user---
- (void)pickerView:(UIPickerView *)thePickerView
      didSelectRow:(NSInteger)row
       inComponent:(NSInteger)component {
    favoriteColorSelected = [colors objectAtIndex:row];
}
```

The color selected will now be saved in the `favoriteColorSelected` object.

Loading the Settings Values

With the user interface of the application ready, it is time to learn how you can programmatically load the values of the preferences settings and then display them in your application, as described in the following Try It Out. This display is useful because it gives users a chance to view the values of the settings without needing to access the Settings application.

TRY IT OUT   Loading Settings Values

1. Using the project created in the previous section, modify the `application:didFinishLaunchingWithOptions:` method in the `ApplicationSettingsAppDelegate.m` file:

```
- (BOOL)application:(UIApplication *)application
  didFinishLaunchingWithOptions:(NSDictionary *)launchOptions
{
    //--- initialize the settings value first;
    // if not all settings values will be null --
    NSUserDefaults *defaults = [NSUserDefaults standardUserDefaults];
    if (![defaults objectForKey:@"login_name"])
        [defaults setObject:@"login name" forKey:@"login_name"];
    if (![defaults objectForKey:@"password"])
        [defaults setObject:@"password" forKey:@"password"];
    if (![defaults objectForKey:@"color"])
        [defaults setObject:@"Green" forKey:@"color"];
    [defaults synchronize];

    self.window =
        [[[UIWindow alloc] initWithFrame:
            [[UIScreen mainScreen] bounds]] autorelease];
    // Override point for customization after application launch.
    self.viewController =
        [[[ApplicationSettingsViewController alloc]
            initWithNibName:@"ApplicationSettingsViewController"
            bundle:nil] autorelease];
    self.window.rootViewController = self.viewController;
    [self.window makeKeyAndVisible];
    return YES;
}
```

2. Insert the following method into the `loadSettings:` method in the `ApplicationSettingsViewController.m` file:

```
-(IBAction) loadSettings: (id) sender {
    NSUserDefaults *defaults = [NSUserDefaults standardUserDefaults];
    loginName.text = [defaults objectForKey:@"login_name"];
    password.text = [defaults objectForKey:@"password"];

    //---find the index of the array for the color saved---
    favoriteColorSelected = [[NSString alloc] initWithString:
                             [defaults objectForKey:@"color"]];
    int selIndex = [colors indexOfObject:favoriteColorSelected];

    //---display the saved color in the Picker view---
    [favoriteColor selectRow:selIndex inComponent:0 animated:YES];
}
```

3. Press Command-R to test the application on the iPhone Simulator. When the application is loaded, click the Load Settings Values button. You should see the settings values displayed in the Text Fields and the Picker View (see Figure 9-14).

FIGURE 9-14

How It Works

To load the values of the preferences settings, you use a class known as `NSUserDefaults`:

```
NSUserDefaults *defaults = [NSUserDefaults standardUserDefaults];
```

The preceding statement returns the one instance of the `NSUserDefaults` class. Think of `NSUserDefaults` as a common database that you can use to store your application preferences settings.

When your application runs for the first time, you need to set the values of the settings *before* you can use them. Hence, the best place to initialize them is in the application delegate.

To retrieve the values of the preferences settings, you use the `objectForKey:` method to check whether each setting is null. If it is, the setting has not been initialized yet and hence you need to set it. To initialize the setting, use the `setObject:forKey:` method:

```
NSUserDefaults *defaults = [NSUserDefaults standardUserDefaults];
if (![defaults objectForKey:@"login_name"])
    [defaults setObject:@"login name" forKey:@"login_name"];
if (![defaults objectForKey:@"password"])
    [defaults setObject:@"password" forKey:@"password"];
if (![defaults objectForKey:@"color"])
    [defaults setObject:@"Green" forKey:@"color"];
[defaults synchronize];
```

Note that to immediately save the settings values to the Settings application, you should call the `synchronize` method of the `NSUserDefaults` instance.

To load the settings value, likewise you use the `objectForKey:` method, specifying the name of the preference setting you want to retrieve:

```
-(IBAction) loadSettings: (id) sender {
    NSUserDefaults *defaults = [NSUserDefaults standardUserDefaults];
    loginName.text = [defaults objectForKey:@"login_name"];
    password.text = [defaults objectForKey:@"password"];

    //---find the index of the array for the color saved---
    favoriteColorSelected = [[NSString alloc] initWithString:
                                [defaults objectForKey:@"color"]];
    int selIndex = [colors indexOfObject:favoriteColorSelected];

    //---display the saved color in the Picker view---
    [favoriteColor selectRow:selIndex inComponent:0 animated:YES];
}
```

Resetting the Preferences Settings Values

Sometimes, you may want to reset the values of the preferences settings of your application. This is especially true if you have made an error in the `Root.plist` file and want to reset all the settings. The easiest way to do this is to remove the application from the device or Simulator. To do so, simply tap (or click the Simulator) and hold the application's icon; and when the icons start to wriggle, tap the X button to remove the application. The preferences settings associated with the application will also be removed.

Another way to clear the values of the preferences settings is to navigate to the folder containing your application (on the iPhone Simulator). The applications on the iPhone Simulator are stored in the following folder: `~/Library/Application Support/iPhone Simulator>/<version_no>/ Applications/` (note that the tilde symbol (~) represents your home directory and not your root directory). Inside this folder, you need to find the folder containing your application. Within the application folder is a `Library/Preferences` folder. Delete the file ending with `<application_name>.plist` (see Figure 9-15) and your preferences settings will be reset.

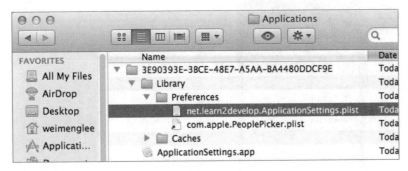

FIGURE 9-15

Saving the Settings Values

Now that you have seen how to load the values of preferences settings, the following Try It Out demonstrates how to save the values back to the preferences settings. This enables users to directly modify their preferences settings from within your application, instead of using the Settings application to do so.

TRY IT OUT Saving Settings Values

1. Using the same project created in the previous section, insert the following method in the `saveSettings:` method in the `ApplicationSettingsViewController.m` file:

```
-(IBAction) saveSettings: (id) sender {
    NSUserDefaults *defaults = [NSUserDefaults standardUserDefaults];
    [defaults setObject:loginName.text forKey:@"login_name"];
    [defaults setObject:password.text forKey:@"password"];
    [defaults setObject:favoriteColorSelected forKey:@"color"];
    [defaults synchronize];

    UIAlertView *alert =
    [[UIAlertView alloc] initWithTitle:@"Settings Value Saved"
                                message:@"Settings Saved"
                              delegate:nil
                     cancelButtonTitle:@"Done"
                     otherButtonTitles:nil];
    [alert show];
    [alert release];
}
```

2. Press Command-R to test the application on the iPhone Simulator. Make some changes to the login name, password, and favorite color. When you click the Save Settings Value button, all the

changes are made to the device (see Figure 9-16). When you check the Settings application, you will see the updated settings values (see Figure 9-17).

FIGURE 9-16

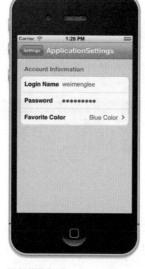

FIGURE 9-17

How It Works

To save the values back to the preferences settings, you used the same approach that you used to retrieve those settings — that is, the NSUserDefaults class:

```
NSUserDefaults *defaults = [NSUserDefaults standardUserDefaults];
[defaults setObject:loginName.text forKey:@"login_name"];
[defaults setObject:password.text forKey:@"password"];
[defaults setObject:favoriteColorSelected forKey:@"color"];
[defaults synchronize];
```

As usual, rather than use the objectForKey: method, you now used the setObject:forKey: method to save the values.

SUMMARY

This chapter explained how you can make use of the Application Preferences feature of the iPhone to save your application preferences to the Settings application. This enables you to delegate most of the mundane tasks of saving and loading an application's preferences settings to the OS. All you need to do is use the NSUserDefaults class to programmatically access the preferences settings.

EXERCISES

1. You have learned that you can use the NSUserDefaults class to access the preferences settings values for your application. What are the methods for retrieving and saving the values?

2. What are the two ways in which you can remove the preferences settings for an application?

Answers to the exercises can be found in Appendix D.

▶ **WHAT YOU LEARNED IN THIS CHAPTER**

TOPIC	KEY CONCEPTS
Adding application preferences to your application	Add a Settings Bundle file to your project and modify the `Root.plist` file.
Loading the value of a preference setting	`NSUserDefaults` *defaults = `[NSUserDefaults standardUserDefaults]`; `loginName`.text = [defaults `objectForKey:@"login_name"`];
Resetting preferences settings values	Remove the entire application either from the Home screen or via the iPhone Simulator folder on your Mac.
Saving the value of a preference setting	`NSUserDefaults` *defaults = [`NSUserDefaults standardUserDefaults`]; [defaults `setObject:loginName`.text forKey:@`"login_name"`]; [defaults `synchronize`];

10

File Handling

WHAT YOU WILL LEARN IN THIS CHAPTER

➤ Where your applications are stored in iOS 5

➤ The various folders within your Applications folder

➤ How to read and write to files in the Documents and tmp folders

➤ How to use a property to store structured data

➤ How to programmatically retrieve values stored in a property list

➤ How to modify the values retrieved from a property list and save the changes to a file

➤ How to copy bundled resources to the application's folder during runtime

➤ How to export a document from your application to another application

➤ How to share your application's Documents folder through iTunes

➤ How to allow other applications to import documents into your application

All the applications you have developed up to this point are pretty straightforward — the application starts, performs something interesting, and ends. In Chapter 9, you saw how you can make use of the Application settings feature to save the preferences of your application to a central location managed by the Settings application. Sometimes, however, you simply need to save some data to your application's folder for use later. For example, rather than keep files you download from a remote server in memory, a more effective and memory-efficient method is to save them in a file so that you can use them later (even after the application has shut down and restarted).

This chapter describes the two available approaches to persisting data in your application so that you can access it later: saving the data as files or as a property list. You also learn how to bundle resources such as text files and database files with your application so that when the application is installed on the user's device, the resources can be copied onto the local storage of the device and used from there. In addition, you will learn how to share files between applications.

UNDERSTANDING THE APPLICATION FOLDERS

Your applications are stored in the iOS file system, so you'll find it useful to understand the folder structure of the iPhone and iPad.

On the desktop, the contents of the iOS Simulator is stored in the ~/Library/Application Support/ iPhone Simulator>/<*version_no*>/ folder.

> **NOTE** *The ~ (tilde) represents the current user's directory. Specifically, the preceding directory is equivalent to the following:*
>
> ```
> /Users/<username>/Library/Application Support/
> iPhone Simulator>/<version_no>/
> ```
>
> *Note that in Lion, the Library folder is now hidden. To view the Library folder, you can select Go ⇨ Go to Folder..., and then enter "~/**Library**."*

Within this folder are five subfolders:

- ➤ Applications
- ➤ Library
- ➤ Media
- ➤ Root
- ➤ tmp

The Applications folder contains all your installed applications (see Figure 10-1). Within it are several folders with long filenames. These filenames are generated by Xcode to uniquely identify each of your applications. Each application's folder holds your application's executable file (the `.app` file, which includes all embedded resources), together with a few other folders, such as Documents, Library, and tmp. On the iPhone and iPad, all applications run within their own sandboxed environments — that is, an application can access only the files stored within its own folder; it cannot access the folders of other applications.

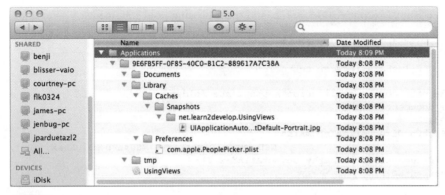

FIGURE 10-1

Using the Documents and Library Folders

The Documents folder is where you can store files used by your application, whereas the Library folder stores the application-specific settings. It also contains snapshots of your application before its goes into the background so that they can be displayed later when they are returned to the foreground, giving the impression that your application is springing back to life instantly. The tmp folder stores temporary data required by your application.

How you do write to these folders? The following Try It Out provides an example of doing just that. You can download the indicated code files to work through the project.

TRY IT OUT **Writing to and Reading from Files**

codefile FilesHandling.zip available for download at Wrox.com

1. Using Xcode, create a new Single View Application (iPhone) project and name it **FilesHandling**. You will also use the project name as the Class Prefix and ensure that you have the Use Automatic Reference Counting option unchecked.

2. In the `FilesHandlingViewController.h` file, add the following bold statements:

```
#import <UIKit/UIKit.h>

@interface FilesHandlingViewController : UIViewController

-(NSString *) documentsPath;
-(NSString *) readFromFile:(NSString *) filePath;
-(void) writeToFile:(NSString *) text
        withFileName:(NSString *) filePath;

@end
```

3. In the `FilesHandlingViewController.m` file, add the following bold statements:

```objc
#import "FilesHandlingViewController.h"

@implementation FilesHandlingViewController

//---finds the path to the application's Documents folder---
-(NSString *) documentsPath {
    NSArray *paths =
    NSSearchPathForDirectoriesInDomains(
                                        NSDocumentDirectory, NSUserDomainMask, YES);
    NSString *documentsDir = [paths objectAtIndex:0];
    return documentsDir;
}

//---write content into a specified file path---
-(void) writeToFile:(NSString *) text
        withFileName:(NSString *) filePath {
    NSMutableArray *array = [[NSMutableArray alloc] init];
    [array addObject:text];
    [array writeToFile:filePath atomically:YES];
    [array release];
}

//---read content from a specified file path---
-(NSString *) readFromFile:(NSString *) filePath {
    //---check if file exists---
    if ([[NSFileManager defaultManager] fileExistsAtPath:filePath]) {
        NSArray *array =
        [[NSArray alloc] initWithContentsOfFile: filePath];
        NSString *data =
        [NSString stringWithFormat:@"%@",
         [array objectAtIndex:0]];
        [array release];
        return data;
    }
    else
        return nil;
}

- (void)viewDidLoad
{
    //---formulate filename---
    NSString *fileName =
    [[self documentsPath] stringByAppendingPathComponent:@"data.txt"];

    //---write something to the file---
    [self writeToFile:@"a string of text" withFileName:fileName];

    //---read it back---
    NSString *fileContent = [self readFromFile:fileName];

    //---display the content read in the Debugger Console window---
    NSLog(@"%@", fileContent);
    [super viewDidLoad];
}
```

4. Press Command-R to test the application on the iPhone Simulator.

5. Go to Finder and navigate to the Documents folder of your application. The `data.txt` file is now visible (see Figure 10-2).

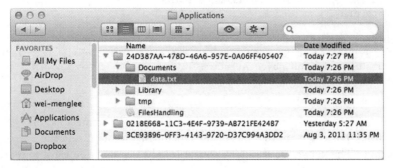

FIGURE 10-2

6. When you deploy the application to a real iOS device, the location of the file on the real device is /var/mobile/Applications/<application_id>/Documents/data.txt.

7. Double-click the `data.txt` file to view its contents as follows:

```
<?xml version="1.0" encoding="UTF-8"?>
<!DOCTYPE plist PUBLIC "-//Apple//DTD PLIST 1.0//EN"
    "http://www.apple.com/DTDs/PropertyList-1.0.dtd">
<plist version="1.0">
<array>
    <string>a string of text</string>
</array>
</plist>
```

8. If you turn on the output window (press Command-Shift-c), you will see that the application prints a string of text (see Figure 10-3).

FIGURE 10-3

How It Works

You first define the `documentsPath` method, which returns the path to the Documents folder:

```
//---finds the path to the application's Documents folder---
-(NSString *) documentsPath {
    NSArray *paths =
    NSSearchPathForDirectoriesInDomains(
                                    NSDocumentDirectory, NSUserDomainMask, YES);
    NSString *documentsDir = [paths objectAtIndex:0];
    return documentsDir;
}
```

Basically, you use the `NSSearchPathForDirectoriesInDomains()` function to create a list of directory search paths, indicating that you want to look for the Documents folder (using the `NSDocumentDirectory` constant). The `NSUserDomainMask` constant indicates that you want to search from the application's home directory, and the `YES` argument indicates that you want to obtain the full path of all the directories found.

To obtain the path to the Documents folder, you simply extract the first item of the `paths` array (because there is only one Documents folder in an iOS application's folder). In fact, this block of code is derived from the Mac OS X API, which might return multiple folders; but in the case of the iOS, there can only be one Documents folder per application.

You next define the `writeToFile:withFileName:` method, which creates an `NSMutableArray` and adds the text to be written to the file to it:

```
//---write content into a specified file path---
-(void) writeToFile:(NSString *) text
        withFileName:(NSString *) filePath {
    NSMutableArray *array = [[NSMutableArray alloc] init];
    [array addObject:text];
    [array writeToFile:filePath atomically:YES];
    [array release];
}
```

To persist the contents (a process known as *serialization*) of the `NSMutableArray` to a file, you use its `writeToFile:atomically:` method. The `atomically:` parameter indicates that the file should first be written to a temporary file before it is renamed to the filename specified. This approach guarantees that the file will never be corrupted, even if the system crashes during the writing process.

To read the contents from a file, you define the `readFromFile:` method:

```
//---read content from a specified file path---
-(NSString *) readFromFile:(NSString *) filePath {
    //--check if file exists--
    if ([[NSFileManager defaultManager] fileExistsAtPath:filePath]) {
        NSArray *array =
        [[NSArray alloc] initWithContentsOfFile: filePath];
        NSString *data =
        [NSString stringWithFormat:@"%@",
         [array objectAtIndex:0]];
```

```
            [array release];
            return data;
        }
        else
            return nil;
}
```

You first use an instance of the `NSFileManager` class to determine whether the specified file exists. If it does, then you read the content of the file into an `NSArray` object. In this case, because you know that the file contains a single line of text, you extract the first element in the array.

With all the methods in place, you are ready to make use of them. When the view is loaded, you create the pathname for a file that you want to save. You then write a string of text into the file and immediately read it back and print it in the output window:

```
- (void)viewDidLoad
{
    //---formulate filename---
    NSString *fileName =
    [[self documentsPath] stringByAppendingPathComponent:@"data.txt"];

    //---write something to the file---
    [self writeToFile:@"a string of text" withFileName:fileName];

    //---read it back---
    NSString *fileContent = [self readFromFile:fileName];

    //---display the content read in the Debugger Console window---
    NSLog(@"%@", fileContent);
    [super viewDidLoad];
}
```

Storing Files in the Temporary Folder

In addition to storing files in the Documents folder, you can store temporary files in the tmp folder. Files stored in the tmp folder are not backed up by iTunes, so you need to find a permanent place for the files you want to keep. To get the path to the tmp folder, you can call the `NSTemporaryDirectory()` function, like this:

```
-(NSString *) tempPath{
    return NSTemporaryDirectory();
}
```

The following statement returns the path of a file (`"data.txt"`) to be stored in the tmp folder:

```
NSString *fileName =
    [[self tempPath] stringByAppendingPathComponent:@"data.txt"];
```

Which Folder Should You Use: Documents or tmp?

All the files stored in the Documents folder (as well as the Library folder, with the exception of the caches folder) of your application are automatically backed up by iTunes when the user connects his or her device to iTunes. Hence, if your applications store a large number of files in the Documents folder, it will take a long time to back up the files each time the user connects to iTunes. If all the applications on the user's device contain a large number of files in their Documents folder, you can easily imagine the amount of time needed for iTunes to synchronize your device. As such, your application should only use the Documents folder sparingly to store files that are absolutely necessary for the running of your application. For example, in the Documents folder, you can store databases that are required by your application. For temporary files that you don't need later (such as results returned from a web service that you will store somewhere else later, images, etc.), you can store them in the tmp folder. Files stored in the tmp folder will not be backed up by iTunes, and it is your responsibility to perform your own housekeeping. Occasionally, iOS may also delete files in the tmp folder when your application is not running.

USING PROPERTY LISTS

In iOS programming, you can use property lists to store structured data using key/value pairs. Property lists are stored as XML files and are highly transportable across file systems and networks. For example, you might want to store a list of App Store application titles in your application. Because applications in the App Store are organized by category, it would be natural to store this information using a property list employing the structure shown in the following table:

CATEGORY	TITLES
Games	"Animal Park", "Biology Quiz", "Calculus Test"
Entertainment	"Eye Balls - iBlower", "iBell", "iCards Birthday"
Utilities	"Battery Monitor", "iSystemInfo"

In Xcode, you can create and add a property list to your project and populate it with items using the built-in Property List Editor. The property list is deployed together with the application. Programmatically, you can retrieve the values stored in a property list using the NSDictionary class. More importantly, if you need to make changes to a property list, you can write the changes to a file so that you can later refer to the file directly instead of the property list.

In the following Try It Out, you create a property list and populate it with some values. You then read the values from the property list during runtime, make some changes, and save the modified values to another property list file in the Documents folder.

 NOTE *To store application-specific settings that users can modify outside your application, consider using the* NSUserDefaults *class to store the settings in the Settings application. Application settings are discussed in Chapter 9.*

TRY IT OUT Creating and Modifying a Property List

1. Using the same project created in the previous section, right-click the project name in Xcode and choose New File . . . .

2. Select the Resource item on the left of the New File dialog and select the Property List template on the right of the dialog (see Figure 10-4). Click Next.

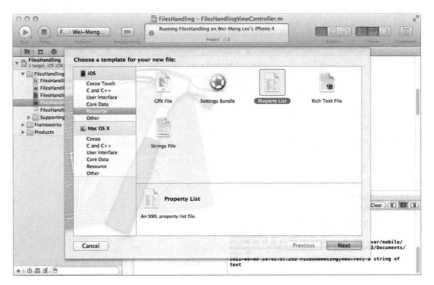

FIGURE 10-4

3. Name the property list **Apps.plist**.

4. Populate `Apps.plist` as shown in Figure 10-5.

FIGURE 10-5

5. Add the following bold statements to the viewDidLoad method:

```
- (void)viewDidLoad
{
    //---formulate filename---
    NSString *fileName =
    [[self documentsPath] stringByAppendingPathComponent:@"data.txt"];

    //NSString *fileName =
    //[[self tempPath] stringByAppendingPathComponent:@"data.txt"];
    //NSLog(@"%@", fileName);

    //---write something to the file---
    [self writeToFile:@"a string of text" withFileName:fileName];

    //---read it back---
    NSString *fileContent = [self readFromFile:fileName];

    //---display the content read in the Debugger Console window---
    NSLog(@"%@", fileContent);

    //---get the path to the property list file---
    NSString *plistFileName =
    [[self documentsPath]
     stringByAppendingPathComponent:@"Apps.plist"];

    //---if the property list file can be found---
    if ([[NSFileManager defaultManager] fileExistsAtPath:plistFileName]) {

        //---load the content of the property list file into a NSDictionary
        // object---
        NSDictionary *dict =
        [[NSDictionary alloc]
         initWithContentsOfFile:plistFileName];

        //---for each category---
        for (NSString *category in dict) {
            NSLog(@"%@", category);
            NSLog(@"========");

            //---return all titles in an array---
            NSArray *titles = [dict valueForKey:category];

            //---print out all the titles in that category---
            for (NSString *title in titles) {
                NSLog(@"%@", title);
            }
        }
        [dict release];
    }
    else {
```

```objc
//---load the property list from the Resources folder---
NSString *pListPath =
[[NSBundle mainBundle] pathForResource:@"Apps"
                               ofType:@"plist"];

NSDictionary *dict =
[[NSDictionary alloc] initWithContentsOfFile:pListPath];

//---make a mutable copy of the dictionary object---
NSMutableDictionary *copyOfDict = [dict mutableCopy];

//---get all the different categories---
NSArray *categoriesArray =
[[copyOfDict allKeys]
 sortedArrayUsingSelector:@selector(compare:)];

//---for each category---
for (NSString *category in categoriesArray) {
    //---get all the app titles in that category---
    NSArray *titles = [dict valueForKey:category];

    //---make a mutable copy of the array---
    NSMutableArray *mutableTitles = [titles mutableCopy];

    //---add a new title to the category---
    [mutableTitles addObject:@"New App title"];

    //---set the array back to the dictionary object---
    [copyOfDict setObject:mutableTitles forKey:category];
    [mutableTitles release];
}

//---write the dictionary to file---
fileName =
[[self documentsPath]
 stringByAppendingPathComponent:@"Apps.plist"];
[copyOfDict writeToFile:fileName atomically:YES];
[dict release];
[copyOfDict release];
}
[super viewDidLoad];
}
```

6. Press Command-R to test the application on the iPhone Simulator.

7. When you first run the application, it creates a new .plist file in the Documents folder. Double-click the .plist file to view it using the Property List Editor; you will see a new item named New App title for each category of applications (see Figure 10-6).

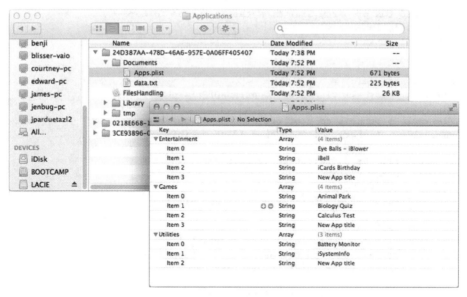

FIGURE 10-6

8. Run the application a second time. It prints the content of the `.plist` file in the Documents folder to the output window (see Figure 10-7), proving the existence of the property list in the Documents folder.

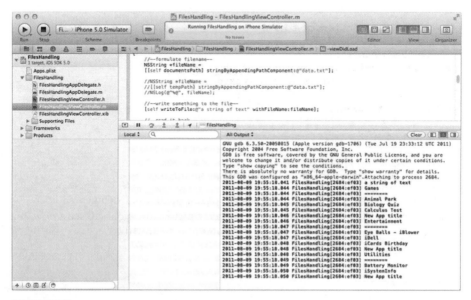

FIGURE 10-7

How It Works

The first part of this example shows how you can add a property list file to your application. In the property list file, you add three keys representing the category of applications in the App Store: Entertainment, Games, and Utilities. Each category contains a list of application titles.

When the view is loaded, you look for a file named `Apps.plist` in the Documents folder of your application:

```
//---get the path to the property list file---
NSString *plistFileName =
[[self documentsPath]
 stringByAppendingPathComponent:@"Apps.plist"];
```

If the file is found, you load its contents into an `NSDictionary` object:

```
//---if the property list file can be found---
if ([[NSFileManager defaultManager] fileExistsAtPath:plistFileName]) {

    //---load the content of the property list file into a NSDictionary
    // object---
    NSDictionary *dict =
    [[NSDictionary alloc]
     initWithContentsOfFile:plistFileName];

    //...
}
```

Next, you enumerate through all the keys in the dictionary object and print the title of each application in the output window:

```
//---for each category---
for (NSString *category in dict) {
    NSLog(@"%@", category);
    NSLog(@"=======");

    //---return all titles in an array---
    NSArray *titles = [dict valueForKey:category];

    //---print out all the titles in that category---
    for (NSString *title in titles) {
        NSLog(@"%@", title);
    }
}
[dict release];
```

When the application is run for the first time, the `Apps.plist` file is not available, so you load it from the Resources folder:

```
else {
    //---load the property list from the Resources folder---
    NSString *pListPath =
```

```
    [[NSBundle mainBundle] pathForResource:@"Apps"
                             ofType:@"plist"];

    NSDictionary *dict =
    [[NSDictionary alloc] initWithContentsOfFile:pListPath];

    //...
}
```

Because you are making changes to the dictionary object, you need to make a mutable copy of it and assign it to an NSMutableDictionary object:

```
//---make a mutable copy of the dictionary object---
NSMutableDictionary *copyOfDict = [dict mutableCopy];
```

This step is important because the NSDictionary object is immutable, meaning that after the items are populated from the property list, you cannot add content to the dictionary object. Using the mutableCopy method of the NSDictionary class allows you to create a mutable instance of the dictionary object, which is NSMutableDictionary.

You then retrieve an array containing all the keys in the mutable dictionary object:

```
//---get all the different categories---
NSArray *categoriesArray =
[[copyOfDict allKeys]
 sortedArrayUsingSelector:@selector(compare:)];
```

You use this array to loop through all the keys in the dictionary so that you can add some additional titles to each category:

```
//---for each category---
for (NSString *category in categoriesArray) {

}
```

Note that you cannot enumerate using the NSMutableDictionary object like this:

```
for (NSString *category in copyOfDict) {
    //...
}
```

That's because you cannot add items to the NSMutableDictionary object while it is being enumerated. Therefore, you need to loop using an NSArray object.

When you're inside the loop, you extract all the titles of the applications in each category and make a mutable copy of the array containing the titles of the applications:

```
//---get all the app titles in that category---
NSArray *titles = [dict valueForKey:category];

//---make a mutable copy of the array---
NSMutableArray *mutableTitles = [titles mutableCopy];
```

You can now add a new title to the mutable array containing the application titles:

```
//---add a new title to the category---
[mutableTitles addObject:@"New App title"];
```

After the additional item is added to the mutable array, you set it back to the mutable dictionary object:

```
//---set the array back to the dictionary object---
[copyOfDict setObject:mutableTitles forKey:category];
[mutableTitles release];
```

Finally, you write the mutable dictionary object to a file using the `writeToFile:atomically:` method:

```
//---write the dictionary to file---
fileName =
[[self documentsPath]
stringByAppendingPathComponent:@"Apps.plist"];
[copyOfDict writeToFile:fileName atomically:YES];
[dict release];
[copyOfDict release];
```

COPYING BUNDLED RESOURCES

In the previous section, you learned how to embed a property list file into your application and then programmatically recreate the property list and save it in the Documents folder during runtime. While that example showed the various ways to manipulate a property list, in general it is much easier to simply copy the resource (such as the property list) into the Documents folder directly.

All resources embedded within your application (commonly known as *bundled resources*) are read-only. In order to make changes to them, you need to copy them into the application's folders, such as the Documents or tmp folders. You can do so by copying the resource when the application starts. The ideal location to perform this is in the application delegate. Using the preceding example, you could define the following `copyFileInBundleToDocumentsFolder:withExtension:` method in the `FilesHandlingAppDelegate.m` file:

```
#import "FilesHandlingAppDelegate.h"

#import "FilesHandlingViewController.h"

@implementation FilesHandlingAppDelegate

@synthesize window = _window;
@synthesize viewController = _viewController;

- (void) copyFileInBundleToDocumentsFolder:(NSString *) fileName
                        withExtension:(NSString *) ext {

    //--get the path of the Documents folder--
    NSArray *paths = NSSearchPathForDirectoriesInDomains(
                            NSDocumentDirectory, NSUserDomainMask, YES);

    NSString *documentsDirectory = [paths objectAtIndex:0];

    //--get the path to the file you want to copy in the Documents folder--
```

```
NSString *filePath =
[documentsDirectory
 stringByAppendingPathComponent:
 [NSString stringWithString:fileName]];

filePath = [filePath stringByAppendingString:@"."];
filePath = [filePath stringByAppendingString:ext];

//--check if file is already in Documents folder,
// if not, copy it from the bundle--
NSFileManager *fileManager = [NSFileManager defaultManager];
if (![fileManager fileExistsAtPath:filePath]) {

    //--get the path of the file in the bundle--
    NSString *pathToFileInBundle =
    [[NSBundle mainBundle] pathForResource:fileName ofType:ext];

    //--copy the file in the bundle to the Documents folder--
    NSError *error = nil;
    bool success =
    [fileManager copyItemAtPath:pathToFileInBundle
                         toPath:filePath error:&error];

    if (success) {
        NSLog(@"File copied");
    }
    else {
        NSLog(@"%@", [error localizedDescription]);
    }
}
}
```

This method simply copies the specified file to the Documents folder if it is not already there.

To copy the property list when the application is starting, call the
copyFileInBundleToDocumentsFolder:withExtension: method in the
application:didFinishLaunchingWithOptions: event:

```
- (BOOL)application:(UIApplication *)application
didFinishLaunchingWithOptions:(NSDictionary *)launchOptions
{
    //---copy the txt files to the Documents folder---
    [self copyFileInBundleToDocumentsFolder:@"Apps" withExtension:@"plist"];

    self.window = [[[UIWindow alloc] initWithFrame:[[UIScreen mainScreen]
bounds]] autorelease];
    // Override point for customization after application launch.
    self.viewController = [[[FilesHandlingViewController alloc]
initWithNibName:@"FilesHandlingViewController" bundle:nil] autorelease];
    self.window.rootViewController = self.viewController;
    [self.window makeKeyAndVisible];
    return YES;
}
```

Doing this ensures that the property list is copied to the Documents folder when the application runs for the first time.

IMPORTING AND EXPORTING FILES

One of the common tasks that iOS developers have to do is import and export documents from their iOS application. For example, suppose you are developing a document reader and you want to allow the user to import documents into your application so that they can be read offline. In addition, your reader might also support the exporting of documents so that other applications can make use of them. In this section, you will learn the different techniques you can employ to allow documents to be imported into or exported from your iOS application.

The following Try It Out creates the project that you will use to learn the various methods to import and export documents.

TRY IT OUT Creating the Project

1. Using Xcode, create a new Single View (iPhone) application and name it **OfflineReader**. You will also use the project name as the Class Prefix and ensure that you have the Use Automatic Reference Counting option unchecked.

2. Select the `OfflineReaderViewController.xib` file to open it in Interface Builder and populate it with a Web View and Round Rect Button (see Figure 10-8):

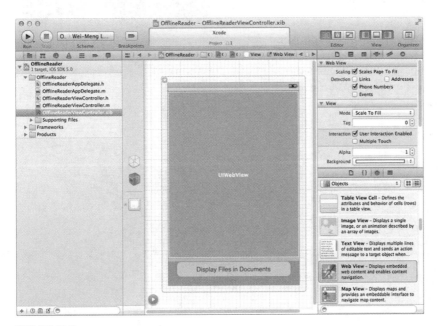

FIGURE 10-8

3. In the Attributes Inspector window for the Web View, ensure that you check the Scales Page to Fit option.

4. In the `OfflineReaderViewController.xib` file, add the following statements in bold:

```
#import <UIKit/UIKit.h>

@interface OfflineReaderViewController : UIViewController
<UIDocumentInteractionControllerDelegate> {
    IBOutlet UIWebView *webView;
}

-(void)openDocumentIn;
-(void)handleDocumentOpenURL:(NSURL *)url;
-(void)displayAlert:(NSString *) str;
-(void)loadFileFromDocumentsFolder:(NSString *) filename;
-(void)listFilesFromDocumentsFolder;

- (IBAction) btnDisplayFiles;

@end
```

5. Back in Interface Builder, connect the outlet and action to the Web View and Round Rect Button. Right-clicking on the File's Owner item should now reveal the connections, as shown in Figure 10-9.

6. Drag and drop two files into the Supporting Files folder of the project (see Figure 10-10). In this example, I have a PDF file named `Courses for Sep and Oct 2011.pdf` and an image file named `icon.jpg`.

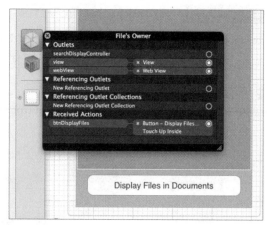

FIGURE 10-9

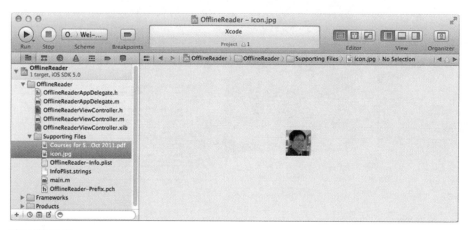

FIGURE 10-10

7. In the `OfflineReader-Info.plist` file, set the first item of the `"Icon files"` key to `"icon.jpg"` (see Figure 10-11).

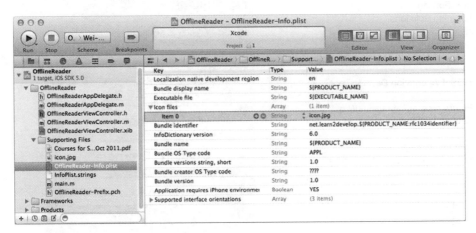

FIGURE 10-11

How It Works

You now have an iPhone project with the icon set. It also has a PDF document in the Supporting Files folder. In the following sections, you will see how you can export the PDF file to external applications and allow other applications to import documents into your application.

Exporting Documents

In this section, you will learn how to export a document from your application. For example, in the Mail application on your iPhone, when you receive a PDF file, you can either tap on the icon (see Figure 10-12) to view the document within the Mail application or tap and hold the icon.

If you do the latter, an action sheet is displayed (see Figure 10-13). You can tap the "Open in . . ." button to see a list of applications to which your document can be exported.

FIGURE 10-12

FIGURE 10-13

The following Try It Out demonstrates how you can export the PDF document in the Supporting Files folder of your application to an external application.

TRY IT OUT Exporting Documents to External Applications

1. Using the same project created in the previous section, add the following lines of code in bold to the `OfflineReaderViewController.m` file:

```
#import "OfflineReaderViewController.h"

@implementation OfflineReaderViewController

UIDocumentInteractionController *documentController;

-(void)openDocumentIn {
    NSString * filePath = [[NSBundle mainBundle] pathForResource:
    @"Courses for Sep and Oct 2011" ofType:@"pdf"];
    documentController = [UIDocumentInteractionController
        interactionControllerWithURL:[NSURL fileURLWithPath:filePath]];
    documentController.delegate = self;
    [documentController retain];
    documentController.UTI = @"com.adobe.pdf";
    [documentController presentOpenInMenuFromRect:CGRectZero
                                inView:self.view
                                animated:YES];
}

-(void)documentInteractionController:(UIDocumentInteractionController *)controller
```

```
            willBeginSendingToApplication:(NSString *)application {

}

-(void)documentInteractionController:(UIDocumentInteractionController *)controller
        didEndSendingToApplication:(NSString *)application {

}

-(void)documentInteractionControllerDidDismissOpenInMenu:
(UIDocumentInteractionController *)controller {

}

- (void)viewDidLoad {
    [self openDocumentIn];
    [super viewDidLoad];
}
-(void) dealloc {
    [documentController release];
    [super dealloc];
}
```

2. Press Command-R to test the application on a real device (the iOS Simulator won't work in this case). When the View window is loaded, you will see an action sheet displaying the list of applications to which you can export your document (see Figure 10-14).

3. If you select iBooks, the PDF document will appear in iBooks (see Figure 10-15).

FIGURE 10-14

FIGURE 10-15

How It Works

The `UIDocumentInteractionController` class provides in-app support for user interaction with files in your application. In this example, you use it to export a document to an external application.

You then define a few methods. The `openDocumentIn` method basically creates the path to point to the PDF document (that you want to export) and then uses it to feed into the `documentController` object. You need to set the UTIs (Uniform Type Identifiers) for the `documentController` object so that it can help the system find the appropriate application to open your document. In this case, it is set to `com.adobe.pdf`, which represents a PDF document. Other common UTIs are `com.apple.quicktime-movie` (QuickTime movies), `public.html` (HTML documents), and `public.jpeg` (JPEG files).

The other three methods (`documentInteractionController:willBeginSendingToApplication:`, `documentInteractionController:didEndSendingToApplication:`, and `documentInteractionControllerDidDismissOpenInMenu:`) are the methods defined in the `UIDocumentInteractionControllerDelegate` protocol. They are fired when the `documentController` object is being invoked. For this example, you don't really need to code anything within these methods.

Finally, in the `viewDidLoad` method, you invoke the `openDocumentIn` method to export the document.

File Sharing

The previous section showed how you can export a document to an external application that can be chosen by the user. What about the reverse — importing a document into your application? In iOS, there are two ways to get files into your application:

➤ File sharing through iTunes

➤ Exchanges between applications (like the one you just saw in the previous section)

The first method presents a very easy and direct way for users to transfer large number of files into or out of an application. The following Try It Out shows you how.

TRY IT OUT File Sharing through iTunes

1. Using the same project created in the previous section, add a new key named **UIFileSharingEnabled** to the `OfflineReader-Info.plist` file and set its value to `YES` (see Figure 10-16).

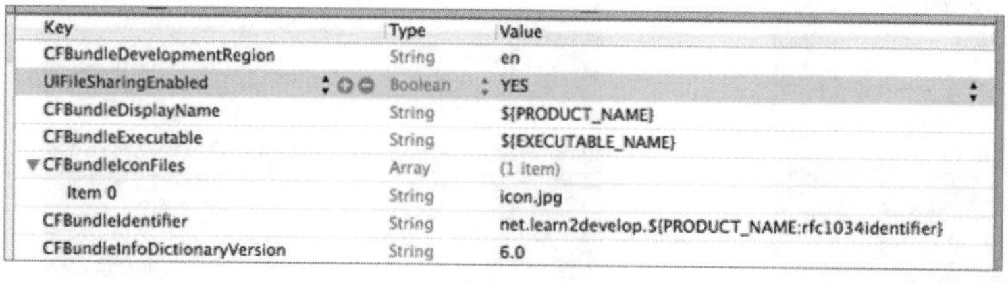

Key	Type	Value
CFBundleDevelopmentRegion	String	en
UIFileSharingEnabled	Boolean	YES
CFBundleDisplayName	String	${PRODUCT_NAME}
CFBundleExecutable	String	${EXECUTABLE_NAME}
▼ CFBundleIconFiles	Array	(1 item)
Item 0	String	icon.jpg
CFBundleIdentifier	String	net.learn2develop.${PRODUCT_NAME:rfc1034identifier}
CFBundleInfoDictionaryVersion	String	6.0

FIGURE 10-16

NOTE The UIFileSharingEnabled *key is also known as "Application supports iTunes File Sharing" in the drop-down menu.*

2. Press Command-R to redeploy the application onto the real device. Launch iTunes and select the device name, followed by the Apps tab. Figure 10-17 shows that the OfflineReader application now appears under the File Sharing section (scroll down to the bottom of the page).

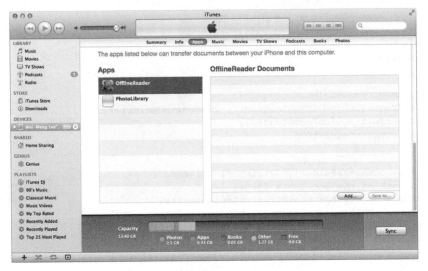

FIGURE 10-17

3. To copy a file into the application, simply drag and drop it into the rectangle labeled OfflineReader Documents. Figure 10-18 shows that I have copied a PDF document into the application. All copied documents will reside in the Documents folder of your application.

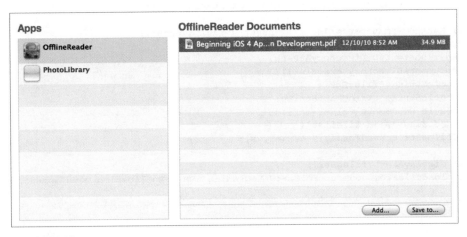

FIGURE 10-18

4. If you want to extract files from the application's Documents folder and save them locally to your computer, select the file(s) and click the "Save to . . ." button.

5. To confirm that the files are copied into the Documents folder of your application, add the following code to the `OfflineReaderViewController.m` file:

```
-(void) displayAlert:(NSString *) str {
    UIAlertView *alert =
    [[UIAlertView alloc] initWithTitle:@"Alert"
                               message:str
                              delegate:self
                     cancelButtonTitle:@"OK"
                     otherButtonTitles:nil];
    [alert show];
    [alert release];
}


- (void)handleDocumentOpenURL:(NSURL *)url {
    NSURLRequest *requestObj = [NSURLRequest requestWithURL:url];
    [webView setUserInteractionEnabled:YES];
    [webView loadRequest:requestObj];
}

-(void)loadFileFromDocumentsFolder:(NSString *) filename {
    //---get the path of the Documents folder---
    NSArray *paths = NSSearchPathForDirectoriesInDomains(
                       NSDocumentDirectory, NSUserDomainMask, YES);
    NSString *documentsDirectory = [paths objectAtIndex:0];
    NSString *filePath = [documentsDirectory
                            stringByAppendingPathComponent:filename];
    NSURL *fileUrl = [NSURL fileURLWithPath:filePath];
    [self handleDocumentOpenURL:fileUrl];
}


-(void)listFilesFromDocumentsFolder {
    //---get the path of the Documents folder---
    NSArray *paths = NSSearchPathForDirectoriesInDomains(
                       NSDocumentDirectory, NSUserDomainMask, YES);
    NSString *documentsDirectory = [paths objectAtIndex:0];

    NSFileManager *manager = [NSFileManager defaultManager];
    NSArray *fileList =
    [manager contentsOfDirectoryAtPath:
        documentsDirectory error:nil];
    NSMutableString *filesStr =
    [NSMutableString stringWithString:
    @"Files in Documents folder \n"];
    for (NSString *s in fileList){
        [filesStr appendFormat:@"%@ \n", s];
    }
    [self displayAlert:filesStr];
    [self loadFileFromDocumentsFolder:@"Beginning iOS 4 Application Development.pdf"];
```

```
    }

    - (IBAction) btnDisplayFiles {
        [self listFilesFromDocumentsFolder];
    }
```

6. Press Command-R to deploy the application on the device again. Tapping the Display Files in Documents button will both display the filename and load the PDF document in the Web View (see Figure 10-19), proving that the file was transferred into the application successfully.

How It Works

The magic for making your application appear under the File Sharing section of iTunes is the UIFileSharingEnabled key. Once this key is set to YES, your application will automatically appear in iTunes, exposing the Documents folder.

In this example, the displayAlert: method is simply a helper method to display an alert view on the screen.

The handleDocumentOpenURL: method takes an NSURL object and loads the Web View with its content.

The loadFileFromDocumentsFolder: method takes a filename and converts its path into an NSURL object. It then calls the handleDocumentOpenURL: method to display the Web View with the content of the file.

The listFilesFromDocumentsFolder method displays the names of all files and folders contained

FIGURE 10-19

within the Documents folder of the application. Besides that, it is also hardcoded to display the PDF document named Beginning iOS 4 Application Development.pdf (which was copied earlier). If the file is loaded successfully on the Web View, this proves that the document is copied correctly through iTunes.

Importing Documents

The second method of transferring documents into an application is through another application. Earlier, you saw how a PDF document in your application can be transferred to the iBooks application for viewing. This time, you will learn how a document can be transferred into your own application.

To begin, the following Try It Out shows you how to modify your application to accept PDF documents. Essentially, you need to get your application to register with the iOS, informing it that it is able to accept PDF documents.

TRY IT OUT   Importing Documents into Your Application

1.   Using the same project created in the previous section, modify the OfflineReader-Info.plist file (right-click on any of the items in this file and select Show Raw Keys/Values) by adding a new CFBundleDocumentTypes key as shown in Figure 10-20.

Key	Type	Value
CFBundleDevelopmentRegion	String	en
▼ CFBundleDocumentTypes	Array	(1 item)
▼ Item 0 (PDF Document)	Diction...	(4 items)
CFBundleTypeName	String	PDF Document
LSHandlerRank	String	Alternate
CFBundleTypeRole	String	Viewer
▼ LSItemContentTypes	Array	(1 item)
Item 0	String	com.adobe.pdf
UIFileSharingEnabled	Boolean	YES
CFBundleDisplayName	String	${PRODUCT_NAME}

FIGURE 10-20

2.   Add the following bold statements to the OfflineReaderAppDelegate.m file:

```
#import "OfflineReaderAppDelegate.h"

#import "OfflineReaderViewController.h"

@implementation OfflineReaderAppDelegate

@synthesize window = _window;
@synthesize viewController = _viewController;

-(BOOL)application:(UIApplication *)application
          openURL:(NSURL *)url
 sourceApplication:(NSString *)sourceApplication
        annotation:(id)annotation {
    if (url != nil && [url isFileURL]) {
        [self.viewController handleDocumentOpenURL:url];
    }
    Return YES;
}

- (BOOL)application:(UIApplication *)application didFinishLaunchingWithOptions:
(NSDictionary *)launchOptions
```

```
{
    self.window = [[[UIWindow alloc] initWithFrame:[[UIScreen mainScreen] bounds]]
     autorelease];
    // Override point for customization after application launch.
    self.viewController = [[[OfflineReaderViewController alloc]
        initWithNibName:@"OfflineReaderViewController"
        bundle:nil] autorelease];
    self.window.rootViewController = self.viewController;
    [self.window makeKeyAndVisible];
    Return YES;
}
```

3. Add the following bold statements to the `handleDocumentOpenURL:` method:

```
- (void)handleDocumentOpenURL:(NSURL *)url {
    [self displayAlert:[url absoluteString]];
    NSURLRequest *requestObj = [NSURLRequest requestWithURL:url];
    [webView setUserInteractionEnabled:YES];
    [webView loadRequest:requestObj];
}
```

4. Press Command-R to redeploy the application onto the real device. This time, if you go back to the same e-mail containing the PDF document and tap and hold onto it, you will find that you have the option to open the document in the OfflineReader application (see Figure 10-21).

5. When the document is opened in OfflineReader, the path of the document is shown (see Figure 10-22).

FIGURE 10-21

FIGURE 10-22

How It Works

The `CFBundleDocumentTypes` key in the `OfflineReader-Info.plist` file will register that the application is capable of handling PDF documents with iOS. Note the following:

➤ The `CFBundleDocumentTypes` key is of type `Array`. It contains an array of dictionaries describing the types of documents supported by your application.

➤ Item 0 is of type `Dictionary`.

➤ The `CFBundleTypeName` key specifies the abstract name for the specified document type.

➤ The `LSHandlerRank` key specifies whether the application is the Owner (creator of this file type), Alternate (secondary viewer of this file type), `None`, or `Default`.

➤ The `CFBundleTypeRole` key specifies the application's role with respect to the type: `Editor`, `Viewer`, `Shell`, or `None`.

➤ The `LSItemContentTypes` key is of type `Array`. It contains an array of UTIs specifying the file type.

When a PDF document is passed into the application, the application fires a particular method: `application:openURL:sourceApplication:annotation:`. This method must be implemented in the application delegate:

```
-(BOOL)application:(UIApplication *)application
         openURL:(NSURL *)url
sourceApplication:(NSString *)sourceApplication
      annotation:(id)annotation {
    if (url != nil && [url isFileURL]) {
        [self.viewController handleDocumentOpenURL:url];
    }
    return YES;
}
```

When a document is passed into your application, it is copied into a folder called Inbox, located within the Documents folder. The `url` argument contains the path to the document in the Inbox folder. In the preceding code, once the document is passed in, you call the `handleDocumentOpenURL:` method defined in the `OfflineReaderViewController` class to load the document in the Web View.

Importing Self-Defined Documents

The previous section showed how to import well-known document types, such as PDF, into your application. What if you want to import your own self-defined document types? For example, suppose you are writing a Sudoku program and want to implement your own file format for saving the state of a game. In this case, your file might have the .sdk extension, which is used only by your application. The following Try It Out shows you how to accomplish this.

Importing Self-Defined Documents into Your Application

1. Using the same project created in the previous section, add the keys shown in Figure 10-23 to the `OfflineReader-Info.plist` file:

Key	Type	Value
CFBundleDevelopmentRegion	String	en
▼ UTExportedTypeDeclarations	Array	(1 item)
▼ Item 0	Diction...	(4 items)
UTTypeDescription	String	Sudoku Game Document
▼ UTTypeConformsTo ⊕⊖	Array	(1 item)
Item 0	String	public.data
UTTypeIdentifier	String	net.learn2develop.offlinereader.sdk
▼ UTTypeTagSpecification	Diction...	(2 items)
public.filename-extension	String	sdk
public.mime-type	String	application/offlinereader
▼ CFBundleDocumentTypes	Array	(2 items)
▼ Item 0 (Sudoku Game Document)	Diction...	(4 items)
CFBundleTypeName	String	Sudoku Game Document
LSHandlerRank	String	Owner
CFBundleTypeRole	String	Editor
▼ LSItemContentTypes	Array	(1 item)
Item 0	String	net.learn2develop.offlinereader.sdk
▼ Item 1 (PDF Document)	Diction...	(4 items)
CFBundleTypeName	String	PDF Document
LSHandlerRank	String	Alternate
CFBundleTypeRole	String	Viewer
▼ LSItemContentTypes	Array	(1 item)
Item 0	String	com.adobe.pdf
UIFileSharingEnabled	Boolean	YES
CFBundleDisplayName	String	${PRODUCT_NAME}

FIGURE 10-23

2. Press Command-R to test the application on a real device again. This time, if your e-mail contains a document of extension .sdk, you will see the icon of your application displayed next to the document name (see Figure 10-24). When you tap on the document name, you will see a list of options to open your documents with (see Figure 10-25).

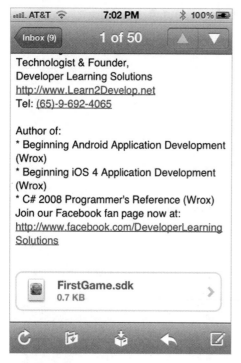

FIGURE 10-24

FIGURE 10-25

How It Works

Observe that you add another key to the `CFBundleDocumentTypes` array. You set the `LSItemContentTypes` to a unique value, using the reverse domain name of your company and the type you are defining. Since this is a self-defined content type, you have to define it using the `UTExportedTypeDeclarations` key.

Once the self-defined document is copied into your application, you can proceed to perform whatever actions you want. The document is saved in the Inbox folder, located within the Documents folder.

NOTE *For more information on UTI, refer to Apple's documentation: "Introduction to Uniform Type Identifiers Overview."* `http://developer.apple .com/library/ios/#documentation/FileManagement/Conceptual/ understanding_utis/understand_utis_intro/understand_utis_intro.html.`

SUMMARY

This chapter demonstrated how to write a file to the file system of the iPhone and how to read it back. In addition, you saw how structured data can be represented using a property list and how you can programmatically work with a property list using a dictionary object. The next chapter shows you how to use databases to store more complex data.

EXERCISES

1. Describe the uses of the various subfolders contained within an application's folder.

2. What is the difference between the `NSDictionary` and `NSMutableDictionary` classes?

3. Name the paths of the Documents and tmp folders on a real device.

4. Name the class that provides in-app support for exporting documents from your application.

5. What key should be set in order to allow file sharing support for your application?

6. What key is used to register a new file type with iOS to inform it that your application is capable of handling it?

Answers to the exercises can be found in Appendix D.

▶ **WHAT YOU LEARNED IN THIS CHAPTER**

TOPIC	KEY CONCEPTS
Subdirectories in each of the applications folders	Documents, Library, and tmp
Getting the path of the Documents folder	NSArray *paths = NSSearchPathForDirectoriesInDomains(NSDocumentDirectory, NSUserDomainMask, YES); NSString *documentsDir = [paths objectAtIndex:0];
Getting the path of the tmp directory	-(NSString *) tempPath{ return NSTemporaryDirectory(); }
Checking whether a file exists	if ([[NSFileManager defaultManager] fileExistsAtPath:filePath]) { }
Loading a property list from the Resources folder	NSString *pListPath = [[NSBundle mainBundle] pathForResource:@"Apps" ofType:@"plist"];
Creating a mutable copy of an NSDictionary object	NSDictionary *dict = [[NSDictionary alloc] initWithContentsOfFile:plistFileName]; NSMutableDictionary *copyOfDict = [dict mutableCopy];
Using bundled resources in your application	Copy the resources into the application's folders, such as Documents or tmp. You should copy the resources in the application's delegate when the application has just finished launching.
Exporting documents from your application	Use the UIDocumentInteractionController class.
Enabling file sharing in your application	Set the UIFileSharingEnabled key to YES in the .plist file of your project.
Importing documents into your application	Implement the application:openURL:sourceApplication:annotation: method in your application delegate.
Defining a file type supported by your application	Set the CFBundleDocumentTypes key in the .plist file.

11

Database Storage Using SQLite

- ➤ How to use the SQLite3 database in your Xcode project
- ➤ Creating and opening a SQLite3 database
- ➤ How to use the various SQLite3 functions to execute SQL strings
- ➤ How to use bind variables to insert values into a SQL string
- ➤ Bundling a pre-built SQLite database with your application

As you continue on your iOS development journey, you will soon realize that your application needs a way to save data. For example, you may want to save the text that the user is entering into a text field, or, in an RSS application, the last item that the user has read.

For simple applications, you can write the data you want to persist to a text file. For more structured data, you can use a property list. For large and complex data, it is more efficient to store it using a database. The iOS comes with the SQLite3 database library, which you can use to store your data. With your data stored in a database, your application can populate a Table view or store a large amount of data in a structured manner.

 NOTE *Besides using SQLite for data storage, developers can also use another framework for storage: Core Data. Core Data is part of the Cocoa API, which was first introduced in the iPhone SDK 3.0. It is basically a framework for manipulating data without worrying about the details of storage and retrieval. A discussion of Core Data is beyond the scope of this book.*

This chapter shows you how to use the embedded SQLite3 database library in your applications.

LINKING TO THE SQLITE3 LIBRARY

To use a SQLite3 database in your application, you first need to add the `libsqlite3.dylib` library to your Xcode project. The following Try It Out demonstrates how. You will need to download the code files indicated for this exercise and the rest of the Try It Out features in this chapter.

TRY IT OUT Preparing Your Project to Use SQLite3

codefile Databases.zip available for download at Wrox.com

1. Using Xcode, create a new Single View Application (iPhone) project and name it **Databases**. Use the project name as the Class Prefix. Ensure that you have the Use Automatic Reference Counting option unchecked.

2. Select the project name and then click the Build Phases tab on the right (see Figure 11-1). Click the "+" button shown in the Link Binary with Libraries section to add the `libsqlite3.dylib` library to it. After this, the library will be added to the project (see Figure 11-2).

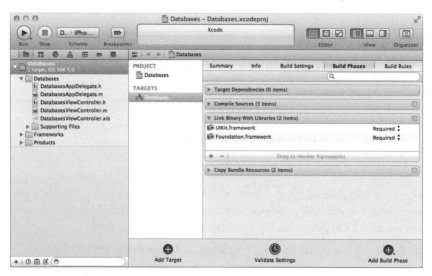

FIGURE 11-1

FIGURE 11-2

3. In the `DatabasesViewController.h` file, declare a variable of type `sqlite3`, as well as a few methods (see the code in bold). You will define the various methods throughout this chapter.

```
#import <UIKit/UIKit.h>
#import "sqlite3.h"

@interface DatabasesViewController : UIViewController
{
    sqlite3 *db;
}

-(NSString *) filePath;
-(void) openDB;
-(void) createTableNamed:(NSString *) tableName
              withField1:(NSString *) field1
              withField2:(NSString *) field2;
-(void) insertRecordIntoTableNamed:(NSString *) tableName
                        withField1:(NSString *) field1
                        field1Value:(NSString *) field1Value
                          andField2:(NSString *) field2
                        field2Value:(NSString *) field2Value;
-(void) getAllRowsFromTableNamed: (NSString *) tableName;

@end
```

4. In the `DatabasesViewController.m` file, define the `filePath` method as shown in bold:

```
#import "DatabasesViewController.h"

@implementation DatabasesViewController

-(NSString *) filePath {
    NSArray *paths =
        NSSearchPathForDirectoriesInDomains(
        NSDocumentDirectory, NSUserDomainMask, YES);

    NSString *documentsDir = [paths objectAtIndex:0];
    return [documentsDir stringByAppendingPathComponent:@"database.sql"];
}
```

How It Works

In order to work with SQLite3, you must link your application to a dynamic library called `libsqlite3.dylib`. The `libsqlite3.dylib` that you selected is an alias to the latest version of the SQLite3 library. On an actual iPhone device, the `libsqlite3.dylib` is located in the `/usr/lib/` directory.

To use a SQLite database, you need to create an object of type `sqlite3`:

```
sqlite3 *db;
```

The `filePath` method returns the full path to the SQLite database that will be created in the `Documents` directory on your iPhone (within your application's sandbox):

```
-(NSString *) filePath {
    NSArray *paths =
        NSSearchPathForDirectoriesInDomains(
    NSDocumentDirectory, NSUserDomainMask, YES);

    NSString *documentsDir = [paths objectAtIndex:0];
    return [documentsDir stringByAppendingPathComponent:@"database.sql"];
```

 NOTE *Chapter 10 discusses the various folders that you can access within your application's sandbox.*

CREATING AND OPENING A DATABASE

After the necessary library is added to the project, you can open a database for usage. You use the various C functions included with SQLite3 to create or open a database, as demonstrated in the following one-step Try It Out.

TRY IT OUT Opening a Database

1. Using the `Databases` project created previously, define the `openDB` method in the `DatabasesViewController.m` file:

```
-(void) openDB {
    //--create database--
    if (sqlite3_open([[self filePath] UTF8String], &db) != SQLITE_OK ) {
        sqlite3_close(db);
        NSAssert(0, @"Database failed to open.");
    }
}

- (void)viewDidLoad
{
    [self openDB];
    [super viewDidLoad];
}
```

How It Works

The `sqlite3_open()` C function opens a SQLite database whose filename is specified as the first argument:

```
[self filePath] UTF8String]
```

In this case, the filename of the database is specified as a C string using the `UTF8String` method of the `NSString` class because the `sqlite3_open()` C function does not understand an `NSString` object.

The second argument contains a handle to the `sqlite3` object, which in this case is `db`.

If the database is available, it is opened. If the specified database is not found, a new database is created. If the database is successfully opened, the function will return a value of `0` (represented using the `SQLITE_OK` constant).

The following list from `www.sqlite.org/c3ref/c_abort.html` shows the result codes returned by the various SQLite functions:

```
#define SQLITE_OK           0    /* Successful result */
#define SQLITE_ERROR        1    /* SQL error or missing database */
#define SQLITE_INTERNAL     2    /* Internal logic error in SQLite */
#define SQLITE_PERM         3    /* Access permission denied */
#define SQLITE_ABORT        4    /* Callback routine requested an abort */
#define SQLITE_BUSY         5    /* The database file is locked */
#define SQLITE_LOCKED       6    /* A table in the database is locked */
#define SQLITE_NOMEM        7    /* A malloc() failed */
#define SQLITE_READONLY     8    /* Attempt to write a readonly database */
#define SQLITE_INTERRUPT    9    /* Operation terminated by sqlite3_interrupt()*/
#define SQLITE_IOERR        10   /* Some kind of disk I/O error occurred */
#define SQLITE_CORRUPT      11   /* The database disk image is malformed */
#define SQLITE_NOTFOUND     12   /* NOT USED. Table or record not found */
#define SQLITE_FULL         13   /* Insertion failed because database is full */
#define SQLITE_CANTOPEN     14   /* Unable to open the database file */
#define SQLITE_PROTOCOL     15   /* NOT USED. Database lock protocol error */
#define SQLITE_EMPTY        16   /* Database is empty */
#define SQLITE_SCHEMA       17   /* The database schema changed */
#define SQLITE_TOOBIG       18   /* String or BLOB exceeds size limit */
#define SQLITE_CONSTRAINT   19   /* Abort due to constraint violation */
#define SQLITE_MISMATCH     20   /* Data type mismatch */
#define SQLITE_MISUSE       21   /* Library used incorrectly */
#define SQLITE_NOLFS        22   /* Uses OS features not supported on host */
#define SQLITE_AUTH         23   /* Authorization denied */
#define SQLITE_FORMAT       24   /* Auxiliary database format error */
#define SQLITE_RANGE        25   /* 2nd parameter to sqlite3_bind out of range */
#define SQLITE_NOTADB       26   /* File opened that is not a database file */
#define SQLITE_ROW          100  /* sqlite3_step() has another row ready */
#define SQLITE_DONE         101  /* sqlite3_step() has finished executing */
```

Examining the Database Created

If the database is created successfully, it can be found in the Documents folder of your application's sandbox on the iPhone Simulator in the ~/Library/Application Support/ iPhone Simulator/5.0/Applications/<App_ID>/ Documents/ folder (see Figure 11-3).

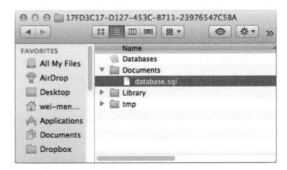

Creating a Table

FIGURE 11-3

After the database is created, you can create a table to store some data. The following one-step Try It Out demonstrates how to create a table with two text fields. For illustration purposes, create a table named Contacts, with two fields called email and name.

TRY IT OUT Creating a Table

1. Using the same Databases project, define the createTableNamed:with-Field1:withField2: method in the DatabasesViewController.m file as follows:

```
-(void) createTableNamed:(NSString *) tableName
            withField1:(NSString *) field1
            withField2:(NSString *) field2 {

    char *err;
    NSString *sql = [NSString stringWithFormat:
                    @"CREATE TABLE IF NOT EXISTS '%@' ('%@' "
                    "TEXT PRIMARY KEY, '%@' TEXT);",
                    tableName, field1, field2];

    if (sqlite3_exec(db, [sql UTF8String], NULL, NULL, &err)
        != SQLITE_OK) {
        sqlite3_close(db);
        NSAssert(0, @"Tabled failed to create.");
    }
}

- (void)viewDidLoad
{
    [self openDB];
    [self createTableNamed:@"Contacts"
            withField1:@"email"
            withField2:@"name"];
    [super viewDidLoad];
}
```

How It Works

The createTableNamed:withField1:withField2: method takes three parameters: tableName, field1, and field2.

Using these parameters, you first formulate a SQL string and then create a table using the `sqlite3_exec()` C function, with the important arguments to this function being the `sqlite3` object, the SQL query string, and a pointer to a variable for error messages. If an error occurs in creating the database, then you use the `NSAssert` method to halt the application and close the database connection.

If the operation is successful, a table named `Contacts` with two fields (`email` and `name`) is created.

 NOTE *For a jump start in the SQL language, check out the SQL tutorial at* `http://w3schools.com/sql/default.asp`*.*

Inserting Records

After the table is created, you can insert some records into it. The following Try It Out shows you how to write three rows of records in the table created in the previous section.

TRY IT OUT   **Inserting Records**

1. In the `Databases` project, define the `insertRecordIntoTableNamed:withField1:field1Value:andField2:field2Value:` method in the `DatabasesViewController.m` file as follows and modify the `viewDidLoad` method as shown in bold:

```
-(void) insertRecordIntoTableNamed:(NSString *) tableName
                      withField1:(NSString *) field1
                     field1Value:(NSString *) field1Value
                       andField2:(NSString *) field2
                     field2Value:(NSString *) field2Value {

    NSString *sql = [NSString stringWithFormat:
               @"INSERT OR REPLACE INTO '%@' ('%@', '%@') "
               "VALUES ('%@','%@')", tableName, field1, field2,
               field1Value, field2Value];

    char *err;
    if (sqlite3_exec(db, [sql UTF8String], NULL, NULL, &err)
        != SQLITE_OK) {
        sqlite3_close(db);
        NSAssert(0, @"Error updating table.");
    }
}

- (void)viewDidLoad
{
    [self openDB];
    [self createTableNamed:@"Contacts"
            withField1:@"email"
            withField2:@"name"];
```

```
for (int i=0; i<=2; i++) {
    NSString *email = [[NSString alloc] initWithFormat:
                        @"user%d@learn2develop.net",i];

    NSString *name = [[NSString alloc] initWithFormat: @"user %d",i];
    [self insertRecordIntoTableNamed:@"Contacts"
                        withField1:@"email" field1Value:email
                          andField2:@"name" field2Value:name];
    [email release];
    [name release];
}

[super viewDidLoad];
```

How It Works

The code in this example is similar to that of the previous one; you formulate a SQL string and use the `sqlite3_exec()` C function to insert a record into the database:

```
NSString *sql = [NSString stringWithFormat:
                @"INSERT OR REPLACE INTO '%@' ('%@', '%@') "
                "VALUES ('%@','%@')", tableName, field1, field2,
                field1Value, field2Value];
//---the above SQL statement to be typed in a single line---

char *err;
if (sqlite3_exec(db, [sql UTF8String], NULL, NULL, &err)
    != SQLITE_OK) {
    sqlite3_close(db);
    NSAssert(0, @"Error updating table.");
}
```

In the `viewDidLoad` method, you insert three records into the database by calling the `insertRecordIntoTableNamed:withField1:field1Value:andField2:field2Value:` method:

```
for (int i=0; i<=2; i++) {
    NSString *email = [[NSString alloc] initWithFormat:
                        @"user%d@learn2develop.net",i];

    NSString *name = [[NSString alloc] initWithFormat: @"user %d",i];
    [self insertRecordIntoTableNamed:@"Contacts"
                        withField1:@"email" field1Value:email
                          andField2:@"name" field2Value:name];
    [email release];
    [name release];
}
```

Bind Variables

When formulating SQL strings, you often need to insert values into the query string and ensure that the string is well formulated and contains no invalid characters. In the preceding section, you saw that in order to insert a row into the database, you had to formulate your SQL statement like this:

```
NSString *sql = [NSString stringWithFormat:
                @"INSERT OR REPLACE INTO '%@' ('%@', '%@') "
                "VALUES ('%@','%@')", tableName, field1, field2,
                field1Value, field2Value];
//--the above SQL statement to be typed in a single line--

char *err;
if (sqlite3_exec(db, [sql UTF8String], NULL, NULL, &err)
    != SQLITE_OK) {
    sqlite3_close(db);
    NSAssert(0, @"Error updating table.");
}
```

SQLite supports a feature known as *bind variables* to help you formulate your SQL string. For example, the preceding SQL string can be formulated as follows using bind variables:

```
NSString *sqlStr = [NSString stringWithFormat:
                @"INSERT OR REPLACE INTO '%@' ('%@', '%@') "
                "VALUES (?,?)", tableName, field1, field2];
const char *sql = [sqlStr UTF8String];
```

Here, the ? is a placeholder; you must replace it with the actual value of the query. In the preceding statement, assuming that `tableName` is `Contacts`, `field1` is `email`, and `field2` is `name`, the `sql` is now as follows:

INSERT OR REPLACE INTO Contacts ('email', 'name') VALUES (?,?)

> **NOTE** *The ? can be inserted only into the* VALUES *and* WHERE *section of the SQL statement; you cannot insert it into a table name, for example. The following statement would be invalid:*
>
> ```
> INSERT OR REPLACE INTO ? ('email', 'name') VALUES (?,?)
> ```

To substitute the values for the ?, create a `sqlite3_stmt` object and use the `sqlite3_prepare_v2()` function to compile the SQL string into a binary form and then insert the placeholder values using the `sqlite3_bind_text()` function, like this:

```
sqlite3_stmt *statement;
if (sqlite3_prepare_v2(db, sql, -1, &statement, nil) == SQLITE_OK) {
    sqlite3_bind_text(statement, 1, [field1Value UTF8String],
                    -1, NULL);
    sqlite3_bind_text(statement, 2, [field2Value UTF8String],
                    -1, NULL);
```

NOTE *To bind integer values, use the* `sqlite3_bind_int()` *function.*

After the preceding call, the SQL string looks like this:

```
INSERT OR REPLACE INTO Contacts ('email', 'name') VALUES
  ('user0@learn2develop.net', 'user0')
```

To execute the SQL statement, you use the `sqlite3_step()` function, followed by the `sqlite3_finalize()` function to delete the prepared SQL statement:

```
if (sqlite3_step(statement) != SQLITE_DONE)
    NSAssert(0, @"Error updating table.");
sqlite3_finalize(statement);
```

Using bind variables, the
`insertRecordIntoTableNamed:withField1:field1Value:andField2:field2Value:` method
could now be rewritten as follows:

```
-(void) insertRecordIntoTableNamed:(NSString *) tableName
                         withField1:(NSString *) field1
                        field1Value:(NSString *) field1Value
                          andField2:(NSString *) field2
                        field2Value:(NSString *) field2Value {

    NSString *sqlStr = [NSString stringWithFormat:
                @"INSERT OR REPLACE INTO '%@' ('%@', '%@') "
                "VALUES (?,?)", tableName, field1, field2];
    const char *sql = [sqlStr UTF8String];


    sqlite3_stmt *statement;
    if (sqlite3_prepare_v2(db, sql, -1, &statement, nil) == SQLITE_OK) {
        sqlite3_bind_text(statement, 1, [field1Value UTF8String],
                          -1, NULL);
        sqlite3_bind_text(statement, 2, [field2Value UTF8String],
                          -1, NULL);
    }


    if (sqlite3_step(statement) != SQLITE_DONE)
        NSAssert(0, @"Error updating table.");
    sqlite3_finalize(statement);
```

NOTE *In the "Inserting Records" section, you used the* `sqlite3_exec()` *function
to execute SQL statements. In this example, you actually use a combination of the*
`sqlite3_prepare()`, `sqlite3_step()`, *and* `sqlite3_finalize()` *functions to
do the same thing. In fact, the* `sqlite3_exec()` *function is actually a wrapper for
these three functions. For nonquery SQL statements (such as for creating tables,
inserting rows, and so on), it is always better to use the* `sqlite3_exec()` *function.*

Retrieving Records

Now that the records have been successfully inserted into the table, it is time to retrieve them. This is a good way to ensure that they have actually been saved. The following Try It Out shows you how to retrieve your records.

TRY IT OUT Retrieving Records from a Table

1. In the Databases project, define the getAllRowsFromTableNamed: method in the DatabasesViewController.m file as follows and modify the viewDidLoad method as shown in bold:

```
-(void) getAllRowsFromTableNamed: (NSString *) tableName {
    //--retrieve rows--
    NSString *qsql = [NSString stringWithFormat:@"SELECT * FROM %@",
                        tableName];

    sqlite3_stmt *statement;
    if (sqlite3_prepare_v2( db, [qsql UTF8String], -1,
                            &statement, nil) == SQLITE_OK) {
        while (sqlite3_step(statement) == SQLITE_ROW) {
            char *field1 = (char *) sqlite3_column_text(statement, 0);
            NSString *field1Str =
            [[NSString alloc] initWithUTF8String: field1];

            char *field2 = (char *) sqlite3_column_text(statement, 1);
            NSString *field2Str =
            [[NSString alloc] initWithUTF8String: field2];

            NSString *str = [[NSString alloc] initWithFormat:@"%@ - %@",
                            field1Str, field2Str];
            NSLog(@"%@", str);

            [field1Str release];
            [field2Str release];
            [str release];
        }

        //--deletes the compiled statement from memory--
        sqlite3_finalize(statement);
    }
}

- (void)viewDidLoad
{
    [self openDB];
    [self createTableNamed:@"Contacts"
            withField1:@"email"
            withField2:@"name"];
    for (int i=0; i<=2; i++) {
        NSString *email = [[NSString alloc] initWithFormat:
                            @"user%d@learn2develop.net",i];

        NSString *name = [[NSString alloc] initWithFormat: @"user %d",i];
        [self insertRecordIntoTableNamed:@"Contacts"
                        withField1:@"email" field1Value:email
                        andField2:@"name" field2Value:name];
```

```
    [email release];
    [name release];
}

[self getAllRowsFromTableNamed:@"Contacts"];
sqlite3_close(db);
[super viewDidLoad];
}
```

2. Press Command-R to test the application. In Xcode, press Command-Shift-C to display the Output window. When the application has loaded, the Debugger Console displays the records (see Figure 11-4), proving that the rows are indeed in the table.

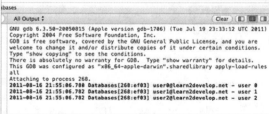

FIGURE 11-4

How It Works

To retrieve the records from the table, you first prepare the SQL statement and then use the `sqlite3_step()` function to execute the prepared statement. The `sqlite3_step()` function returns a value of 100 (represented by the `SQLITE_ROW` constant) if another row is ready. In this case, you call the `sqlite3_step()` function using a `while` loop, continuing as long as it returns a `SQLITE_ROW`:

```
if (sqlite3_prepare_v2( db, [qsql UTF8String], -1,
                        &statement, nil) == SQLITE_OK) {
    while (sqlite3_step(statement) == SQLITE_ROW) {
        char *field1 = (char *) sqlite3_column_text(statement, 0);
        NSString *field1Str =
        [[NSString alloc] initWithUTF8String: field1];

        char *field2 = (char *) sqlite3_column_text(statement, 1);
        NSString *field2Str =
        [[NSString alloc] initWithUTF8String: field2];

        NSString *str = [[NSString alloc] initWithFormat:@"%@ - %@",
                        field1Str, field2Str];
        NSLog(@"%@", str);

        [field1Str release];
        [field2Str release];
        [str release];
    }
    //---deletes the compiled statement from memory---
    sqlite3_finalize(statement);
}
```

To retrieve the value for the first field in the row, you use the `sqlite3_column_text()` function by passing it the `sqlite3_stmt` object as well as the index of the field you are retrieving. For example, you use the following to retrieve the first field of the returned row:

```
char *field1 = (char *) sqlite3_column_text(statement, 0);
```

To retrieve an integer column (field), use the `sqlite3_column_int()` function.

NOTE *If the method you are calling is defined below the viewDidLoad, the compiler will generate a warning.*

BUNDLING SQLITE DATABASES WITH YOUR APPLICATION

Although programmatically creating a SQLite database and using it during runtime is very flexible, most of the time you just need to create the database file during the designing stage of your development, and bundle the database with your application so that it can be used during runtime. Therefore, rather than create the database file using code, you need to create it in Mac OS X.

Fortunately, you can easily create a SQLite database file in Mac OS X by using the `sqlite3` application in Terminal. Figure 11-5 shows the command that you need to create a database named `mydata.sql`, containing a table named `Contacts` with two fields: `email` and `name`. It also inserts a row into the table and then retrieves it to verify that it is inserted properly.

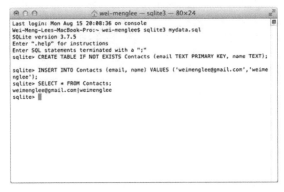

FIGURE 11-5

The commands are as follows:

➤ `sqlite3 mydata.sql`

➤ `CREATE TABLE IF NOT EXISTS Contacts (email TEXT PRIMARY KEY, name TEXT);`

➤ `INSERT INTO Contacts (email, name) VALUES ('weimenglee@gmail.com', 'weimenglee');`

➤ `SELECT * FROM Contacts;`

 NOTE *Remember to end each command with a semicolon (;). Also, by default, when you launch Terminal, you are in your home directory. Hence, running the `sqlite3` application will save your database file in your home directory.*

Even though you could use the `sqlite3` application to insert records into the database, it would be much easier to use a graphical tool to do that. You can use the SQLite Database Browser

(see Figure 11-6), which you can download free from `http://sourceforge.net/projects/`
`sqlitebrowser/`. Using the SQLite Database Browser, you can perform a wide variety of functions
with the database file.

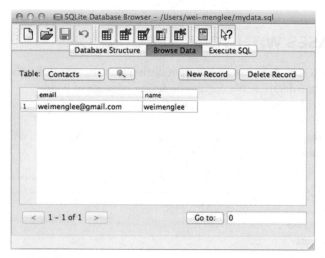

FIGURE 11-6

SUMMARY

This chapter provided a brief introduction to the SQLite3 database used in the iPhone. With
SQLite3, you can now store all your structured data in an efficient manner and perform complex
aggregations on your data. To learn more about SQLite, visit its official page at `www.sqlite.org`.

EXERCISES

1. Explain the difference between the `sqlite3_exec()` function and the three functions `sqlite3_prepare()`, `sqlite3_step()`, and `sqlite3_finalize()`.

2. How do you obtain a C-style string from an `NSString` object?

3. Write the code segment to retrieve a set of rows from a table.

Answers to the exercises can be found in Appendix D.

▶ **WHAT YOU LEARNED IN THIS CHAPTER**

TOPIC	KEY CONCEPTS
Using a SQLite3 database in your application	Add a reference to the `libsqlite3.dylib` library to your project.
Obtaining a C-style string from an `NSString` object	Use the `UTF8String` method of the `NSString` class.
Creating and opening a SQLite3 database	Use the `sqlite3_open()` C function.
Executing a SQL query	Use the `sqlite3_exec()` C function.
Closing a database connection	Use the `sqlite3_close()` C function.
Using bind variables	Create a `sqlite3_stmt` object. Use the `sqlite3_prepare_v2()` C function to prepare the statement. Use the `sqlite3_bind_text()` (or `sqlite3_bind_int()`, and so on) C function to insert the values into the statement. Use the `sqlite3_step()` C function to execute the statement. Use the `sqlite3_finalize()` C function to delete the statement from memory.
Retrieving records	Use the `sqlite3_step()` C function to retrieve each individual row.
Retrieving columns from a row	Use the `sqlite3_column_text()` (or `sqlite3_column_int()`, and so on) C function.

12

Programming iCloud

WHAT YOU WILL LEARN IN THIS CHAPTER

➤   How to enable iCloud storage for your iOS application

➤   How to store documents for your application on iCloud

➤   How to store key-value data for your application on iCloud

One of the major new features in iOS 5 is iCloud. Using iCloud, all the information stored on your devices is stored on remote servers (commonly known as *cloud computing*) maintained by Apple. For example, all the contacts on your iPhone can be synced to iCloud. When you purchase a new iPad, all the contacts on your iPhone can automatically be downloaded from iCloud wirelessly, saving you all the time of transferring the information (either manually or through iTunes) to the new device; and when you make changes to a contact on the iPad, the changes are automatically synced to the iPhone. In addition to syncing content, you can also use iCloud to automatically download songs, apps, and books that you have purchased on other iOS devices.

In iOS 5, iCloud is available free to all users. When you sign up for iCloud, you get 5GB of free storage (you can purchase additional storage if you need more). Using this free storage, you can use iCloud to back up your devices so that in the unfortunate event that you lose your iPhone (or iPad), you can simply restore all your content onto a new replacement device.

In this chapter, you will learn how to make use of iCloud to save documents and data in your application so that they are available to the same application running on all your other devices.

STORING AND USING DOCUMENTS IN ICLOUD

From an iOS developer's perspective, iCloud presents two different usage scenarios:

➤ **Document storage** — Saves all your application documents on iCloud so that it accessible to other devices

➤ **Key-value data storage** — Saves small amounts of application-specific data to the application so that it can be shared with other devices

The first usage involves saving documents in your application on the iCloud. For example, in an eBook reader application, a user may purchase an eBook (or simply copy a PDF document into the application's Documents folder; see Chapter 10). The user would expect the newly purchased eBook to be available to the same application on another device. Instead of storing the eBook on your application's sandbox, your application can make use of iCloud's document storage to store the eBook. Documents stored in the iCloud's document storage are automatically available to your application on all other devices. This way, all your application's documents are stored in a central location and available to all the user's devices.

The second usage allows you to store application-specific data on iCloud. Data that is specific to an application (such as application preferences) can be saved onto iCloud and made visible to the same application on all your other devices. Using the eBook reader example, the page number of a book that the reader is currently reading is a perfect example of an application-specific data that can be stored on the iCloud and made available on other devices, with the result being the reader can start reading a book on one device, turn that device off, and then later start reading the same book at the same place they left off, on another device.

The following sections describe these two usage scenarios.

Enabling iCloud Storage for Your Application

Even though iCloud is free for iOS 5 users, you need to register for iCloud on your device before you can use it. To register for iCloud, go to the Settings application on your iOS device, tap the iCloud item, and follow the instructions on screen.

 NOTE *The following sections describe how to write an application to make use of iCloud. Because several steps are involved, I have divided them into individual sections so that you can understand each part of the process before continuing.*

The following Try It Out shows you how to take the first step to enabling iCloud for your application: creating an iCloud-enabled App ID and provisioning profile.

TRY IT OUT Creating the App ID and Provisioning Profile for iCloud

1. Log in to the iOS Provisioning Portal at `http://developer.apple.com/devcenter/ios/index.action` to create a new App ID.

> **NOTE** For more information on how to log in to the iOS Provisioning Portal, please refer to Appendix A.

2. On the Manage tab of the App IDs page, create an App ID and give it a description of **DemoiCloudAppID**. Select Use Team ID as the Bundle Seed and name the Bundle Identifier **net.learn2develop.DemoiCloud** (see Figure 12-1).

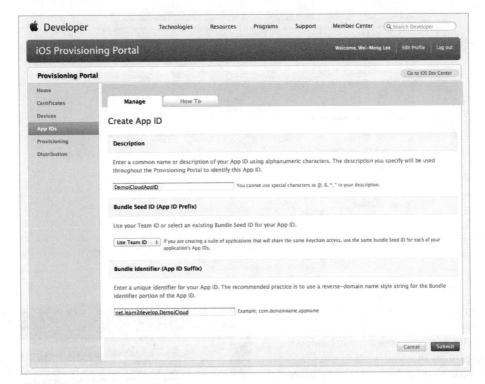

FIGURE 12-1

> **NOTE** The Bundle Identifier must be globally unique; hence be sure to use your organization's reverse domain name so that you can minimize the chances that someone has the same Bundle Identifier as you. In any case, if there is a conflict you will be asked to provide another unique Bundle Identifier.

3. With the App ID created, you need to enable the App ID for iCloud. Click the Configure link shown on the right of the App ID that you have just created to configure it. Check the Enable for iCloud option, as shown in Figure12-2.

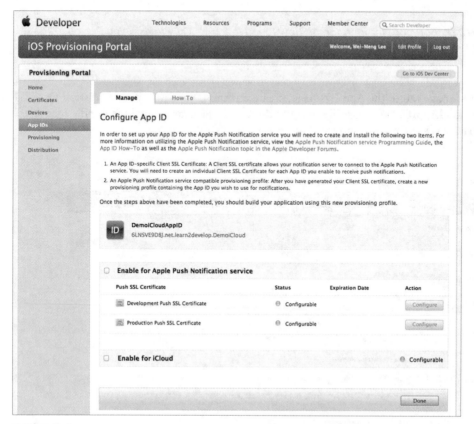

FIGURE 12-2

4. A pop-up will appear, warning you that all new provisioning profiles you create using this App ID will be enabled for iCloud. All existing profiles that you wish to use for iCloud must be modified and reinstalled on your devices again. Click OK to continue (see Figure 12-3).

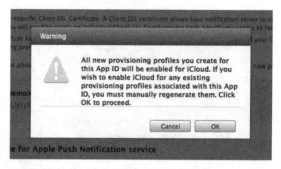

FIGURE 12-3

5. You now need to create a new provisioning profile to use with this new App ID. On the Development tab of the Provisioning page, create a new Profile named **DemoiCloudProfile**, associate it with this new App ID, and select the devices on which you wish to test (see Figure 12-4). Click Submit to continue.

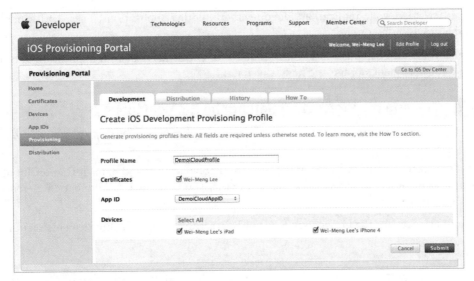

FIGURE 12-4

6. Once the profile is created, download and install it onto any devices that you will use to test your application. For the example in this chapter, you need two iOS devices; the Simulator does not support iCloud.

> **NOTE** *Refer to Appendix A if you are unsure how to install the provisioning profile onto your devices. To test the iCloud feature, you need a real device; the iOS Simulator will not work.*

How It Works

To use iCloud for storage of your documents, you need to have an App ID that is enabled for iCloud. Note that for the Bundle Identifier, you need to specify a unique identifier string (using your reverse-domain name is recommended); the wildcard character (*) is not allowed. Also, the provisioning profiles that you will use to deploy your application onto real devices must use this iCloud-enabled App ID. If you already have existing provisioning profiles created and want to use this iCloud-enabled App ID, you need to modify these provisioning profiles to use this new App ID, and then download and install them onto your devices again. The easiest way to get this example to work is to create a new provisioning profile.

Setting Project Entitlements

When your application uses iCloud to store documents, folders will be created in iCloud to uniquely identify the owner. Hence, you need to request specific entitlements in your application so that iCloud can differentiate your application's documents from other applications. These entitlements are tied to the provisioning profile.

The following Try It Out demonstrates how to request for entitlements in your application in order to use iCloud for document storage and key-value data.

TRY IT OUT Creating the Project and Setting the Entitlements

codefile DemoiCloud.zip available for download at Wrox.com

1. Using Xcode, create a new Single View Application (iPhone) project and name it **DemoiCloud**. Use the project name as the Class Prefix and ensure that you have the Use Automatic Reference Counting option unchecked.

2. In the Summary page for the project (see Figure 12-5), scroll down to the Entitlements section.

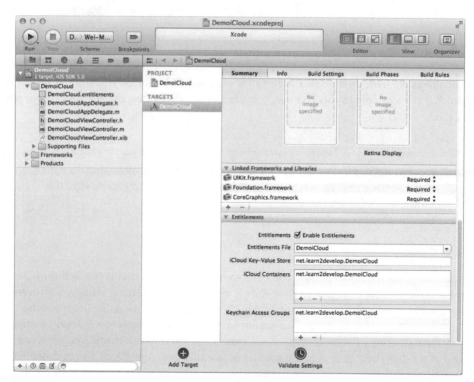

FIGURE 12-5

3. Check the Enable Entitlements option and set the values as follows: (shown in Figure 12-5)

- ➤ **Entitlements File** — `DemoiCloud`
- ➤ **iCloud-Key-Value Store** — `net.learn2develop.DemoiCloud`
- ➤ **iCloud Containers** — `net.learn2develop.DemoiCloud`
- ➤ **Keychain Access Groups** — `net.learn2develop.DemoiCloud`

How It Works

You need to set two entitlements in your application if you want to use iCloud.

If you want to use iCloud document storage, you need to request the iCloud Containers entitlement. This is done by simply setting it to a value of the following format: `<TEAM_ID>.<CUSTOM_STRING>`. The `Team_ID` is the unique ten-character identifier associated with your developer account (refer to Figure 12-2). Note that in this example you do not need to enter the `TEAM_ID`, as it is set for you automatically (more on this shortly).The `CUSTOM_STRING` is a string that you set to uniquely identify the iCloud storage container used by your application. It is recommended that you use the reverse domain name of your organization for the custom string, just like the Bundle Identifier used in your App ID. You can set more than one iCloud Containers entitlement if you want to create multiple containers to be used by multiple applications. The first iCloud containers entitlement is always the main container used by your application.

If you want to use iCloud key-value data storage, you need to request the iCloud Key-Value Store entitlement. You only need to set a single value for this entitlement.

In the preceding example, the entitlements are saved in the `DemoiCloud.entitlements` file in the project. To see its raw content, right-click on the file and select Open As ⇨ Source Code. Its raw content looks like this:

```
<?xml version="1.0" encoding="UTF-8"?>
<!DOCTYPE plist PUBLIC "-//Apple//DTD PLIST 1.0//EN" "
    http://www.apple.com/DTDs/PropertyList-1.0.dtd">
<plist version="1.0">
<dict>
<key>com.apple.developer.ubiquity-container-identifiers</key>
<array>
<string>$(TeamIdentifierPrefix)net.learn2develop.DemoiCloud</string>
</array>
<key>com.apple.developer.ubiquity-kvstore-identifier</key>
<string>$(TeamIdentifierPrefix)net.learn2develop.DemoiCloud</string>
<key>keychain-access-groups</key>
<array>
<string>$(AppIdentifierPrefix)net.learn2develop.DemoiCloud</string>
</array>
</dict>
</plist>
```

Notice the inclusion of the `$(TeamIdentifierPrefix)` placeholder (which is shown in bold above). Hence, you do not need to enter your `TEAM_ID` earlier when you set the entitlements for your application.

As mentioned, you can add multiple strings for the iCloud Containers entitlement. For example, suppose you add a second string to it as shown here:

```
<key>com.apple.developer.ubiquity-container-identifiers</key>
<array>
<string>$(TeamIdentifierPrefix)net.learn2develop.DemoiCloud</string>
<string>$(TeamIdentifierPrefix)net.learn2develop.DemoiCloud.Free</string>
</array>
```

In this case, besides being able to access the documents stored in the container identified by `$(TeamIdentifierPrefix)net.learn2develop.DemoiCloud`, your application will also be able to access the container identified by `$(TeamIdentifierPrefix)net.learn2develop.DemoiCloud.Free`, which is created by another separate application.

Managing iCloud Documents Using the UIDocument Class

To manage documents stored in iCloud, Apple recommends you use the `UIDocument` class. This class does all the work of reading and writing to files stored in iCloud. Using the `UIDocument` class, there is no need for you to manage the complexity of resolving conflicts when two devices try to update the same file at the same time. To use the `UIDocument` class, you need to subclass it and then implement a few methods.

The following Try It Out shows how to subclass the `UIDocument` class so that you can use it to manage your documents in iCloud.

TRY IT OUT Managing iCloud Documents

1. Using the project created in the previous section, add a new Objective-C class and name it **MyCloudDocument**. Make it a subclass of `UIDocument` (see Figure 12-6).

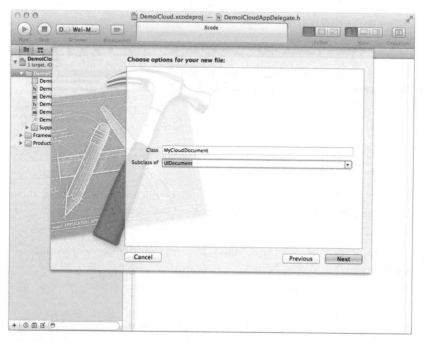

FIGURE 12-6

2. Populate the `MyCloudDocument.h` file as follows:

```objc
#import <UIKit/UIKit.h>
@class MyCloudDocument;

@protocol MyCloudDocumentDelegate <NSObject>
- (void)documentContentsDidUpdate:(MyCloudDocument *)document;
@end

@interface MyCloudDocument : UIDocument

@property (assign, nonatomic) id <MyCloudDocumentDelegate> delegate;
@property (copy, nonatomic) NSString *contents;

@end
```

3. Populate the `MyCloudDocument.m` file as follows:

```objc
#import "MyCloudDocument.h"

@implementation MyCloudDocument

@synthesize delegate = _delegate;
@synthesize contents = _contents;

- (void)dealloc {
    [_contents release];
    [super dealloc];
}

//---create the file at the specified URL and init it with some content---
- (id)initWithFileURL:(NSURL *)url {
    self = [super initWithFileURL:url];
    return self;
}

//---load the content of the document---
- (BOOL)loadFromContents:(id)contents
                  ofType:(NSString *)
            typeName error:(NSError **)outError {
    if ([contents length] > 0)
    {
        self.contents =
            [[[NSString alloc] initWithData:contents
                                   encoding:NSUTF8StringEncoding]
                                   autorelease];
    } else {
        //---if nothing, set it to empty string---
        self.contents = @"";
    }

    //---if the object implements this delegate, call it---
    if ([_delegate respondsToSelector:
        @selector(documentContentsDidUpdate:)]) {
        //---tell the delegate that the content of the document has changed---
        [self.delegate documentContentsDidUpdate:self];
    }
```

```
        return YES;
    }

    //---save the content of the document---
    - (id)contentsForType:(NSString *)typeName
                    error:(NSError **)outError {
        return [self.contents dataUsingEncoding:NSUTF8StringEncoding];
    }

    @end
```

How It Works

In the preceding example, you defined a protocol named `MyCloudDocumentDelegate`, which contains a method named `documentContentsDidUpdate`.

In the class, you implemented the following methods:

➤ `initWithFileURL:` — This method is called when you are creating a new document in iCloud. It takes a single argument, which is the URL for the file to be created.

➤ `loadFromContents:ofType:error:` — This method is called when your application tries to load the content of the document from iCloud. For this example, the document is a simple text file; therefore, you will only deal with strings by converting the data from `NSData` to `NSString`. When a document is loaded, you also invoke the `documentContentsDidUpdate` delegate so that the application knows that it has managed to load the document from iCloud.

➤ `contentsForType:error:` — This method is called when you try to save the file to iCloud. Here, you simply convert the string content of the file to the `NSData` type.

To create documents on iCloud, you need to create instances of subclasses of `UIDocument`, which in this case is the `MyCloudDocument` class. The next Try It Out shows how this is done.

Storing Documents on iCloud

Now that you have seen how to use the `UIDocument` class, it is time to put everything together and create an application that stores your documents in iCloud.

The following Try It Out shows how your application can make use of the `UIDocument` class to save a document on iCloud, and then access the same document from other iOS devices running the same application. If you are eager to see how things work first, follow the steps and try it out on two iOS devices. For those of you who want to understand the details of how this works, jump to the How It Works section, which dissects the code. After that you can try it out on your devices.

TRY IT OUT Saving Documents on iCloud

1. Using the project created in the previous section, select the `DemoiCloudViewController.xib` file to edit it in Interface Builder.

2. Add the following views to the View window (see also Figure 12-7):

➤ Two Labels (set their text properties to "Enter some text here" and "Files on iCloud")

➤ Text Field

➤ Two Round Rect Buttons (set their text properties to "Create file on iCloud" and "Save to file on iCloud")

➤ Text View (remember to delete the text displayed inside it)

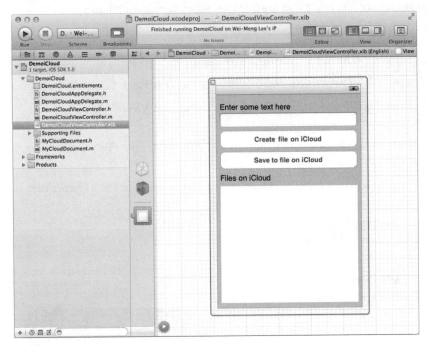

FIGURE 12-7

3. In the `DemoiCloudViewController.h` file, add the following lines in bold:

```objective-c
#import <UIKit/UIKit.h>
#import "MyCloudDocument.h"

@interface DemoiCloudViewController : UIViewController
<MyCloudDocumentDelegate>
{
    IBOutlet UITextField *txtContent;
    IBOutlet UITextView *txtFilesOniCloud;

    NSURL *documentiCloudPath;
    MyCloudDocument *myCloudDocument;
    NSMutableArray *documentURLs;
}

@property (nonatomic, retain) UITextField *txtContent;
```

```
@property (nonatomic, retain) UITextView *txtFilesOniCloud;
@property (nonatomic, retain) NSMetadataQuery *query;

-(IBAction) btnSave:(id)sender;
-(IBAction) createFileOniCloud:(id)sender;
-(IBAction) doneEditing:(id)sender;

- (NSURL *)ubiquitousDocumentsURL;
- (void)updateUbiquitousDocuments:(NSNotification *)notification;
- (void) searchFilesOniCloud;
- (void) displayAlert:(NSString *) title withmessage:(NSString *) msg;

@end
```

4. Back in Interface Builder, perform the following actions:

➤ Control-click the File's Owner item and drag it over the Text Field. Select `txtContent`.

➤ Control-click the File's Owner item and drag it over the Text View. Select `txtFilesOniCloud`.

➤ Control-click the Create File on iCloud button and drag it over the File's Owner item. Select `createFileOniCloud:`.

➤ Control-click the Save to file on iCloud button and drag it over the File's Owner item. Select `btnSave:`.

➤ Right-click on the Text Field and connect the Did End On Exit item to the File's Owner item. Select `doneEditing:`.

5. Right-click on the File's Owner item and you should see the connections as shown in Figure 12-8.

6. In the `DemoiCloudViewController.m` file, add the following lines in bold:

FIGURE 12-8

```
#import "DemoiCloudViewController.h"

@implementation DemoiCloudViewController

@synthesize txtContent, txtFilesOniCloud;
@synthesize query = _query;

NSString *FILENAME = @"MyFile.txt";

-(IBAction)doneEditing:(id)sender {
    [sender resignFirstResponder];
}

- (void) displayAlert:(NSString *) title withmessage:(NSString *) msg {
    UIAlertView *alert =
        [[UIAlertView alloc] initWithTitle:title
                                   message:msg
                                  delegate:self
                         cancelButtonTitle:@"OK"
```

```
                            otherButtonTitles: nil];
    [alert show];
    [alert release];
}

//---get the root URL for the iCloud storage's Documents folder---
- (NSURL *)ubiquitousDocumentsURL {
    //---use the string that you added earlier when setting the
    // entitlement for the iCloud container---
    return
    [[[NSFileManager defaultManager] URLForUbiquityContainerIdentifier:
      @"6LNSVE9D8J.net.learn2develop.DemoiCloud"]
     URLByAppendingPathComponent:@"Documents"];
}




//---search for files on iCloud---
-(void) searchFilesOniCloud {
    NSURL *ubiquitousDocumentsURL = [self ubiquitousDocumentsURL];
    if (ubiquitousDocumentsURL) {
        NSMetadataQuery *query = [[[NSMetadataQuery alloc] init] autorelease];
        query.predicate = [NSPredicate predicateWithFormat:@"%K like '*'",
                                NSMetadataItemFSNameKey];
        query.searchScopes = [NSArray arrayWithObject:
                                    NSMetadataQueryUbiquitousDocumentsScope];
        [query startQuery];
        self.query = query;
    } else {
        [self displayAlert:@"iCloud"
                withmessage:@"iCloud storage not enabled on this device.
Please enable it and try again."];
    }
}

//---called when there are changes to the files in iCloud---
- (void)updateUbiquitousDocuments:(NSNotification *)notification {
    [documentURLs removeAllObjects];
    txtFilesOniCloud.text = @"";

    for (NSMetadataItem *item in self.query.results) {
        NSURL *url = [item valueForAttribute:NSMetadataItemURLKey];
        NSLog(@"%@", [url absoluteString]);

        //---add the URL of the document to the array---
        if (![documentURLs containsObject:(url)]) {
            [documentURLs addObject:url];
            txtFilesOniCloud.text = [txtFilesOniCloud.text
                stringByAppendingFormat:@"%@\n",[url absoluteString]];
        }
    }
}

//---content of the document from iCloud is retrieved---
- (void)documentContentsDidUpdate:(MyCloudDocument *)document {
```

```objc
        txtContent.text = document.contents;
}

-(IBAction)createFileOniCloud:(id)sender {
    //---get the path of the Documents folder in iCloud (local)---
    documentiCloudPath = [self ubiquitousDocumentsURL];

    //---create the full pathname for document to sync to iCloud---
    documentiCloudPath = [documentiCloudPath
                            URLByAppendingPathComponent:FILENAME];

    //---create the UIDocument document---
    myCloudDocument =
        [[MyCloudDocument alloc] initWithFileURL:documentiCloudPath];
    myCloudDocument.delegate = self;

    //---check if the document already exists on iCloud---
    if ([documentURLs containsObject:(documentiCloudPath)]) {
        [self displayAlert:@"Document exists on iCloud"
                withmessage:@"Document already exists on iCloud. Retrieving
it..."];

        //---open the existing file---
        [myCloudDocument openWithCompletionHandler:^(BOOL success) {}];
    } else {
        [self displayAlert:@"Creating Document on iCloud"
                withmessage:@"Document is currently being created on iCloud."];
        //---save the content---
        myCloudDocument.contents = txtContent.text;
        [myCloudDocument updateChangeCount:UIDocumentChangeDone];
    }
}

-(IBAction) btnSave:(id)sender {
    //---save the content---
    myCloudDocument.contents = txtContent.text;
    [myCloudDocument updateChangeCount:UIDocumentChangeDone];
}

- (void)viewDidLoad {
    //---used for storing the filenames of files in iCloud---
    documentURLs = [[NSMutableArray alloc] init];

    //---register for notifications; used for searching of files on iCloud---
    [[NSNotificationCenter defaultCenter]
        addObserver:self
          selector:@selector(updateUbiquitousDocuments:)
              name:NSMetadataQueryDidFinishGatheringNotification
            object:nil];
    [[NSNotificationCenter defaultCenter]
        addObserver:self
          selector:@selector(updateUbiquitousDocuments:)
              name:NSMetadataQueryDidUpdateNotification
            object:nil];

    //---search for all the files in iCloud---
```

```
    [self searchFilesOniCloud];

    [super viewDidLoad];
}
```

7. You are now ready to deploy the application on two iOS devices to see if it works. For illustration purposes, I have deployed the application onto an iPhone and an iPad.

8. On the iPhone, first type some text into the Text Field. Then tap on the Create File on iCloud button to save the file on iCloud. Because this is the first time you are saving this file onto iCloud, you will see the alert shown in Figure 12-9.

9. A little later (about 10-15 seconds typically), the Text View will display the path of the document (see Figure 12-10). This proves that the file has been saved successfully. Note that the path points to a location on your local device, indicating that the file is saved there. The UIDocument subclass takes care of synchronizing all the documents saved in this folder to iCloud.

10. On the iPad, the application automatically displays the path of the file saved on iCloud (see Figure 12-11).

FIGURE 12-9

FIGURE 12-10

FIGURE 12-11

11. Tap on the Create File on iCloud button. Because the file already exists on iCloud, you will see the alert shown in Figure 12-12. Click OK to dismiss the alert.

12. You will now see the content of the file displayed in the Text Field (see Figure 12-13). The content of the file has been fetched from iCloud.

FIGURE 12-12

FIGURE 12-13

13. Tap on the Text Field and type some text into it (see Figure 12-14). Tap on the Save to file on iCloud button to save the changes to the file on iCloud.

14. On the iPhone, after a while (typically 10-15 seconds), you will see that the change made on the iPad is now displayed automatically in the Text Field (see Figure 12-15).

FIGURE 12-14

FIGURE 12-15

How It Works

To create documents in iCloud, you first create a variable of type `MyCloudDocument` (which is a subclass of `UIDocument`):

```
MyCloudDocument *myCloudDocument;
```

You also create an `NSMutableArray` object to store all the files that are found on iCloud:

```
//---used for storing the filenames of files in iCloud---
documentURLs = [[NSMutableArray alloc] init];
```

When the application starts, you first register for two notifications — one for searching (which you will see next) and one for getting updates when documents are updated:

```
//---register for notifications; used for searching of files on iCloud---
[[NSNotificationCenter defaultCenter]
    addObserver:self
        selector:@selector(updateUbiquitousDocuments:)
            name:NSMetadataQueryDidFinishGatheringNotification
          object:nil];
[[NSNotificationCenter defaultCenter]
    addObserver:self
        selector:@selector(updateUbiquitousDocuments:)
            name:NSMetadataQueryDidUpdateNotification
          object:nil];
```

When new files are found on iCloud or when changes are found on files on iCloud, the `updateUbiquitousDocuments:` method is called.

Then you search for all the files on your iCloud directory:

```
//---search for all the files in iCloud---
[self searchFilesOniCloud];
```

The `searchForFilesOniCloud` method first calls the `ubiquitousDocumentsURL` method to obtain the URL for your iCloud's `Documents` folder:

```
//---search for files on iCloud---
-(void) searchFilesOniCloud {
    NSURL *ubiquitousDocumentsURL = [self ubiquitousDocumentsURL];
    if (ubiquitousDocumentsURL) {
        NSMetadataQuery *query = [[[NSMetadataQuery alloc] init] autorelease];
        query.predicate = [NSPredicate predicateWithFormat:@"%K like '*'",
                              NSMetadataItemFSNameKey];
        query.searchScopes = [NSArray arrayWithObject:
                                 NSMetadataQueryUbiquitousDocumentsScope];
        [query startQuery];
        self.query = query;
    } else {
        [self displayAlert:@"iCloud"
             withmessage:@"iCloud storage not enabled on this device.
Please enable it and try again."];
    }
}
```

The `ubiquitousDocumentsURL` method calls the `URLForUbiquityContainerIdentifier:` method of the `NSFileManager` object using the string that you added earlier when setting the entitlement for the iCloud container(note the `TEAM ID`, which you can obtain from Figure 12-2) of the `NSFileManager` object to obtain the user's iCloud directory. It then appends the `Documents` folder to this directory and returns it:

```
//---get the root URL for the iCloud storage's Documents folder---
- (NSURL *)ubiquitousDocumentsURL
{
    return
    [[[NSFileManager defaultManager] URLForUbiquityContainerIdentifier:
        @"6LNSVE9D8J.net.learn2develop.DemoiCloud"]
            URLByAppendingPathComponent:@"Documents"];
}
```

You are free to create additional directories inside the iCloud directory, but Apple recommends that you create a `Documents` folder inside it to store the user's documents. One benefit of doing so is that the all the files stored inside the `Documents` folder will be exposed via Settings ⇨ iCloud ⇨ Storage & Backup ⇨ Manage Storage on the user's device. Users will then be able to delete these files directly through the Settings application.

The path of the iCloud's Documents folder looks like this: `/private/var/mobile/Library/ Mobile Documents/6LNSVE9D8J~net~learn2develop~DemoiCloud/Documents/`. Note that this is a path on your local device. All the files that you want to save on iCloud are saved in this directory. The `UIDocument` class takes care of moving the documents to iCloud, synchronizing the changes, and so on. If iCloud is not enabled or the entitlement string supplied is not correct, the `URLForUbiquityContainerIdentifier:` method will return `nil`.

Continuing with the search, you create an `NSMetadataQuery` object to search for all files in the `Documents` folder of the iCloud container. You use the `NSMetadataQueryUbiquitousDocumentsScope` constant to search for files in the `Documents` folder; if you want to search for files elsewhere, you should use the `NSMetadataQueryUbiquitousDataScope` constant:

```
    if (ubiquitousDocumentsURL) {
        NSMetadataQuery *query = [[[NSMetadataQuery alloc] init] autorelease];
        query.predicate = [NSPredicate predicateWithFormat:@"%K like '*'",
                            NSMetadataItemFSNameKey];
        query.searchScopes = [NSArray arrayWithObject:
                                    NSMetadataQueryUbiquitousDataScope];
        [query startQuery];
        self.query = query;
    } else {
        [self displayAlert:@"iCloud"
                withmessage:@"iCloud storage not enabled on this device.
Please enable it and try again."];
    }
```

To start the search, you use the `startQuery` method. When files are found on the iCloud container, the `updateUbiquitousDocuments:` method is called:

```
//---called when there are changes to the files in iCloud---
- (void)updateUbiquitousDocuments:(NSNotification *)notification {
```

```
        [documentURLs removeAllObjects];
        txtFilesOniCloud.text = @"";

        for (NSMetadataItem *item in self.query.results) {
            NSURL *url = [item valueForAttribute:NSMetadataItemURLKey];
            NSLog(@"%@", [url absoluteString]);

            //---add the URL of the document to the array---
            if (![documentURLs containsObject:(url)]) {
                [documentURLs addObject:url];
                txtFilesOniCloud.text = [txtFilesOniCloud.text
                    stringByAppendingFormat:@"%@\n",[url absoluteString]];
            }
        }
    }
```

Here, you simply add the file paths of each document found in the search result into the array and then display the path on the Text View.

To create a document on iCloud, you instantiate the `MyCloudDocument` class and pass it the full URL of the document you want to create:

```
-(IBAction)createFileOniCloud:(id)sender {
    //---get the path of the Documents folder in iCloud (local)---
    documentiCloudPath = [self ubiquitousDocumentsURL];

    //---create the full pathname for document to sync to iCloud---
    documentiCloudPath = [documentiCloudPath
                            URLByAppendingPathComponent:FILENAME];

    //---create the UIDocument document---
    myCloudDocument =
        [[MyCloudDocument alloc] initWithFileURL:documentiCloudPath];
    myCloudDocument.delegate = self;

    //---check if the document already exists on iCloud---
    if ([documentURLs containsObject:(documentiCloudPath)]) {
        [self displayAlert:@"Document exists on iCloud"
                withmessage:@"Document already exists on iCloud. Retrieving
it..."];

        //---open the existing file---
        [myCloudDocument openWithCompletionHandler:^(BOOL success) {}];
    } else {
        [self displayAlert:@"Creating Document on iCloud"
                withmessage:@"Document is currently being created on iCloud."];
        //---save the content---
        myCloudDocument.contents = txtContent.text;
        [myCloudDocument updateChangeCount:UIDocumentChangeDone];
    }
}
```

If the document you want to create already exists in the iCloud container, you open it using the `openWithCompletionHandler:` method. This method opens and reads the content of the file asynchronously. If the file does not exist, you assign its content with the value of the Text File. You then call the `updateChangeCount:` method of the `UIDocument` to signal that there are changes to your document so that `UIDocument` can make the changes to iCloud.

To save changes to a file, you simply modify the `contents` property of the `MyCloudDocument` instances and then call the `updateChangeCount:` method:

```
-(IBAction) btnSave:(id)sender {
    //---save the content---
    myCloudDocument.contents = txtContent.text;
    [myCloudDocument updateChangeCount:UIDocumentChangeDone];
}
```

When your document is modified in iCloud, the `documentContentsDidUpdate:` method is called:

```
//---content of the document from iCloud is retrieved---
- (void)documentContentsDidUpdate:(MyCloudDocument *)document {
    txtContent.text = document.contents;
}
```

In this case, you simply display the updated content in the Text Field. To confirm that the document is created in iCloud, go to your device and examine the Settings ➪ iCloud ➪ Storage & Backup ➪ Manage Storage page (see Figure 12-16). Tapping on the Documents & Data item will display the file `MyFile.txt`, which was created by your application. If you want to delete the file, you can tap on the Edit button.

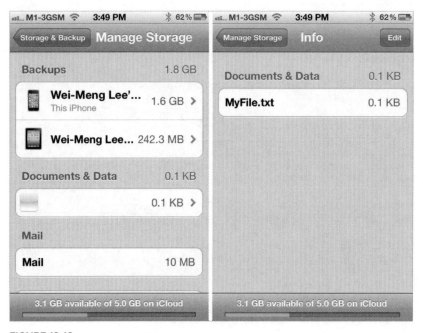

FIGURE 12-16

STORING KEY-VALUE DATA IN ICLOUD

In Chapter 9, you learned about the use of the NSUserDefaults class to save user's preferences data in the Settings application. You do so via the use of key-value pairs, which can be simple data types like numbers, strings, arrays, and so on. However, data stored using the NSUserDefaults class is available only to the application on that particular device; if you have the same application on multiple devices, these values cannot be shared. Imagine you are writing an eBook reader application that runs on both the iPhone and iPad platforms. Users may install your application on multiple devices. When they stop reading at a particular page on their iPhone, they might want to continue from where they left off by reading it on their iPad later. In this case, there must be a way for the application on both devices to retrieve the user's last page number. Of course, you could devise your own server solution whereby the application can sync the information back to the server, but that would mean you have to write an additional application (such as JSON web services, or a socket server).

Fortunately, besides saving user documents, you can use iCloud to save small chunks of information so that the same application running on different devices can share them. It does impose some restrictions, most of which should not be a major problem for most applications. Using iCloud, you can save key-value data with the following restrictions:

➤   The maximum amount of space in a key-value store is 64KB.

➤   The maximum size of a single key is 4KB.

The following Try It Out demonstrates how you can store key-value data on iCloud. It uses the same project you created in the previous section of this chapter.

TRY IT OUT   **Using iCloud to Store Key-Value Data**

1.   Using the project created in the previous section, add the following lines in bold to the DemoiCloudViewController.h file:

```
- (void)viewDidLoad {
    //---used for storing the filenames of files in iCloud---
    documentURLs = [[NSMutableArray alloc] init];

    //---register for notifications; used for searching of files on iCloud---
    [[NSNotificationCenter defaultCenter]
        addObserver:self
          selector:@selector(updateUbiquitousDocuments:)
              name:NSMetadataQueryDidFinishGatheringNotification
            object:nil];
    [[NSNotificationCenter defaultCenter]
        addObserver:self
          selector:@selector(updateUbiquitousDocuments:)
              name:NSMetadataQueryDidUpdateNotification
            object:nil];

    //---search for all the files in iCloud---
    [self searchFilesOniCloud];

    //---get the ubiquitous key store from iCloud---
    NSUbiquitousKeyValueStore *keyValue =
```

```
        [NSUbiquitousKeyValueStore defaultStore];

    NSString *lastUsed = [keyValue stringForKey:@"lastUsed"];
    if ([lastUsed length]>0) {
        [self displayAlert:@"Last Used"
                withmessage:[NSString stringWithFormat:
                    @"Application was last used on: %@", lastUsed]];
    }

    //---get the current date and time---
    NSDate *currentDateTime = [NSDate date];
    NSDateFormatter *dateFormatter =
        [[[NSDateFormatter alloc] init] autorelease];
    [dateFormatter setDateFormat:@"yyyy-MM-dd HH:mm:ss"];
    NSString *dateInString = [dateFormatter stringFromDate:currentDateTime];

    //---save the current date and time---
    [keyValue setString:dateInString forKey:@"lastUsed"];
    [keyValue synchronize];

    [super viewDidLoad];
}
```

2. Deploy the application onto the iPad, wait a few seconds (e.g., 20 seconds) and then deploy onto the iPhone. When the application loads onto the iPhone, you will see the alert shown in Figure 12-17, indicating the date and time when the application was last used.

FIGURE 12-17

How It Works

In order to store key-value data on the iCloud, you need to specify the string for the iCloud key-value Store in your entitlements file, which you have done earlier in this chapter. This string is represented by the `com.apple.developer.ubiquity-kvstore-identifier` key:

```
<?xml version="1.0" encoding="UTF-8"?>
<!DOCTYPE plist PUBLIC "-//Apple//DTD PLIST
1.0//EN" "http://www.apple.com/DTDs/PropertyList-1.0.dtd">
<plist version="1.0">
<dict>
<key>com.apple.developer.ubiquity-container-identifiers</key>
<array>
<string>$(TeamIdentifierPrefix)net.learn2develop.DemoiCloud</string>
</array>
<key>com.apple.developer.ubiquity-kvstore-identifier</key>
<string>$(TeamIdentifierPrefix)net.learn2develop.DemoiCloud</string>
<key>keychain-access-groups</key>
<array>
<string>$(AppIdentifierPrefix)net.learn2develop.DemoiCloud</string>
</array>
</dict>
</plist>
```

To store key-value data on iCloud, you first need to obtain an instance of the NSUbiquitousKeyValueStore object:

```
//---get the ubiquitous key store from iCloud---
NSUbiquitousKeyValueStore *keyValue =
    [NSUbiquitousKeyValueStore defaultStore];
```

To retrieve the string value of a key, you use the stringForKey: method:

```
NSString *lastUsed = [keyValue stringForKey:@"lastUsed"];
if ([lastUsed length]>0) {
    [self displayAlert:@"Last Used"
          withmessage:[NSString stringWithFormat:
              @"Application was last used on: %@", lastUsed]];
}
```

Besides using the stringForKey: method, you can also use the following methods for other data types:

➤ arrayForKey:

➤ boolForKey:

➤ dataForKey:

➤ dictionaryForKey:

➤ doubleForKey:

➤ longLongForKey:

➤ objectForKey:

To store string key-value data, use the setString:forKey: method:

```
[keyValue setString:dateInString forKey:@"lastUsed"];
[keyValue synchronize];
```

To synchronize the changes back to iCloud, use the synchronize method. To store key-value data of other data types, you can also use the following methods:

➤ setArray:forKey:

➤ setBool:forKey:

➤ setData:forKey:

➤ setDictionary:forKey:

➤ setDouble:forKey:

➤ setLongLong:forKey:

➤ setObject:forKey:

➤ setString:forKey:

While the NSUbiquitousKeyValueStore class performs an almost identical service to that of the NSUserDefaults class, it should not be used as a replacement for it. Try to save all application-specific data to the local device using the NSUserDefaults class first. Only then do you make a copy on iCloud using the NSUbiquitousKeyValueStore class. This enables your application to always have a copy of the application's data regardless of whether the user has network connectivity or whether he or she has enabled iCloud.

SUMMARY

In this chapter, you had a good look at how you can store your documents and data on iCloud. Using iCloud, you can automatically synchronize your documents and data across applications running on multiple devices. Best of all, the iOS SDK provides the UIDocument class, which provides all the heavy-lifting needed to ensure that documents are synced and updated correctly, thus leaving you with more time to develop your application.

EXERCISES

1. Name the method you can use to obtain the path of your iCloud storage container.

2. What is the advantage of saving your documents in the Documents folder of your iCloud storage container?.

3. What is the advantage of storing key-value data on iCloud?

Answers to the exercises can be found in Appendix D.

▶ **WHAT YOU LEARNED IN THIS CHAPTER**

TOPIC	KEY CONCEPTS
Two main uses for iCloud	Use for document storage and data storage.
Setting entitlements for iCloud	Set the iCloud Containers entitlement and the iCloud Key-Value Store entitlement.
Managing iCloud documents	Subclass the `UIDocument` class.

Methods to implement in subclass of `UIDocument`	The three methods are:
	`initWithFileURL:`
	`loadFromContents:ofType:error:`
	`contentsForType:error:`

Create a `Documents` folder in iCloud to store your documents	Doing so allows users to manage the files directly through the Settings application.
Storing key-value data on iCloud	Use the `NSUbiquitousKeyValueStore` class.

13

Performing Simple Animations and Video Playback

Up to this point, the applications you have written have all made use of the standard views provided by the iOS SDK. As Apple has reiterated, the iPhone is not just for serious work; it is also a gaming platform.

In this chapter, you have some fun creating something visual. You learn how to perform some simple animations using a timer object and then perform some transformations on a view. Although it is beyond the scope of this book to show you how to create animations using OpenGL ES, this chapter does demonstrate some interesting techniques that you can use to make your applications come alive. In addition, you will also learn how to play back a video in your iPhone application.

USING THE NSTIMER CLASS

One of the easiest ways to get started with animation is to use the NSTimer class. The NSTimer class creates timer objects, which enable you to call a method at a regular time interval. Using an NSTimer object, you can update the position of an image at regular time intervals, thereby creating the impression that it is being animated.

In the following Try It Out, you learn how to display a bouncing ball on the screen using the NSTimer class. When the ball touches the sides of the screen, it bounces off in the opposite direction. You also learn how to control the frequency with which the ball animates. Download the code files indicated for this and other Try It Out features within this chapter.

TRY IT OUT   Animating a Ball

codefile Animation.zip is available for download at Wrox.com

1. Using Xcode, create a new Single View Application (iPhone) project and name it **Animation**. You will also use the project name as the Class Prefix and ensure that you have the Use Automatic Reference Counting option unchecked.

2. Drag and drop an image named tennisball.jpg to the Supporting Files folder in Xcode. When the Add dialog appears, check the Copy Item into the Destination Group's Folder (If Needed) option so that the image is copied into the project (see Figure 13-1).

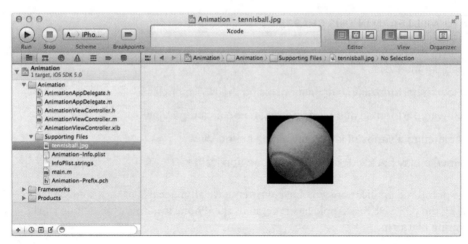

FIGURE 13-1

3. Select the AnimationViewController.xib file to edit it in Interface Builder.

4. Drag and drop an Image View onto the View window and set its Image property to tennisball .jpg (see Figure 13-2).

Ensure that the size of the Image View accommodates the entire tennis ball image. Later, you will move the Image View on the screen, so it is important not to fill the entire screen with the Image View.

5. Select the View (outside the Image View) and change the background color to black (see Figure 13-3).

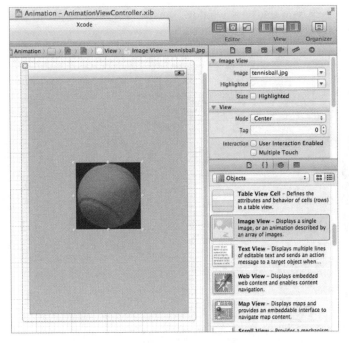

FIGURE 13-2

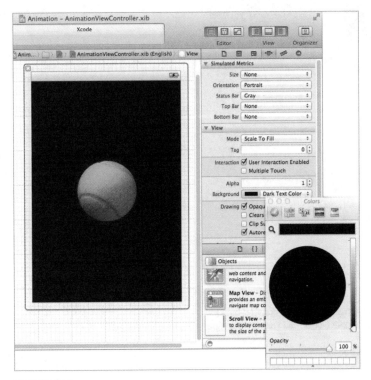

FIGURE 13-3

6. Add a Label and a Slider from the Library onto the View window (see the lower-left corner of Figure 13-4). Set the Current property of the Slider view to 0.01.

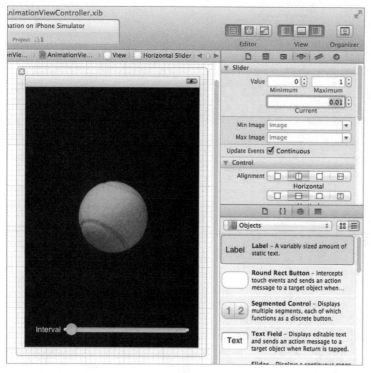

FIGURE 13-4

7. In the AnimationViewController.h file, declare the following outlets, fields, and actions (shown in bold):

```objc
#import <UIKit/UIKit.h>

@interface AnimationViewController : UIViewController
{
    IBOutlet UIImageView *imageView;
    IBOutlet UISlider *slider;

    CGPoint delta;
    NSTimer *timer;
    float ballRadius;
}

@property (nonatomic, retain) UIImageView *imageView;
@property (nonatomic, retain) UISlider *slider;

-(IBAction) sliderMoved:(id) sender;

@end
```

8. Back in Interface Builder, connect the outlets and actions as follows (see Figure 13-5 for the connections after all the outlets and actions are connected):

> ➤ Control-click and drag the File's Owner item to the Image View and select `imageView`.

> ➤ Control-click and drag the File's Owner item to the Slider and select `slider`.

> ➤ Control-click and drag the Slider to the File's Owner item and select `sliderMoved:`.

9. Add the following bold statements to the `AnimationViewController.m` file:

FIGURE 13-5

```objc
#import "AnimationViewController.h"

@implementation AnimationViewController

@synthesize imageView;
@synthesize slider;

-(void) onTimer {
    imageView.center = CGPointMake(imageView.center.x + delta.x,
                                   imageView.center.y + delta.y);

    if (imageView.center.x > self.view.bounds.size.width - ballRadius ||
        imageView.center.x < ballRadius)
        delta.x = -delta.x;

    if (imageView.center.y > self.view.bounds.size.height - ballRadius ||
        imageView.center.y < ballRadius)
        delta.y = -delta.y;
}

- (void) viewDidLoad {
    ballRadius = imageView.bounds.size.width / 2;
    [slider setShowValue:YES];
    delta = CGPointMake(12.0,4.0);
    timer = [NSTimer scheduledTimerWithTimeInterval:slider.value
                                             target:self
                                           selector:@selector(onTimer)
                                           userInfo:nil
                                            repeats:YES];
    [super viewDidLoad];
}

-(IBAction) sliderMoved:(id) sender {
    [timer invalidate];
    timer = [NSTimer scheduledTimerWithTimeInterval:slider.value
                                             target:self
```

```
                                        selector:@selector(onTimer)
                                        userInfo:nil
                                         repeats:YES];
    }

    - (void)dealloc {
        [timer invalidate];
        [imageView release];
        [slider release];
        [super dealloc];
    }
```

10. Press Command-R to test the application on the iPhone Simulator. The tennis ball should now be animated on the screen (see Figure 13-6). Vary the speed of the animation by moving the slider — to the right to slow it down and to the left to speed it up.

How It Works

When the view is loaded, the first thing you do is get the radius of the tennis ball, which in this case is half the width of the image:

```
    ballRadius = imageView.bounds.size.width / 2;
```

This value is used during the animation to check whether the tennis ball has touched the edges of the screen.

FIGURE 13-6

To set the slider to show its value, you used the setShowValue: method:

```
    [slider setShowValue:YES];
```

> **NOTE** The setShowValue: method is undocumented; hence, the compiler will sound a warning. Be forewarned that using any undocumented methods may result in your application being rejected when you submit it to Apple for approval. In general, use undocumented methods only for debugging purposes.

You also initialized the delta variable:

```
    delta = CGPointMake(12.0,4.0);
```

The delta variable is used to specify how many pixels the image must move every time the timer fires. The preceding code tells it to move 12 points horizontally and 4 points vertically.

You next called the scheduledTimerWithTimeInterval:target:selector:userInfo:repeats: class method of the NSTimer class to create a new instance of the NSTimer object:

```
    timer = [NSTimer scheduledTimerWithTimeInterval:slider.value
                                target:self
```

```
selector:
    @selector(onTimer)
userInfo:nil
 repeats:YES];
```

The `scheduledTimerWithTimeInterval:` parameter specifies the number of seconds between firings of the timer. Here, you set it to the value of the Slider view, which accepts a value from 0.0 to 1.0. For example, if the slider's value is 0.5, the timer object will fire every half-second.

The `selector:` parameter specifies the method to call when the timer fires, and the `repeats:` parameter indicates whether the timer object will repeatedly reschedule itself. In this case, when the timer fires, it calls the `onTimer` method, which you defined next.

In the `onTimer` method, you changed the position of the Image View by setting its `center` property to a new value. After repositioning, you checked whether the image touched the edges of the screen; if it has, the value of the `delta` variable is negated:

```
-(void) onTimer {
    imageView.center = CGPointMake(imageView.center.x + delta.x,
                                   imageView.center.y + delta.y);
    if (imageView.center.x >
            self.view.bounds.size.width - ballRadius ||
        imageView.center.x < ballRadius)
        delta.x = -delta.x;

    if (imageView.center.y >
            self.view.bounds.size.height - ballRadius ||
        imageView.center.y < ballRadius)
        delta.y = -delta.y;
}
```

When you move the slider, the `sliderMoved:` method is called. In this method, you first invalidated the timer object and then created another instance of the `NSTimer` class:

```
-(IBAction) sliderMoved:(id) sender {
    [timer invalidate];
    timer = [NSTimer scheduledTimerWithTimeInterval:slider.value
                                  target:self
                                  selector:
                                      @selector(onTimer)
                                  userInfo:nil
                                   repeats:YES];
}
```

Moving the slider enables you to change the frequency at which the image is animated.

NOTE *After an* NSTimer *object is started, you cannot change its firing interval. The only way to change the interval is to invalidate the current object and create a new* NSTimer *object.*

Animating the Visual Change

You may have noticed that as you move the slider toward the right, the animation slows and becomes choppy. To make the animation smoother, you can animate the visual changes by using one of the *block-based animation* methods. One such block-based animation method is the `animateWithDuration:delay:options:animations:completion:` class method of the `UIView` class:

```
[UIView animateWithDuration:slider.value
                delay:0.0f
              options:UIViewAnimationOptionAllowUserInteraction |
                      UIViewAnimationOptionCurveLinear
           animations:^{
               imageView.center = CGPointMake(imageView.center.x + delta.x,
                                              imageView.center.y + delta.y);
           }
           completion:nil];
```

The preceding code performs the specified animations immediately using the `UIViewAnimationOptionCurveLinear` (constant speed) and `UIViewAnimationOptionAllowUserInteraction` (allows the user to interact with the views while they are being animated) animation options. This results in a much smoother animation.

TRANSFORMING VIEWS

You can use the `NSTimer` class to simulate a simple animation by continuously changing the position of the Image View, but you can also use the transformation techniques supported by the iOS SDK to achieve the same effect.

Transforms are defined in Core Graphics (a C-based API that is based on the Quartz advanced drawing engine; you use this framework to handle things such as drawings, transformations, image creation, etc.), and the iOS SDK supports standard affine 2D transforms. You can use the iOS SDK to perform the following affine 2D transforms:

➤ **Translation** — Moves the origin of the view by the amount specified using the *x* and *y* axes

➤ **Rotation** — Moves the view by the angle specified

➤ **Scaling** — Changes the scale of the view by the *x* and *y* factors specified

> **NOTE** *An* affine transformation *is a linear transformation that preserves co-linearity and ratio of distances. This means that all the points lying on a line initially will remain in a line after the transformation, with the respective distance ratios between them maintained.*

Figure 13-7 shows the effects of the various transformations.

Translation

To perform an affine transform on a view, simply use its `transform` property. Recall that in the previous example, you set the new position of the view through its `center` property:

```
imageView.center = CGPointMake(imageView.center.x + delta.x,
                               imageView.center.y + delta.y);
```

Translated

Rotated

Scaled

FIGURE 13-7

Using 2D transformation, you can use its `transform` property and set it to a `CGAffineTransform` data structure returned by the `CGAffineTransformMakeTranslation()` function, like this:

```
//---add the following bold line in the AnimationViewController.h file---
#import <UIKit/UIKit.h>

@interface AnimationViewController : UIViewController
{
    IBOutlet UIImageView *imageView;
    IBOutlet UISlider *slider;
    CGPoint delta;
    NSTimer *timer;
```

```
    float ballRadius;

    //---add this line---
    CGPoint translation;
}

@property (nonatomic, retain) UIImageView *imageView;
@property (nonatomic, retain) UISlider *slider;

-(IBAction) sliderMoved:(id) sender;

@end


//---add the following bold lines in the AnimationViewController.m file---
- (void)viewDidLoad {
    ballRadius = imageView.bounds.size.width / 2;
    [slider setShowValue:YES];
    delta = CGPointMake(12.0,4.0);

    translation = CGPointMake(0.0,0.0);

    timer = [NSTimer scheduledTimerWithTimeInterval:slider.value
                                    target:self
                                  selector:@selector(onTimer)
                                  userInfo:nil
                                   repeats:YES];
    [super viewDidLoad];
}

-(void) onTimer {
    [UIView animateWithDuration:slider.value
                          delay:0.0f
                        options:UIViewAnimationOptionAllowUserInteraction |
                                UIViewAnimationOptionCurveLinear
                     animations:^{
        imageView.transform =
            CGAffineTransformMakeTranslation(translation.x, translation.y);
                     }
                     completion:nil];

    translation.x += delta.x;
    translation.y += delta.y;

    if (imageView.center.x + translation.x >
        self.view.bounds.size.width - ballRadius ||
        imageView.center.x + translation.x < ballRadius)
        delta.x = -delta.x;

    if (imageView.center.y + translation.y >
        self.view.bounds.size.height - ballRadius ||
        imageView.center.y + translation.y < ballRadius)
        delta.y = -delta.y;
}
```

The `CGAffineTransformMakeTranslation()` function takes two arguments: the value to move for the *x* axis and the value to move for the *y* axis.

The preceding code achieves the same effect as setting the `center` property of the Image View.

Rotation

The rotation transformation enables you to rotate a view using the angle you specify. In the following Try It Out, you modify the code from the previous example so that the tennis ball rotates as it bounces across the screen.

TRY IT OUT   Rotating the Tennis Ball

1. In the `AnimationViewController.h` file, add the declaration for the `angle` variable as shown in bold:

    ```
    #import <UIKit/UIKit.h>

    @interface AnimationViewController : UIViewController
    {
        IBOutlet UIImageView *imageView;
        IBOutlet UISlider *slider;
        CGPoint delta;
        NSTimer *timer;
        float ballRadius;

        CGPoint translation;

        //---add this line---
        float angle;
    }

    @property (nonatomic, retain) UIImageView *imageView;
    @property (nonatomic, retain) UISlider *slider;

    -(IBAction) sliderMoved:(id) sender;

    @end
    ```

2. In the `AnimationViewController.m` file, add the following bold statements:

    ```
    - (void)viewDidLoad {

        //--set the angle to 0--
        angle = 0;

        ballRadius = imageView.bounds.size.width / 2;
        [slider setShowValue:YES];
        delta = CGPointMake(12.0,4.0);

        translation = CGPointMake(0.0,0.0);

        timer = [NSTimer scheduledTimerWithTimeInterval:slider.value
    ```

```
                                                    target:self
                                              selector:@selector(onTimer)
                                              userInfo:nil
                                               repeats:YES];
        [super viewDidLoad];
    }

    -(void) onTimer {
        [UIView animateWithDuration:slider.value
                              delay:0.0f
                            options:UIViewAnimationOptionAllowUserInteraction |
                                    UIViewAnimationOptionCurveLinear
                         animations:^{
            imageView.transform = CGAffineTransformMakeRotation(angle);
                            }
                         completion:nil];

        angle += 0.02;
        if (angle>6.2857) angle = 0;

        imageView.center = CGPointMake(imageView.center.x + delta.x,
                                       imageView.center.y + delta.y);

        if (imageView.center.x > self.view.bounds.size.width - ballRadius ||
            imageView.center.x < ballRadius)
            delta.x = -delta.x;

        if (imageView.center.y > self.view.bounds.size.height - ballRadius ||
            imageView.center.y < ballRadius)
            delta.y = -delta.y;
    }
```

3.   Press Command-R to test the application. The tennis ball now rotates as it bounces across the screen.

How It Works

To rotate a view, set its `transform` property using a `CGAffineTransform` data structure returned by the `CGAffineTransformMakeRotation()` function. The `CGAffineTransformMakeRotation()` function takes a single argument, which contains the angle to rotate (in radians). After each rotation, you increment the angle by 0.02:

```
    //—-rotation—-
    imageView.transform = CGAffineTransformMakeRotation(angle);
    ...
    angle += 0.02;
```

A full rotation takes 360 degrees, which works out to be 2PI radians (recall that PI is equal to 22/7, which is approximately 3.142857). If the angle exceeds 6.2857 (=2*3.142857), you reset `angle` to 0:

```
    if (angle>6.2857) angle = 0;
```

Interestingly, you can combine multiple transformations into one, using the `CGAffineTransformConcat` function:

```
[UIView animateWithDuration:slider.value
                  delay:0.0f
                options:UIViewAnimationOptionAllowUserInteraction |
                       UIViewAnimationOptionCurveLinear
             animations:^{
                 imageView.transform =
                     CGAffineTransformConcat(
                         CGAffineTransformMakeRotation(angle),
                         CGAffineTransformMakeTranslation(
                             translation.x, translation.y));
             }
             completion:nil];
```

The above code snippet applies a rotation and translation transformation to the Image View.

Scaling

To scale views, you use the `CGAffineTransformMakeScale()` function to return a `CGAffineTransform` data structure and set it to the `transform` property of the view:

```
imageView.transform = CGAffineTransformMakeScale(angle,angle);
```

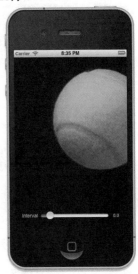

`CGAffineTransformMakeScale()` takes two arguments: the factor to scale for the *x* axis and the factor to scale for the *y* axis. For simplicity, I have used the `angle` variable for the scale factor for both the *x* and *y* axes.

If you modify the previous Try It Out with the preceding statement, the tennis ball gets bigger as it bounces on the screen (see Figure 13-8). It then resets back to its original size and grows again.

ANIMATING A SERIES OF IMAGES

So far, you have seen that you can use an Image View to display a static image. In addition, you can use it to display a series of images and then alternate between them.

The following Try It Out shows how this is done using an Image View.

FIGURE 13-8

TRY IT OUT | **Displaying a Series of Images**

codefile Animations2.zip is available for download at Wrox.com

1. Using Xcode, create a new Single View Application (iPhone) project and name it **Animations2**.

2. Add a series of images to the project by dragging and dropping them into the `Supporting Files` folder in Xcode. When the Add dialog appears, check the Copy Item into Destination Group's Folder (If Needed) option so that each of the images will be copied into the project. Figure 13-9 shows the images added.

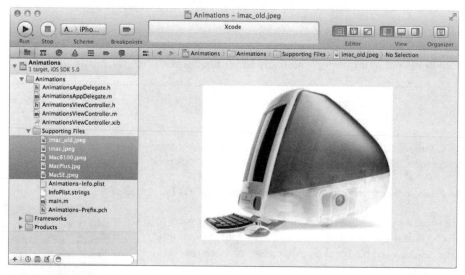

FIGURE 13-9

3. In the `Animations2ViewController.m` file, add the following bold statements:

```objc
- (void)viewDidLoad {
    NSArray *images = [NSArray arrayWithObjects:
                    [UIImage imageNamed:@"MacSE.jpeg"],
                    [UIImage imageNamed:@"imac.jpeg"],
                    [UIImage imageNamed:@"MacPlus.jpg"],
                    [UIImage imageNamed:@"imac_old.jpeg"],
                    [UIImage imageNamed:@"Mac8100.jpeg"],
                    nil];

    CGRect frame = CGRectMake(0,0,320,460);
    UIImageView *imageView = [[UIImageView alloc] initWithFrame:frame];
    imageView.animationImages = images;
    imageView.contentMode = UIViewContentModeScaleAspectFit;

    //---seconds to complete one set of animation---
    imageView.animationDuration = 3;

    //---continuous---
```

```
    imageView.animationRepeatCount = 0;

    //---start the animation---
    [imageView startAnimating];

    //---add the image view to the View window---
    [self.view addSubview:imageView];

    [imageView release];
    [super viewDidLoad];
}
```

4. Press Command-R to view the series of images on the iPhone Simulator. The images are displayed in the Image View (see Figure 13-10), one at a time.

FIGURE 13-10

How It Works

You first created an NSArray object and initialized it with a few UIImage objects:

```
NSArray *images = [NSArray arrayWithObjects:
                    [UIImage imageNamed:@"MacSE.jpeg"],
                    [UIImage imageNamed:@"imac.jpeg"],
```

```
                     [UIImage imageNamed:@"MacPlus.jpg"],
                     [UIImage imageNamed:@"imac_old.jpeg"],
                     [UIImage imageNamed:@"Mac8100.jpeg"],
                     nil];
```

You then instantiated a `UIImageView` object:

```
          CGRect frame = CGRectMake(0,0,320,460);
          UIImageView *imageView = [[UIImageView alloc] initWithFrame:frame];
```

To get the Image View to display the series of images, you had to set its `animationImages` property to the `images` object. You also set the display mode of the Image View:

```
          imageView.animationImages = images;
          imageView.contentMode = UIViewContentModeScaleAspectFit;
```

To control how fast the images are displayed, you set the `animationDuration` property to a value. This value indicates the number of seconds it takes the Image View to display one complete set of images. The `animationRepeatCount` property enables you to specify how many times you want the animation to occur. Set it to 0 if you want it to be displayed indefinitely:

```
          //---seconds to complete one set of animation---
          imageView.animationDuration = 3;

          //---continuous---
          imageView.animationRepeatCount = 0;
```

Finally, you started the animation by calling the `startAnimating` method. You also needed to add the Image View to the View window by calling the `addSubView:` method:

```
          //---start the animation---
          [imageView startAnimating];

          //---add the image view to the View window---
          [self.view addSubview:imageView];
```

Note that the animation technique described in this section is suitable for a moderate number of animating objects. For more complex animation, you might want to explore OpenGL ES.

PLAYING VIDEO ON THE IPHONE

Playing videos is one of the most commonly performed tasks on the iPhone. Prior to iOS 4 for the iPhone, all videos had to be played full-screen. However, starting with iOS 4, this rule has been relaxed; you can now embed videos within your iPhone applications. This makes it possible for you to embed more than one video in any View window. This section shows you how to enable video playback in your iPhone applications.

Enabling Video Playback

codefile PlayVideo.zip is available for download at Wrox.com

1. Using Xcode, create a new Single View Application (iPhone) project and name it `PlayVideo`. You will also use the project name as the Class Prefix and ensure that you have the Use Automatic Reference Counting option unchecked.

2. Drag a sample video into the Supporting Files folder of your Xcode project (see Figure 13-11).

FIGURE 13-11

3. Double-click on the project name in Xcode and select the PlayVideo target. Select the Build Phases tab on the right and expand the section Link Binary With Libraries (3 items). Click the "+" button (see Figure 13-12).

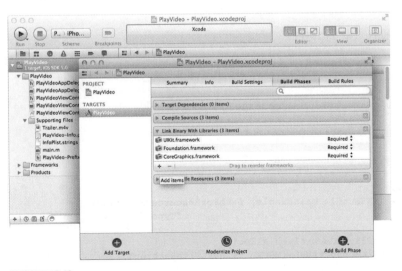

FIGURE 13-12

4. Select `MediaPlayer.framework` to add it to your project (see Figure 13-13).

FIGURE 13-13

5. In the `PlayVideoViewController.h` file, code the following in bold:

```
#import <UIKit/UIKit.h>
#import <MediaPlayer/MediaPlayer.h>

@interface PlayVideoViewController : UIViewController
{
    MPMoviePlayerController *player;
}

@end
```

6. In the `PlayVideoViewController.m` file, code the following in bold:

```
#import "PlayVideoViewController.h"

@implementation PlayVideoViewController

- (void)viewDidLoad {
    NSString *url = [[NSBundle mainBundle] pathForResource:@"Trailer"
                                                    ofType:@"m4v"];

    player = [[MPMoviePlayerController alloc]
                initWithContentURL:[NSURL fileURLWithPath:url]];

    [[NSNotificationCenter defaultCenter]
```

```
            addObserver:self
                selector:@selector(movieFinishedCallback:)
                    name:MPMoviePlayerPlaybackDidFinishNotification
                  object:player];

    //---set the size of the movie view and then add it to the View window---
    player.view.frame = CGRectMake(10, 10, 300, 300);
    [self.view addSubview:player.view];

    //---play movie---
    [player play];
    [super viewDidLoad];
}

//---called when the movie is done playing---
- (void) movieFinishedCallback:(NSNotification*) aNotification {
    MPMoviePlayerController *moviePlayer = [aNotification object];
    [[NSNotificationCenter defaultCenter]
        removeObserver:self
                  name:MPMoviePlayerPlaybackDidFinishNotification
                object:moviePlayer];
    [moviePlayer.view removeFromSuperview];
    [player release];
}
```

7. To test the application on the iPhone Simulator, press Command-R. Figure 13-14 shows the movie playing on the iPhone Simulator.

8. Click the movie and you will be able to display the movie full-screen. Figure 13-15 shows two different scenes from the same movie; the one on the right is shown in full-screen width.

FIGURE 13-14

FIGURE 13-15

How It Works

Basically, you used the `MPMoviePlayerController` class to control the playback of a video:

```
player = [[MPMoviePlayerController alloc]
            initWithContentURL:[NSURL fileURLWithPath:url]];
```

You then used the `NSNotificationCenter` class to register a notification so that when the movie is done playing (i.e., it ends), the `movieFinishedCallback:` method can be called:

```
[[NSNotificationCenter defaultCenter]
    addObserver:self
        selector:@selector(movieFinishedCallback:)
            name:MPMoviePlayerPlaybackDidFinishNotification
          object:player];
```

To display the movie on the View window, you set the size of the movie, added its `view` property to the View window, and then played it:

```
//—set the size of the movie view and then add it to the View window—
player.view.frame = CGRectMake(10, 10, 300, 300);
[self.view addSubview:player.view];

//—play movie—
[player play];
```

When the movie stops playing, you should unregister the notification, remove the movie, and then release the `player` object:

```
//—called when the movie is done playing—
- (void) movieFinishedCallback:(NSNotification*) aNotification {
    MPMoviePlayerController *moviePlayer = [aNotification object];
    [[NSNotificationCenter defaultCenter]
        removeObserver:self
                name:MPMoviePlayerPlaybackDidFinishNotification
              object:moviePlayer];
    [moviePlayer.view removeFromSuperview];
    [player release];
}
```

The `MPMoviePlayerController` class can play any movie or audio files (both fixed-length or streamed content) supported in iOS. Typical file extensions supported are: .mov, .mp4, .mpv, and .3GP.

SUMMARY

In this chapter, you have seen the usefulness of the `NSTimer` class and how it can help you perform some simple animations. You have also learned about the various affine transformations supported by the iOS SDK. Next, you learned how the Image View enables you to animate a series of images at a regular time interval. Last, but not least, you learned how to play back a video in your iPhone application.

EXERCISES

1. Name the three affine transformations supported by the iPhone SDK.

2. How do you pause an `NSTimer` object and then resume it?

3. What is the purpose of enclosing your block of code using the `animateWithDuration:delay:options:animations:completion:` method of the `UIView` class, as shown in the following code snippet?

```
[UIView animateWithDuration:slider.value
                delay:0.0f
              options:UIViewAnimationOptionAllowUserInteraction |
                      UIViewAnimationOptionCurveLinear
           animations:^{
               //---code to effect visual change---
           }
           completion:nil];
```

4. Name the class that you can use for video playback.

Answers to the exercises can be found in Appendix D.

▶ WHAT YOU LEARNED IN THIS CHAPTER

TOPIC	KEY CONCEPTS
| **Using the `NSTimer` object to create timers** | Create a timer object that will call the `onTimer` method every half-second:<br><br>```
timer = [NSTimer scheduledTimerWithTimeInterval: 0.5
                   target:self
                   selector:@selector(onTimer)
                   userInfo:nil
                   repeats:YES];
``` |
| **Stopping the `NSTimer` object** | `[timer invalidate];` |
| **Animating visual changes** | ```
[UIView animateWithDuration:slider.value
        animations:^{
  //---code to effect visual change---
}];
``` |
Performing affine transformations	Use the `transform` property of the view.
Translation	Use the `CGAffineTransformMakeTranslation()` function to return a `CGAffineTransform` data structure and set it to the `transform` property.
Rotation	Use the `CGAffineTransformMakeRotation()` function to return a `CGAffineTransform` data structure and set it to the `transform` property.
Scaling	Use the `CGAffineTransformMakeScale()` function to return a `CGAffineTransform` data structure and set it to the `transform` property.
Animating a series of images using an Image View	Set the `animationImages` property to an array containing `UIImage` objects. Set the `animationDuration` property. Set the `animationRepeatCount` property. Call the `startAnimating` method.
Playing back a video	Use the `MPMoviePlayerController` class.

14

Accessing Built-In Applications

WHAT YOU WILL LEARN IN THIS CHAPTER

➤ How to send e-mails from within your application

➤ Invoking Safari from within your application

➤ How to invoke the phone from within your application

➤ How to send SMS messages from within your application

➤ Accessing the camera and Photo Library

The iPhone comes with a number of built-in applications that make it one of the most popular mobile devices of all time. Some of these applications are Mail, Phone, Safari, SMS, and Calendar. These applications perform most of the tasks you would expect from a mobile phone. As an iPhone developer, you can also programmatically invoke these applications from within your application using the various APIs provided by the iOS SDK.

In this chapter, you learn how to invoke some of the built-in applications that are bundled with the iPhone, as well as how to interact with them from within your iPhone application.

SENDING E-MAIL

Sending e-mail is one of the many tasks performed by iPhone users. Sending e-mail on the iPhone is accomplished using the built-in Mail application, which is a rich HTML mail client that supports POP3, IMAP, and Exchange e-mail systems, and most web-based e-mail such as Yahoo! and Gmail.

There are times where you need to allow your user to send an e-mail message in your iPhone application. A good example is embedding a feedback button in your application that users can click to send feedback to you directly. You have two ways to send e-mail programmatically:

➤ Build your own e-mail client and implement all the necessary protocols necessary to communicate with an e-mail server.

➤ Invoke the built-in Mail application and ask it to send the e-mail for you.

Unless you are well versed in network communications and familiar with all the e-mail protocols, your most logical choice is the second option — invoke the Mail application to do the job. The following Try It Out shows you how.

TRY IT OUT Sending E-Mail Using the Mail Application

Codefile [Emails.zip] is available for download at Wrox.com

1. Using Xcode, create a Single View Application (iPhone) project and name it **Emails**. You need to also use the project name as the Class Prefix and ensure that you have the Use Automatic Reference Counting option unchecked.

2. Select the `EmailsViewController.xib` file to edit it in Interface Builder. Populate the View window with the following views (see Figure 14-1):

➤ `Label`

➤ `TextField`

➤ `TextView` (remember to delete the sample text inside the view)

➤ `Button`

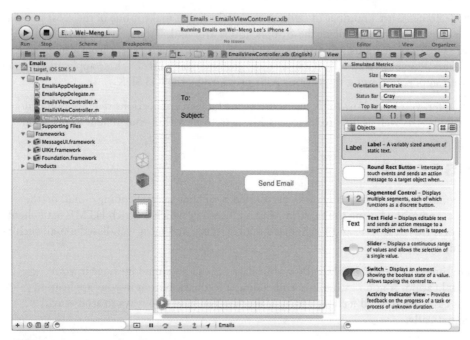

FIGURE 14-1

3. Insert the following statements in bold into the `EmailsViewController.h` file:

```
#import <UIKit/UIKit.h>

@interface EmailsViewController : UIViewController
{
    IBOutlet UITextField *to;
    IBOutlet UITextField *subject;
    IBOutlet UITextView *body;
}

@property (nonatomic, retain) UITextField *to;
@property (nonatomic, retain) UITextField *subject;
@property (nonatomic, retain) UITextView *body;

-(IBAction) btnSend: (id) sender;

@end
```

4. Back in Interface Builder, Control-click and drag the File's Owner item to each of the three views (the two Text Field and oneText View) and select to, subject, and body, respectively.

5. Control-click and drag the Round Rect Button to the File's Owner item and select btnSend:.

6. Insert the following code in bold into the `EmailsViewController.m` file:

```
#import "EmailsViewController.h"

@implementation EmailsViewController

@synthesize to, subject, body;

- (void) sendEmailTo:(NSString *) toStr
        withSubject:(NSString *) subjectStr
            withBody:(NSString *) bodyStr {

    NSString *emailString =
        [[NSString alloc] initWithFormat:@"mailto:?to=%@&subject=%@&body=%@",
            [toStr stringByAddingPercentEscapesUsingEncoding: NSASCIIStringEncoding],
            [subjectStr stringByAddingPercentEscapesUsingEncoding:NSASCIIStringEncoding],
            [bodyStr stringByAddingPercentEscapesUsingEncoding:NSASCIIStringEncoding]];

    [[UIApplication sharedApplication] openURL:[NSURL URLWithString:emailString]];
    [emailString release];
}

-(IBAction) btnSend: (id) sender{
    [self sendEmailTo:to.text withSubject:subject.text withBody:body.text];
}

- (void)dealloc {
    [to release];
    [subject release];
    [body release];
    [super dealloc];
}
```

7. Press Command-R to test the application on a real iPhone. Figure 14-2 shows the application in action. After you have filled in the TextFields and TextView with the necessary information, click the Send button to invoke the Mail application and fill it with all the information you have typed in your application. Clicking the Send button in Mail sends the e-mail.

FIGURE 14-2

How It Works

The magic of invoking the Mail application lies in the string that you create in the `sendEmailTo:withSubject:withBody:` method that you have defined:

```
NSString *emailString =
    [[NSString alloc] initWithFormat:@"mailto:?to=%@&subject=%@&body=%@",
        [toStr stringByAddingPercentEscapesUsingEncoding: NSASCIIStringEncoding],
        [subjectStr stringByAddingPercentEscapesUsingEncoding:NSASCIIStringEncoding],
        [bodyStr stringByAddingPercentEscapesUsingEncoding:NSASCIIStringEncoding]];
```

Basically, this is a URL string with the `mailto:` protocol indicated. The various parameters, such as `to`, `subject`, and `body`, are inserted into the string. Note that you use the `stringByAddingPercentEscapesUsingEncoding:` method of the `NSString` class to encode the various parameters with the correct percent escapes so that the result is a valid URL string.

To invoke the Mail application, simply call the `sharedApplication` method to return the singleton application instance and then use the `openURL:` method to invoke the Mail application:

```
[[UIApplication sharedApplication] openURL:[NSURL URLWithString:emailString]];
```

 NOTE *Remember that this example works only on a real device. Testing it on the iPhone Simulator will not work. Appendix A discusses how to prepare your iPhone for testing.*

The downside of using this approach is that when you tap the Send button, the application is pushed to the background when the Mail application takes over. When the e-mail is sent, you have to manually bring the application to the foreground again; otherwise, it will not appear. To compose the e-mail from within your application and then get the Mail application to send it for you, you can use the `MFMailComposeViewController` class. The following Try It Out shows how this can be done.

TRY IT OUT **Sending E-Mail without Leaving the Application**

1. Using the same project created in the previous Try It Out, add a new Round Rect button to the `EmailViewController.xib` file (see Figure 14-3).

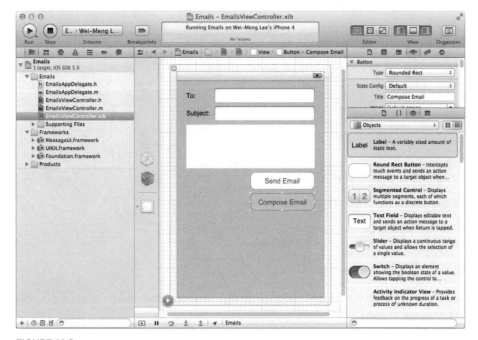

FIGURE 14-3

2. In Xcode, add the `MessageUI.framework` file to your project (see Figure 14-4).

FIGURE 14-4

 NOTE *If you are not familiar with how to add a framework to your project, please refer to Appendix B for more details.*

3. Add the following statement in bold to the `EmailsViewController.h` file:

```objc
#import <UIKit/UIKit.h>
#import <MessageUI/MFMailComposeViewController.h>

@interface EmailsViewController : UIViewController
<MFMailComposeViewControllerDelegate>
{
    IBOutlet UITextField *to;
    IBOutlet UITextField *subject;
    IBOutlet UITextView *body;
}

@property (nonatomic, retain) UITextField *to;
@property (nonatomic, retain) UITextField *subject;
@property (nonatomic, retain) UITextView *body;

-(IBAction) btnSend: (id) sender;
-(IBAction) btnComposeEmail: (id) sender;

@end
```

4. In Interface Builder, Control-click and drag the Compose E-mail button over the File's Owner item. Select `btnComposeEmail:`.

5. Add the following statement in bold to the `EmailsViewController.m` file:

```
#import "EmailsViewController.h"

@implementation EmailsViewController

@synthesize to, subject, body;

-(IBAction) btnComposeEmail: (id) sender {
    MFMailComposeViewController *picker =
    [[MFMailComposeViewController alloc] init];
    picker.mailComposeDelegate = self;

    [picker setSubject:@"Email subject here"];
    [picker setMessageBody:@"Email body here" isHTML:NO];
    [self presentModalViewController:picker animated:YES];
    [picker release];
}

- (void)mailComposeController:(MFMailComposeViewController*)controller
        didFinishWithResult:(MFMailComposeResult)result
                    error:(NSError*)error {
    [controller dismissModalViewControllerAnimated:YES];
}
```

6. Press Command-R to test the application on a real iPhone. Like the previous Try It Out, you will see the Mail application's compose screen (see Figure 14-5). However, unlike the previous example, when the e-mail is sent, control is returned to the application.

FIGURE 14-5

How It Works

The `MFMailComposeViewController` class presents the window for composing a message modally and does not cause the current application to go into the background. This is very useful when you want to resume with the current application after the e-mail has been sent.

Invoking Safari

If you want to invoke the Safari web browser on your iPhone, you can also make use of a URL string and then use the `openURL:` method of the application instance, like this:

```
[[UIApplication sharedApplication]
    openURL:[NSURL URLWithString: @"http://www.apple.com"]];
```

The preceding code snippet invokes Safari to open the `www.apple.com` page (see Figure 14-6).

Invoking the Phone

To make a phone call using the iPhone's phone dialer, use the following URL string:

```
[[UIApplication sharedApplication]
    openURL:[NSURL URLWithString: @"tel:1234567890"]];
```

The preceding statement invokes the dialer of the iPhone using the phone number specified.

FIGURE 14-6

 NOTE *The preceding statement works only for the iPhone, not the iPod touch, of course, because the iPod touch does not have phone capabilities. Also, you would need to use a real device to test this out; the code does not have an effect on the iPhone Simulator. Appendix A discusses how to prepare your iPhone for testing.*

Invoking SMS

You can also use a URL string to send SMS messages using the SMS application:

```
[[UIApplication sharedApplication]
    openURL:[NSURL URLWithString: @"sms:1234567890"]];
```

The preceding statement invokes the SMS application (see Figure 14-7). Note that the current application will be sent to the background.

FIGURE 14-7

 NOTE As noted in the preceding section, this statement works only for the iPhone, not the iPod touch, because the iPod touch does not have a phone, and therefore messaging capabilities. Also, you would need to use a real device to test this out; the code does not have an effect on the iPhone Simulator. Appendix A discusses how to prepare your iPhone for testing.

Just like sending e-mail messages, you can also send SMS messages without leaving your application. The following Try It Out shows how to do this.

TRY IT OUT Sending SMS Messages without Leaving Your Application

1. Using the previous project, `Emails`, add the following statements in bold to the `EmailsViewController.h` file:

```
#import <UIKit/UIKit.h>
#import <MessageUI/MFMailComposeViewController.h>
#import <MessageUI/MFMessageComposeViewController.h>

@interface EmailsViewController : UIViewController
<MFMailComposeViewControllerDelegate,
```

```
    MFMessageComposeViewControllerDelegate> {
        IBOutlet UITextField *to;
        IBOutlet UITextField *subject;
        IBOutlet UITextView *body;
    }

    @property (nonatomic, retain) UITextField *to;
    @property (nonatomic, retain) UITextField *subject;
    @property (nonatomic, retain) UITextView *body;

    -(IBAction) btnSend: (id) sender;
    -(IBAction) btnComposeEmail: (id) sender;
    -(IBAction) btnComposeSMS: (id) sender;

    @end
```

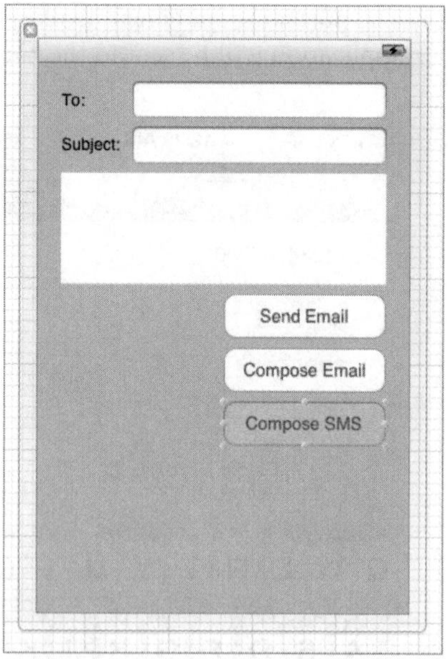

2. Add a Round Rect Button to the View window in the EmailsViewController.xib file (see Figure 14-8).

3. Add the following statements in bold to the EmailsViewController.m file:

```
    #import "EmailsViewController.h"

    @implementation EmailsViewController

    @synthesize to, subject, body;

    -(IBAction) btnComposeSMS:(id)sender {
        MFMessageComposeViewController *picker =
        [[MFMessageComposeViewController alloc] init];
        picker.messageComposeDelegate = self;

        [picker setBody:@"This message sent from the application."];
        [self presentModalViewController:picker animated:YES];
        [picker release];
    }

    - (void)messageComposeViewController:(MFMessageComposeViewController *)controller
                    didFinishWithResult:(MessageComposeResult)result {
        [controller dismissModalViewControllerAnimated:YES];
    }
```

FIGURE 14-8

4. In Interface Builder, Control-click and drag the Compose SMS button over the File's Owner item. Select btnComposeSMS:.

5. Press Command-R to test the application on an iPhone device. You will be able to compose your SMS message. When the message is sent, control is returned to your application.

How It Works

The MFMessageComposeViewController class presents the SMS composer window modally and does not cause the current application to go into the background. This is very useful when you want to resume with the current application after the SMS message has been sent.

INTERCEPTING SMS MESSAGES

One of the most frequently requested features of the iOS SDK is the capability to intercept incoming SMS messages from within an iPhone application. Unfortunately, the current version of the SDK does not provide a means to do this.

Likewise, you cannot send SMS messages directly from within your application; the messages must be sent from the built-in SMS application itself. This requirement prevents rogue applications from sending SMS messages without the user's knowledge.

ACCESSING THE CAMERA AND THE PHOTO LIBRARY

The iPhone 4 (and 4S) (as well as the iPad 2) has a camera (in fact two – one front facing and one rear facing) that enables users to both take pictures and record videos. These pictures and videos are saved in the Photos application. As a developer, you have two options to manipulate the camera and to access the pictures and videos stored in the Photos application:

➤   You can invoke the camera to take pictures or record a video.

➤   You can invoke the Photos application to allow users to select a picture or video from the photo albums. You can then use the picture or video selected in your application.

Accessing the Photo Library

Every iOS device includes the Photos application, in which pictures are stored. Using the iOS SDK, you can use the `UIImagePickerController` class to programmatically display a UI that enables users to select pictures from the Photos application. The following Try It Out demonstrates how you can do that in your application.

TRY IT OUT   Accessing the Photos in the Photo Library

Codefile [PhotoLibrary.zip] is available for download at Wrox.com

1.   Using Xcode, create a Single View Application (iPhone) project and name it `PhotoLibrary`. You will also use the project name as the Class Prefix and ensure that you have the Use Automatic Reference Counting option unchecked.

2.   Select the `PhotoLibraryViewController.xib` file to edit it in Interface Builder.

3.   Populate the View window with the following views (see Figure 14-9):

➤   Round Rect Button

➤   ImageView

4.   In the Attributes Inspector window for the ImageView view, set the Mode to Aspect Fit (see Figure 14-10).

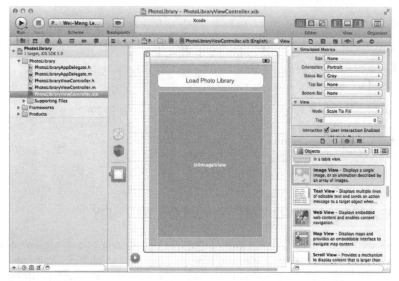

FIGURE 14-9

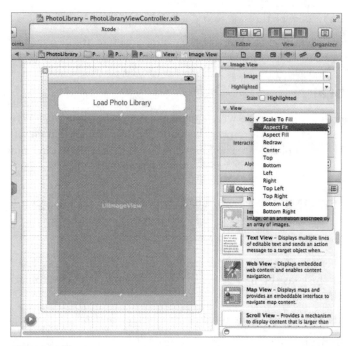

FIGURE 14-10

5. In the `PhotoLibraryViewController.h` file, insert the following statements that appear in bold:

```
#import <UIKit/UIKit.h>

@interface PhotoLibraryViewController : UIViewController
<UINavigationControllerDelegate,
```

```
    UIImagePickerControllerDelegate>
{
    IBOutlet UIImageView *imageView;
    UIImagePickerController *imagePicker;
}

@property (nonatomic, retain) UIImageView *imageView;

-(IBAction) btnClicked: (id) sender;

@end
```

6. Back in Interface Builder, Control-click and drag the File's Owner item to the ImageView view and select imageView.

7. Control-click and drag the Button view to the File's Owner item and select btnClicked:.

8. In the PhotoLibraryViewController.m file, insert the following statements that appear in bold:

```
#import "PhotoLibraryViewController.h"

@implementation PhotoLibraryViewController

@synthesize imageView;

- (void)viewDidLoad {
    imagePicker = [[UIImagePickerController alloc] init];
    [super viewDidLoad];
}

- (IBAction) btnClicked: (id) sender{
    imagePicker.delegate = self;
    imagePicker.sourceType =
    UIImagePickerControllerSourceTypePhotoLibrary;

    //---show the Image Picker---
    [self presentModalViewController:imagePicker animated:YES];
}

- (void)imagePickerController:(UIImagePickerController *)picker
didFinishPickingMediaWithInfo:(NSDictionary *)info {
    UIImage *image;
    NSURL *mediaUrl;
    mediaUrl = (NSURL *)[info valueForKey:
                        UIImagePickerControllerMediaURL];

    if (mediaUrl == nil) {
        image = (UIImage *) [info valueForKey:
                            UIImagePickerControllerEditedImage];
        if (image == nil) {
            //---original image selected---
            image = (UIImage *)
            [info valueForKey:UIImagePickerControllerOriginalImage];

            //---display the image---
            imageView.image = image;
```

```
        }
        else { //---edited image picked---
            //---get the cropping rectangle applied to the image---
            CGRect rect =
            [[info valueForKey:UIImagePickerControllerCropRect]
             CGRectValue];

            //---display the image---
            imageView.image = image;
        }
    }
    //---hide the Image Picker---
    [picker dismissModalViewControllerAnimated:YES];
}

- (void)imagePickerControllerDidCancel:(UIImagePickerController *)picker {
    //---user did not select image; hide the Image Picker---
    [picker dismissModalViewControllerAnimated:YES];
}

- (void)dealloc {
    [imageView release];
    [imagePicker release];
    [super dealloc];
}
```

9. Press Command-R to test the application on the iPhone Simulator.

10. When the application is loaded, tap the Load Photo Library button. The Photo Albums on the iPhone Simulator appear. Select a particular album (see Figure 14-11), and then select a picture. The selected picture will then be displayed on the ImageView view (see Figure 14-12).

FIGURE 14-11

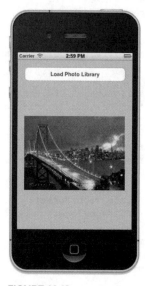

FIGURE 14-12

NOTE *Because the iPhone Simulator does not contain any built-in photo albums, you might not be able to test this application on the simulator. Thus, I suggest you test this on a real device. Appendix A discusses how to test your application on real devices.*

How It Works

Access to the Photo Library is provided by the UIImagePickerController class, which provides the UI for choosing and taking pictures and videos on your iPhone. All you need to do is create an instance of this class and provide a delegate that conforms to the UIImagePickerControllerDelegate protocol. In addition, your delegate must conform to the UINavigationControllerDelegate protocol because the UIImagePickerController class uses the Navigation Controller to enable users to select photos from the Photo Library. Therefore, you first needed to specify the protocols in PhotoLibraryViewController.h:

```
@interface PhotoLibraryViewController : UIViewController
    <UINavigationControllerDelegate,
    UIImagePickerControllerDelegate>
{
```

When the Load Library button is clicked, you set the type of picker interface displayed by the UIImagePickerController class and then display it modally:

```
- (IBAction) btnClicked: (id) sender{
    imagePicker.delegate = self;
    imagePicker.sourceType =
    UIImagePickerControllerSourceTypePhotoLibrary;
    //---show the Image Picker---
    [self presentModalViewController:imagePicker animated:YES];
}
```

Note that if you want the picture to be editable when the user chooses it, you can add the following statement:

```
    imagePicker.allowsEditing = YES;
```

By default, the source type is always UIImagePickerControllerSourceTypePhotoLibrary, but you can change it to one of the following:

➤ UIImagePickerControllerSourceTypeCamera — For taking photos directly with the camera

➤ UIImagePickerControllerSourceTypeSavedPhotosAlbum — For directly going to the Photo Albums application

When a picture has been selected by the user, the imagePickerController:didFinishPickingMediaWithInfo: event fires, which you handle by checking the type of media selected by the user:

```
- (void)imagePickerController:(UIImagePickerController *)picker
didFinishPickingMediaWithInfo:(NSDictionary *)info {
    UIImage *image;
```

```
    NSURL *mediaUrl;
    mediaUrl = (NSURL *)[info valueForKey:
                        UIImagePickerControllerMediaURL];

    if (mediaUrl == nil) {
        image = (UIImage *) [info valueForKey:
                            UIImagePickerControllerEditedImage];
      if (image == nil) {
          //---original image selected---
          image = (UIImage *)
          [info valueForKey:UIImagePickerControllerOriginalImage];

          //---display the image---
          imageView.image = image;
      }
       else { //---edited image picked---
           //---get the cropping rectangle applied to the image---
            CGRect rect =
            [[info valueForKey:UIImagePickerControllerCropRect]
            CGRectValue];

           //---display the image---
            imageView.image = image;
        }
    }
    //---hide the Image Picker---
    [picker dismissModalViewControllerAnimated:YES];
}
```

The type of media selected by the user is encapsulated in the `info:` parameter. You use the `valueForKey:` method to extract the appropriate media type and then typecast it to the respective type:

```
    mediaUrl = (NSURL *)
      [info valueForKey:UIImagePickerControllerMediaURL];
```

If the user cancels the selection, the `imagePickerControllerDidCancel:` event fires. In this case, you simply dismiss the Image Picker:

```
- (void)imagePickerControllerDidCancel:(UIImagePickerController *)
  picker {
    //---user did not select image; hide the Image Picker---
    [picker dismissModalViewControllerAnimated:YES];
}
```

Accessing the Camera

Besides accessing the Photo Library, you can also access the camera on your iPhone. Although accessing the hardware is the focus of the next chapter, this section takes a look at how to access the camera because it is also accomplished using the `UIImagePickerController` class.

In the following Try It Out, you modify the existing project created in the previous section. There isn't much to modify because most of the code you have written still applies.

TRY IT OUT   **Activating the Camera**

1.   Using the same project created in the previous section, edit the `PhotoLibraryViewController.m` file by changing the source type of the Image Picker to camera (see code highlighted in bold):

```
- (IBAction) btnClicked: (id) sender{
    imagePicker.delegate = self;

    //---comment this out---
    /*
    imagePicker.sourceType = UIImagePickerControllerSourceTypePhotoLibrary;
    */

    //---invoke the camera---
    imagePicker.sourceType = UIImagePickerControllerSourceTypeCamera;
    NSArray *mediaTypes =
        [NSArray arrayWithObjects:kUTTypeImage, nil];
    imagePicker.mediaTypes = mediaTypes;

    imagePicker.cameraCaptureMode = UIImagePickerControllerCameraCaptureModePhoto;
    imagePicker.allowsEditing = YES;

    //--show the Image Picker--
    [self presentModalViewController:imagePicker animated:YES];
}
```

2.   In the `PhotoLibraryViewController.m` file, define the following two methods:

```
- (NSString *) filePath: (NSString *) fileName {
    NSArray *paths =
        NSSearchPathForDirectoriesInDomains(
            NSDocumentDirectory, NSUserDomainMask, YES);
    NSString *documentsDir = [paths objectAtIndex:0];
    return [documentsDir stringByAppendingPathComponent:fileName];
}

- (void) saveImage{
    //---get the data from the ImageView---
    NSData *imageData =
    [NSData dataWithData:UIImagePNGRepresentation(imageView.image)];

    //---write the data to file---
    [imageData writeToFile:[self filePath:@"MyPicture.png"] atomically:YES];
}
```

3.   Insert the following statements that appear in bold:

```
- (void)imagePickerController:(UIImagePickerController *)picker
didFinishPickingMediaWithInfo:(NSDictionary *)info {
    UIImage *image;
    NSURL *mediaUrl;
    mediaUrl = (NSURL *)[info valueForKey:UIImagePickerControllerMediaURL];

    if (mediaUrl == nil) {
        image = (UIImage *) [info valueForKey:UIImagePickerControllerEditedImage];
```

```
        if (image == nil) {
            //---original image selected---
            image = (UIImage *)
            [info valueForKey:UIImagePickerControllerOriginalImage];

            //---display the image---
            imageView.image = image;
        }
        else { //---edited image picked---

            //---get the cropping rectangle applied to the image---
            CGRect rect =
                [[info valueForKey:UIImagePickerControllerCropRect]
                    CGRectValue];

            //---display the image---
            imageView.image = image;
        }
        //---save the image captured---
        [self saveImage];
    }
    //---hide the Image Picker---
    [picker dismissModalViewControllerAnimated:YES];
}
```

4. Press Command-R to test the application on a real iPhone.

5. Tap the Load Photo Library button. You can now use your iPhone's camera to take photos. Once a photo is taken (see Figure 14-13), the picture is saved to the Documents folder of your application.

FIGURE 14-13

How It Works

In this exercise you modified the source type of the Image Picker to camera:

```
imagePicker.sourceType = UIImagePickerControllerSourceTypeCamera;
```

When the camera takes a picture, the picture is passed back in the
`imagePickerController:didFinishPickingMediaWithInfo:` method and displayed in the
ImageView view. However, it is your responsibility to manually save the image to a location on the
phone. In this case, you defined the `filePath:` method to save the picture to the Documents folder of
your application:

```
- (NSString *) filePath: (NSString *) fileName {
    NSArray *paths =
        NSSearchPathForDirectoriesInDomains(
            NSDocumentDirectory, NSUserDomainMask, YES);
    NSString *documentsDir = [paths objectAtIndex:0];
    return [documentsDir stringByAppendingPathComponent:fileName];
}
```

The `saveImage:` method extracts the image data on the ImageView view and then calls the `filePath:`
method to save the data into a file named `MyPicture.png`:

```
- (void) saveImage{
    //---get the date from the ImageView---
    NSData *imageData =
    [NSData dataWithData:UIImagePNGRepresentation(imageView.image)];

    //---write the date to file---
    [imageData writeToFile:[self filePath:@"MyPicture.png"] atomically:YES];
}
```

 NOTE *By default on the iPhone 4 and iPhone 4S, the rear camera is
always activated when you use the* `UIImagePickerController` *class. If you
want to activate the front camera instead, you can set the* `cameraDevice`
property of the `UIImagePickerController` *class, which can be either of the
following values:* `UIImagePickerControllerCameraDeviceRear` *(default) or*
`UIImagePickerControllerCameraDeviceFront`*.*

Appendix A discusses how to prepare your iPhone for testing.

SUMMARY

In this chapter, you learned how you can easily integrate the various built-in applications into your
own iPhone applications. In particular, you saw how you can invoke the built-in SMS, Mail, Safari,
and Phone simply by using a URL string. In addition, you learned how to send SMS and e-mail

messages without leaving your application. You also learned about accessing the Photo Library applications using the classes provided by the iPhone SDK.

EXERCISES

1. Name the various URL strings for invoking the Safari, Mail, SMS, and Phone applications.

2. What is the class name for invoking the Image Picker UI in the iPhone?

3. What is the class name for invoking the Mail Composer UI in the iPhone?

4. What is the class name for invoking the Message Composer UI in the iPhone?

Answers to the exercises can be found in Appendix D.

▶ **WHAT YOU LEARNED IN THIS CHAPTER**

TOPIC	KEY CONCEPTS
Sending e-mail from within your application	`NSString` *emailString = `@"mailto:?to=user@email.com&subject=Subject&body=Body";` `[[UIApplication` sharedApplication] openURL:`[NSURL` URLWithString:emailString]];
Invoking Safari	`[[UIApplication` sharedApplication] openURL:`[NSURL` URLWithString: `@"http://www.apple.com"]];`
Invoking the Phone	`[[UIApplication` sharedApplication] openURL:`[NSURL` URLWithString: `@"tel:12345678*2"]];`
Invoking SMS	`[[UIApplication` sharedApplication] openURL:`[NSURL` URLWithString: `@"sms:12345678*2"]];`
Accessing the Photo Library	Use the `UIImagePickerController` class and ensure that your View Controller conforms to the `UINavigationControllerDelegate` protocol.
Invoking the Mail Composer UI	Use the `MFMailComposeViewController` class.
Invoking the Message Composer UI	Use the `MFMessageComposeViewController` class.

15

Accessing the Sensors

WHAT YOU WILL LEARN IN THIS CHAPTER

➤ How to obtain the gyroscope data from your iOS device

➤ How to obtain accelerometer data from your iOS device

➤ How to detect shakes to your device

Beginning with iPhone 4, Apple introduced a new gyroscopic sensor in addition to the original accelerometer sensor available since the first iPhone. Using the gyroscope, you can measure the device's angular acceleration around the x, y, and z axes. This enables you to accurately measure the yaw, pitch, and roll of the device. In addition to the gyroscope, the built-in accelerometer measures the linear acceleration of the device along the three axes. With these two sensors, your application can determine how far, how fast, and in which direction it is moving in space.

In this chapter, you learn how to access the gyroscope and accelerometer data and use the Shake API to detect shakes to your iPhone.

USING THE GYROSCOPE AND ACCELEROMETER

The gyroscope in an iOS device enables you to measure the device's angular acceleration around the x, y, and z axes. Figure 15-1 shows how this enables you to accurately measure the yaw, pitch, and roll of the device.

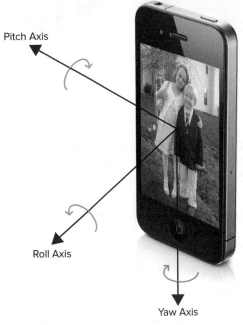

Pitch Axis

Roll Axis

Yaw Axis

FIGURE 15-1

The accelerometer in iOS devices measures the acceleration of the device relative to freefall. A value of 1 indicates that the device is experiencing 1 g of force exerted on it (1 g of force being the gravitational pull of the earth, which your device experiences when it is stationary). The accelerometer measures the acceleration of the device in three different axes: *x*, *y*, and *z*. Figure 15-2 shows the different axes measured by the accelerometer.

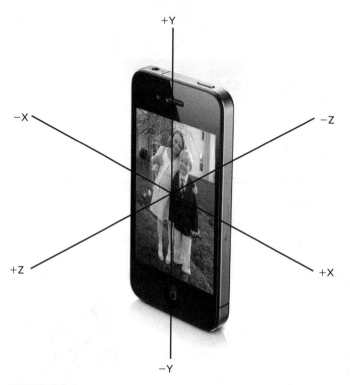

FIGURE 15-2

Table 15-1 shows example readings of the three axes when the device is in the various positions. Bear in mind that you won't see the exact same values as these, because they are always fluctuating due to the accelerometer's sensitivity.

TABLE 15-1: Example Readings of the X, Y, and Z Axes

POSITION	X	Y	Z
Vertical upright position	0.0	−1.0	0.0
Landscape left	1.0	0.0	0.0
Landscape right	−1.0	0.0	0.0

POSITION	X	Y	Z
Upside down	0.0	1.0	0.0
Flat up	0.0	0.0	−1.0
Flat down	0.0	0.0	1.0

If the iPhone is held upright and moved to the right quickly, the value of the *x*-axis will increase from 0 to a positive value. If it is moved to the left quickly, the value of the *x*-axis will decrease from 0 to a negative value. If the device is moved upward quickly, the value of the *y*-axis will increase from −1.0 to a larger value. If the device is moved downward quickly, the value of the *y*-axis will decrease from −1.0 to a smaller value.

If the device is horizontal and then moved downward, the value of the *z*-axis will decrease from −1.0 to a smaller number. If it is moved upward, the value of the *z*-axis will increase from −1.0 to a bigger number.

 NOTE *The accelerometer used on the iPhone gives a maximum reading of about +/− 2.3 g, with a resolution of about 0.018 g.*

In the iOS SDK, the device's accelerometer and gyroscope data are all encapsulated within the `CMMotionManager` class. The `CMMotionManager` class exposes a number of properties containing the accelerometer data, rotation-rate data, and other device-motion data such as attitude.

The following Try It Out shows you how you can use the `CMMotionManager` class to access the gyroscope and accelerometer of an iOS device.

TRY IT OUT Accessing the Gyroscope and Accelerometer Data

codefile Gyroscope.zip available for download at Wrox.com

1. Using Xcode, create a new Single View Application (iPhone) project and name it `Gyroscope`. Use the project name as the Class Prefix and ensure that you have the Use Automatic Reference Counting option unchecked.

2. Add the `CoreMotion.framework` to your project (see Figure 15-3).

3. In the `GyroscopeViewController.h` file, add the following statements that appear in bold:

```
#import <UIKit/UIKit.h>
#import <CoreMotion/CoreMotion.h>

@interface GyroscopeViewController : UIViewController
```

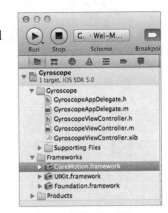

FIGURE 15-3

```
{
    IBOutlet UITextField *txtRoll;
    IBOutlet UITextField *txtPitch;
    IBOutlet UITextField *txtYaw;

    IBOutlet UITextField *txtX;
    IBOutlet UITextField *txtY;
    IBOutlet UITextField *txtZ;

    CMMotionManager *mm;
}

@property (nonatomic, retain) UITextField *txtRoll;
@property (nonatomic, retain) UITextField *txtPitch;
@property (nonatomic, retain) UITextField *txtYaw;

@property (nonatomic, retain) UITextField *txtX;
@property (nonatomic, retain) UITextField *txtY;
@property (nonatomic, retain) UITextField *txtZ;

@end
```

4. Select the `GyroscopeViewController.xib` file to edit it in Interface Builder.

5. Add the following views to the View window (see Figure 15-4):

➤ Label (name them as **Roll, Pitch, Yaw, x, y,** and **z**)

➤ TextField

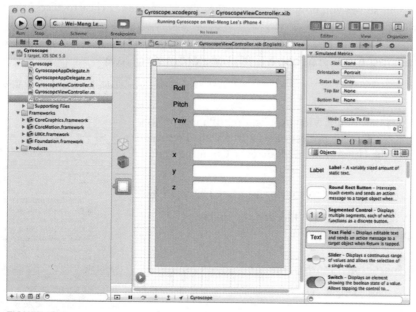

FIGURE 15-4

6. Connect the respective outlets to the TextField views by control-clicking the File's Owner item and dragging each outlet over each TextField.

7. In the `GyroscopeViewController.m` file, add the following statements that appear in bold:

```objc
#import "GyroscopeViewController.h"

@implementation GyroscopeViewController

@synthesize txtRoll;
@synthesize txtPitch;
@synthesize txtYaw;

@synthesize txtX;
@synthesize txtY;
@synthesize txtZ;

- (void)viewDidLoad
{
    mm = [[CMMotionManager alloc] init];
    if (mm.isDeviceMotionAvailable) {
        mm.deviceMotionUpdateInterval = 1.0/60.0;
        [mm startDeviceMotionUpdatesToQueue:[NSOperationQueue currentQueue]
                                withHandler:^(CMDeviceMotion *motion, NSError *error)
         {
             CMAttitude *currentAttitude = motion.attitude;
             float roll = currentAttitude.roll;
             float pitch = currentAttitude.pitch;
             float yaw = currentAttitude.yaw;

             txtRoll.text = [NSString stringWithFormat:@"%f",roll];
             txtPitch.text = [NSString stringWithFormat:@"%f",pitch];
             txtYaw.text = [NSString stringWithFormat:@"%f",yaw];

             CMAcceleration currentAcceleration = motion.userAcceleration;
             txtX.text = [NSString stringWithFormat:@"%f",currentAcceleration.x];
             txtY.text = [NSString stringWithFormat:@"%f",currentAcceleration.y];
             txtZ.text = [NSString stringWithFormat:@"%f",currentAcceleration.z];
         }];
    }
    [super viewDidLoad];
}

-(void) dealloc
{
    [txtRoll release];
    [txtPitch release];
    [txtYaw release];
    [txtX release];
    [txtY release];
    [txtZ release];
    [mm stopDeviceMotionUpdates];
    [super dealloc];
}
```

8. Debug the application on a real iPhone device by pressing Command-R. Figure 15-5 shows a snapshot of the values on the device as it is moved.

How It Works

As mentioned earlier, you use the `CMMotionManager` class to obtain the gyroscope data. Before you start obtaining the result, you should first check whether the device supports the gyroscope and accelerometer sensors:

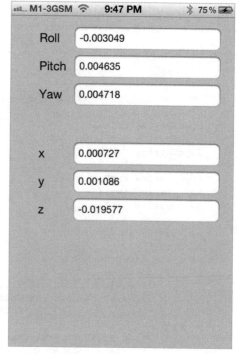

```
mm = [[CMMotionManager alloc] init];
if (mm.isDeviceMotionAvailable) {
    //...
}
```

Because all the iOS devices support the accelerometer, the preceding check is essentially confirming whether the gyroscope is available on the device.

Next, you set the interval in which the motion manager updates its data through the block handler defined in the `startDeviceMotionUpdatesToQueue:withHandler:` method:

FIGURE 15-5

```
mm.deviceMotionUpdateInterval = 1.0/60.0; //---in seconds---
[mm startDeviceMotionUpdatesToQueue:[NSOperationQueue currentQueue]
                        withHandler:^(CMDeviceMotion *motion, NSError *error)
{
    CMAttitude *currentAttitude = motion.attitude;
    float roll = currentAttitude.roll;
    float pitch = currentAttitude.pitch;
    float yaw = currentAttitude.yaw;

    txtRoll.text = [NSString stringWithFormat:@"%f",roll];
    txtPitch.text = [NSString stringWithFormat:@"%f",pitch];
    txtYaw.text = [NSString stringWithFormat:@"%f",yaw];

    CMAcceleration currentAcceleration = motion.userAcceleration;
    txtX.text = [NSString stringWithFormat:@"%f",currentAcceleration.x];
    txtY.text = [NSString stringWithFormat:@"%f",currentAcceleration.y];
    txtZ.text = [NSString stringWithFormat:@"%f",currentAcceleration.z];
}];
```

The `deviceMotionUpdateInterval` property specifies the interval in seconds — that is, the number of seconds between updates. In this case, you want the sensor data to be updated 60 times per second.

The block handler passes in a `CMDeviceMotion` object (`motion`), which encapsulates the measures of the attitude and acceleration of a device. The attitude of a device is its orientation relative to a given frame of reference. Essentially, the `attitude` object represents the roll, pitch, and yaw of a device. To obtain the accelerometer data, you use the `userAcceleration` structure of the `CMDeviceMotion` object.

Besides using the block handler, you could actually schedule an NSTimer object to read the sensors' values at regular time intervals. The preceding code could be rewritten as follows:

```
- (void)onTimer {
    CMAttitude *currentAttitude = mm.deviceMotion.attitude;
    float roll = currentAttitude.roll;
    float pitch = currentAttitude.pitch;
    float yaw = currentAttitude.yaw;

    txtRoll.text = [NSString stringWithFormat:@"%f",roll];
    txtPitch.text = [NSString stringWithFormat:@"%f",pitch];
    txtYaw.text = [NSString stringWithFormat:@"%f",yaw];

    CMAcceleration currentAcceleration = mm.deviceMotion.userAcceleration;
    txtX.text = [NSString stringWithFormat:@"%f",currentAcceleration.x];
    txtY.text = [NSString stringWithFormat:@"%f",currentAcceleration.y];
    txtZ.text = [NSString stringWithFormat:@"%f",currentAcceleration.z];
}

- (void)viewDidLoad
{
    mm = [[CMMotionManager alloc] init];
    if (mm.isDeviceMotionAvailable) {
        [NSTimer scheduledTimerWithTimeInterval:1.0/60.0
                                         target:self
                                       selector:@selector(onTimer)
                                       userInfo:nil
                                        repeats:YES];
        [mm startDeviceMotionUpdates];
    }
    [super viewDidLoad];
}
```

Here, you use the startDeviceMotionUpdates method to start the sensors. The onTimer method will be fired 60 times per second, and this is where you read the sensors' values.

VISUALIZING THE SENSOR DATA

Printing out the raw values of the gyroscope and accelerometer data is not very exciting. Instead, the following Try It Out shows you how to modify the application so that you can use the gyroscope data to move a soccer ball on the screen.

TRY IT OUT Visualizing the Gyroscope Data

1. Using the same project created in the previous section, add the CoreGraphics.framework to the project (see Figure 15-6).

2. Add an image of a soccer ball to the Supporting Files folder, as shown in Figure 15-7.

FIGURE 15-6

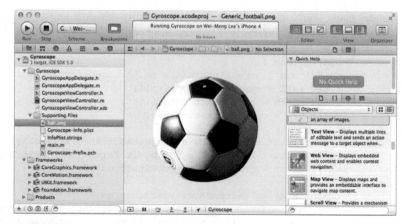

FIGURE 15-7

3. Select the `GyroscopeViewController.xib` file to edit it in Interface Builder.

4. Add an ImageView to the View window and set its `Image` attribute to `ball.png` (see Figure 15-8).

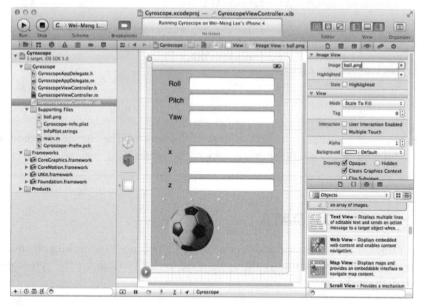

FIGURE 15-8

5. In the `GyroscopeViewController.h` file, add the following code in bold:

```
#import <UIKit/UIKit.h>
#import <CoreMotion/CoreMotion.h>

@interface GyroscopeViewController : UIViewController
```

```
{
    IBOutlet UITextField *txtRoll;
    IBOutlet UITextField *txtPitch;
    IBOutlet UITextField *txtYaw;

    IBOutlet UITextField *txtX;
    IBOutlet UITextField *txtY;
    IBOutlet UITextField *txtZ;

    CMMotionManager *mm;

    IBOutlet UIImageView *imageView;
    CGPoint delta;
    CGPoint translation;
    float ballRadius;
}

@property (nonatomic, retain) UITextField *txtRoll;
@property (nonatomic, retain) UITextField *txtPitch;
@property (nonatomic, retain) UITextField *txtYaw;

@property (nonatomic, retain) UITextField *txtX;
@property (nonatomic, retain) UITextField *txtY;
@property (nonatomic, retain) UITextField *txtZ;

@property (nonatomic, retain) UIImageView *imageView;

@end
```

6. In Interface Builder, Control-click and drag the File's Owner item over the Image View. Select imageView.

7. In the GyroscopeViewController.m file, add the following code in bold:

```
#import "GyroscopeViewController.h"

@implementation GyroscopeViewController

@synthesize txtRoll;
@synthesize txtPitch;
@synthesize txtYaw;

@synthesize txtX;
@synthesize txtY;
@synthesize txtZ;

@synthesize imageView;

- (void)viewDidLoad
{
    ballRadius = imageView.frame.size.width / 2;
    delta = CGPointMake(12.0,4.0);
    translation = CGPointMake(0.0,0.0);

    mm = [[CMMotionManager alloc] init];
```

```objc
    if (mm.isDeviceMotionAvailable) {
        mm.deviceMotionUpdateInterval = 1.0/60.0;
        [mm startDeviceMotionUpdatesToQueue:[NSOperationQueue currentQueue]
                        withHandler:^(CMDeviceMotion *motion, NSError *error)
        {
            CMAttitude *currentAttitude = motion.attitude;
            float roll = currentAttitude.roll;
            float pitch = currentAttitude.pitch;
            float yaw = currentAttitude.yaw;

            txtRoll.text = [NSString stringWithFormat:@"%f",roll];
            txtPitch.text = [NSString stringWithFormat:@"%f",pitch];
            txtYaw.text = [NSString stringWithFormat:@"%f",yaw];

            CMAcceleration currentAcceleration = motion.userAcceleration;
            txtX.text = [NSString stringWithFormat:@"%f",currentAcceleration.x];
            txtY.text = [NSString stringWithFormat:@"%f",currentAcceleration.y];
            txtZ.text = [NSString stringWithFormat:@"%f",currentAcceleration.z];

            //---animating the ball---
            if (currentAttitude.roll>0)
                delta.x = 2;
            else
                delta.x = -2;
            if (currentAttitude.pitch>0)
                delta.y = 2;
            else
                delta.y = -2;

            [UIView animateWithDuration:0.5
                        animations:^
            {
                imageView.transform =
                    CGAffineTransformMakeTranslation(
                        translation.x, translation.y);
            }];

            translation.x = translation.x + delta.x;
            translation.y = translation.y + delta.y;

            if (imageView.center.x + translation.x > 320 - ballRadius ||
                imageView.center.x + translation.x < ballRadius) {
                translation.x -= delta.x;
            }

            if (imageView.center.y + translation.y > 460 - ballRadius ||
                imageView.center.y + translation.y < ballRadius) {
                translation.y -= delta.y;
            }
        }];
    }
    [super viewDidLoad];
}

-(void) dealloc
```

```
{
    [txtRoll release];
    [txtPitch release];
    [txtYaw release];
    [txtX release];
    [txtY release];
    [txtZ release];
    [mm stopDeviceMotionUpdates];

    [imageView release];
    [super dealloc];
}

- (BOOL)shouldAutorotateToInterfaceOrientation:(UIInterfaceOrientation)
interfaceOrientation
{
    // Return YES for supported orientations
    return (interfaceOrientation == UIInterfaceOrientationPortrait);
}
```

8. Press Command-R to test the application on a real iPhone device. Observe that as you move the device, the ball moves in the same direction as your hand (see Figure 15-9).

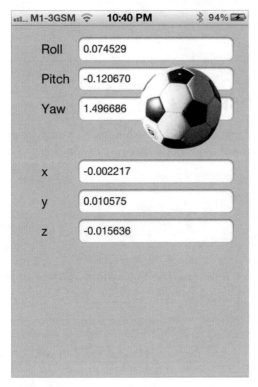

FIGURE 15-9

NOTE *If you test this on an iPhone4 and find that the update rate of 60Hz over-drives the UI, causing slow updates and image delays from changes in the gyroscope, drop the rate to 30hz. It should be more responsive.*

How It Works

This exercise enables you to visually examine the data reported by the gyroscope. In this case, only the roll and pitch data are used. The `delta` variable represents the amount to move, both in the *x*-axis and the *y*-axis.

To move the image, you apply a translation via the Image View's `transform` property:

```
[UIView animateWithDuration:0.5
                  animations:^
{
    imageView.transform =
        CGAffineTransformMakeTranslation(
            translation.x, translation.y);
}];
```

The `translation` variable keeps track of the current translation so that the image animates smoothly.

You also restricted the View window to only display upright in the portrait mode so that you can see the ball moving when you rotate the device.

USING THE SHAKE API TO DETECT SHAKES

Beginning with the iPhone OS 3, Apple introduced the Shake API, which helps your application to detect shakes to the device. In reality, this API comes in the form of three events that you can handle in your code:

➤ `motionBegan:`

➤ `motionEnded:`

➤ `motionCancelled:`

These three events are defined in the `UIResponder` class, which is the superclass of `UIApplication`, `UIView`, and its subclasses (including `UIWindow`). The following Try It Out shows you how to detect shakes to your device using these three events.

TRY IT OUT Using the Shake API

codefile Shake.zip available for download at Wrox.com

1. Using Xcode, create a new Single View Application (iPhone) project and name it **Shake**. You will also use the project name as the Class Prefix and ensure that you have the Use Automatic Reference Counting option unchecked.

2. Select the `ShakeViewController.xib` file to edit it in Interface Builder.

3. Populate the View window with the following views (the result will look like Figure 15-10):

➤ TextField

➤ DatePicker

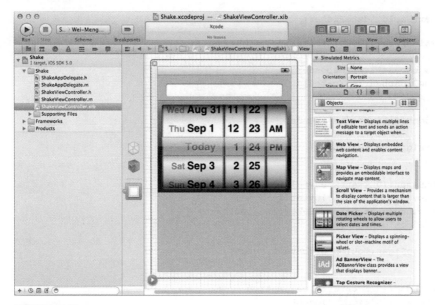

FIGURE 15-10

4. Insert the following statements that appear in bold into the `ShakeViewController.h` file:

```
#import <UIKit/UIKit.h>

@interface ShakeViewController : UIViewController
{
    IBOutlet UITextField *textField;
    IBOutlet UIDatePicker *datePicker;
}

@property (nonatomic, retain) UITextField *textField;
@property (nonatomic, retain) UIDatePicker *datePicker;

-(IBAction) doneEditing: (id) sender;
- (void)ResetDatePicker;

@end
```

5. In Interface Builder, perform the following actions:

➤ Control-click and drag the File's Owner item to the TextField view and select `textField`.

➤ Control-click and drag the File's Owner item to the DatePicker view and select `datePicker`.

➤ Right-click the TextField view and connect its `Did End on Exit` event to the File's Owner item. Select `doneEditing:`.

6. Insert the following statements that appear in bold in the `ShakeViewController.m` file:

```objc
#import "ShakeViewController.h"

@implementation ShakeViewController

@synthesize textField, datePicker;

- (void) viewDidAppear:(BOOL) animated
{
    [self.view becomeFirstResponder];
    [super viewDidAppear:animated];
}

- (IBAction) doneEditing: (id) sender
{
    [sender resignFirstResponder];
}

- (void)motionBegan:(UIEventSubtype) motion
        withEvent:(UIEvent *)event {
    if (event.subtype == UIEventSubtypeMotionShake) {
        NSLog(@"motionBegan:");
    }
    [super motionBegan:motion withEvent:event];
}

- (void)motionEnded:(UIEventSubtype) motion
        withEvent:(UIEvent *)event {
    if (event.subtype == UIEventSubtypeMotionShake) {
        NSLog(@"motionEnded:");
        [self ResetDatePicker];
    }
    [super motionEnded:motion withEvent:event];
}

- (void)motionCancelled:(UIEventSubtype) motion
          withEvent:(UIEvent *)event {
    if (event.subtype == UIEventSubtypeMotionShake) {
        NSLog(@"motionCancelled:");
    }
    [super motionCancelled:motion withEvent:event];
}

- (void)ResetDatePicker {
    [datePicker setDate:[NSDate date]];
}

- (void)dealloc {
    [textField release];
    [datePicker release];
    [super dealloc];
}
```

7. Right-click the project name in Xcode and choose New File. . . . Choose the Cocoa Touch Class item on the left and select the Objective-C class template. Choose the UIView subclass (see Figure 15-11) and name the file ShakeView.m. Click Next.

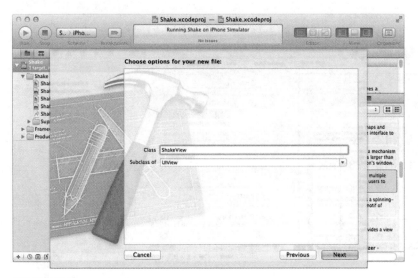

FIGURE 15-11

8. Insert the following statements in bold in ShakeView.m:

```objectivec
#import "ShakeView.h"

@implementation ShakeView

- (id)initWithFrame:(CGRect)frame
{
    self = [super initWithFrame:frame];
    if (self) {
        // Initialization code
    }
    return self;
}

- (BOOL)canBecomeFirstResponder {
    return YES;
}

/*
// Only override drawRect: if you perform custom drawing.
// An empty implementation adversely affects performance during animation.
- (void)drawRect:(CGRect)rect
{
    // Drawing code
}
*/

@end
```

9. In Interface Builder, select the View window and view its Identity Inspector window. Set `ShakeView` as its class name (see Figure 15-12).

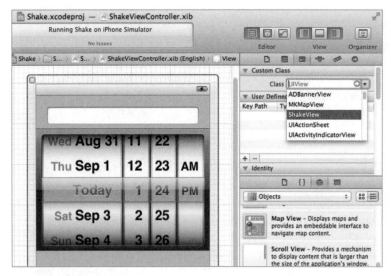

FIGURE 15-12

10. Press Command-R to test the application on the iPhone Simulator. Open the output window by pressing Command-Shift-C in Xcode.

11. With the application in the iPhone Simulator, choose Hardware ⇨ Shake Gesture to simulate shaking the device. Note the information printed in the Debugger Console window:

```
2011-09-02 13:53:08.142 Shake[2402:707] motionBegan:
2011-09-02 13:53:08.851 Shake[2402:707] motionEnded:
```

12. Tap the TextField view to make the keyboard appear, and type some text into it. Choose Hardware ⇨ Shake Gesture to simulate shaking the device again. Note the values printed in the output window, and the alert on the screen (see Figure 15-13).

13. Close the keyboard by clicking the return key on the keyboard. Simulate shaking the device again and observe the output on the Debugger Console window.

14. Set the DatePicker view to any date. Choose Hardware ⇨ Shake Gesture to simulate shaking the device again. Notice that the DatePicker view resets to the current date.

FIGURE 15-13

How It Works

Be aware that the three events used for monitoring shakes are fired only when there is a first responder in your View. Hence, the first thing you do when your View appears is set it to become the first responder (in the ShakeViewController.m file):

```
- (void) viewDidAppear:(BOOL)animated
{
    [self.view becomeFirstResponder];
    [super viewDidAppear:animated];
}
```

However, by default, the View cannot be a first responder, so you need to create a UIView subclass (ShakeView.m) so that you can override the default canBecomeFirstResponder method to return a YES:

```
- (BOOL)canBecomeFirstResponder {
    return YES;
}
```

Doing so allows your View to become a first responder. By default, Interface Builder wires your View with the UIView base class (with which you need not do anything most of the time). You now need to tell Interface Builder to use the newly created ShakeView subclass.

Next, you handle the three events in the ShakeViewController.m file:

```
- (void)motionBegan:(UIEventSubtype) motion
        withEvent:(UIEvent *)event {
    if (event.subtype == UIEventSubtypeMotionShake) {
        NSLog(@"motionBegan:");
    }
    [super motionBegan:motion withEvent:event];
}

- (void)motionEnded:(UIEventSubtype) motion
        withEvent:(UIEvent *)event {
    if (event.subtype == UIEventSubtypeMotionShake) {
        NSLog(@"motionEnded:");
        [self ResetDatePicker];
    }
    [super motionEnded:motion withEvent:event];
}

- (void)motionCancelled:(UIEventSubtype) motion
            withEvent:(UIEvent *)event {
    if (event.subtype == UIEventSubtypeMotionShake) {
        NSLog(@"motionCancelled:");
    }
    [super motionCancelled:motion withEvent:event];
}
```

For each event, you first check that the motion is indeed a shake; then, you print a debugging statement in the Debugger Console.

The `motionBegan:` event is fired when the OS suspects that the device is being shaken. If eventually the OS determines that the action is not a shake, the `motionCancelled:` event is fired. When the OS finally determines that the action is a shake action, the `motionEnded:` event is fired.

You also added a `ResetDatePicker` method to reset the DatePicker to the current date:

```
- (void)ResetDatePicker {
    [datePicker setDate:[NSDate date]];
}
```

When the device is shaken, you called the `ResetDatePicker` method to reset the DatePicker to the current date:

```
- (void)motionEnded:(UIEventSubtype) motion
          withEvent:(UIEvent *)event {
    if (event.subtype == UIEventSubtypeMotionShake) {
        NSLog(@"motionEnded:");
        [self ResetDatePicker];
    }
    [super motionEnded:motion withEvent:event];
}
```

SUMMARY

In this chapter, you have seen how to obtain the gyroscope and accelerometer data of your iOS device. You also saw how to use the Shake API to help you determine whether your device is being shaken. Combining this knowledge enables you to create very compelling applications (such as shaking the device to refresh the data displayed in a Table View).

EXERCISES

1. Name the class to use to obtain the gyroscope and accelerometer data on your iOS device.

2. Name the three events in the Shake API in the iOS SDK.

Answers to the exercises can be found in Appendix D.

▶ WHAT YOU LEARNED IN THIS CHAPTER

TOPIC	KEY CONCEPTS
Accessing the gyroscope and accelerometer data	Use the `CMMotionManager` class.
Detecting shakes	You can use either the accelerometer data or the Shake API in the iOS SDK. For the Shake API, handle the following events: `motionBegan:`, `motionEnded:`, and `motionCancelled:`.

16

Using Web Services

WHAT YOU WILL LEARN IN THIS CHAPTER

➤ Understanding the various ways to consume Web services in your iPhone applications

➤ How to communicate with a Web service using SOAP

➤ How to communicate with a Web service using HTTP GET

➤ How to communicate with a Web service using HTTP POST

➤ How to communicate with a JSON Web service

➤ Parsing the result of a Web service call using the NSXMLParser class

➤ How to integrate Twitter into your application

Communicating with the outside world is one of the ways to make your iOS applications interesting and useful. This is especially true today when so many Web services provide such useful functionality. However, consuming Web services in an iOS is not for the fainthearted. Unlike other development tools (such as Microsoft Visual Studio), Xcode does not have built-in tools that make consuming Web services easy. Everything must be done by hand, and you need to know how to form the relevant XML messages to send to the Web services and then parse the returning XML result.

This chapter explains how to communicate with XML Web services from within your iOS application. Working through the examples in this chapter will give you a solid foundation for consuming other Web services that you will need in your own projects. Besides consuming XML Web services, you will also learn how to consume a much more efficient type of Web service — JSON Web services.

In addition, this chapter covers one of the new APIs in iOS 5 — integrating with Twitter. You will learn how to enable your users to post tweets from within your application.

> **NOTE** *For an introduction to XML Web services, check out this link:* www.w3schools.com/webservices/ws_intro.asp.

BASICS OF CONSUMING XML WEB SERVICES

Before you create an Xcode project to consume a Web service, it is good to examine a real Web service to see the different ways you can consume it. My favorite example is to use an ASMX XML Web service created using .NET. For the purposes of this discussion, we'll look at a Web service called CurrencyConvertor, which enables you to convert one currency to another.

The CurrencyConvertor Web service is located at http://www.webservicex.net/currencyconvertor.asmx. If you use Safari to load this URL, you will see that it exposes one Web method: ConversionRate, as shown in Figure 16-1.

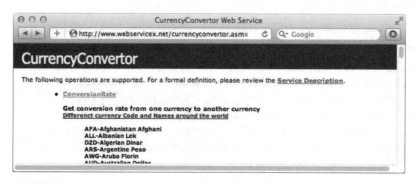

FIGURE 16-1

The ConversionRate method returns the result (the exchange rate between two specified currencies) as an XML string. Clicking the ConversionRate link reveals the page shown in Figure 16-2.

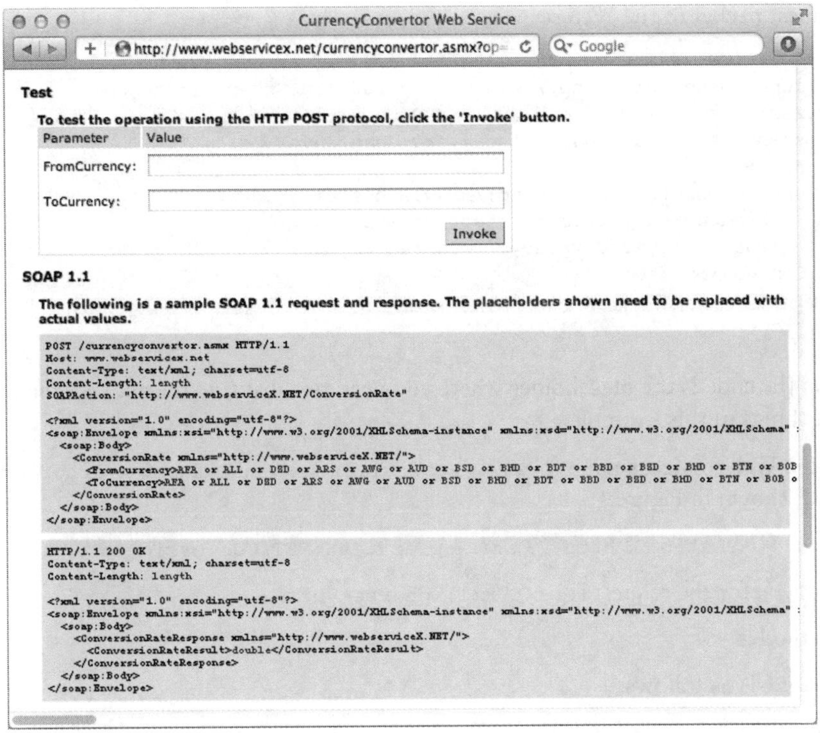

FIGURE 16-2

The important parts are the sections following the Test section shown on the page. They detail the various ways in which you can consume the Web service: SOAP, and optionally, HTTP GET and HTTP POST. In the .NET world, accessing the Web service is a pretty straightforward affair — Visual Studio provides a built-in tool to create a Web proxy service object for the Web service simply by downloading the WSDL document. For iOS development, you need to get your hands dirty, so you must understand the underlying mechanics of how to consume a Web service.

Using SOAP 1.1

The most common way to consume a Web service is using SOAP (Simple Object Access Protocol). When using SOAP, you need to use the POST method to send the following header to the Web service:

```
POST /currencyconvertor.asmx HTTP/1.1
Host: www.webservicex.net
Content-Type: text/xml; charset=utf-8
Content-Length: length
SOAPAction: "http://www.webserviceX.NET/ConversionRate"
```

You then send the request packet to the Web service:

```
<?xml version="1.0" encoding="utf-8"?>
<soap:Envelope xmlns:xsi="http://www.w3.org/2001/XMLSchema-instance"
    xmlns:xsd="http://www.w3.org/2001/XMLSchema"
    xmlns:soap="http://schemas.xmlsoap.org/soap/envelope/">
    <soap:Body>
        <ConversionRate xmlns="http://www.webserviceX.NET/">
            <FromCurrency>fromCurrency</FromCurrency>
            <ToCurrency>toCurrency</ToCurrency>
        </ConversionRate>
    </soap:Body>
</soap:Envelope>
```

The bold italic word in the code is the placeholder where you need to substitute the actual value. Note a few important things in this example:

➤   The URL for the Web service is `http://www.webservicex.net/currencyconvertor.asmx`. This is the URL shown in Figure 16-1.

➤   The URL for the `SOAPAction` is `http://www.webserviceX.NET/ConversionRate`.

➤   The `Content-Type` for the request is `text/xml; charset=utf-8`.

➤   The HTTP method is `POST`.

➤   The `SOAP` request is as follows:

```
<?xml version="1.0" encoding="utf-8"?>
<soap:Envelope xmlns:xsi="http://www.w3.org/2001/XMLSchema-instance"
    xmlns:xsd="http://www.w3.org/2001/XMLSchema"
    xmlns:soap="http://schemas.xmlsoap.org/soap/envelope/">
    <soap:Body>
        <ConversionRate xmlns="http://www.webserviceX.NET/">
            <FromCurrency>currency1</FromCurrency>
            <ToCurrency>currency2</ToCurrency>
        </ConversionRate>
    </soap:Body>
</soap:Envelope>
```

➤   The `Content-Length` of the SOAP request is the total number of characters in the SOAP request.

➤   The Web service will return the following header response followed by the SOAP Response packet:

```
HTTP/1.1 200 OK
Content-Type: text/xml; charset=utf-8
Content-Length: length

<?xml version="1.0" encoding="utf-8"?>
<soap:Envelope xmlns:xsi="http://www.w3.org/2001/XMLSchema-instance"
    xmlns:xsd="http://www.w3.org/2001/XMLSchema"
    xmlns:soap="http://schemas.xmlsoap.org/soap/envelope/">
    <soap:Body>
        <ConversionRateResponse xmlns="http://www.webserviceX.NET/">
            <ConversionRateResult>double</ConversionRateResult>
        </ConversionRateResponse>
    </soap:Body>
</soap:Envelope>
```

The result (exchange rate) will be enclosed within the block of XML results (shown in bold above). You would need to extract it from the XML result.

Using SOAP 1.2

Using SOAP 1.2 is very similar to using SOAP 1.1. The following shows the SOAP request for SOAP 1.2:

```
POST /currencyconvertor.asmx HTTP/1.1
Host: www.webservicex.net
Content-Type: application/soap+xml; charset=utf-8
Content-Length: length

<?xml version="1.0" encoding="utf-8"?>
<soap12:Envelope xmlns:xsi="http://www.w3.org/2001/XMLSchema-instance"
    xmlns:xsd="http://www.w3.org/2001/XMLSchema"
    xmlns:soap12="http://www.w3.org/2003/05/soap-envelope">
    <soap12:Body>
        <ConversionRate xmlns="http://www.webserviceX.NET/">
            <FromCurrency>fromCurrency</FromCurrency>
            <ToCurrency>toCurrency</ToCurrency>
        </ConversionRate>
    </soap12:Body>
</soap12:Envelope>
```

The SOAP response for SOAP 1.2 would be as follows:

```
HTTP/1.1 200 OK
Content-Type: application/soap+xml; charset=utf-8
Content-Length: length

<?xml version="1.0" encoding="utf-8"?>
<soap12:Envelope xmlns:xsi="http://www.w3.org/2001/XMLSchema-instance"
    xmlns:xsd="http://www.w3.org/2001/XMLSchema"
    xmlns:soap12="http://www.w3.org/2003/05/soap-envelope">
    <soap12:Body>
        <ConversionRateResponse xmlns="http://www.webserviceX.NET/">
            <ConversionRateResult>double</ConversionRateResult>
        </ConversionRateResponse>
    </soap12:Body>
</soap12:Envelope>
```

The key difference between SOAP 1.1 and 1.2 is that SOAP 1.1 requires the specification of the SOAP Action in the header, which is not needed in SOAP 1.2.

Using HTTP GET

If you do not want to use SOAP, you can use the simpler HTTP GET method, passing the data required by the Web service through the query string. Here is the format for sending the request header:

```
GET /currencyconvertor.asmx/ConversionRate?FromCurrency=string&
ToCurrency=string HTTP/1.1
Host: www.webservicex.net
HTTP/1.1 200 OK
Content-Type: text/xml; charset=utf-8
Content-Length: length
```

Take note of the following:

➤ The URL for the Web service is `http://www.webservicex.net/currencyconvertor`
  `.asmx/ConversionRate?FromCurrency=`*fromCurrency*`&ToCurrency=`*toCurrency*.

➤ The `Content-Type` for the request is `text/xml; charset=utf-8`.

➤ The `Content-Length` of the SOAP request is 0, since there is nothing you need to send
  separately (everything is sent through the query string in the header).

➤ The HTTP method is `GET`.

The result will be returned in the following packet:

```
<?xml version="1.0" encoding="utf-8"?>
<double xmlns="http://www.webserviceX.NET/">double</double>
```

Using HTTP POST

In addition to using HTTP GET, you can also use HTTP POST. Here is the format for sending the
request header:

```
POST /currencyconvertor.asmx/ConversionRate HTTP/1.1
Host: www.webservicex.net
Content-Type: application/x-www-form-urlencoded
Content-Length: length

FromCurrency=fromCurrency&ToCurrency=toCurrency
```

Take note of the following:

➤ The URL for the Web service is `http://www.webservicex.net/currencyconvertor`
  `.asmx/ConversionRate`.

➤ The `Content-Type` for the request is `application/x-www-form-urlencoded`.

➤ The `Content-Length` of the SOAP request is the length of
  `FromCurrency=`*fromCurrency*`&ToCurrency=`*toCurrency*.

➤ The HTTP method is `POST`.

The result will be returned in the following header and packet:

```
HTTP/1.1 200 OK
Content-Type: text/xml; charset=utf-8
Content-Length: length

<?xml version="1.0" encoding="utf-8"?>
<double xmlns="http://www.webserviceX.NET/">double</double>
```

CONSUMING WEB SERVICES USING SOAP, HTTP GET, AND HTTP POST

As you can see here, besides using SOAP to communicate with a Web service, two more methods are available: HTTP GET and HTTP POST. Using HTTP GET (the simplest), all the information you need to pass to the Web service can be sent through the query string. For example, you can invoke a Web service through the query string like this:

```
www.somewebservice.com/webservice.asmx?key1=value1&key2=value2
```

However, the query string length is limited (recommended to be less than 256 characters), and is hence not suitable if you need to pass a lot of data to the Web service.

An alternative to this would be to use the HTTP POST method, which allows more data to be sent. Using the example just used, instead of passing all the keys and their values through the URL, you would send them through the HTTP header. However, HTTP POST has its limitations as well. As with HTTP GET, the data to be sent must be formatted as key/value pairs, but each key/value pair is limited in size to 1,024 characters. HTTP POST is also a little more secure than HTTP GET, because it is more difficult (but not impossible) to modify the values sent in the header than the query string. The most versatile method is to use the SOAP method, which allows complex data types to be sent to the Web service through the SOAP request.

CONSUMING A WEB SERVICE IN YOUR iOS APPLICATION USING SOAP

Now you're ready to tackle the exciting task of consuming a Web service in your iOS application! In the following Try It Out, you learn how to communicate with the Web service using the SOAP method.

TRY IT OUT   Consuming Web Services Using SOAP

codefile WebServices.zip available for download at Wrox.com

1. Using Xcode, create a Single View Application (iPhone) project and name it **WebServices**. Use the project name as the Class Prefix and ensure that you have the Use Automatic Reference Counting option unchecked.

2. Select the `WebServicesViewController.xib` file to edit it in Interface Builder.

3. Populate the View window with the views as follows (see also Figure 16-3):

➤ Label (name it **Enter amount to convert**)

➤ Text Field

➤ Round Rect Button (name it **Convert**)

4. In Xcode, edit the `WebServicesViewController.h` file by adding the following bold statements:

```
#import <UIKit/UIKit.h>

@interface WebServicesViewController : UIViewController
<NSURLConnectionDelegate>
{
    IBOutlet UITextField *txtAmount;
    NSMutableData *webData;
    NSURLConnection *conn;
    NSString *matchingElement;
}

@property (nonatomic, retain) UITextField *txtAmount;

- (IBAction)buttonClicked:(id)sender;

@end
```

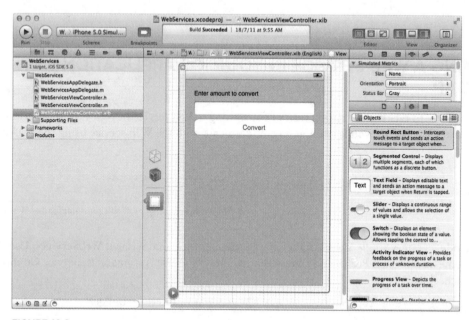

FIGURE 16-3

5. In Interface Builder, perform the following actions:

➤ Control-click the File's Owner item and drag it over the TextField. Select `txtAmount`.

➤ Control-click the Round Rect Button and drag it over the File's Owner item. Select `buttonClicked:`.

6. Right-click the File's Owner item now and you should see the connections as shown in Figure 16-4.

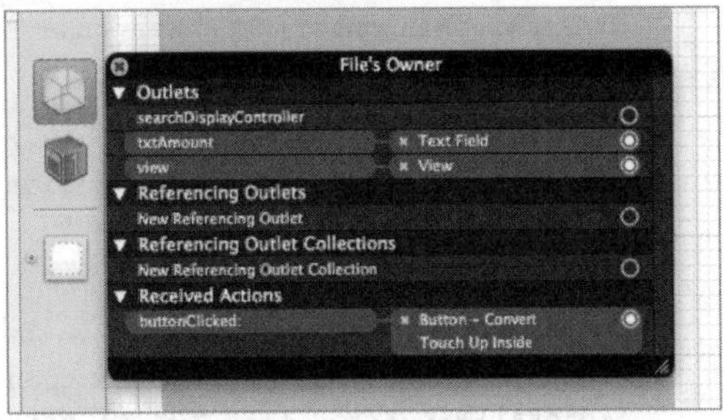

FIGURE 16-4

7. In the `WebServicesViewController.m` file, add the following bold statements:

```
#import "WebServicesViewController.h"

@implementation WebServicesViewController

@synthesize txtAmount;

- (IBAction)buttonClicked:(id)sender {
    //---using SOAP 1.2 here---
    matchingElement = @"ConversionRateResult";
    NSString *soapMsg = [NSString stringWithFormat:
                        @"<?xml version=\"1.0\" encoding=\"utf-8\"?>"
                        "<soap12:Envelope xmlns:xsi=\"http://www.w3.org/2001/
XMLSchema-instance\" xmlns:xsd=\"http://www.w3.org/2001/XMLSchema\"
xmlns:soap12=\"http://www.w3.org/2003/05/soap-envelope\">"
                        "<soap12:Body>"
                        "<ConversionRate xmlns=\"http://www.webserviceX.NET/\">"
                        "<FromCurrency>%@</FromCurrency>"
                        "<ToCurrency>%@</ToCurrency>"
                        "</ConversionRate>"
                        "</soap12:Body>"
                        "</soap12:Envelope>", @"USD", @"SGD"];

    //---print the XML to examine---
    NSLog(@"%@", soapMsg);

    NSURL *url = [NSURL URLWithString: @"http://www.webservicex.net/
currencyconvertor.asmx"];
    NSMutableURLRequest *req = [NSMutableURLRequest requestWithURL:url];
    NSString *msgLength = [NSString stringWithFormat:@"%d", [soapMsg length]];

    //---need this only if using SOAP 1.1---
    //[req addValue:@"http://www.webserviceX.NET/ConversionRate" forHTTPHeaderField:@
"SOAPAction"];

    [req addValue:@"text/xml; charset=utf-8" forHTTPHeaderField:@"Content-Type"];
    [req addValue:msgLength forHTTPHeaderField:@"Content-Length"];
    [req setHTTPMethod:@"POST"];
    [req setHTTPBody: [soapMsg dataUsingEncoding:NSUTF8StringEncoding]];

    conn = [[NSURLConnection alloc] initWithRequest:req delegate:self];
```

```objc
        if (conn) {
            webData = [[NSMutableData data] retain];
        }
    }

    -(void) connection:(NSURLConnection *)connection
    didReceiveResponse:(NSURLResponse *) response{
        [webData setLength: 0];
    }

    -(void) connection:(NSURLConnection *)connection
    didReceiveData:(NSData *) data {
        [webData appendData:data];
    }

    -(void) connection:(NSURLConnection *)connection
      didFailWithError:(NSError *) error {
        [conn release];
        [webData release];
    }

    -(void) connectionDidFinishLoading:(NSURLConnection *) connection {
        [conn release];
        NSLog(@"DONE. Received Bytes: %d", [webData length]);
        NSString *theXML = [[NSString alloc] initWithBytes:[webData mutableBytes]
                                                    length:[webData length]
                                                  encoding:NSUTF8StringEncoding];

        //---prints the XML received---
        NSLog(@"%@", theXML);
        [theXML release];
    }

    - (void)dealloc {
        [txtAmount release];
        [super dealloc];
    }
```

8. Press Command-R to test the application on the iPhone Simulator. Enter a number in the Text Field, and click the Convert button.

9. In Xcode, press Shift-Command-C to open the output window. Observe that the following was sent to the Web service:

```xml
<?xml version="1.0" encoding="utf-8"?>
<soap12:Envelope
    xmlns:xsi="http://www.w3.org/2001/XMLSchema-instance"
    xmlns:xsd="http://www.w3.org/2001/XMLSchema"
    xmlns:soap12="http://www.w3.org/2003/05/soap-envelope">
    <soap12:Body>
        <ConversionRate xmlns="http://www.webserviceX.NET/">
            <FromCurrency>USD</FromCurrency>
            <ToCurrency>SGD</ToCurrency>
        </ConversionRate>
    </soap12:Body>
</soap12:Envelope>
```

10. The Web service responded with the following:

```
<?xml version="1.0" encoding="utf-8"?>
<soap:Envelope
    xmlns:soap="http://www.w3.org/2003/05/soap-envelope"
    xmlns:xsi="http://www.w3.org/2001/XMLSchema-instance"
    xmlns:xsd="http://www.w3.org/2001/XMLSchema">
    <soap:Body>
        <ConversionRateResponse xmlns="http://www.webserviceX.NET/">
            <ConversionRateResult>1.205</ConversionRateResult>
        </ConversionRateResponse>
    </soap:Body>
</soap:Envelope>
```

The response from the Web service indicates that you have managed to communicate with it. The challenge now is how to parse the XML to extract the relevant result that you want. In this case, the result you want is encapsulated in the `<ConversionRateResult>` element. In the next section you'll learn how to parse the XML response.

How It Works

Now, spend some time examining what you just did. First, you created the SOAP request packet:

```
NSString *soapMsg = [NSString stringWithFormat:
                    @"<?xml version=\"1.0\" encoding=\"utf-8\"?>"
                    "<soap12:Envelope xmlns:xsi=\"http://www.w3.org/2001/
XMLSchema-instance\" xmlns:xsd=\"http://www.w3.org/2001/XMLSchema\"
xmlns:soap12=\"http://www.w3.org/2003/05/soap-envelope\">"
                    "<soap12:Body>"
                    "<ConversionRate xmlns=\"http://www.webserviceX.NET/\">"
                    "<FromCurrency>%@</FromCurrency>"
                    "<ToCurrency>%@</ToCurrency>"
                    "</ConversionRate>"
                    "</soap12:Body>"
                    "</soap12:Envelope>", @"USD", @"SGD"];
```

Here, you were hardcoding the two currencies, USD and SGD (Singapore Dollars), to obtain the exchange rate. Next, you created a URL load request object using an instance of the `NSMutableURLRequest` and `NSURL` objects:

```
NSURL *url = [NSURL URLWithString: @"http://www.webservicex.net/
currencyconvertor.asmx"];
NSMutableURLRequest *req = [NSMutableURLRequest requestWithURL:url];
```

You then populated the request object with the various headers, such as Content-Type, SOAPAction, and Content-Length. You also set the HTTP method and HTTP body:

```
[req addValue:@"text/xml; charset=utf-8" forHTTPHeaderField:@"Content-Type"];
[req addValue:msgLength forHTTPHeaderField:@"Content-Length"];
[req setHTTPMethod:@"POST"];
[req setHTTPBody: [soapMsg dataUsingEncoding:NSUTF8StringEncoding]];
```

To establish the connection with the Web service, you used the NSURLConnection class together with the request object just created:

```
conn = [[NSURLConnection alloc] initWithRequest:req delegate:self];
if (conn) {
    webData = [[NSMutableData data] retain];
}
```

The NSURLConnection object proceeded to send the request to the Web service and asynchronously call the various methods (which you will define next) when responses are received from the Web service. The data method of the NSMutableData class returns an empty data object. The NSMutableData object represents a wrapper for byte buffers, which you use to receive incoming data from the Web service.

When data starts streaming in from the Web service, the connection:didReceiveResponse: method is called, which you implemented here:

```
-(void) connection:(NSURLConnection *)connection
didReceiveResponse:(NSURLResponse *) response{
    [webData setLength: 0];
}
```

Then, you initialized the length of webData to zero.

As the data progressively comes in from the Web service, the connection:didReceiveData: method is called. Next, you appended the data received to the webData object:

```
-(void) connection:(NSURLConnection *)connection
didReceiveData:(NSData *) data {
    [webData appendData:data];
}
```

If an error occurs during the transmission, the connection:didFailWithError: method is called:

```
-(void) connection:(NSURLConnection *)connection
  didFailWithError:(NSError *) error {
    [conn release];
    [webData release];
}
```

It is important that you handle a communication failure gracefully so that the user can try again later.

When the connection has finished and successfully downloaded the response, the connectionDidFinishLoading: method is called:

```
-(void) connectionDidFinishLoading:(NSURLConnection *) connection {
    [conn release];
    NSLog(@"DONE. Received Bytes: %d", [webData length]);
    NSString *theXML = [[NSString alloc] initWithBytes:[webData mutableBytes]
                                         length:[webData length]
                                         encoding:NSUTF8StringEncoding];

    //---prints the XML received---
```

```
NSLog(@"%@", theXML);
[theXML release];
```

Finally, you simply print the XML response received from the Web service to the output window.

Besides using SOAP, you might want to use the simpler HTTP GET or POST method, which eliminates the need to create lengthy SOAP request packets. The following two Try It Outs show you how to modify the application to use HTTP GET and HTTP POST.

TRY IT OUT Consuming Web Services Using HTTP GET

1. Using the same project created in the previous project, modfy the `buttonClicked:` method as shown in bold:

```
- (IBAction)buttonClicked:(id)sender {
    //---using HTTP GET---
    matchingElement = @"double";
    NSURL *url =
        [NSURL URLWithString:
            [NSString stringWithFormat:
                @"http://www.webservicex.net/currencyconvertor.asmx/ConversionRate?From
Currency=%@&ToCurrency=%@",@"USD",@"SGD"]];

    NSMutableURLRequest *req = [NSMutableURLRequest requestWithURL:url];
    NSString *msgLength = @"0";

    [req addValue:@"text/xml; charset=utf-8" forHTTPHeaderField:@"Content-Type"];
    [req addValue:msgLength forHTTPHeaderField:@"Content-Length"];
    [req setHTTPMethod:@"GET"];

    conn = [[NSURLConnection alloc] initWithRequest:req delegate:self];
    if (conn) {
        webData = [[NSMutableData data] retain];
    }
}
```

2. Press Command-R to test the application. Click the Convert button and observe the results in the output window:

```
2011-08-30 14:00:54.650 WebServices[1029:f203] DONE. Received Bytes: 98
2011-08-30 14:00:54.651 WebServices[1029:f203] <?xml version="1.0"
    encoding="utf-8"?>
<double xmlns="http://www.webserviceX.NET/">1.205</double>
```

How It Works

In this exercise, you used the HTTP GET method to connect to the Web service. You formulated the query string to convert the USD to SGD and send it directly to the Web service. Observe that the response from the Web service is much simpler than using the SOAP method.

The next Try It Out will show you an alternative to using HTTP GET – HTTP POST. You might recall that HTTP GET imposes a restriction on the length of your query string. Hence, it is not suitable if you have a lot of data to send to your Web service. In this case, you could use HTTP POST.

TRY IT OUT Consuming Web Services Using HTTP POST

1. Using the same project used in the previous example, modify the `buttonClicked:` method as shown in bold:

```
- (IBAction)buttonClicked:(id)sender {
    //---using HTTP POST---
    matchingElement = @"double";
    NSString *postStr =
        [NSString stringWithFormat:@"FromCurrency=%@&ToCurrency=%@",@"USD",@"SGD"];
    NSURL *url = [NSURL URLWithString:
                    @"http://www.webservicex.net/currencyconvertor.asmx/
ConversionRate"];
    NSMutableURLRequest *req = [NSMutableURLRequest requestWithURL:url];
    NSString *strLength = [NSString stringWithFormat:@"%d", [postStr length]];

    [req addValue:@"application/x-www-form-urlencoded" forHTTPHeaderField:@"Content-
Type"];
    [req addValue:strLength forHTTPHeaderField:@"Content-Length"];
    [req setHTTPMethod:@"POST"];
    [req setHTTPBody: [postStr dataUsingEncoding:NSUTF8StringEncoding]];

    conn = [[NSURLConnection alloc] initWithRequest:req delegate:self];
    if (conn) {
        webData = [[NSMutableData data] retain];
    }
}
```

2. Press Command-R to test the application. Click the Convert button and observe the results in the output window:

```
2011-08-30 14:06:24.688 WebServices[1075:f203] DONE. Received Bytes: 99
2011-08-30 14:06:24.689 WebServices[1075:f203] <?xml version="1.0"
    encoding="utf-8"?>
<double xmlns="http://www.webserviceX.NET/">1.2055</double>
```

How It Works

In this exercise, you used the HTTP POST method to communicate with the Web service. Notice that the request information is sent to the Web service separately from the query string. Like the HTTP GET method, the response is much simpler than using the SOAP method.

PARSING THE XML RESPONSE

In the iOS SDK, you can use the NSXMLParser object to parse an XML response returned by the Web service. The NSXMLParser class is an implementation of the Simple API for the XML (SAX) mechanism, which parses an XML document serially.

An NSXMLParser object reads an XML document, scanning it from beginning to end. As it encounters the various items in the document (such as elements, attributes, comments, and so on), it notifies its delegates so that appropriate actions can be taken (such as extracting the value of an element, etc.).

In the following Try It Out, you will parse the XML result returned by the Web service so that you can obtain the exchange rate of the two currencies you sent to the Web service.

TRY IT OUT **Parsing the XML Result Returned by the Web Service**

1. Using the WebServices project created in the previous section, add the following statements to the WebServicesViewController.h file to parse the response from the Web service:

```
#import <UIKit/UIKit.h>

@interface WebServicesViewController : UIViewController
<NSXMLParserDelegate, NSURLConnectionDelegate>
{
    IBOutlet UITextField *txtAmount;
    NSMutableData *webData;
    NSString *matchingElement;
    NSURLConnection *conn;
    NSMutableString *soapResults;
    NSXMLParser *xmlParser;
    BOOL elementFound;
}

@property (nonatomic, retain) UITextField *txtAmount;

- (IBAction)buttonClicked:(id)sender;

@end
```

2. In the WebServicesViewController.m file, add the following bold statements to the connectionDidFinishLoading: method:

```
-(void) connectionDidFinishLoading:(NSURLConnection *) connection {
    [conn release];
    NSLog(@"DONE. Received Bytes: %d", [webData length]);
    NSString *theXML = [[NSString alloc] initWithBytes:[webData mutableBytes]
                                                length:[webData length]
                                              encoding:NSUTF8StringEncoding];

    //---prints the XML received---
    NSLog(@"%@", theXML);
```

```
        [theXML release];

        if (xmlParser) {
            [xmlParser release];
        }
        xmlParser = [[NSXMLParser alloc] initWithData: webData];
        [xmlParser setDelegate: self];
        [xmlParser setShouldResolveExternalEntities: YES];
        [xmlParser parse];
        [webData release];
    }
```

3. In the `WebServicesViewController.m` file, add the following methods:

```
//---when the start of an element is found---
-(void)  parser:(NSXMLParser *) parser
didStartElement:(NSString *) elementName
   namespaceURI:(NSString *) namespaceURI
  qualifiedName:(NSString *) qName
     attributes:(NSDictionary *) attributeDict {

    if ([elementName isEqualToString:matchingElement]) {
        if (!soapResults) {
            soapResults = [[NSMutableString alloc] init];
        }
        elementFound = YES;
    }
}

//---when the text of an element is found---
-(void)parser:(NSXMLParser *) parser foundCharacters:(NSString *)string {
    if (elementFound) {
        [soapResults appendString: string];
    }
}

//---when the end of element is found---
-(void)parser:(NSXMLParser *)parser
didEndElement:(NSString *)elementName
 namespaceURI:(NSString *)namespaceURI
qualifiedName:(NSString *)qName {

    if ([elementName isEqualToString:matchingElement]) {
        //---displays the conversion rate---
        NSLog(@"%@", soapResults);

        float conversionRate = [soapResults floatValue];
        float result = [txtAmount.text floatValue] * conversionRate;

        UIAlertView *alert = [[UIAlertView alloc] initWithTitle:@"Result"
                                                        message:[NSString
stringWithFormat:@"Converted Amount is $%.2f", result]
                                                       delegate:self
                                              cancelButtonTitle:@"OK"
                                              otherButtonTitles:nil];
        [alert show];
        [alert release];
```

```
            elementFound = FALSE;
            [xmlParser abortParsing];
        }
    }

    - (void)parserDidEndDocument:(NSXMLParser *)parser {
        if (soapResults) {
            [soapResults release];
            soapResults = nil;
        }
    }

    - (void)    parser:(NSXMLParser *)parser
    parseErrorOccurred:(NSError *)parseError {
        if (soapResults) {
            [soapResults release];
            soapResults = nil;
        }
    }

    - (void)dealloc {
        if (xmlParser) {
            [xmlParser release];
        }
        if (soapResults) {
            [soapResults release];
        }
        [txtAmount release];
        [super dealloc];
    }
```

4. Test the application on the iPhone Simulator by pressing Command-R. Enter a number and click the Convert button. The application displays the result, as shown in Figure 16-5.

How It Works

To parse the XML result, you created an instance of the NSXMLParser class and then initialized it with the response returned by the Web service. The NSXMLParser is an implementation of the Simple API for the XML (SAX) parser. It parses an XML document sequentially, in an event-driven manner. As the parser encounters the various elements, attributes, and so forth, in an XML document, it raises events where you can insert your own event handlers to do your processing.

As the NSXMLParser object encounters the various items in the XML document, it fires off several methods, which you need to define:

➤ parser:didStartElement:namespaceURI:qualifiedName: attributes: — Fired when the start tag of an element is found:

```
//---when the start of an element is found---
-(void)  parser:(NSXMLParser *) parser
didStartElement:(NSString *) elementName
   namespaceURI:(NSString *) namespaceURI
```

FIGURE 16-5

```
    qualifiedName:(NSString *) qName
      attributes:(NSDictionary *) attributeDict {

    if ([elementName isEqualToString:matchingElement]) {
        if (!soapResults) {
            soapResults = [[NSMutableString alloc] init];
        }
        elementFound = YES;
    }
}
```

Then, you checked whether the tag matched the string saved in the `matchingElement` string (which may be `ConversionRateResult` or `double`, depending on whether SOAP, HTTP GET, or HTTP POST is used). If it matched, you set the Boolean variable `elementFound` to YES.

➤ `parser:foundCharacters:` — Fired when the text of an element is found:

```
//---when the text of an element is found---
-(void)parser:(NSXMLParser *) parser foundCharacters:(NSString *)string {
    if (elementFound) {
        [soapResults appendString: string];
    }
}
```

Next, when the correct start tag was found, you extracted the value of the element into the `soapResults` object.

➤ `parser:didEndElement:namespaceURI:qualifiedName:` — Fired when the end of an element is found:

```
//---when the end of element is found---
-(void)parser:(NSXMLParser *)parser
didEndElement:(NSString *)elementName
 namespaceURI:(NSString *)namespaceURI
qualifiedName:(NSString *)qName {

    if ([elementName isEqualToString:matchingElement]) {
        //---displays the conversion rate---
        NSLog(@"%@", soapResults);

        float conversionRate = [soapResults floatValue];
        float result = [txtAmount.text floatValue] * conversionRate;

        UIAlertView *alert = [[UIAlertView alloc] initWithTitle:@"Result"
                                                        message:[NSString
        stringWithFormat:@"Converted Amount is $%.2f", result]
                                                       delegate:self
                                              cancelButtonTitle:@"OK"
                                              otherButtonTitles:nil];
        [alert show];
        [alert release];
        elementFound = FALSE;
        [xmlParser abortParsing];
    }
}
```

Finally, you simply looked for the closing tag to confirm that the value of the element has been correctly extracted. You then calculated the converted amount and printed the value using a `UIAlertView` object.type="note"

 NOTE *The Web service might take a while to return the result. Hence, once you have clicked on the button, be sure to wait a while for the result.*

CONSUMING JSON WEB SERVICES

While most Web services currently in use were developed using XML and SOAP, they are inefficient for one primary reason: The use of XML makes data transfer expensive and slow (the start and end tags take up a huge portion of the document). Because the request and response packets use XML, it takes longer to transmit them, and parsing XML messages on the mobile device takes considerable effort.

Hence, if you are developing an end-to-end solution today, it is much better to use a non-XML based solution for the server side. A JSON Web service is one good candidate. JSON is a lightweight text-based open standard designed for human-readable data interchange. Using JSON, a Web service returns the result using a JSON string instead of an XML string. The following shows an example JSON string:

```json
{
    "firstName": "John",
    "lastName": "Smith",
    "age": 25,
    "address":
    {
        "streetAddress": "21 2nd Street",
        "city": "New York",
        "state": "NY",
        "postalCode": "10021"
    },
    "phoneNumber":
    [
        {
          "type": "home",
          "number": "212 555-1234"
        },
        {
          "type": "fax",
          "number": "646 555-4567"
        }
    ]
}
```

Instead of using angle brackets to enclose data, JSON uses a series of braces, brackets, and colons to format the data. This formatting makes it very easy to parse the data into arrays and dictionary objects so that the relevant data can be extracted.

In the following Try It Out, you will learn how to consume a JSON Web service from your iPhone application.

TRY IT OUT Consuming a JSON Web Service

codefile UsingJSON.zip available for download at Wrox.com

1. Using Xcode, create a Single View Application (iPhone) project and name it **UsingJSON**. Be sure to use the project name as the Class Prefix and ensure that you have the Use Automatic Reference Counting option unchecked.

2. Download the SBJson_v3.0.4.zip package from https://github.com/stig/json-framework/.

3. Add a new group in your project and name it **SBJson** (see Figure 16-6).

4. Unzip the downloaded package and drag all the files in the Classes folder into the newly created SBJson group in your Xcode project. Ensure that you check the "Copy items into destination group's folder (if needed)" option (see Figure 16-7).

FIGURE 16-6

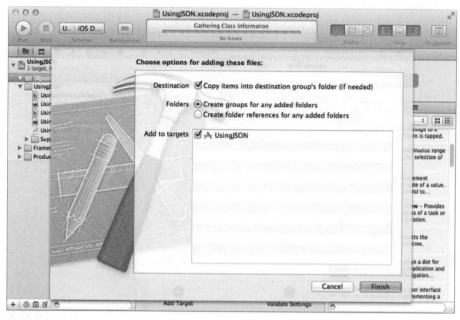

FIGURE 16-7

5. Select the `UsingJSONViewController.xib` file to edit it in Interface Builder.

6. Populate the View window with the following views (see Figure 16-8):

➤ Label (name it **Lat** and **Lng**)

➤ Text Field

➤ Round Rect Button (name it **Get Weather**)

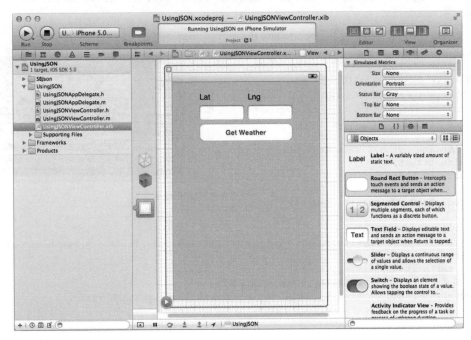

FIGURE 16-8

7. Add the following bold code to the `UsingJSONViewController.h` file:

```
#import <UIKit/UIKit.h>
#import "SBJson.h"

@interface UsingJSONViewController : UIViewController
<NSURLConnectionDelegate>
{
    IBOutlet UITextField *txtLat;
    IBOutlet UITextField *txtLng;
    NSURLConnection *conn;
    NSMutableData *webData;
}

@property (nonatomic, retain) UITextField *txtLat;
@property (nonatomic, retain) UITextField *txtLng;
-(IBAction) btnGetWeather:(id)sender;

@end
```

8. Back in Interface Builder, perform the following actions:

➤ Control-click on the File's Owner item and drag it over the first TextField. Select `txtLat`.

➤ Control-click on the File's Owner item and drag it over the first TextField. Select `txtLng`.

➤ Control-click on the Round Rect Button and drag it over the File's Owner item. Select `btnGetWeather:`.

9. Right-click on the File's Owner item and view the connections (see Figure 16-9).

10. Add the following bold code to the `UsingJSONViewController.m` file:

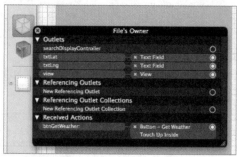

FIGURE 16-9

```
#import "UsingJSONViewController.h"

@implementation UsingJSONViewController
@synthesize txtLat;
@synthesize txtLng;

-(IBAction) btnGetWeather:(id)sender
{
    NSString *queryURL =
        [NSString stringWithFormat:@"http://ws.geonames.org/findNearByWeatherJSON?lat=%@&lng=%@",
            txtLat.text, txtLng.text];
    NSURL *url = [NSURL URLWithString: queryURL];
    NSMutableURLRequest *req = [NSMutableURLRequest requestWithURL:url];
    conn = [[NSURLConnection alloc] initWithRequest:req
                                           delegate:self];
    if (conn) {
        webData = [[NSMutableData data] retain];
    }
}

-(void) connection:(NSURLConnection *)connection
didReceiveResponse:(NSURLResponse *) response{
    [webData setLength: 0];
}

-(void) connection:(NSURLConnection *)connection
    didReceiveData:(NSData *) data {
    [webData appendData:data];
}

-(void) connection:(NSURLConnection *)connection
  didFailWithError:(NSError *) error {
    [conn release];
```

```
        [webData release];
}

-(void) connectionDidFinishLoading:(NSURLConnection *) connection
{
    [conn release];
    NSLog(@"DONE. Received Bytes: %d", [webData length]);
    NSString *strResult = [[NSString alloc] initWithBytes:[webData mutableBytes]
                                            length:[webData length]
                                          encoding:NSUTF8StringEncoding];

    NSDictionary *result = [strResult JSONValue];
    for (id theKey in result) {
        NSDictionary *detailedItems = [result objectForKey:theKey];
        UIAlertView *alert = [[UIAlertView alloc] initWithTitle:@"Result"
                                                message:strResult
                                                delegate:self
                                       cancelButtonTitle:@"OK"
                                       otherButtonTitles:nil];
        [alert show];
        [alert release];
        NSLog(@"Key is %@, Value is %@", theKey, detailedItems);

        //---print out individual keys and their values---
        for (id detailedKey in detailedItems) {
            id detailedValue = [detailedItems objectForKey:detailedKey];
            NSLog(@"Key is %@, Value is %@", detailedKey, detailedValue);
        }
    }
    [strResult release];
    [webData release];
}

-(void) dealloc
{
    [txtLat release];
    [txtLng release];
    [super dealloc];
}
```

11. Press Command-R to debug the application on the iPhone Simulator. Enter the latitude and longitude of a location (see Figure 16-10) and then click the Get Weather button. You should see the result in an alert view.

12. In Xcode, press Command-Shift-C to view the output window (see Figure 16-11).

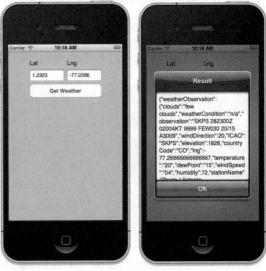

FIGURE 16-10

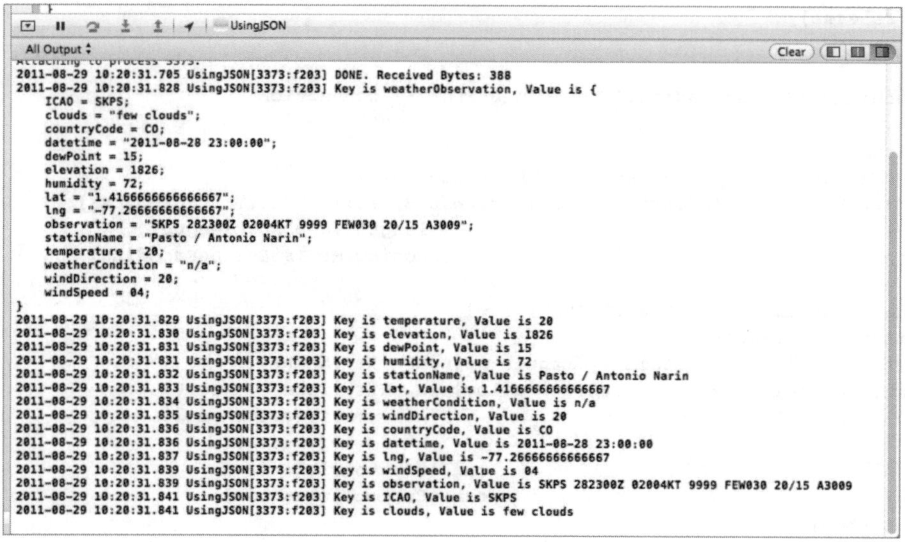

FIGURE 16-11

How It Works

To parse JSON strings, you use the json-framework, located at: `https://github.com/stig/json-framework`. To use the framework, you need to copy all the class files from this framework into your project and then import its header file.

The JSON Web service you used in this example enables you to check the weather information of a location given its latitude and longitude. You call this Web service just as you call a Web service using the HTTP GET method described earlier:

```
NSString *queryURL =
    [NSString stringWithFormat:@"http://ws.geonames.org/findNearByWeatherJSON?lat
=%@&lng=%@",
        txtLat.text, txtLng.text];
NSURL *url = [NSURL URLWithString: queryURL];
NSMutableURLRequest *req = [NSMutableURLRequest requestWithURL:url];
conn = [[NSURLConnection alloc] initWithRequest:req
                                       delegate:self];
if (conn) {
    webData = [[NSMutableData data] retain];
}
```

The latitude and longitude are passed in via the query string. When the Web service returns the result as a JSON string, you convert the JSON string into an NSDictionary object. This can be done by calling the JSONValue method (which belongs to the json-framework) on the NSString object:

```
NSDictionary *result = [strResult JSONValue];
```

You then iterate through the dictionary object to find out the individual results in the JSON string:

```
for (id theKey in result) {
    NSDictionary *detailedItems = [result objectForKey:theKey];
    UIAlertView *alert = [[UIAlertView alloc] initWithTitle:@"Result"
                                                    message:strResult
                                                   delegate:self
                                          cancelButtonTitle:@"OK"
                                          otherButtonTitles:nil];
    [alert show];
    [alert release];
    NSLog(@"Key is %@, Value is %@", theKey, detailedItems);

    //---print out individual keys and their values---
    for (id detailedKey in detailedItems) {
        id detailedValue = [detailedItems objectForKey:detailedKey];
        NSLog(@"Key is %@, Value is %@", detailedKey, detailedValue);
    }
}
```

INTEGRATING TWITTER INTO YOUR APPLICATION

In iOS 5, Twitter integration has been built right into the OS. A lot of built-in applications now support Twitter — Safari, Photos, Camera, YouTube, Maps, etc. In order to tweet directly from within all these applications, you first need to set up your Twitter account in the Settings application. Figure 16-12 shows the Twitter item in the Settings application on the iPhone Simulator. Clicking on the Twitter item allows you to sign in to your existing Twitter account, or create a new one if you do not already have an account.

FIGURE 16-12

Besides the built-in applications' support for Twitter, you can also integrate Twitter support in your own application. The following Try It Out shows you how easy it is to enable users to tweet directly from your application.

codefile Twitter.zip available for download at Wrox.com

1. Using Xcode, create a new Single View Application (iPhone) project and name it `Twitter`. Use the project name as the Class Prefix and ensure that you have the Use Automatic Reference Counting option unchecked.

2. Add the Twitter.framework to your project (see Figure 16-13).

3. Select the `TwitterViewController.xib` file to edit it in Interface Builder.

4. Add the following views to the View window (see Figure 16-14):

➤ Label (name it **Enter your tweets** and **URL**)

➤ Text Field

➤ Round Rect Button (name it **Tweet!**)

FIGURE 16-13

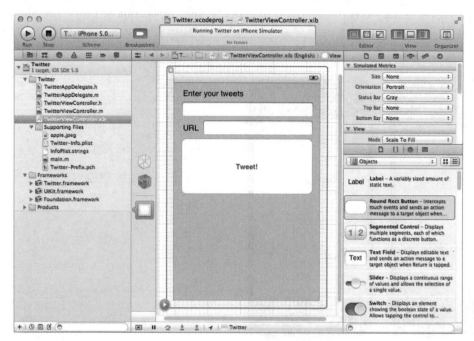

FIGURE 16-14

5. Add the following bold statements to `TwitterViewController.h`:

```
#import <UIKit/UIKit.h>
#import <Twitter/Twitter.h>

@interface TwitterViewController : UIViewController
{
    IBOutlet UITextField *txtText;
    IBOutlet UITextField *txtURL;
}

@property (nonatomic, retain) UITextField *txtText;
@property (nonatomic, retain) UITextField *txtURL;

-(IBAction) btnTweet:(id)sender;
-(void) displayAlert:(NSString *) msg;

@end
```

6. Back in Interface Builder, perform the following actions:

➤ Control-click the File's Owner item and drag it over the first TextField. Select `txtText`.

➤ Control-click the File's Owner item and drag it over the second TextField. Select `txtURL`.

➤ Control-click on the Round Rect Button and drag it over the File's Owner item. Select `btnTweet:`.

7. Right-click on the File's Owner item and note the connections as shown in Figure 16-15.

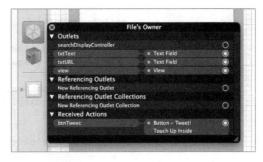

FIGURE 16-15

8. Drag and drop an image named `apple.jpeg` into the Supporting Files folder (see Figure 16-16).

FIGURE 16-16

9. Add the following bold statements to `TwitterViewController.m`:

```objc
#import "TwitterViewController.h"

@implementation TwitterViewController
@synthesize txtText;
@synthesize txtURL;

-(IBAction) btnTweet:(id)sender
{
    if ([TWTweetComposeViewController class]) {
        //---twitter available---
        if ([TWTweetComposeViewController canSendTweet]) {
            //---twitter is configured---
            TWTweetComposeViewController *twitter =
                [[TWTweetComposeViewController alloc] init];
            [twitter setInitialText:txtText.text];
            [twitter addURL:[NSURL URLWithString:txtURL.text]];
            [twitter addImage:[UIImage imageNamed:@"apple.jpeg"]];

            [self presentViewController:twitter animated:YES completion:nil];
            twitter.completionHandler = ^(TWTweetComposeViewControllerResult result)
            {
                switch (result)
                {
                    case TWTweetComposeViewControllerResultCancelled:
                        [self displayAlert:@"Cancelled"];
                        break;
                    case TWTweetComposeViewControllerResultDone:
                        [self displayAlert:@"Done!"];
                        break;
                }
                [self dismissViewControllerAnimated:YES completion:NULL];
            };
            [twitter release];
        }
    } else {
        //--twitter is not available---
        [self displayAlert:@"Twitter not available."];
    }
}

-(void) displayAlert:(NSString *) msg
{
    UIAlertView *alert = [[UIAlertView alloc] initWithTitle:@"Message"
                                                    message:msg
                                                   delegate:self
                                          cancelButtonTitle:@"OK"
                                          otherButtonTitles:nil];
```

```
    [alert show];
    [alert release];
}

-(void) dealloc
{
    [txtText release];
    [txtURL release];
    [super dealloc];
}
```

10. Press Command-R to debug the application on the iPhone Simulator. Enter some text and an URL (see Figure 16-17). Then, click the Tweet! button.

11. You will see the Tweet Composer window showing the text that you have entered (see Figure 16-18). You can modify the text here before you post the tweet. When you are done, click the Send button to post the tweet.

FIGURE 16-17

FIGURE 16-18

12. To verify that the tweet was actually posted successfully, you can use Safari on your Mac to navigate to http://www.twitter.com to view the tweet posted (see Figure 16-19).

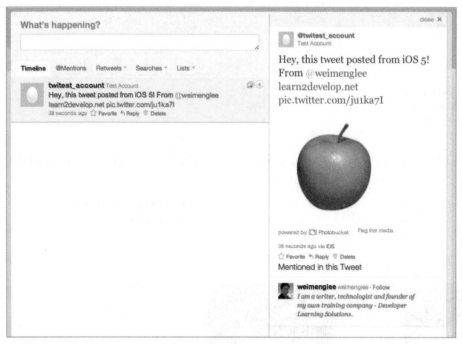

FIGURE 16-19

How It Works

To integrate Twitter into your application, you first needed to add the Twitter framework into your project.

For composing tweets, the Twitter framework provides the `TWTweetComposeViewController` class, which presents a modal window for users to enter the content of the tweet. As this class is only available in iOS 5 or later, it is important that you check for the availability of this class before actually calling it. You can did so by calling its `class` method, like this:

```
if ([TWTweetComposeViewController class]) {
    //---twitter available---
    //...
} else {
    //--twitter is not available---
    [self displayAlert:@"Twitter not available."];
}
```

Once the `TWTweetComposeViewController` class was confirmed to be available, you checked whether the user has configured his or her Twitter account in the Settings application. This can be confirmed using the `canSendTweet` method:

```
if ([TWTweetComposeViewController canSendTweet]) {
    //---twitter is configured---
    //...
}
```

Once you created an instance of the `TWTweetComposeViewController` class, you set the initial text of the tweet, as well as the URL and image:

```
TWTweetComposeViewController *twitter =
    [[TWTweetComposeViewController alloc] init];
[twitter setInitialText:txtText.text];
[twitter addURL:[NSURL URLWithString:txtURL.text]];
[twitter addImage:[UIImage imageNamed:@"apple.jpeg"]];
```

To display the composer window, you used the `presentViewController:animated:completion:` method of the current view window:

```
[self presentViewController:twitter animated:YES completion:nil];
```

From there, the user can modify the text of the tweet and post the Tweet by clicking the Send button on the compose window. You cannot programmatically send the tweet for the user.

To get the result of the compose window, you created a block and set it to the `completionHandler` property of the `TWTweetComposeViewController` object:

```
twitter.completionHandler = ^(TWTweetComposeViewControllerResult result)
{
    switch (result)
    {
        case TWTweetComposeViewControllerResultCancelled:
            [self displayAlert:@"Cancelled"];
            break;
        case TWTweetComposeViewControllerResultDone:
            [self displayAlert:@"Done!"];
            break;
    }
    [self dismissViewControllerAnimated:YES completion:NULL];
};
[twitter release];
```

You can monitor whether the user has cancelled the posting or proceeded to send the posting. After this, you dismiss the composer window.

SUMMARY

This chapter explored the various ways you can consume a Web service in your iOS applications: SOAP, HTTP GET, HTTP POST, and JSON. You also learned how to extract data from an XML document. Finally, you learned how to integrate Twitter into your application using the new API in iOS 5.

EXERCISES

1. Name the four ways in which you can consume a Web service in your iOS applications.

2. Name the three key events you need to handle when using the NSURLConnection class.

3. Describe the steps with which the NSXMLParser class parses the content of an XML document.

4. Name the class new in iOS 5 for composing Tweets.

Answers to the exercises can be found in Appendix D.

▶ WHAT YOU LEARNED IN THIS CHAPTER

TOPIC	KEY CONCEPTS
Ways to consume a Web service	SOAP 1.1/1.2, HTTP GET, HTTP POST, and JSON
Formulating a URL request	Use the NSMutableURLRequest class.
Establishing a URL connection	Use the NSURLConnection class.
Class for storing byte buffers	Use the NSMutableData class.
Events fired by the NSURLConnection class	connection:didReceiveResponse: connection:didReceiveData: connection:didFailWithError: connectionDidFinishLoading:
Parsing XML content	Use the NSXMLParser class.
Events fired by the NSXMLParser class	*parser:didStartElement:namespaceURI: qualifiedName:attributes: *parser:foundCharacters: *parser:didEndElement:namespaceURI: qualifiedName:
Parsing JSON strings	Use the json-framework and add the classes to your project.
Class for composing Tweets	Use the TWTweetComposeViewController class.

17

Bluetooth Programming

WHAT YOU WILL LEARN IN THIS CHAPTER

➤ Using the various APIs within the Game Kit framework for Bluetooth communications

➤ How to look for peer Bluetooth devices using the GKPeerPickerController class

➤ Sending and receiving data from a connected device

➤ How to implement Bluetooth voice chat

The iPhone and iPad include built-in Bluetooth functionality, enabling them to communicate with other Bluetooth devices, such as Bluetooth headsets, iPhone, iPod touch, and iPad. This chapter shows you how to write iPhone and iPad applications that use Bluetooth to communicate with another device, performing tasks such as sending and receiving text messages, as well as voice chatting. Daunting as it may sound, Bluetooth programming is actually quite simple using the iOS SDK. All the Bluetooth functionalities are encapsulated within the Game Kit framework.

 NOTE To test the concepts covered in this chapter, you need at least one device: iPad, iPhone (4S, 4, 3G or 3GS), or iPod touch (second generation or later) running iPhone OS 3.0 or later.

USING THE GAME KIT FRAMEWORK

One of the neat features available in the iOS SDK is the Game Kit framework, which contains APIs that enable communications over a Bluetooth network. You can use these APIs to create peer-to-peer games and applications with ease. Unlike other mobile platforms, using Bluetooth as a communication channel in the iOS is much easier than you might expect.

In this section, you will learn how to build a simple application that enables two iOS devices to communicate with each other.

Searching for Peer Devices

Before any exchanges of data can take place, the first step to Bluetooth communication is for the devices to locate each other. The following Try It Out shows you how to use the Game Kit framework to locate your Bluetooth peer.

1. Using Xcode, create a new Single View Application (iPhone) project and name it **Bluetooth**. You need to use the project name as the Class Prefix and ensure that you have the Use Automatic Reference Counting option unchecked.

2. Add the `GameKit.framework` to your project (see Figure 17-1).

3. Select the `BluetoothViewController.xib` file to edit it in Interface Builder. As shown in Figure 17-2, add the following views to the View window:

➤ Text Field

➤ Round Rect buttons (name them **Send, Connect,** and **Disconnect**)

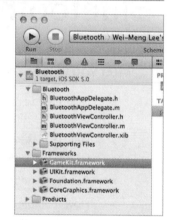

FIGURE 17-1

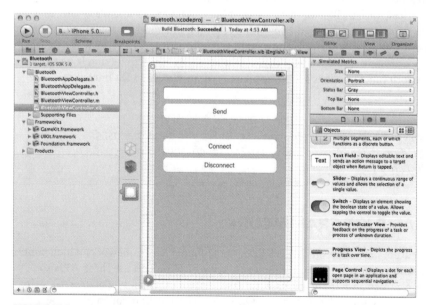

FIGURE 17-2

4. In the `BluetoothViewController.h` file, add the following statements shown in bold:

```
#import <UIKit/UIKit.h>
#import <GameKit/GameKit.h>

@interface BluetoothViewController : UIViewController
<GKSessionDelegate, GKPeerPickerControllerDelegate>
{
    GKSession *currentSession;
    IBOutlet UITextField *txtMessage;
    IBOutlet UIButton *connect;
    IBOutlet UIButton *disconnect;
}

@property (nonatomic, retain) GKSession *currentSession;
@property (nonatomic, retain) UITextField *txtMessage;
@property (nonatomic, retain) UIButton *connect;
@property (nonatomic, retain) UIButton *disconnect;

-(IBAction) btnSend:(id) sender;
-(IBAction) btnConnect:(id) sender;
-(IBAction) btnDisconnect:(id) sender;

@end
```

5. Back in Interface Builder, perform the following actions:

➤ Control-click the File's Owner item and drag and drop it over the Text Field view. Select `txtMessage`.

➤ Control-click the File's Owner item and drag and drop it over the Connect button. Select `connect`.

➤ Control-click the File's Owner item and drag and drop it over the Disconnect button. Select `disconnect`.

➤ Control-click the Send button and drag and drop it over the File's Owner item. Select `btnSend:`.

➤ Control-click the Connect button and drag and drop it over the File's Owner item. Select `btnConnect:`.

➤ Control-click the Disconnect button and drag and drop it over the File's Owner item. Select `btnDisconnect:`.

6. Right-click on the File's Owner item to verify that all the connections are made correctly (see Figure 17-3).

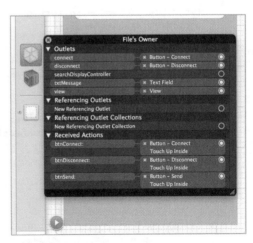

FIGURE 17-3

7. In the `BluetoothViewController.m` file, add the following statements in bold:

```
#import "BluetoothViewController.h"

@implementation BluetoothViewController

@synthesize currentSession;
@synthesize txtMessage;
@synthesize connect;
@synthesize disconnect;

GKPeerPickerController *picker;

-(IBAction) btnConnect:(id) sender {
    picker = [[GKPeerPickerController alloc] init];
    picker.delegate = self;
    picker.connectionTypesMask = GKPeerPickerConnectionTypeNearby;
    [connect setHidden:YES];
    [disconnect setHidden:NO];
    [picker show];
}

- (void)peerPickerController:(GKPeerPickerController *)picker
            didConnectPeer:(NSString *)peerID
                toSession:(GKSession *)session {
    self.currentSession = session;
    session.delegate = self;
    [session setDataReceiveHandler:self withContext:nil];
    picker.delegate = nil;

    [picker dismiss];
    [picker autorelease];
}

- (void)peerPickerControllerDidCancel:(GKPeerPickerController *)picker {
    picker.delegate = nil;
    [picker autorelease];

    [connect setHidden:NO];
    [disconnect setHidden:YES];
}

-(IBAction) btnDisconnect:(id) sender {
    [self.currentSession disconnectFromAllPeers];
    self.currentSession = nil;

    [connect setHidden:NO];
    [disconnect setHidden:YES];
}

- (void)session:(GKSession *)session
           peer:(NSString *)peerID
 didChangeState:(GKPeerConnectionState)state {
    switch (state) {
```

```objc
        case GKPeerStateAvailable:
            NSLog(@"State Available");
            break;
        case GKPeerStateConnecting:
            NSLog(@"State Connecting");
            break;
        case GKPeerStateUnavailable:
            NSLog(@"State Unavailable");
            break;
        case GKPeerStateConnected:
            NSLog(@"State Connected");
            break;
        case GKPeerStateDisconnected:
            NSLog(@"State Disconnected");
            self.currentSession = nil;
            [connect setHidden:NO];
            [disconnect setHidden:YES];
            break;
    }
}

- (void)viewDidLoad
{
    [connect setHidden:NO];
    [disconnect setHidden:YES];
    [super viewDidLoad];
}


- (void)dealloc {
    [txtMessage release];
    [currentSession release];
    [super dealloc];
}
```

8. Press Command-R to run the application on the iPhone Simulator first, followed by on a real device (iPhone, iPad, or iPod touch).

> **NOTE** When testing your Bluetooth application using the Simulator and a real device, you need to ensure that both the Mac and the real device are connected to a wireless network belonging to the same subnet. In addition, the Mac must be connected using Wi-Fi in order for the Simulator to find the real device.

9. If Bluetooth is not turned on, you will be asked to turn it on. Tap the Connect button on each device. You will see the standard UI to discover other devices (see Figure 17-4).

10. After a few seconds, both devices should be able to find each other (see Figure 17-5). When testing on a Simulator and a real device, the Simulator will always be able to locate the real device (not the reverse). Tap the name of the found device; the application will attempt to connect to it.

11. When another device tries to connect to your device, a popup is displayed, as shown in Figure 17-6. Tap Accept to connect or tap Decline to decline the connection.

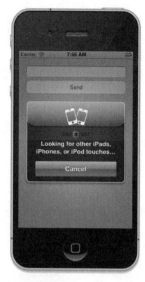

FIGURE 17-4

FIGURE 17-5

FIGURE 17-6

 NOTE *To ensure that the application only installs on devices that support Bluetooth, you should add the* `UIRequiredDeviceCapabilities` *key to the project's* `Info.plist` *file and set its value to* `peer-peer`.

How It Works

The `GKSession` object is used to represent a session between two connected Bluetooth devices. You use it to send and receive data between the two devices. Hence, you first created a variable of type `GKSession`:

```
GKSession *currentSession;
```

The GKPeerPickerController class provides a standard UI to enable your application to discover and connect to another Bluetooth device. This is the easiest way to connect to another Bluetooth device.

To discover and connect to another Bluetooth device, you implemented the btnConnect: method as follows:

```
-(IBAction) btnConnect:(id) sender {
    picker = [[GKPeerPickerController alloc] init];
    picker.delegate = self;
    picker.connectionTypesMask = GKPeerPickerConnectionTypeNearby;
    [connect setHidden:YES];
    [disconnect setHidden:NO];
    [picker show];
}
```

The connectionTypesMask property indicates the types of connections from which the user can choose. Two types are available: GKPeerPickerConnectionTypeNearby and GKPeerPickerConnectionTypeOnline. For Bluetooth communication, use the GKPeerPickerConnectionTypeNearby constant. The GKPeerPickerConnectionTypeOnline constant indicates an Internet-based connection.

When remote Bluetooth devices are detected and the user has selected and connected to one of them, the peerPickerController:didConnectPeer:toSession: method is called. It is implemented as follows:

```
- (void)peerPickerController:(GKPeerPickerController *)picker
            didConnectPeer:(NSString *)peerID
                toSession:(GKSession *)session {
    self.currentSession = session;
    session.delegate = self;
    [session setDataReceiveHandler:self withContext:nil];
    picker.delegate = nil;

    [picker dismiss];
    [picker autorelease];
}
```

The peerID argument allows you to identify the party with whom you are communicating. Your application can communicate with multiple parties using the peerID as the identifier.

When the user has connected to the peer Bluetooth device, you save the GKSession object to the currentSession property. This enables you to use the GKSession object to communicate with the remote device.

If the user cancels the Bluetooth Picker, the peerPickerControllerDidCancel: method is called. It's defined as follows:

```
- (void)peerPickerControllerDidCancel:(GKPeerPickerController *)
picker {
    picker.delegate = nil;
```

```
    [picker autorelease];

    [connect setHidden:NO];
    [disconnect setHidden:YES];
}
```

To disconnect from a connected device, use the `disconnectFromAllPeers` method from the `GKSession` object:

```
-(IBAction) btnDisconnect:(id) sender {
    [self.currentSession disconnectFromAllPeers];
    self.currentSession = nil;

    [connect setHidden:NO];
    [disconnect setHidden:YES];
}
```

The `disconnectFromAllPeers` method disconnects your application from all the parties that are currently connected to you. You can also use the `disconnectPeerFromAllPeers:` method to selectively disconnect a specific party.

When a device is connected or disconnected, the `session:peer:didChangeState:` method is called:

```
- (void)session:(GKSession *)session
           peer:(NSString *)peerID
  didChangeState:(GKPeerConnectionState)state {
    switch (state) {
        case GKPeerStateAvailable:
            NSLog(@"State Available");
            break;
        case GKPeerStateConnecting:
            NSLog(@"State Connecting");
            break;
        case GKPeerStateUnavailable:
            NSLog(@"State Unavailable");
            break;
        case GKPeerStateConnected:
            NSLog(@"State Connected");
            break;
        case GKPeerStateDisconnected:
            NSLog(@"State Disconnected");
            self.currentSession = nil;
            [connect setHidden:NO];
            [disconnect setHidden:YES];
            break;
    }
}
```

Handling this event enables you to determine when a connection is established or ended. For example, when the connection is established, you might want to immediately start sending data to the other device.

DISCOVERING EACH OTHER

Why is it that your application can only see another device running the same application, and not other Bluetooth applications running on the same device?

The reason is simple. When you use the `GKPeerPickerController` class to look for other Bluetooth devices, it creates a session ID. Applications will only be able to see each other if the session IDs are identical. By default, the session ID is the application's Bundle Identifier (you can see this in the `Info.plist` file in the Xcode project). Hence, if an application is installed on two devices, each should be able to see the other because they have the same Bundle Identifier. By default, the bundle identifier is set to: `<Company_Identifier>.${PRODUCT_NAME:rfc1034identifier}`. Therefore, if two applications have a different Company Identifier and Product Name, they won't be able to see each other.

If you want to customize the session ID by creating your own, just implement the following method:

```
- (GKSession *)peerPickerController:(GKPeerPickerController *)picker
        sessionForConnectionType:(GKPeerPickerConnectionType)type
{
    if (!self.currentSession) {
        self.currentSession =
        [[[GKSession alloc] initWithSessionID:@"Session_ID_Here"
                                  displayName:nil
                                  sessionMode:GKSessionModePeer]
                            autorelease];
        self.currentSession.delegate = self;
    }
    return self.currentSession;
}
```

In this case, devices can only see each other if their session IDs are the same. The `displayName` argument enables you to specify the name of the device that will be seen by the other party. If you set it to `nil`, iOS will use the device's name.

Sending and Receiving Data

Once two devices are connected via Bluetooth, you can begin to send data between them. The data is transmitted using the `NSData` object (which is actually a bytes buffer), so you are free to define your own data format to send any types of data (such as images, text files, binary files, and so on).

The following Try It Out demonstrates how to send a simple text message to another Bluetooth-connected device.

TRY IT OUT Sending Text to Another Device

1. Using the project created in the previous section, add the following statement in bold to the
    `BluetoothViewController.h` file:

    ```
    #import <UIKit/UIKit.h>
    #import <GameKit/GameKit.h>

    @interface BluetoothViewController : UIViewController
    <GKSessionDelegate, GKPeerPickerControllerDelegate>
    {
        GKSession *currentSession;
        IBOutlet UITextField *txtMessage;
        IBOutlet UIButton *connect;
        IBOutlet UIButton *disconnect;
    }

    @property (nonatomic, retain) GKSession *currentSession;
    @property (nonatomic, retain) UITextField *txtMessage;
    @property (nonatomic, retain) UIButton *connect;
    @property (nonatomic, retain) UIButton *disconnect;

    -(IBAction) btnSend:(id) sender;
    -(IBAction) btnConnect:(id) sender;
    -(IBAction) btnDisconnect:(id) sender;
    -(void) mySendDataToPeers:(NSData *) data;

    @end
    ```

2. Add the following methods to the `BluetoothViewController.m` file:

    ```
    - (void) mySendDataToPeers:(NSData *) data {
        if (currentSession)
            [self.currentSession sendDataToAllPeers:data
                                      withDataMode:GKSendDataReliable
                                             error:nil];
    }

    -(IBAction) btnSend:(id) sender {
        //---convert an NSString object to NSData---
        NSData* data;
        NSString *str = [NSString stringWithString:txtMessage.text];
        data = [str dataUsingEncoding: NSASCIIStringEncoding];
        [self mySendDataToPeers:data];
    }

    - (void) receiveData:(NSData *)data
                fromPeer:(NSString *)peer
               inSession:(GKSession *)session
                 context:(void *)context {
        //---convert the NSData to NSString---
        NSString* str;

        str = [[NSString alloc] initWithData:data
    ```

```
                                    encoding:NSASCIIStringEncoding];
    UIAlertView *alert = [[UIAlertView alloc] initWithTitle:@"Data received"
                                              message:str
                                              delegate:self
                                      cancelButtonTitle:@"OK"
                                      otherButtonTitles:nil];

    [alert show];
    [alert release];
    [str release];
}
```

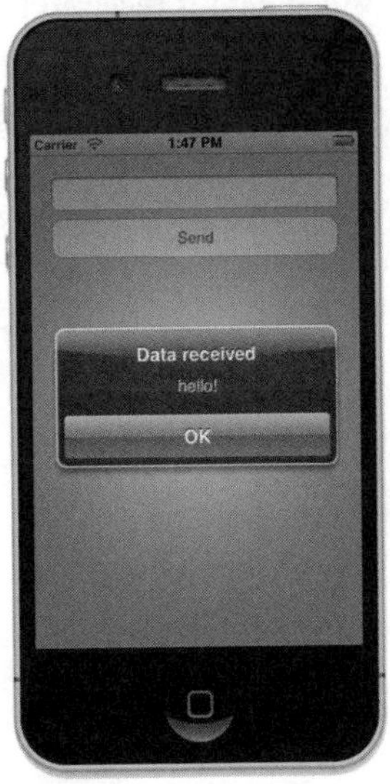

3. Deploy the application onto two devices (or the Simulator and a real device). Connect the devices using Bluetooth. Now enter some text and start sending it to the other device. Data received from another device is shown in an Alert view (see Figure 17-7).

How It Works

To send data to the connected Bluetooth device, you used the `sendDataToAllPeers:withDataMode:` method of the `GKSession` object. The data that you send is transmitted via an `NSData` object.

The `mySendDataToAllPeers:` method is defined as follows:

```
- (void) mySendDataToPeers:(NSData *) data {
    if (currentSession)
        [self.currentSession sendDataToAllPeers:data
                         withDataMode:GKSendDataReliable
                                error:nil];
}
```

FIGURE 17-7

In this example, you are sending data to all connected peers using the `sendDataToAllPeers:withDataMode:` method. To send data to a particular peer, use the `sendData:toPeers:withDataMode:` method.

> **NOTE** Note the use of the `GKSendDataReliable` constant. This constant means that the `GKSession` object continues to send the data until it is successfully transmitted or the connection times out. The data is delivered in the order it is sent. Use this constant when you need to ensure guaranteed delivery. Conversely, the `GKSendDataUnreliable` constant indicates that the `GKSession` object sends the data once and does not retry if an error occurs. The data sent can be received out of order by recipients. Use this constant for small packets of data that must arrive quickly in order to be useful to the recipient.

The `btnSend:` method enables text entered by the user to be sent to the remote device:

```
-(IBAction) btnSend:(id) sender {
    //---convert an NSString object to NSData---
```

```
        NSData* data;
        NSString *str = [NSString stringWithString:txtMessage.text];
        data = [str dataUsingEncoding: NSASCIIStringEncoding];
        [self mySendDataToPeers:data];
}
```

When data is received from the other device, the `receiveData:fromPeer:inSession:context:` method is called:

```
- (void) receiveData:(NSData *)data
            fromPeer:(NSString *)peer
           inSession:(GKSession *)session
             context:(void *)context {
    //---convert the NSData to NSString---
    NSString* str;

    str = [[NSString alloc] initWithData:data
                                encoding:NSASCIIStringEncoding];
    UIAlertView *alert = [[UIAlertView alloc] initWithTitle:@"Data received"
                                                    message:str
                                                   delegate:self
                                          cancelButtonTitle:@"OK"
                                          otherButtonTitles:nil];
    [alert show];
    [alert release];
    [str release];
}
```

Here, the received data is in the NSData format. To display it using the UIAlertView class, you convert it to an NSString object.

Note that for Bluetooth data exchange, the maximum data size is 87KB per block. That is, you can send no more than 87KB of data every time you call the `sendDataToAllPeers:withDataMode:` method. Even so, Apple recommends that you send no more than 1,000 bytes at any time. If you need to transfer large amounts of data, you need to split them up into multiple blocks and reassemble them at the destination.

IMPLEMENTING VOICE CHATTING

Another cool feature of the Game Kit framework is its support for voice chat.

The Voice Chat service in the Game Kit enables two devices to establish a voice chat. The voice chat takes place over either an Internet connection or a Bluetooth connection. This section shows you how to implement voice chatting over a Bluetooth communication channel.

TRY IT OUT   Enabling Bluetooth Voice Chatting

codefile BluetoothChat.zip available for download at Wrox.com

1. Using Xcode, create a new Single View Application (iPhone) project and name it **BluetoothChat**. You need to use the project name as the Class Prefix and ensure that you have the Use Automatic Reference Counting option unchecked.

2. Add the GameKit and AVFoundation frameworks to the Frameworks folder of the project (see Figure 17-8).

3. Drag and drop a WAV file (see Figure 17-9) onto the Resources folder in Xcode.

FIGURE 17-8

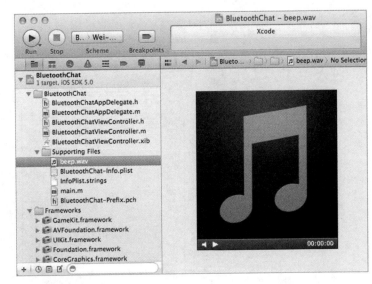

FIGURE 17-9

4. Select the BluetoothViewController.xib file to edit it in Interface Builder.

5. Populate the View window with three Round Rect Button views (see Figure 17-10). Label them MUTE, Disconnect, and Connect.

6. Add the following bold statements to the BluetoothChatViewController.h file:

```
#import <UIKit/UIKit.h>
#import <GameKit/GameKit.h>
#import <AVFoundation/AVFoundation.h>

@interface BluetoothChatViewController : UIViewController
    <GKVoiceChatClient,
    GKPeerPickerControllerDelegate,
    GKSessionDelegate>
```

```
{
    GKSession *currentSession;
    IBOutlet UIButton *connect;
    IBOutlet UIButton *disconnect;
    GKPeerPickerController *picker;
}

@property (nonatomic, retain) GKSession *currentSession;
@property (nonatomic, retain) UIButton *connect;
@property (nonatomic, retain) UIButton *disconnect;
-(IBAction)btnMute:(id) sender;
-(IBAction)btnUnmute:(id) sender;
-(IBAction)btnConnect:(id) sender;
-(IBAction)btnDisconnect:(id) sender;

@end
```

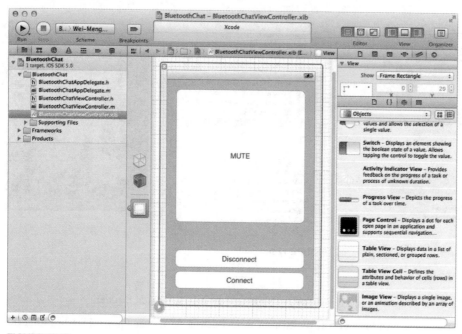

FIGURE 17-10

7. In the `BluetoothViewController.xib` window, perform the following connections:

➤ Control-click the File's Owner item and drag and drop it over the Connect button. Select `connect`.

➤ Control-click the File's Owner item and drag and drop it over the Disconnect button. Select `disconnect`.

➤ Control-click the Connect button and drag and drop it over the File's Owner item. Select btnConnect:.

➤ Control-click the Disconnect button and drag and drop it over the File's Owner item. Select btnDisconnect:.

➤ Right-click the Mute button and connect the Touch Down event to the File's Owner item. Select btnMute:.

➤ Right-click the MUTE button and connect the Touch Up Inside event to the File's Owner item. Select btnUnmute:.

8. To verify that all the connections are made correctly, right-click the File's Owner item and view its connections (see Figure 17-11).

9. Add the following bold statements to the BluetoothViewController.m file:

FIGURE 17-11

```objc
#import "BluetoothChatViewController.h"

@implementation BluetoothChatViewController


@synthesize currentSession;
@synthesize connect;
@synthesize disconnect;

NSString *recorderFilePath;
AVAudioPlayer *audioPlayer;

- (void)viewDidLoad
{
    [connect setHidden:NO];
    [disconnect setHidden:YES];
    [super viewDidLoad];
}

- (GKSession *)peerPickerController:(GKPeerPickerController *)picker
        sessionForConnectionType:(GKPeerPickerConnectionType)type {
    if (!self.currentSession) {
        self.currentSession =
        [[[GKSession alloc] initWithSessionID:@"Session_ID_Here"
                            displayName:nil
                            sessionMode:GKSessionModePeer] autorelease];
        self.currentSession.delegate = self;
    }
    return self.currentSession;
}

//---select a nearby Bluetooth device---
```

```objc
-(IBAction) btnConnect:(id) sender {
    picker = [[GKPeerPickerController alloc] init];
    picker.delegate = self;
    picker.connectionTypesMask = GKPeerPickerConnectionTypeNearby;
    [connect setHidden:YES];
    [disconnect setHidden:NO];
    [picker show];
}


//---disconnect from the other device---
-(IBAction) btnDisconnect:(id) sender {
    [self.currentSession disconnectFromAllPeers];
    currentSession = nil;
    [connect setHidden:NO];
    [disconnect setHidden:YES];
}


//---did connect to a peer---
-(void) peerPickerController:(GKPeerPickerController *)pk
                didConnectPeer:(NSString *)peerID
                     toSession:(GKSession *) session {
    self.currentSession = session;
    session.delegate = self;
    [session setDataReceiveHandler:self withContext:nil];
    picker.delegate = nil;
    [picker dismiss];
    [picker autorelease];
}


//---connection was cancelled---
-(void) peerPickerControllerDidCancel:(GKPeerPickerController *)pk {
    picker.delegate = nil;
    [picker autorelease];
    [connect setHidden:NO];
    [disconnect setHidden:YES];
}


//---mute the voice chat---
-(IBAction) btnMute:(id) sender {
    [GKVoiceChatService defaultVoiceChatService].microphoneMuted = YES;
}


//---unmute the voice chat---
-(IBAction) btnUnmute:(id) sender {
    [GKVoiceChatService defaultVoiceChatService].microphoneMuted = NO;
}


//---returns a unique ID that identifies the local user---
-(NSString *) participantID {
    return currentSession.peerID;
}


//---sends voice chat configuration data to the other party---
-(void) voiceChatService:(GKVoiceChatService *) voiceChatService
```

```
                    sendData:(NSData *) data
            toParticipantID:(NSString *) participantID {
    [currentSession sendData:data
                    toPeers:[NSArray arrayWithObject:participantID]
               withDataMode:GKSendDataReliable error:nil];
}


//---session state changed---
-(void) session:(GKSession *)session
           peer:(NSString *)peerID
 didChangeState:(GKPeerConnectionState)state {
    switch (state) {
        case GKPeerStateAvailable:
            NSLog(@"State Available");
            break;
        case GKPeerStateConnecting:
            NSLog(@"State Connecting");
            break;
        case GKPeerStateUnavailable:
            NSLog(@"State Unavailable");
            break;
        case GKPeerStateConnected: {
            //---plays an audio file---
            NSString *soundFilePath =
                [[NSBundle mainBundle] pathForResource:@"beep"
                                                ofType:@"wav"];
            NSURL *fileURL =
                [[NSURL alloc] initFileURLWithPath:soundFilePath];
            AVAudioPlayer *audioPlayer =
                [[[AVAudioPlayer alloc] initWithContentsOfURL:fileURL
                                                error:nil] autorelease];
            [fileURL release];
            [audioPlayer play];

            NSError *error;
            AVAudioSession *audioSession = [AVAudioSession sharedInstance];
            if (![audioSession
                    setCategory:AVAudioSessionCategoryPlayAndRecord
                  error:&error]) {
                NSLog(@"Error setting category: %@",
                    [error localizedDescription]);
            }
            if (![audioSession setActive:YES error:&error]) {
                NSLog(@"Error activating audioSession: %@",
                    [error description]);
            }
            [GKVoiceChatService defaultVoiceChatService].client = self;

            //---initiating the voice chat---
            if (![[GKVoiceChatService defaultVoiceChatService]
                    startVoiceChatWithParticipantID:peerID error:&error]) {
                NSLog(@"Error starting startVoiceChatWithParticipantID:%@",
                    [error userInfo]);
            }
```

```
            } break;
            case GKPeerStateDisconnected: {
                [[GKVoiceChatService defaultVoiceChatService]
                    stopVoiceChatWithParticipantID:peerID];
                currentSession = nil;
                [connect setHidden:NO];
                [disconnect setHidden:YES];
            } break;
        }
    }

//---data received from the other party---
-(void) receiveData:(NSData *)data
        fromPeer:(NSString *)peer
      inSession:(GKSession *)session
        context:(void *)context {
    //---start the voice chat when initiated by the client---
    [[GKVoiceChatService defaultVoiceChatService]
        receivedData:data fromParticipantID:peer];
}

//---session failed with error---
-(void) session:(GKSession *)session
didFailWithError:(NSError *)error {
    NSLog(@"%@",[error description]);
}

- (void)dealloc {
    [currentSession release];
    [connect release];
    [disconnect release];
    [super dealloc];
}
```

10. To test the application, deploy it onto two devices (or the Simulator and a real device). For the iPod touch, you need to connect it to an external microphone, as it does not include one. Then run the application and press the Connect button to use Bluetooth to connect the two devices. As soon as the two devices are connected, you can start chatting! To temporarily mute the conversation, press and hold the MUTE button. When it is released, the conversation resumes. Have fun!

How It Works

When two Bluetooth devices are connected, you first play the beep sound and start the audio session (via the `session:peer:didChangeState:` method):

```
            //---plays an audio file---
            NSString *soundFilePath =
                [[NSBundle mainBundle] pathForResource:@"beep"
                                            ofType:@"wav"];
            NSURL *fileURL =
                [[NSURL alloc] initFileURLWithPath:soundFilePath];
            AVAudioPlayer *audioPlayer =
```

```
            [[[AVAudioPlayer alloc] initWithContentsOfURL:fileURL
                                            error:nil] autorelease];
        [fileURL release];
        [audioPlayer play];

        NSError *error;
        AVAudioSession *audioSession = [AVAudioSession sharedInstance];
        if (![audioSession
                setCategory:AVAudioSessionCategoryPlayAndRecord
                error:&error]) {
            NSLog(@"Error setting category: %@",
                [error localizedDescription]);
        }
        if (![audioSession setActive:YES error:&error]) {
            NSLog(@"Error activating audioSession: %@",
                [error description]);
        }
        [GKVoiceChatService defaultVoiceChatService].client = self;
```

You then retrieve a singleton instance of the GKVoiceChatService class and call its startVoiceChatWithParticipantID:error: method to start the voice chat:

```
        //---initiating the voice chat---
        if (![[GKVoiceChatService defaultVoiceChatService]
                startVoiceChatWithParticipantID:peerID error:&error]) {
            NSLog(@"Error starting startVoiceChatWithParticipantID:%@",
                [error userInfo]);
        }
```

Notice that you needed to implement the participantID method declared in the GKVoiceChatClient protocol:

```
    //---returns a unique ID that identifies the local user---
    -(NSString *) participantID {
        return currentSession.peerID;
    }
```

This method should return a string that uniquely identifies the current user. Since you are using Bluetooth, you used the peerID property of the GKSession object.

Calling the startVoiceChatWithParticipantID:error: method invokes the voiceChatService:sendData:toParticipantID: method (defined in the GKVoiceChatClient protocol), which makes use of the current Bluetooth session to send the configuration data to the other connected device:

```
    //---sends voice chat configuration data to the other party---
    -(void) voiceChatService:(GKVoiceChatService *) voiceChatService
                    sendData:(NSData *) data
            toParticipantID:(NSString *) participantID {
        [currentSession sendData:data
                    toPeers:[NSArray arrayWithObject:participantID]
                    withDataMode:GKSendDataReliable error:nil];
    }
```

When it has received the configuration data, the other device starts the Voice Chat service by calling the `receivedData:fromParticipantID:` method (also defined in the `GKVoiceChatClient` protocol):

```
//---data received from the other party---
-(void) receiveData:(NSData *)data
        fromPeer:(NSString *)peer
        inSession:(GKSession *)session
        context:(void *)context {
    //---start the voice chat when initiated by the client---
    [[GKVoiceChatService defaultVoiceChatService]
        receivedData:data fromParticipantID:peer];
}
```

The `GKVoiceChatService` uses the configuration information that was exchanged between the two devices and creates its own connection to transfer voice data.

You can mute the microphone by setting the `microphoneMuted` property to YES:

```
[GKVoiceChatService defaultVoiceChatService].microphoneMuted = YES;
```

SUMMARY

This chapter has demonstrated how easy it is to connect two iOS devices using Bluetooth. Using the concepts shown in this chapter, you can build networked games and other interesting applications easily. You also saw how the Game Kit framework provides the `GKVoiceChatService` class, which makes voice communication between two devices seamless. It is not necessary to understand how the voices are transported between two devices — all you need to know is how to call the relevant methods to initialize the chat. However, there is one important thing you should know: Voice chat works not only over Bluetooth, but over any communication channel. In fact, if you have two devices connected using TCP/IP, you can stream the voices over the wire.

EXERCISES

1. What class can you use to locate peer Bluetooth devices?

2. Name the object that is responsible for managing the session between two connected Bluetooth devices.

3. Name the method from the `GKVoiceChatService` class that you need to call to establish a voice chat.

4. Name the two methods defined in the `GKVoiceChatClient` protocol that establish a voice chat channel.

Answers to the exercises can be found in Appendix D.

▶ WHAT YOU LEARNED IN THIS CHAPTER

TOPIC	KEY CONCEPTS
Looking for peer Bluetooth devices	Use the `GKPeerPickerController` class.
Communicating between two Bluetooth devices	Use the `GKSession` class.
Establishing a voice chat	Call the `startVoiceChatWithParticipantID:error:` method from the `GKVoiceChatService` class. On the initiator, call the `voiceChatService:sendData:toParticipantID:` method defined in the `GKVoiceChatClient` protocol. On the receiver, call the `receivedData:fromParticipantID:` method defined in the `GKVoiceChatClient` protocol.
Muting the microphone	`[GKVoiceChatService defaultVoiceChatService].microphoneMuted = YES;`

18

Bonjour Programming

WHAT YOU WILL LEARN IN THIS CHAPTER

➤ How to publish a service on the network using the NSNetService class

➤ Discovering services on the network using the NSNetServiceBrowser class

➤ How to resolve the IP addresses of services on the network

Bonjour is Apple's implementation of the Zeroconf protocol, which enables the automatic discovery of computers, devices, and services on an IP network. In this chapter, you will learn how to implement Bonjour on the iOS by using the NSNetService class to publish a service. You will also use the NSNetServiceBrowser class to discover services that have been published.

CREATING THE APPLICATION

In this section, you create the user interface for the application. You'll use a Table View to display the users that you have discovered on the network. As users are discovered, they will be added to the Table View.

TRY IT OUT Creating the Application's UI

1. Using Xcode, create a Single View Application (iPhone) project and name it **Bonjour**. Use this project name as the Class Prefix and ensure that you have the Use Automatic Reference Counting option unchecked.

2. Select the BonjourViewController.xib file to edit it in Interface Builder. Populate the View window with the following views (see Figure 18-1):

➤ Label (set its text to **Discovered Users** and **Debug statements**)

➤   Table View

➤   Text View

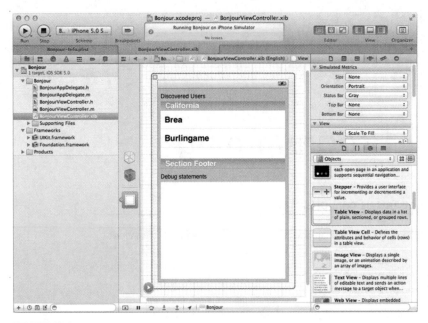

FIGURE 18-1

3.   In the BonjourViewController.h file, add the following bold statements:

```
#import <UIKit/UIKit.h>

@interface BonjourViewController : UIViewController
<UITableViewDelegate, UITableViewDataSource>
{
    IBOutlet UITableView *tbView;
    IBOutlet UITextView *debug;
}

@property (nonatomic, retain) UITableView *tbView;
@property (nonatomic, retain) UITextView *debug;

-(void) resolveIPAddress:(NSNetService *)service;
-(void) browseServices;

@end
```

4.   In the BonjourViewController.xib window, perform the following connections:

➤   Control-click the File's Owner item and drag and drop it over the TableView. Select tbView.

➤   Control-click the File's Owner item and drag and drop it over the Text View. Select debug.

➤   Right-click the Table View and connect the dataSource outlet to the File's Owner item.

➤ Right-click the Table View and connect the `delegate` outlet to the File's Owner item.

5. To verify that all the connections are made correctly, right-click the File's Owner item and view its connections (see Figure 18-2).

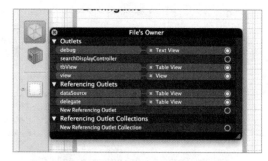

How It Works

Because you'll use the Table View to display the list of users discovered on the network, you need to set the `dataSource` and `delegate` outlets to the File's Owner

FIGURE 18-2

item. The Text View is used to show the various things happening in the background. This is very useful for debugging your application and understanding what happens as services are discovered on the network.

PUBLISHING A SERVICE

With all the views and outlets wired up, you can publish a service using the `NSNetService` class. The following Try It Out shows you how.

TRY IT OUT   Publishing a Service on the Network

1. Using the same project created in the previous section, add the following bold statements to the `BonjourAppDelegate.h` file:

```
#import <UIKit/UIKit.h>

@class BonjourViewController;

@interface BonjourAppDelegate : UIResponder
<UIApplicationDelegate, NSNetServiceDelegate>
{
    NSNetService *netService;
}

@property (strong, nonatomic) UIWindow *window;

@property (strong, nonatomic) BonjourViewController *viewController;

@end
```

2. In the `BonjourAppDelegate.m` file, add the following statements in bold:

```
#import "BonjourAppDelegate.h"

#import "BonjourViewController.h"

@implementation BonjourAppDelegate

@synthesize window = _window;
```

```objc
@synthesize viewController = _viewController;

- (BOOL)application:(UIApplication *)application didFinishLaunchingWithOptions:
  (NSDictionary *)launchOptions
{
    //---publish the service---
    netService = [[NSNetService alloc]
                    initWithDomain:@""
                    type:@"_MyService._tcp."
                    name:@"iOS 5 Simulator"
                    port:9876];
    netService.delegate = self;
    [netService publish];

    self.window = [[[UIWindow alloc] initWithFrame:[[UIScreen mainScreen] bounds]]
                                                              autorelease];
    // Override point for customization after application launch.
    self.viewController = [[[BonjourViewController alloc] initWithNibName:
        @"BonjourViewController" bundle:nil] autorelease];
    self.window.rootViewController = self.viewController;
    [self.window makeKeyAndVisible];
    return YES;
}

-(void)netService:(NSNetService *)aNetService
    didNotPublish:(NSDictionary *)dict {
    NSLog(@"Service did not publish: %@", dict);
}

- (void)applicationWillTerminate:(UIApplication *)application {
    //---stop the service when the application is terminated---
    [netService stop];
}

- (void)applicationDidEnterBackground:(UIApplication *)application
{
    //---stop the service when the application goes into background---
    [netService stop];
}

- (void)applicationWillEnterForeground:(UIApplication *)application
{
    //---start the service when the application comes into foreground---
    [netService publish];
}

- (void)dealloc {
    [netService release];
    [super dealloc];
}
```

How It Works

To publish a service on the network, you use the NSNetService class to advertise your presence on the network:

```
//—-use this to publish a service—-
NSNetService *netService;
```

Here, you advertised your presence on the network by publishing a network service when your application has finished launching (application:DidFinishLaunchingWithOptions:). You publish a network service first by instantiating it with several parameters to the NSNetService class:

```
//---publish the service---
netService = [[NSNetService alloc]
               initWithDomain:@""
               type:@"_MyService._tcp."
               name:@"iOS 5 Simulator"
               port:9876];
```

The first argument specifies the domain for the service. You used @"" to denote the default domain. The second argument indicates the service type and transport layer. In this example, you named the service MyService and it uses TCP as the protocol. Note that you need to prefix the service name and protocol with an underscore (_) and end the protocol with a period (.). The service type will be used by other applications to locate your service. The third argument specifies the name of the service — you can either provide a unique name or use an empty string. The name set here will be visible to other applications that locate you. Finally, you specify the port number on which the service is published via the fourth argument.

To publish the service, you use the publish method of the NSNetService class:

```
netService.delegate = self;
[netService publish];
```

You also implemented the netService:didNotPublish: method so that in the event that the service is not published successfully, you write a message to the Debugger Console window (or perhaps display an alert to the user):

```
-(void)netService:(NSNetService *)aNetService
    didNotPublish:(NSDictionary *)dict {
    NSLog(@"Service did not publish: %@", dict);
```

When the application exits (applicationWillTerminate:) or goes into background mode (applicationDidEnterBackground:), you stop publishing the service:

```
- (void)applicationWillTerminate:(UIApplication *)application {
    //---stop the service when the application is terminated---
    [netService stop];
}

- (void)applicationDidEnterBackground:(UIApplication *)application
{
    //---stop the service when the application goes into background---
    [netService stop];
```

When the application returns to the foreground (applicationWillEnterForeground:), you publish the service again:

```
- (void)applicationWillEnterForeground:(UIApplication *)application
```

```
    {
        //---start the service when the application comes into foreground---
        [netService publish];
    }
```

BROWSING FOR SERVICES

Now that you have seen how to publish a service, this section demonstrates how you can browse for services that have been published on the network. You will use the NSNetServiceBrowser class to discover services published on the network.

TRY IT OUT Browsing for Services on the Network

1. Using the Bonjour project from the previous Try it Out, add the following bold statements to the BonjourViewController.h file:

```
#import <arpa/inet.h>

@interface BonjourViewController : UIViewController
<UITableViewDelegate, UITableViewDataSource,
 NSNetServiceDelegate, NSNetServiceBrowserDelegate>
{
    IBOutlet UITableView *tbView;
    IBOutlet UITextView *debug;
    NSNetServiceBrowser *browser;
    NSMutableArray *services;
}

@property (nonatomic, retain) UITableView *tbView;
@property (nonatomic, retain) UITextView *debug;
@property (nonatomic, retain) NSNetServiceBrowser *browser;
@property (nonatomic, retain) NSMutableArray *services;

-(void) resolveIPAddress:(NSNetService *)service;
-(void) browseServices;

@end
```

2. In the BonjourViewController.m file, add the following bold statements:

```
#import "BonjourViewController.h"

@implementation BonjourViewController

@synthesize tbView;
@synthesize debug;

@synthesize browser;
@synthesize services;

-(NSInteger) tableView:(UITableView *)tableView
  numberOfRowsInSection:(NSInteger)section {
    return [self.services count];
```

```
}

-(UITableViewCell *) tableView:(UITableView *)tableView  cellForRowAtIndexPath:
        (NSIndexPath *)indexPath {
    static NSString *CellIdentifier = @"Cell";

    UITableViewCell *cell = [tableView
                dequeueReusableCellWithIdentifier:CellIdentifier];
    if (cell == nil) {
        cell = [[[UITableViewCell alloc]
                initWithStyle:UITableViewCellStyleDefault
                reuseIdentifier:CellIdentifier] autorelease];
    }
    //---display the name of each service---
    cell.textLabel.text = [[self.services objectAtIndex:indexPath.row] name];

    return cell;
}

-(void) netServiceBrowser:(NSNetServiceBrowser *)aBrowser
        didFindService:(NSNetService *)aService moreComing:(BOOL)more {
    [self.services addObject:aService];
    debug.text = [debug.text stringByAppendingString:
                @"Found service. Resolving address...\n"];
    [self resolveIPAddress:aService];
}

-(void) netServiceBrowser:(NSNetServiceBrowser *)aBrowser
        didRemoveService:(NSNetService *)aService moreComing:(BOOL)more {
    [self.services removeObject:aService];
    debug.text = [debug.text stringByAppendingFormat:@"Removed: %@\n",
            [aService hostName]];
    [self.tbView reloadData];
}

-(void) resolveIPAddress:(NSNetService *)service {
    NSNetService *remoteService = service;
    remoteService.delegate = self;
    [remoteService resolveWithTimeout:0];
}

-(void) netServiceDidResolveAddress:(NSNetService *)service {
    NSData              *address = nil;
    struct sockaddr_in *socketAddress = nil;
    NSString            *ipString = nil;
    int                 port;

    for (int i=0;i < [[service addresses] count]; i++ ) {
        address = [[service addresses] objectAtIndex: i];
        socketAddress = (struct sockaddr_in *) [address bytes];
        ipString = [NSString stringWithFormat: @"%s",
                inet_ntoa(socketAddress->sin_addr)];
        port = socketAddress->sin_port;
        debug.text = [debug.text stringByAppendingFormat:
                    @"Resolved: %@-->%@:%hu\n",
                    [service hostName], ipString, port];
```

```
        }
        [self.tbView reloadData];
    }

-(void) netService:(NSNetService *)service
        didNotResolve:(NSDictionary *)errorDict {
        debug.text = [debug.text stringByAppendingFormat:
                        @"Could not resolve: %@\n", errorDict];
    }

-(void) browseServices {
        self.services = [[NSMutableArray new] autorelease];
        self.browser = [[NSNetServiceBrowser new] autorelease];
        self.browser.delegate = self;
        [self.browser searchForServicesOfType:@"_MyService._tcp." inDomain:@""];
    }

- (void) viewDidLoad
{
        [self browseServices];
        [super viewDidLoad];
}

- (void)dealloc {
        [tbView release];
        [debug release];
        [browser release];
        [services release];
        [super dealloc];
}
```

3. That's it! Deploy the application onto the iPhone Simulator.

4. In the `BonjourAppDelegate.m` file, change the following in bold:

```
        //---publish the service---
        netService = [[NSNetService alloc]
                        initWithDomain:@""
                        type:@"_MyService._tcp."
                        name:@"iOS 5 Device"
                        port:9876];
        netService.delegate = self;
        [netService publish];
```

5. Deploy the application onto a real iPhone.

6. When the application is running, it will search for all services published on the same network. As services are discovered, their names appear in the Table View. Figure 18-3 shows the Table View displaying the hostname of the devices it has discovered.

How It Works

There is quite a bit of coding involved here, so let's take a more detailed look.

FIGURE 18-3

First, you defined the `browseServices` method, which uses the `NSNetServiceBrowser` class to search for the service named "`_MyService._tcp.`" in the default domain:

```
-(void) browseServices {
    self.services = [[NSMutableArray new] autorelease];
    self.browser = [[NSNetServiceBrowser new] autorelease];
    self.browser.delegate = self;
    [self.browser searchForServicesOfType:@"_MyService._tcp." inDomain:@""];
}
```

As services are discovered, the `netServiceBrowser:didFindService:moreComing:` method is called. In this method, you add all the discovered services to the `services` mutable array:

```
(void) netServiceBrowser:(NSNetServiceBrowser *)aBrowser
            didFindService:(NSNetService *)aService moreComing:(BOOL)more {
    [self.services addObject:aService];
    debug.text = [debug.text stringByAppendingString:
                @"Found service. Resolving address...\n"];
    [self resolveIPAddress:aService];
}
```

You also try to resolve the IP address of the discovered service by calling the `resolveIPhonedress:` method, which you define.

The `resolveIPAddress:` method uses the `resolveWithTimeout:` method of the `NSNetService` instance (representing the service that was discovered) to obtain its IP addresses:

```
(void) resolveIPAddress:(NSNetService *)service {
    NSNetService *remoteService = service;
    remoteService.delegate = self;
    [remoteService resolveWithTimeout:0];
}
```

If it manages to resolve the IP addresses of the service, the `netServiceDidResolveAddress:` method is called. If it does not manage to resolve the IP address, the `netService:didNotResolve:` method is called.

In the `netServiceDidResolveAddress:` method, you extracted all the available IP addresses of the service and displayed them on the Text View. You then try to reload the Table View using the `reloadData` method of the `UITableView` class:

```
-(void) netServiceDidResolveAddress:(NSNetService *)service {
    NSData             *address = nil;
    struct sockaddr_in *socketAddress = nil;
    NSString           *ipString = nil;
    int                port;

    for (int i=0;i < [[service addresses] count]; i++ ) {
        address = [[service addresses] objectAtIndex: i];
```

```
                socketAddress = (struct sockaddr_in *) [address bytes];
                ipString = [NSString stringWithFormat: @"%s",
                              inet_ntoa(socketAddress->sin_addr)];
                port = socketAddress->sin_port;
                debug.text = [debug.text stringByAppendingFormat:
                                @"Resolved: %@-->%@:%hu\n",
                                [service hostName], ipString, port];
            }
        [self.tbView reloadData];
    }
```

When services are removed from the network, the netServiceBrowser:didRemoveService: method is called; therefore, in this method you remove the service from the services mutable array:

```
(void) netServiceBrowser:(NSNetServiceBrowser *)aBrowser
        didRemoveService:(NSNetService *)aService moreComing:(BOOL)more {
    [self.services removeObject:aService];
    debug.text = [debug.text stringByAppendingFormat:@"Removed: %@\n",
                    [aService hostName]];
    [self.tbView reloadData];
}
```
The rest of the code involves loading the Table View with the hostname of the
    services that have been discovered. In particular, you display the host name
    of each service in the Table View:-(NSInteger) tableView:(UITableView *)tableView
    numberOfRowsInSection:(NSInteger)section {
        return [self.services count];
}

```
-(UITableViewCell *) tableView:(UITableView *)tableView
    cellForRowAtIndexPath:(NSIndexPath *)indexPath {
    static NSString *CellIdentifier = @"Cell";

    UITableViewCell *cell = [tableView
                            dequeueReusableCellWithIdentifier:CellIdentifier];
    if (cell == nil) {
        cell = [[[UITableViewCell alloc]
                initWithStyle:UITableViewCellStyleDefault
                reuseIdentifier:CellIdentifier] autorelease];
    }

    //---display the name of each service---
    cell.textLabel.text = [[self.services objectAtIndex:indexPath.row] name];

    return cell;
}
```

DOING MORE WITH TCP/IP

With peers on the network discovered, what can you do next? You can use TCP/IP to connect with your network peers and send messages to them. A discussion of using TCP/IP for networking is beyond the scope of this book, but interested users can download a working application from the author's website — www.learn2develop .net — that illustrates how to build a chat application using Bonjour (see Figure 18-4).

FIGURE 18-4

SUMMARY

This chapter explained how to publish a service on the network using the NSNetService class and how to discover services on the local network using the NSNetServiceBrowser class. Once peers are discovered on the network, you can connect to them and initiate peer-to-peer communication. A chat application is a good example of a Bonjour application.

EXERCISES

1. What class can you use to publish a service on the network?

2. What class can you use to discover services on the network?

3. Name the method that is called when a service is discovered.

4. Name the method that is called when a service is removed.

Answers to the exercises can be found in Appendix D.

▶ **WHAT YOU LEARNED IN THIS CHAPTER**

TOPIC	KEY CONCEPTS
Publishing a service	Use the `NSNetService` class.
Discovering services	Use the `NSNetServiceBrowser` class.
Resolving the IP address of a service	Use the `resolveWithTimeout:` method of an `NSNetService` object.
Getting the IP addresses of a service	Use the `addresses` method of an `NSNetService` object.
Method that is called when a service is discovered	`netServiceBrowser:didFindService:moreComing:`
Method that is called when a service is removed	`netServiceBrowser:didRemoveService:moreComing:`

19

Programming Remote Notifications Using Apple Push Notification Services

WHAT YOU WILL LEARN IN THIS CHAPTER

➤ How to use the Apple Push Notification service

➤ Generating a certificate request

➤ Generating a development certificate

➤ How to create an App ID

➤ How to configure an App ID for push notification

➤ Creating a provisioning profile

➤ How to provision a device

➤ How to deploy an iOS application onto a device

➤ Using a push notification provider application

One of the key limitations of iOS is its constraint on running applications in the background, which means that applications requiring a constant state of connectivity (such as social networking applications) cannot receive timely updates when the user switches to another application.

To overcome this limitation, Apple uses the Apple Push Notification service (APNs). The APNs enables your device to remain connected to Apple's push notification server (PNS). When you want to send a push notification to an application installed on the users' devices, you (the provider) can contact the APNs so that it can deliver a push message to the particular application installed on the intended device.

In this chapter, you will learn how to use the APNs to push messages to users who have installed your application.

USING APPLE PUSH NOTIFICATION SERVICE

When your iOS application uses the Apple Push Notification service, the device remains connected to the APNs server using an open TCP/IP connection. To send notifications to your application running on iOS devices, you need to write a *provider application* that communicates with that server. Your provider application will send messages to the APNs server, which in turn relays the message to the various devices running your application by pushing the message to these devices through the TCP/IP connection.

 NOTE *Chapter 21 discusses the multi-tasking feature of iOS 5. While you have the capability to run your application in the background, the types of applications that are allowed to do so are limited. Also, applications running in the background are not allowed to have any network connectivity. While the steps for using the APNs are straightforward, you need to be aware of several details in order to enable messages to be pushed successfully to the devices. In this section, you learn how to create an iOS application that uses the APNs. The following sections take you through the steps for APNs programming in more detail.*

Generating a Certificate Request

The first step to using the APNs is to generate a *certificate request file* so that you can request two development certificates — one for code-signing your application (so that it can be deployed on real devices) and one to be used by your provider to send notifications to the APNs server. The following Try It Out shows you how to generate the certificate request.

TRY IT OUT Generating a Certificate Request

1. Launch the Keychain Access application (an application in Mac OS X that manages your security credentials) in your Mac OS X (you can do so by typing **Keychain in Spotlight**).

2. Select Keychain Access ⇨ Certificate Assistant ⇨ Request a Certificate From a Certificate Authority (see Figure 19-1).

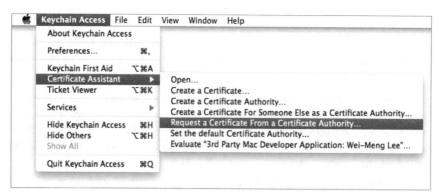

FIGURE 19-1

3. Enter the information required, select the Saved to disk option, and click Continue (see Figure 19-2).

4. Save the certificate request using the suggested name and click Save (see Figure 19-3). Click Continue and then Done in the next two screens.

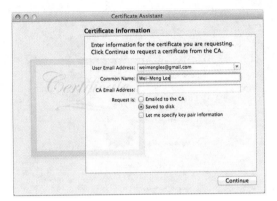

FIGURE 19-2

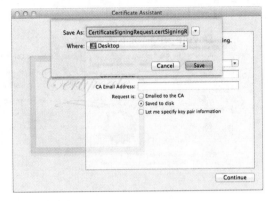

FIGURE 19-3

How It Works

This part is straightforward — use the Keychain Access application to generate a certificate request so that you can send it to Apple later to request for certificates.

Generating a Development Certificate

Once the certificate request is generated, you use it to request a development certificate from Apple. The development certificate is used for code-signing your application so that you can deploy it on a real device.

TRY IT OUT   Generating a Development Certificate

1. Sign in to the iOS Dev Center at `http://developer.apple.com/devcenter/ios/index .action`. Click the iOS Provisioning Portal link on the right side of the page (see Figure 19-4). The welcome page opens.

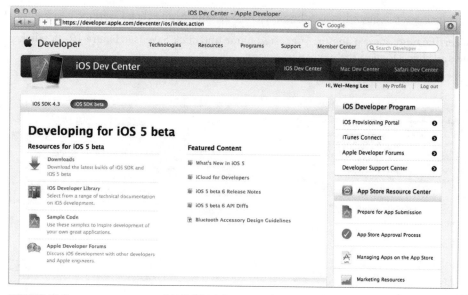

FIGURE 19-4

2. Click the Certificates tab on the left.

3. Click the Request Certificate button in the lower-right corner. Click the Choose File button and select the certificate request file that you created in the previous section, and then click Submit.

4. Your certificate is now pending approval. Refresh the page. After a few seconds the certificate will be ready and you can download it (see Figure 19-5).

FIGURE 19-5

5. Once the certificate is downloaded, double-click it to install it in the Keychain Access application. Figure 19-6 shows the development certificate installed in the Keychain Access application.

FIGURE 19-6

How It Works

This Try It Out generated the development certificate that you need to code-sign your application so that it can be deployed to a real iOS device for testing. The certificate installed in the Keychain Access application contains the private and public key pair. It is a good idea to back up the certificate at this juncture so that in the event that you need to shift your development work to another computer, you can simply restore the certificate from the backup. Downloading the certificate directly from the iOS Dev Center and installing the certificate to another computer will not work because the certificate downloaded from Apple contains only the public key, not the private key. The private key is stored on the machine that created the certificate request.

Creating an Application ID

Each iOS application that uses the APNs must have a unique application ID that identifies itself. In the following Try It Out, you create an App ID for push notification.

TRY IT OUT Creating an App ID for Your Application

1. In the iOS Provisioning Portal, click the App IDs tab on the left and then click the New App ID button (see Figure 19-7).

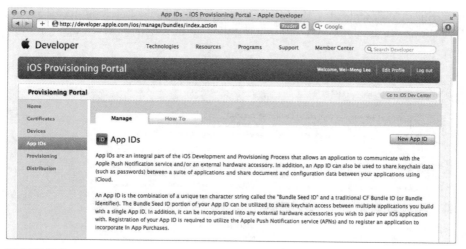

FIGURE 19-7

2. Enter **BegiOS5PushAppID** for the Description and select Use Team ID for the Bundle Seed ID. For the Bundle Identifier, enter **net.learn2develop.BegiOS5PushAppID**. When you are done, click Submit.

> **NOTE** App IDs are globally unique, even among developers. Therefore, in this step, rather than enter `net.learn2develop.BegiOS5PushAppID` for the Bundle Identifier, you should enter your own unique Bundle Identifier. A good recommendation is to use your reverse domain name, such as `com .yourcompany.MyPushAppID`.

3. You should now see the App ID that you have created, together with any you may have previously created (see Figure 19-8).

Description		Apple Push Notification service	In App Purchase	Game Center	iCloud	Action
6LNSVE9D8J.net.learn2deve... BegiOS5PushAppID		Configurable for Development Configurable for Production	Enabled	Enabled	Enabled	Configure

FIGURE 19-8

How It Works

For applications using the APNs, you need to specifically create an App ID to uniquely identify the application. The next section demonstrates how to configure the new App ID for push notifications.

Configuring an App ID for Push Notifications

Once an App ID is created, you need to configure it for push notifications. The following Try It Out shows you how to do this.

Configuring an App ID for Push Notifications

1. To configure an App ID for push notification, click the Configure link displayed to the right of the App ID (refer to Figure 19-8). The Configure option (see Figure 19-9) becomes available.

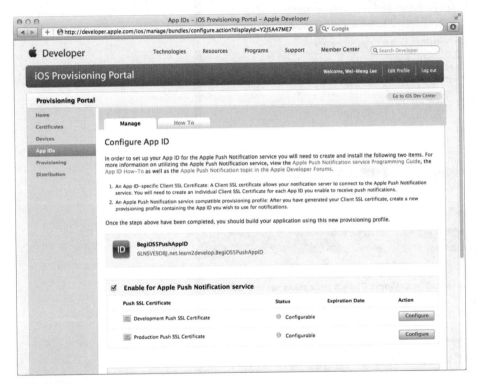

FIGURE 19-9

2. Check the Enable for Apple Push Notification service option, and click the Configure button on the right of the Development Push SSL Certificate.

3. The Apple Push Notification service SSL Certificate Assistant screen opens (see Figure 19-10). Click Continue.

4. Click the Choose File button to locate the certificate request file that you saved earlier, and then click Generate.

5. Your SSL certificate will now be generated. Click Continue.

6. Click the Download button to download the SSL certificate, and then click Done (see Figure 19-11).

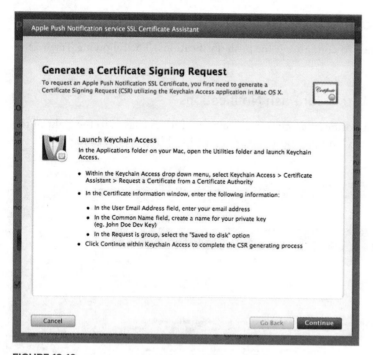

FIGURE 19-10

FIGURE 19-11

7. The filename for the SSL certificate you download is named `aps.developer.identity.cer`. Double-click it to install it in the Keychain Access application (see Figure 19-12). The SSL certificate is used by your provider application in order to contact the APNs to send push notifications to your applications.

FIGURE 19-12

How It Works

When the App ID is configured for push notifications, you need to upload the certificate signing request that you generated earlier to Apple so that you can obtain an SSL certificate for your provider application. Once the SSL certificate is downloaded, you install it into your Keychain Access application. The SSL certificate is for your provider application to use so that it can communicate securely with Apple's Push Server to send push notifications to your application.

Creating a Provisioning Profile

Next, you create a provisioning profile so that your application can be installed onto a real iOS device.

TRY IT OUT   Creating a Provisioning Profile

1. In the iOS Provisioning Portal, select the Provisioning tab on the left and click the New Profile button (see Figure 19-13).

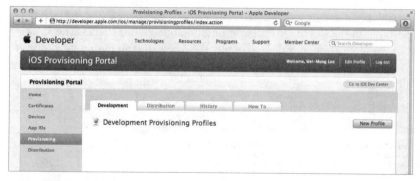

FIGURE 19-13

2. Enter **MyiOS5DevicesProfile** as the profile name, and select BegiOS5PushAppID as the App ID (see Figure 19-14). Finally, check all the devices that you want to provision (you can register these devices with the iOS Provisioning Portal through the Devices tab). When you are done, click Submit.

 NOTE *Appendix A describes how to register your devices through the iOS Provisioning Portal.*

3. The provisioning profile is now pending approval. After a few seconds, it appears (if not, just refresh the browser). Click the Download button to download the provisioning profile (see Figure 19-15).The downloaded provisioning profile is named `MyiOS5DevicesProfile .mobileprovision`.

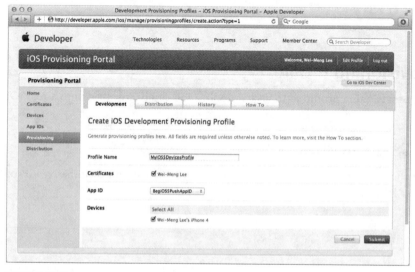

FIGURE 19-14

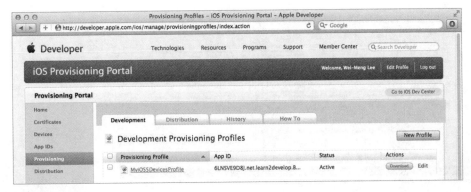

FIGURE 19-15

How It Works

The provisioning profile associates one development certificate with one or more devices and an App ID so that you can install your signed iOS application on a real iOS device.

Provisioning a Device

With the provision profile created, you will now install it onto a real device. Once a device is provisioned, your signed application will be able to run on your iOS devices.

Any devices on which you want to test your application must be provisioned. If a device is not provisioned, you will not be able to install your application on it. The following Try It Out shows you how to provision your iOS device.

TRY IT OUT   Provisioning a Device

1. Connect your iPhone (or iPad) to your Mac. For the example in this chapter, I will use an iPhone.

2. Drag and drop the downloaded MyiOS5DevicesProfile.mobileprovision file onto the Xcode icon on the Dock.

3. Launch the Organizer application from within Xcode and select the device currently connected to your Mac. You should see the MyiOS5DevicesProfile installed on the device (see Figure 19-16).

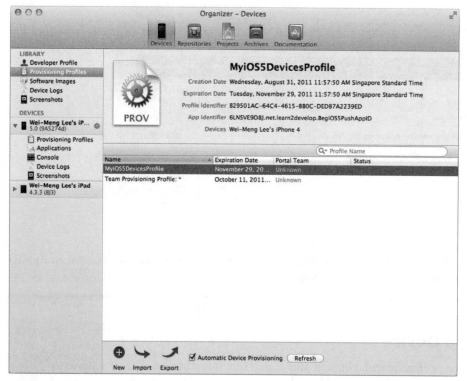

FIGURE 19-16

How It Works

Provisioning your iOS device is straight-forward — simply connect your iOS device to the Mac and then drag and drop the provisioning profile onto the Xcode. Xcode will then automatically install the provisioning profile onto the devices connected to your Mac.

CREATING THE IOS APPLICATION

Finally, you can write your iOS application to receive push notifications. The following Try It Out shows how you can programmatically receive notifications received from the APNs server.

TRY IT OUT   Creating an iOS Application

codefile ApplePushNotification.zip available for download at Wrox.com

1. In Xcode, create a new Single View Application (iPhone) project and name it **ApplePushNotification**. You will also use the project name as the Class Prefix and ensure that you have the Use Automatic Reference Counting option unchecked.

2. Drag and drop a WAV file (shown as `beep.wav` in this example) onto the Supporting Files folder in Xcode (see Figure 19-17).

3. Double-click on the project name in Xcode and select the ApplePushNotification target. Select the Info tab, and set the Bundle Identifier to `net.learn2develop.BegiOS5PushAppID` (see Figure 19-18). This is the Bundle Identifier you set when you created the App ID earlier. As mentioned earlier, you should use your own unique Bundle Identifier.

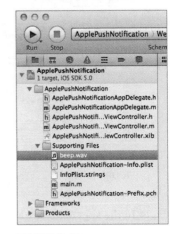

FIGURE 19-17

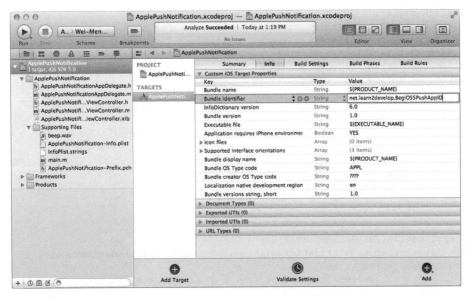

FIGURE 19-18

4. Click the Build Settings tab and type **Code Signing** in the search box. In the Any iOS Device item (under Debug), select the profile that matches the Bundle Identifier, as shown in Figure 19-19.

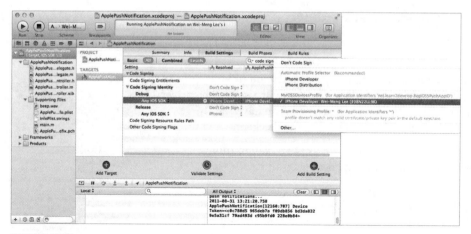

FIGURE 19-19

5. In the `ApplePushNotificationAppDelegate.m` file, type the following bold code:

```
- (BOOL)application:(UIApplication *)application
    didFinishLaunchingWithOptions:(NSDictionary *)launchOptions
{
    NSLog(@"Registering for push notifications...");
    [[UIApplication sharedApplication]
     registerForRemoteNotificationTypes:
     (UIRemoteNotificationTypeAlert |
      UIRemoteNotificationTypeBadge |
      UIRemoteNotificationTypeSound)];

    self.window = [[[UIWindow alloc] initWithFrame:[[UIScreen mainScreen]
    bounds]]autorelease];
    // Override point for customization after application launch.
    self.viewController = [[[ApplePushNotificationViewController alloc]
    initWithNibName:@"ApplePushNotificationViewController" bundle:nil] autorelease];
    self.window.rootViewController = self.viewController;
    [self.window makeKeyAndVisible];
    return YES;
}

- (void)application:(UIApplication *)app
    didRegisterForRemoteNotificationsWithDeviceToken:(NSData *)deviceToken {
    NSString *str = [NSString
                    stringWithFormat:@"Device Token=%@",deviceToken];
    NSLog(@"%@",str);
}

- (void)application:(UIApplication *)app
    didFailToRegisterForRemoteNotificationsWithError:(NSError *)err {
    NSString *str = [NSString stringWithFormat: @"Error: %@", err];
    NSLog(@"%@", str);
}
```

```
    }

- (void)application:(UIApplication *)application
    didReceiveRemoteNotification:(NSDictionary *)userInfo {
    for (id key in userInfo) {
        NSLog(@"key: %@, value: %@", key, [userInfo objectForKey:key]);
    }
}
```

6. Press Command-R to test the application on a real device. When the application is loaded, you will be asked to enable Push Notification so that your application can receive notifications (see Figure 19-20). Tap the OK button to turn on notifications.

7. Press Shift-Command-C in Xcode to display the output window. Carefully observe the device token that is printed (see Figure 19-21). It is formatted as follows: xxxxxxxx xxxxxxxx xxxxxxxx xxxxxxxx xxxxxxxx xxxxxxxx xxxxxxxx xxxxxxxx. Record this device token (you might want to cut and paste it into a text file). You will need it later so your provider application can uniquely identify the devices that will receive push notifications.

FIGURE 19-20

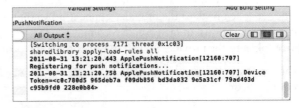

FIGURE 19-21

8. If you click the Settings application on your iPhone, you will notice that you have the Notifications item. Selecting the Notifications item displays a list of apps on your device that use notifications. Select ApplePushNotification and you can configure how the notifications are displayed (see Figure 19-22).

How It Works

To receive push notifications, you first configured your application with the App ID that you created earlier. You then configured your application so it is signed with the correct provisioning profile associated with your development certificate.

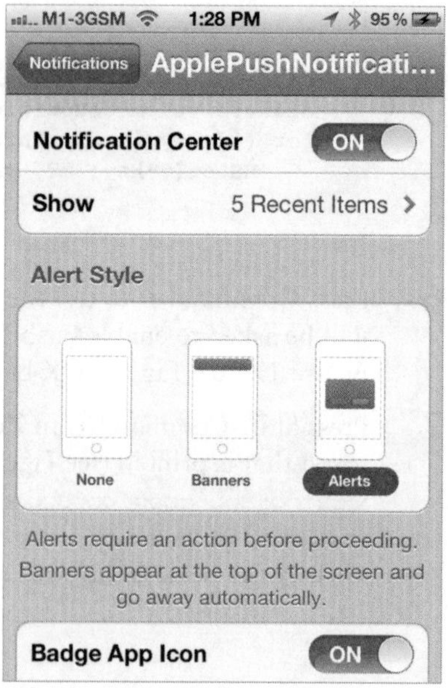

To register your application for push notification, you used the `registerForRemoteNotificationTypes:` method of the `UIApplication` class:

```
NSLog(@"Registering for push notifications...");
[[UIApplication sharedApplication]
 registerForRemoteNotificationTypes:
 (UIRemoteNotificationTypeAlert |
  UIRemoteNotificationTypeBadge |
  UIRemoteNotificationTypeSound)];
```

This registers your application for the three types of notifications — alert, badge, and sound.

If the registration is successful, the `application:didRegisterForRemoteNotificationsWithDeviceToken:` event is called:

FIGURE 19-22

```
- (void)application:(UIApplication *)app
    didRegisterForRemoteNotificationsWithDeviceToken:(NSData *)deviceToken {
    NSString *str = [NSString
                     stringWithFormat:@"Device Token=%@",deviceToken];
    NSLog(@"%@",str);
}
```

At this juncture, you printed out the device token. In a real application, you should programmatically send the device token back to the provider application so that it can maintain a list of devices that need to be sent the notifications. In fact, Apple recommends that every time your application starts up, you send the device token to the provider application to inform the provider that the application is still in use.

If the registration fails, the `application:didFailToRegisterForRemoteNotificationsWithError:` event is called:

```
- (void)application:(UIApplication *)app
    didFailToRegisterForRemoteNotificationsWithError:(NSError *)err {
    NSString *str = [NSString stringWithFormat: @"Error: %@", err];
    NSLog(@"%@", str);
}
```

If the application is running when it receives a push notification, the `application:didReceiveRemoteNotification:` event is called:

```
- (void)application:(UIApplication *)application
    didReceiveRemoteNotification:(NSDictionary *)userInfo {
```

```
    for (id key in userInfo) {
        NSLog(@"key: %@, value: %@", key, [userInfo objectForKey:key]);
    }
}
```

Here, you can examine the content of the message received. If the application is not running when it receives a push notification, the user is prompted with an alert (see Figure 19-23).

Clicking the Launch button launches the application and fires the `application:didReceiveRemoteNotification:` event. The next section shows how you can get a server application to send a notification to your iOS application.

FIGURE 19-23

CREATING THE PUSH NOTIFICATION PROVIDER

A *push notification provider* is an application written by the application's developer to send push notifications to the iOS application through the APNs. Here are the basic steps to send push notifications to your applications via the APNs server:

1. Communicate with the APNs server using the SSL Certificate you created earlier.
2. Construct the payload for the message you want to send.
3. Send the push notification containing the payload to the APNs.

The APNs is a stream TCP socket that your provider can communicate with using a SSL secured communication channel. You send the push notification (containing the payload) as a binary stream. Once you are connected to the APNs, you can send as many push notifications as you want within the duration of the connection.

NOTE *Refrain from opening and closing the connections to the APNs for each push notification that you want to send. Rapid opening and closing of connections to the APNs will be deemed a denial-of-service (DOS) attack and may prevent your provider from sending push notifications to your applications.*

The format of a push notification message looks like Figure 19-24 (taken from Apple's documentation).

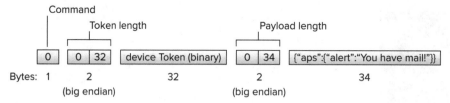

FIGURE 19-24

 NOTE *For more details on APNs, refer to the* Apple Push Notification Service Programming Guide. *The full path to this guide is* `http://developer.apple.com/library/ios/#documentation/NetworkingInternet/Conceptual/RemoteNotificationsPG/Introduction/Introduction.html`.

The payload is a JSON-formatted string (maximum 256 bytes) carrying the information you want to send to your application. An example of a payload looks like the following:

```
{
    "aps":
    {
        "alert":"You got a new message!",
        "badge":5,          "sound":"beep.wav"
    },
    "acme1":"bar",
    "acme2":42
}
```

To save yourself the trouble of developing a push notification provider from scratch, you can use the PushMeBaby application (for Mac OS X) written by Stefan Hafeneger (available at `http://stefan.hafeneger.name/download/PushMeBabySource.zip`).

The following Try It Out shows how to modify the PushMeBaby application to send a notification to your application.

TRY IT OUT   Modifying the Provider Application

1. Download the source of the `PushMeBaby` application and then open it in Xcode.

2. Drag and drop the `aps_developer_identity.cer` file that you downloaded earlier onto the Resources folder of the project (see Figure 19-25).

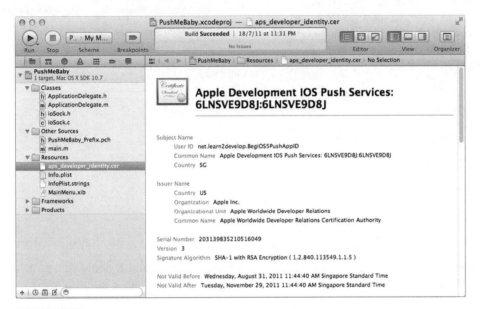

FIGURE 19-25

3. In the `ApplicationDelegate.m` file, modify the code as shown in bold, replacing the device_token with the actual device token you obtained earlier:

```
- (id)init {
    self = [super init];
    if(self != nil) {

        self.deviceToken = @"device_token";

        self.payload = @"{\"aps\":{\"alert\":\"You got a new message!\",\"badge\":5,\"
sound\":\"beep.wav\"},\"acme1\":\"bar\",\"acme2\":42}";
        self.certificate = [[NSBundle mainBundle] pathForResource:@"aps_developer_
identity" ofType:@"cer"];
    }
    return self;
}
```

4. Press Command-R to test the application. You will be asked to grant access to the certificate. Click Always Allow (see Figure 19-26).

5. On the iPhone, ensure that the `ApplePushNotification` application is not running. To send a message to the device, click the Push button. The server essentially sends the following message to the APNs:

FIGURE 19-26

```
{
    "aps":
    {
        "alert":"You got a new message!",
        "badge":5,
        "sound":"beep.wav"
    },
    "acme1":"bar",
    "acme2":42
}
```

6. If the message is pushed correctly, you will see the notification shown earlier in Figure 19-23.

7. Debug the `ApplePushNotification` application by pressing Command-R and send a push message from the `PushMeBaby` application; the Debugger Console window will display the following output:

```
2011-08-31 13:30:52.077 ApplePushNotification[12160:707] key: aps, value: {
    alert = "You got a new message!";
    badge = 5;
    sound = "beep.wav";
}
2011-08-31 13:30:52.079 ApplePushNotification[12160:707] key: acme1, value: bar
2011-08-31 13:30:52.084 ApplePushNotification[12160:707] key: acme2, value: 42
```

How It Works

Basically, the role of the provider is to send notifications to the APNs server for relaying to the devices. Hence, you are sending a message of the following format:

```
{
    "aps":
    {
        "alert":"You got a new message!",
        "badge":5,
        "sound":"beep.wav"
    },
    "acme1":"bar",
    "acme2":42
}
```

The beep.wav filename indicates to the client to play the beep.wav file when the notification is received. If you specified an audio file that cannot be found on the target application (the one receiving the notification), the application will use the default sound for the alert.

SUMMARY

In this chapter, you have seen the various steps required to build an iOS application that utilizes the Apple Push Notification service. Take some time to go through the steps to obtain your development certificates and provisioning profile, for they commonly trip up a developer. Once you get the service working, however, the effort is well worth it!

EXERCISES

1. Name the two certificates that you need to generate in order to use the Apple Push Notification service.

2. Why is it recommended that you back up the development certificate in the Keychain Access application?

3. Name the method used for registering for push notifications.

4. What is the use of the device token?

5. Name the event used to obtain the notification pushed to your device.

Answers to the exercises can be found in Appendix D.

▶ **WHAT YOU LEARNED IN THIS CHAPTER**

TOPIC	KEY CONCEPTS
Steps to using APNs	Generate a certificate request.
	Generate a development certificate.
	Create an App ID.
	Configure the App ID for Push Notification.
	Create a provisioning profile.
	Provision a device.
	Create the iOS application.
	Deploy the application onto a device.
	Create the Push Notification Provider application.
Development certificate	The certificate you download from Apple contains only the public key; the private key is saved in Keychain Access when you generate the certificate request.
	It is recommended that you back up the development certificate.
Provisioning profile	Specifies which devices can be allowed to deploy your applications
Registering for push notification	Use the `registerForRemoteNotificationTypes:` method of the `UIApplication` class.
Obtaining the device token	Obtainable from the `application:didRegisterForRemoteNotificationsWith DeviceToken:` event
Obtaining the push notification sent to the device	Obtainable from the `application:didReceiveRemoteNotification:` event

20

Displaying Maps

With the advent of mobile devices, users have become accustomed to having access to locale information at their fingertips. In this chapter, you will learn how to use the Map Kit to give users that information quickly and easily. You will also learn how to obtain the geographical position of your device using the Core Location Manager, and how to use this information to create a compelling iOS Location-Based Services application.

DISPLAYING MAPS AND MONITORING CHANGES USING THE MAP KIT

The iOS SDK ships with the Map Kit framework, a set of libraries that work with the Google Mobile Maps Service. You can use the Map Kit to display maps within your iOS application, as well as to display your current location. In fact, you can enable the Map Kit to track your current location simply by setting a single property, and the Map Kit will then automatically display your current location as you move.

In the following Try It Out, you will get started with the Map Kit. In particular, you will use the Map Kit to display your current location on the map.

TRY IT OUT   Getting Started with Map Kit

codefile Maps.zip available for download at Wrox.com

1. Using Xcode, create a Single View Application (iPhone) project and name it **Maps**. You also need to use the project name (Maps) as the Class Prefix and ensure that you have the Use Automatic Reference Counting option unchecked.

2. Add the `MapKit.framework` to the Frameworks folder of the project (see Figure 20-1).

3. Select the `MapsViewController.xib` file to edit it in Interface Builder.

4. Populate the View window with the following views (see Figure 20-2):

   ➤   Map View

   ➤   Round Rect Button (label it "Show My Location"; be sure to do this correctly, including capitalization)

5. In the `MapsViewController.h` file, add the following bold statements:

FIGURE 20-1

```
#import <UIKit/UIKit.h>
#import <MapKit/MapKit.h>

@interface MapsViewController : UIViewController
{
    IBOutlet UIButton *btnShowLocation;
    IBOutlet MKMapView *mapView;
}

@property (nonatomic, retain) UIButton *btnShowLocation;
@property (nonatomic, retain) MKMapView *mapView;

-(IBAction) showLocation:(id) sender;
@end
```

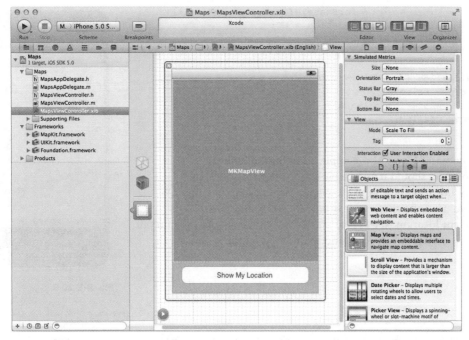

FIGURE 20-2

6. Back in Interface Builder, perform the following actions:

➤ Control-click and drag the File's Owner item and drop it over the Map View. Select `mapView`.

➤ Control-click and drag the File's Owner item and drop it over the Show My Location button. Select `btnShowLocation`.

➤ Control-click and drag the Show My Location button and drop it over the File's Owner item. Select `showLocation:`.

7. In the `MapsViewController.m` file, add the following bold statements:

```
#import "MapsViewController.h"

@implementation MapsViewController

@synthesize btnShowLocation;
@synthesize mapView;

-(IBAction) showLocation:(id) sender {
    if ([[btnShowLocation titleForState:UIControlStateNormal]
        isEqualToString:@"Show My Location"]) {
        [btnShowLocation setTitle:@"Hide My Location"
                        forState:UIControlStateNormal];
        mapView.showsUserLocation = YES;
    } else {
        [btnShowLocation setTitle:@"Show My Location"
```

```
                           forState:UIControlStateNormal];
          mapView.showsUserLocation = NO;
      }
}

- (void)dealloc {
     [mapView release];
     [btnShowLocation release];
     [super dealloc];
}
```

8. Press Command-R to test the application on the iPhone Simulator. You should now be able to see the map. Click the Show My Location button to view your current location and iOS will ask to use your current location. Click OK and you will see your current location (see Figure 20-3). You can also zoom in and out of the map by Option-clicking and then dragging the mouse on the screen.

FIGURE 20-3

 NOTE *It may take up to 20 seconds for the map to locate your current location. In addition, the initial location displayed in the iPhone Simulator is locked on Apple's headquarters in Cupertino, CA, not your actual location.*

How It Works

To show your current location on the map, you simply set the showsUserLocation property of the MKMapView object to YES:

```
          mapView.showsUserLocation = YES;
```

The map will automatically obtain the device's location using the Core Location framework (discussed in the second part of this chapter).

Note that this property merely specifies whether the user's location is displayed on the map (represented as a throbbing blue circle); it does not center the map to display the user's location. Hence, if you are viewing the map of another location, your current location indicator may not be visible on the map.

Note that as you Option-click and drag the map to zoom it in or out, it is important to keep track of the zoom level of the map so that when the user restarts the application, you can display the map using the previous zoom level.

In the following Try It Out, you keep track of the map zoom level as the user changes it.

Printing Out the Map's Zoom Level

1. Using the Maps project created in the previous section, edit the `MapsViewController.h` file by adding the following bold statement:

```
#import <UIKit/UIKit.h>
#import <MapKit/MapKit.h>

@interface MapsViewController : UIViewController
<MKMapViewDelegate>
{
    IBOutlet UIButton *btnShowLocation;
    IBOutlet MKMapView *mapView;
}

@property (nonatomic, retain) UIButton *btnShowLocation;
@property (nonatomic, retain) MKMapView *mapView;

-(IBAction) showLocation:(id) sender;

@end
```

2. In the `MapsViewController.m` file, add the following bold statements:

```
#import "MapsViewController.h"

@implementation MapsViewController

@synthesize btnShowLocation;
@synthesize mapView;

- (void)viewDidLoad
{
    //---connect the delegate of the MKMapView object to
    // this view controller programmatically; you can also connect
    // it via Interface Builder---
    mapView.delegate = self;
    mapView.mapType = MKMapTypeHybrid;
    [super viewDidLoad];
}

-(void)mapView:(MKMapView *)mv regionWillChangeAnimated:(BOOL)animated {
    //---print out the region span - aka zoom level---
    MKCoordinateRegion region = mapView.region;
    NSLog(@"%f",region.span.latitudeDelta);
    NSLog(@"%f",region. span.longitudeDelta);
}
```

3. Press Command-R to test the application on the iPhone Simulator. Zoom in and out of the map and observe the values displayed on the Debugger Console window (see Figure 20-4).

FIGURE 20-4

How It Works

Whenever the zoom level of the map changes, the mapView:regionWillChangeAnimated: event is fired. Hence, you implement the event handler for this event if you want to know when a map is pinched. The mapView:regionWillChangeAnimated: event is defined in the MKMapViewDelegate protocol, so you needed to implement this protocol in the View Controller:

```
@interface MapsViewController : UIViewController
<MKMapViewDelegate>
```

The region displayed by the map is defined by the region property, which is a structure of type MKCoordinateRegion:

```
//---print out the region span - aka zoom level---
MKCoordinateRegion region = mapView.region;
```

The MKCoordinateRegion structure contains a member called center (of type CLLocationCoordinate2D) and another member called span (of type MKCoordinateSpan).

The `MKCoordinateSpan` structure in turn contains two members: `latitudeDelta` and `longitudeDelta` (both of type `CLLocationDegrees`, which is a `double`):

```
NSLog(@"%f",region.span.latitudeDelta);
NSLog(@"%f",region.span.longitudeDelta);
```

Both members define the amount of distance to display for the map:

➤ `latitudeDelta` — One degree of latitude is approximately 111 kilometers (69 miles).

➤ `longitudeDelta` — One degree of longitude spans a distance of approximately 111 kilometers (69 miles) at the equator but shrinks to 0 kilometers at the poles.

Examine the value of these two structures as you zoom in and out of the map — they are a representation of the map's zoom level.

GETTING LOCATION DATA

Nowadays, mobile devices are commonly equipped with GPS receivers. Because of the many satellites orbiting the earth, courtesy of the U.S. government, you can use a GPS receiver to find your location easily. However, GPS requires a clear sky to work and hence does not always work indoors or where satellites can't penetrate (such as a tunnel through a mountain).

Another effective way to locate your position is through cell tower triangulation. When a mobile phone is switched on, it is constantly in contact with base stations surrounding it. By knowing the identity of cell towers, it is possible to correlate this information into a physical location through the use of various databases containing the cell towers' identities and their exact geographical locations. Cell tower triangulation has its advantages over GPS because it works indoors, without the need to obtain information from satellites. However, it is not as precise as GPS because its accuracy depends on the area you are in. Cell tower triangulation works best in densely populated areas where the cell towers are closely located.

A third method of locating your position is to rely on Wi-Fi triangulation. Rather than connect to cell towers, the device connects to a Wi-Fi network and checks the service provider against databases to determine the location serviced by the provider. Of the three methods described here, Wi-Fi triangulation is the least accurate.

On iOS devices, Apple provides the Core Location framework to help you determine your physical location. The beauty of this framework is that it makes use of all three approaches, and whichever method it uses is totally transparent to the developer. You simply specify the accuracy you need, and Core Location determines the best way to obtain the results for you.

Sound amazing? It is. The following Try It Out shows you how this is done in code.

TRY IT OUT | **Obtaining Location Coordinates**

codefile LBS.zip available for download at Wrox.com

1. Using Xcode, create a Single View Application (iPhone) project and name it **LBS**. You also need to use the project name (LBS) as the Class Prefix and ensure that you have the Use Automatic Reference Counting option unchecked.

2. Add the `CoreLocation.framework` to the Frameworks folder (see Figure 20-5).

3. Select the `LBSViewController.xib` file to edit it in Interface Builder. Populate the View window with the following views (see Figure 20-6):

➤ Label (name them **Latitude, Longitude,** and **Accuracy**)

➤ Text Field

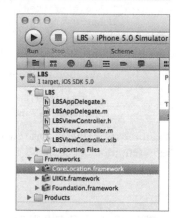

FIGURE 20-5

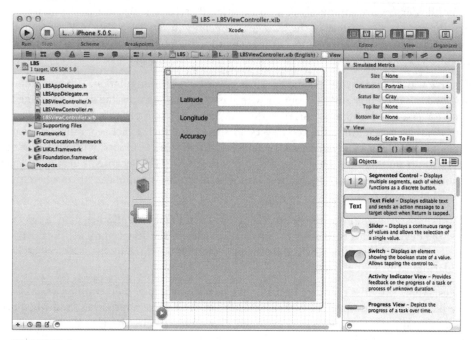

FIGURE 20-6

4. In the `LBSViewController.h` file, add the following statements that appear in bold:

```
#import <UIKit/UIKit.h>
#import <CoreLocation/CoreLocation.h>

@interface LBSViewController : UIViewController
<CLLocationManagerDelegate> {
```

```
    IBOutlet UITextField *accuracyTextField;
    IBOutlet UITextField *latitudeTextField;
    IBOutlet UITextField *longitudeTextField;
    CLLocationManager *lm;
}

@property (retain, nonatomic) UITextField *accuracyTextField;
@property (retain, nonatomic) UITextField *latitudeTextField;
@property (retain, nonatomic) UITextField *longitudeTextField;

@end
```

5. In Interface Builder, perform the following actions:

➤ Control-click and drag the File's Owner item and drop it over the first Text Field view. Select latitudeTextField.

➤ Control-click and drag the File's Owner item and drop it over the second Text Field view. Select longitudeTextField.

➤ Control-click and drag the File's Owner item and drop it over the third Text Field view. Select accuracyTextField.

6. In the LBSViewController.m file, add the following statements that appear in bold:

```
#import "LBSViewController.h"

@implementation LBSViewController

@synthesize latitudeTextField;
@synthesize longitudeTextField;
@synthesize accuracyTextField;

- (void)viewDidLoad
{
    lm = [[CLLocationManager alloc] init];
    lm.delegate = self;
    lm.desiredAccuracy = kCLLocationAccuracyBest;
    lm.distanceFilter = kCLDistanceFilterNone;
    [lm startUpdatingLocation];
    [super viewDidLoad];
}

- (void) locationManager:(CLLocationManager *) manager
       didUpdateToLocation:(CLLocation *) newLocation
              fromLocation:(CLLocation *) oldLocation {

    //---display latitude---
    NSString *lat = [[NSString alloc] initWithFormat:@"%f",
                        newLocation.coordinate.latitude];
    latitudeTextField.text = lat;

    //---display longitude---
    NSString *lng = [[NSString alloc] initWithFormat:@"%f",
                        newLocation.coordinate.longitude];
    longitudeTextField.text = lng;

    //---display accuracy---
```

```
        NSString *acc = [[NSString alloc] initWithFormat:@"%f",
                        newLocation.horizontalAccuracy];
        accuracyTextField.text = acc;

        [acc release];
        [lat release];
        [lng release];
}

- (void) locationManager:(CLLocationManager *) manager
        didFailWithError:(NSError *) error {
    NSString *msg = [[NSString alloc]
                    initWithString:@"Error obtaining location"];
    UIAlertView *alert = [[UIAlertView alloc] initWithTitle:@"Error"
                                        message:msg
                                        delegate:nil
                                cancelButtonTitle:@"Done"
                                otherButtonTitles:nil];

        [alert show];
        [msg release];
        [alert release];
}

- (void)dealloc {
        [lm stopUpdatingLocation];
        [lm release];
        [latitudeTextField release];
        [longitudeTextField release];
        [accuracyTextField release];
        [super dealloc];
}
```

7. Press Command-R to test the application on the iPhone Simulator. The Simulator will ask for permission to use your current location, so click OK. Observe the latitude, longitude, and accuracy reported (see Figure 20-7). The accuracy value indicates the radius of uncertainty for the location, measured in meters.

How It Works

First, to use the CLLocationManager class, you needed to implement the CLLocationManagerDelegate protocol in your View Controller:

FIGURE 20-7

```
@interface LBSViewController : UIViewController
<CLLocationManagerDelegate> {
```

When the View is loaded, you create an instance of the CLLocationManager class:

```
- (void)viewDidLoad
{
    lm = [[CLLocationManager alloc] init];
    lm.delegate = self;
    lm.desiredAccuracy = kCLLocationAccuracyBest;
    lm.distanceFilter = kCLDistanceFilterNone;
```

```
    [lm startUpdatingLocation];
    [super viewDidLoad];
}
```

You then proceeded to specify the desired accuracy using the desiredAccuracy property. You can use the following constants to specify the accuracy that you want:

➤   kCLLocationAccuracyBestForNavigation

➤   kCLLocationAccuracyBest

➤   kCLLocationAccuracyNearestTenMeters

➤   kCLLocationAccuracyHundredMeters

➤   kCLLocationAccuracyKilometer

➤   kCLLocationAccuracyThreeKilometers

While you can specify the accuracy that you want, the actual accuracy is not guaranteed. Also, specifying a location with greater accuracy takes a significant amount of time and your device's battery power.

The distanceFilter property enables you to specify the distance a device must move laterally before an update is generated. The unit for this property is in meters, relative to its last position. To be notified of all movements, use the kCLDistanceFilterNone constant.

Finally, you start the location manager using the startUpdatingLocation method. The user can enable/disable location services in the Settings application. If the service is not enabled and you proceed with the location update, the application asks the user if he or she would like to enable the location services. To stop the location manager, simply use the stopUpdatingLocation method. Remember to do this when you are done with the location tracking; otherwise, the battery of your device will run down quickly.

To obtain location information, you need to handle two events:

➤   locationManager:didUpdateToLocation:fromLocation:

➤   locationManager:didFailWithError:

When a new location value is available, the locationManager:didUpdateToLocation:fromLocation: event is fired. If the location manager cannot determine the location, it fires the locationManager:didFailWithError: event.

When a location value is obtained, you display its latitude and longitude, along with its accuracy, using the CLLocation object:

```
- (void) locationManager:(CLLocationManager *) manager
    didUpdateToLocation:(CLLocation *) newLocation
        fromLocation:(CLLocation *) oldLocation {

    //---display latitude---
    NSString *lat = [[NSString alloc] initWithFormat:@"%f",
                    newLocation.coordinate.latitude];
    latitudeTextField.text = lat;

    //---display longitude---
    NSString *lng = [[NSString alloc] initWithFormat:@"%f",
```

```
                        newLocation.coordinate.longitude];
        longitudeTextField.text = lng;

        //---display accuracy---
        NSString *acc = [[NSString alloc] initWithFormat:@"%f",
                        newLocation.horizontalAccuracy];
        accuracyTextField.text = acc;

        [acc release];
        [lat release];
        [lng release];
    }
```

The `horizontalAccuracy` property of the `CLLocation` object specifies the radius of accuracy, in meters.

Specifying the Hardware Requirement for Location Tracking

While most iOS devices support GPS capabilities, there are still some models that do not support it. For example, the iPod touch does not have a built-in GPS receiver. Hence, if your application uses location-based services, it is strongly recommended that you specify the hardware requirements using the `UIRequiredDeviceCapabilities` key in the .plist file. As shown in Figure 20-8, this key has two items: `gps` and `location-services`. If you only want higher-accuracy location data using GPS, you just need to add the `gps` item. If you want to use the GPS as well as cellular and wireless network triangulation, you need to specify both `gps` and `location-services`.

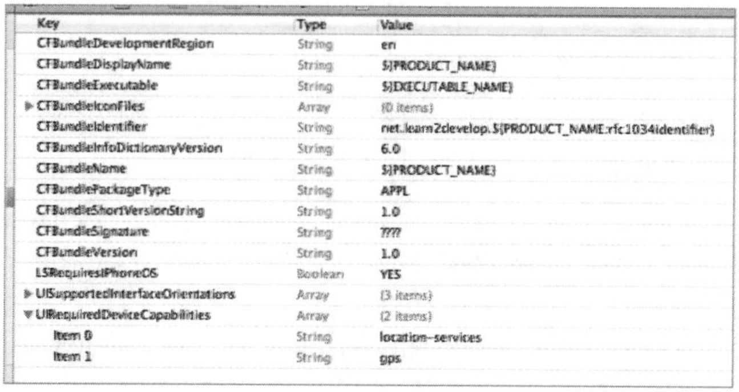

Key	Type	Value
CFBundleDevelopmentRegion	String	en
CFBundleDisplayName	String	${PRODUCT_NAME}
CFBundleExecutable	String	${EXECUTABLE_NAME}
▶ CFBundleIconFiles	Array	(0 items)
CFBundleIdentifier	String	net.learn2develop.${PRODUCT_NAME:rfc1034identifier}
CFBundleInfoDictionaryVersion	String	6.0
CFBundleName	String	${PRODUCT_NAME}
CFBundlePackageType	String	APPL
CFBundleShortVersionString	String	1.0
CFBundleSignature	String	????
CFBundleVersion	String	1.0
LSRequiresIPhoneOS	Boolean	YES
▶ UISupportedInterfaceOrientations	Array	(3 items)
▼ UIRequiredDeviceCapabilities	Array	(2 items)
Item 0	String	location-services
Item 1	String	gps

FIGURE 20-8

Setting the key in the .plist file ensures that AppStore will only install your application on devices that satisfy your hardware requirements. For example, if you specify only the `gps` item, then iPod touch users will not be able to install your application.

Displaying Location Using a Map

Obtaining the location value of a position is interesting, but it isn't very useful if you can't visually locate it on a map. Hence, the ideal situation would be to use the location information to display the location on a map. In the following Try It Out, you will use the Map Kit that you learned how to use in the first part of this chapter to display the map of the location coordinates returned by the Core Location framework. You will also learn how to create the map programmatically, instead of creating it in Interface Builder.

TRY IT OUT Displaying the Location Using a Map

1. Using the LBS project that you just created, add the MapKit .framework to the Frameworks folder (see Figure 20-9).

2. Add the following bold statements to the LBSViewController.h file:

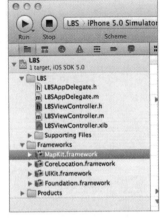

FIGURE 20-9

```objc
#import <UIKit/UIKit.h>
#import <CoreLocation/CoreLocation.h>
#import <MapKit/MapKit.h>

@interface LBSViewController : UIViewController
<CLLocationManagerDelegate, MKMapViewDelegate> {
    IBOutlet UITextField *accuracyTextField;
    IBOutlet UITextField *latitudeTextField;
    IBOutlet UITextField *longitudeTextField;
    CLLocationManager *lm;
    MKMapView *mapView;
}

@property (retain, nonatomic) UITextField *accuracyTextField;
@property (retain, nonatomic) UITextField *latitudeTextField;
@property (retain, nonatomic) UITextField *longitudeTextField;

@end
```

3. In the LBSViewController.m file, add the following bold statements:

```objc
#import "LBSViewController.h"

@implementation LBSViewController

@synthesize latitudeTextField;
@synthesize longitudeTextField;
@synthesize accuracyTextField;

- (void)viewDidLoad
{
    lm = [[CLLocationManager alloc] init];
    lm.delegate = self;
    lm.desiredAccuracy = kCLLocationAccuracyBest;
    lm.distanceFilter = kCLDistanceFilterNone;
    [lm startUpdatingLocation];

    //---display the map in a region---
    mapView = [[MKMapView alloc]
               initWithFrame:CGRectMake(0, 130, 320, 340)];
```

```objc
    mapView.delegate = self;
    mapView.mapType = MKMapTypeHybrid;
    [self.view addSubview:mapView];

    [super viewDidLoad];
}

- (void) locationManager:(CLLocationManager *) manager
        didUpdateToLocation:(CLLocation *) newLocation
             fromLocation:(CLLocation *) oldLocation {

    //---display latitude---
    NSString *lat = [[NSString alloc] initWithFormat:@"%f",
                      newLocation.coordinate.latitude];
    latitudeTextField.text = lat;

    //---display longitude---
    NSString *lng = [[NSString alloc] initWithFormat:@"%f",
                      newLocation.coordinate.longitude];
    longitudeTextField.text = lng;

    //---display accuracy---
    NSString *acc = [[NSString alloc] initWithFormat:@"%f",
                      newLocation.horizontalAccuracy];
    accuracyTextField.text = acc;

    [acc release];
    [lat release];
    [lng release];

    //---update the map---
    MKCoordinateSpan span;
    span.latitudeDelta = .001;
    span.longitudeDelta = .001;

    MKCoordinateRegion region;
    region.center = newLocation.coordinate;
    region.span = span;
    [mapView setRegion:region animated:TRUE];
}

- (void)dealloc {
    [mapView release];
    [lm stopUpdatingLocation];
    [lm release];
    [latitudeTextField release];
    [longitudeTextField release];
    [accuracyTextField release];
    [super dealloc];
```

4. Press Command-R to test the application on the iPhone Simulator. Observe the map displaying the location reported by the location manager (see Figure 20-10). The center of the map is the location reported.

FIGURE 20-10

NOTE *If you test the application on an actual iPhone device, you will see that the map updates itself dynamically when you move about. On the iPhone Simulator, you can simulate movement by selecting Debug ⇨ Location and choosing the desired location simulation (see Figure 20-11).*

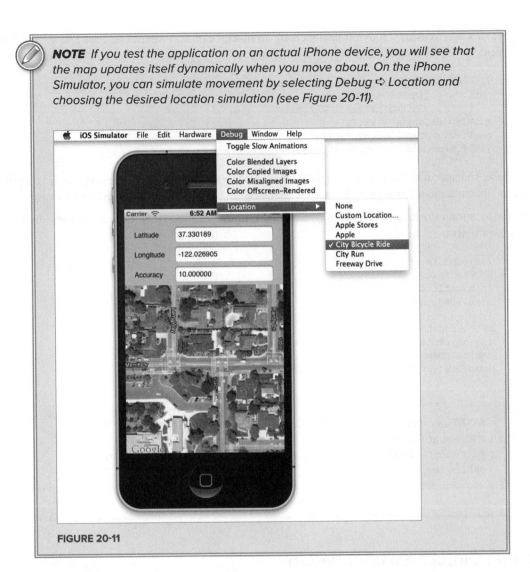

FIGURE 20-11

How It Works

To use the Map Kit in your application, you first needed to add the `MapKit.framework` to your project.

Then, you implemented the `MKMapViewDelegate` protocol in the View Controller to handle the various methods associated with the MapView:

```
@interface LBSViewController : UIViewController
<CLLocationManagerDelegate, MKMapViewDelegate> {
```

When the view has loaded, you dynamically create an instance of the `MKMapView` class and set the map type (hybrid — map and satellite) to display:

```
//---display the map in a region---
mapView = [[MKMapView alloc]
            initWithFrame:CGRectMake(0, 130, 320, 340)];
mapView.delegate = self;
mapView.mapType = MKMapTypeHybrid;
[self.view addSubview:mapView];
```

In this case, you specified the size of the map to display. You set the `delegate` property to `self` so that the View Controller can implement the methods declared in the `MKMapViewDelegate` protocol.

When the location information is updated, you zoom into the location using the `setRegion:` method of the `mapView` object:

```
//---update the map---
MKCoordinateSpan span;
span.latitudeDelta = .001;
span.longitudeDelta = .001;

MKCoordinateRegion region;
region.center = newLocation.coordinate;
region.span = span;
[mapView setRegion:region animated:TRUE];
```

> **NOTE** For more information on the `MKMapView` class, refer to Apple's documentation at `http://developer.apple.com/library/ios/#documentation/MapKit/Reference/MKMapView_Class/MKMapView/MKMapView.html`.

Getting Directional Information

Most iOS devices come with a built-in compass. The following Try It Out shows you how to programmatically obtain directional information using this feature.

TRY IT OUT   Incorporating a Compass

You need a real device (iPhone) to test this application.

1. Using the LBS project, add an image named **Compass.gif** to the Supporting Files folder of the project (see Figure 20-12).

2. In Interface Builder, drag and drop an Image View onto the View window and set its Image attribute to `Compass.gif` and the View Mode attribute to `Aspect Fit` in the Attributes Inspector window. Also, add a Label to the View window (see Figure 20-13).

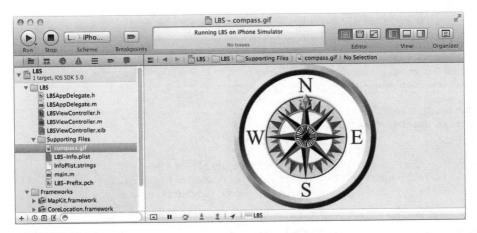

FIGURE 20-12

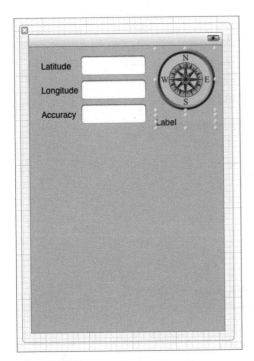

FIGURE 20-13

3. In the `LBSViewController.h` file, add the following bold statements:

```
#import <UIKit/UIKit.h>
#import <CoreLocation/CoreLocation.h>
#import <MapKit/MapKit.h>

@interface LBSViewController : UIViewController
```

```
<CLLocationManagerDelegate, MKMapViewDelegate> {
    IBOutlet UITextField *accuracyTextField;
    IBOutlet UITextField *latitudeTextField;
    IBOutlet UITextField *longitudeTextField;
    CLLocationManager *lm;
    MKMapView *mapView;

    IBOutlet UIImageView *compass;
    IBOutlet UILabel *heading;
}

@property (retain, nonatomic) UITextField *accuracyTextField;
@property (retain, nonatomic) UITextField *latitudeTextField;
@property (retain, nonatomic) UITextField *longitudeTextField;

@property (nonatomic, retain) UIImageView *compass;
@property (nonatomic, retain) UILabel *heading;

@end
```

4. In Interface Builder, perform the following actions:

➤ Control-click and drag the File's Owner item and drop it over the Image View. Select compass.

➤ Control-click and drag the File's Owner item and drop it over the Label. Select heading.

5. In the LBSViewController.m file, add the following bold statements:

```
#import "LBSViewController.h"

@implementation LBSViewController

@synthesize latitudeTextField;
@synthesize longitudeTextField;
@synthesize accuracyTextField;

@synthesize compass;
@synthesize heading;

- (void)locationManager:(CLLocationManager *)manager
      didUpdateHeading:(CLHeading *)newHeading {

    heading.text = [NSString stringWithFormat:@"%.2f degrees",
                    newHeading.magneticHeading];

    //---headings is in degrees---
    double d = newHeading.magneticHeading;

    //---convert degrees to radians---
    double radians = d / 57.2957795;

    compass.transform = CGAffineTransformMakeRotation(-radians);
}
```

```
- (void)viewDidLoad
{
    lm = [[CLLocationManager alloc] init];
    lm.delegate = self;
    lm.desiredAccuracy = kCLLocationAccuracyBest;
    lm.distanceFilter = kCLDistanceFilterNone;
    [lm startUpdatingLocation];

    //---get the compass readings---
    [lm startUpdatingHeading];

    //---display the map in a region---
    mapView = [[MKMapView alloc]
            initWithFrame:CGRectMake(0, 130, 320, 340)];
    mapView.delegate = self;
    mapView.mapType = MKMapTypeHybrid;
    [self.view addSubview:mapView];

    [super viewDidLoad];
}

- (void)dealloc {
    [compass release];
    [heading release];
    [mapView release];
    [lm stopUpdatingLocation];
    [lm release];
    [latitudeTextField release];
    [longitudeTextField release];
    [accuracyTextField release];
    [super dealloc];
}
```

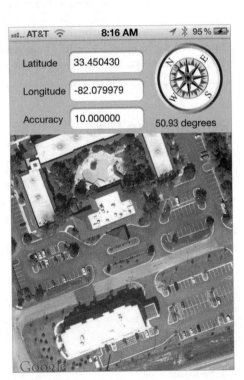

6. Add the `CoreGraphics.framework` to your project if it is not already added to the project (in the beta version of the SDK, this framework is not added in by default).

7. Press Command-R to test the application on an actual iPhone. Observe the image as you turn the device (see Figure 20-14).

FIGURE 20-14

How It Works

Getting directional information is similar to getting location data; you use the Core Location framework. Instead of calling the `startUpdatingLocation` method of the `CLLocationManager` object, you call the `startUpdatingHeading` method:

```
//---get the compass readings---
[lm startUpdatingHeading];
```

When directional information is available, the `locationManager:didUpdateHeading:` method will continually fire:

```
- (void)locationManager:(CLLocationManager *)manager
        didUpdateHeading:(CLHeading *)newHeading {

    heading.text = [NSString stringWithFormat:@"%.2f degrees",
                    newHeading.magneticHeading];

    //---headings is in degrees---
    double d = newHeading.magneticHeading;

    //---convert degrees to radians---
    double radians = d / 57.2957795;

    compass.transform = CGAffineTransformMakeRotation(-radians);
```

The `magneticHeading` property of the `CLHeading` parameter will contain the readings in degrees, with 0 representing magnetic North. The `ImageView` is then rotated based on the value of the heading. Note that you need to convert the degrees into radians for the `CGAffineTransformMakeRotation()` method.

Rotating the Map

The previous section showed how you can programmatically rotate the image of a compass based on the directional heading information obtained from the Core Location framework. Using this concept, you could also rotate the map whenever the direction of your device changes. This is very useful when you are using the map for navigational purposes. The following Try It Out shows how you can rotate the map based on your headings.

TRY IT OUT   **Rotating the Map**

1. Using the LBS project, select the `LBSViewController.xib` file to edit it in Interface Builder.

2. Drag and drop a View view from the Object Library and set its size and location via its Size Inspector window as follows (see also Figure 20-15):

   ➤   **X:** 0

   ➤   **Y:** 130

   ➤   **W:** 320

   ➤   **H:** 330

3. In the Attributes Inspector window for the View, check the Clip Subviews option (see Figure 20-16).

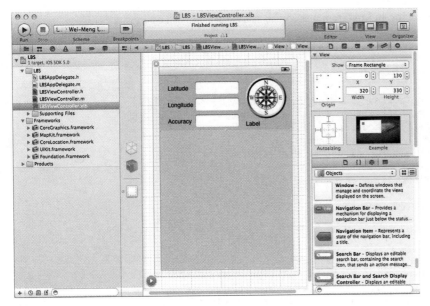

FIGURE 20-15

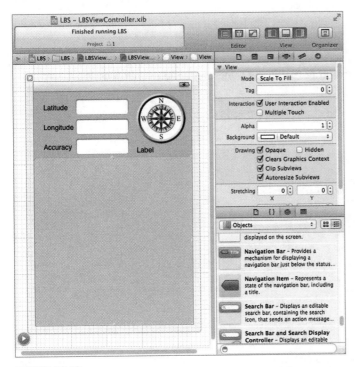

FIGURE 20-16

4. In Xcode, add the following bold statements to the `LBSViewController.h` file:

```
#import <UIKit/UIKit.h>
#import <CoreLocation/CoreLocation.h>
#import <MapKit/MapKit.h>

@interface LBSViewController : UIViewController
<CLLocationManagerDelegate, MKMapViewDelegate> {
    IBOutlet UITextField *accuracyTextField;
    IBOutlet UITextField *latitudeTextField;
    IBOutlet UITextField *longitudeTextField;
    CLLocationManager *lm;
    MKMapView *mapView;

    IBOutlet UIImageView *compass;
    IBOutlet UILabel *heading;
    IBOutlet UIView *viewForMap;
}

@property (retain, nonatomic) UITextField *accuracyTextField;
@property (retain, nonatomic) UITextField *latitudeTextField;
@property (retain, nonatomic) UITextField *longitudeTextField;

@property (nonatomic, retain) UIImageView *compass;
@property (nonatomic, retain) UILabel *heading;
@property (nonatomic, retain) UIView *viewForMap;

@end
```

5. In Interface Builder, Control-click and drag the File's Owner item and drop it over the newly added View view. Select `viewForMap`.

6. Add the following bold statements to the `LBSViewController.m` file:

```
#import "LBSViewController.h"

@implementation LBSViewController

@synthesize latitudeTextField;
@synthesize longitudeTextField;
@synthesize accuracyTextField;

@synthesize compass;
@synthesize heading;

@synthesize viewForMap;

- (void)viewDidLoad
{
    lm = [[CLLocationManager alloc] init];
    lm.delegate = self;
    lm.desiredAccuracy = kCLLocationAccuracyBest;
    lm.distanceFilter = kCLDistanceFilterNone;
```

```
        [lm startUpdatingLocation];

        //---get the compass readings---
        [lm startUpdatingHeading];

        //---display the map in a region---
        mapView = [[MKMapView alloc]
                    initWithFrame:CGRectMake(-90, -85, 500,500)];

        //initWithFrame:CGRectMake(0, 130, 320, 340)];
        mapView.delegate = self;
        mapView.mapType = MKMapTypeHybrid;

        // [self.view addSubview:mapView];
        [self.viewForMap addSubview:mapView];

        [super viewDidLoad];
}

- (void)locationManager:(CLLocationManager *)manager
        didUpdateHeading:(CLHeading *)newHeading {

    heading.text = [NSString stringWithFormat:@"%.2f degrees",
                    newHeading.magneticHeading];

    //---headings is in degrees---
    double d = newHeading.magneticHeading;

    //----convert degrees to radians----
    double radians = d / 57.2957795;

    compass.transform = CGAffineTransformMakeRotation(-radians);

    //---rotate the map---
    mapView.transform = CGAffineTransformMakeRotation(-radians);

}

- (void)dealloc {
    [viewForMap release];
    [compass release];
    [heading release];
    [mapView release];
    [lm stopUpdatingLocation];
    [lm release];
    [latitudeTextField release];
    [longitudeTextField release];
    [accuracyTextField release];
    [super dealloc];
```

7. Deploy the application to a real iPhone device. Observe that as you rotate the iPhone, the map rotates as well.

How It Works

Rotating the map is actually very simple. While you might first assume that the easiest way would be to apply the transformation to the mapView, doing that rotates not only the map, but the entire rectangle (see Figure 20-17).

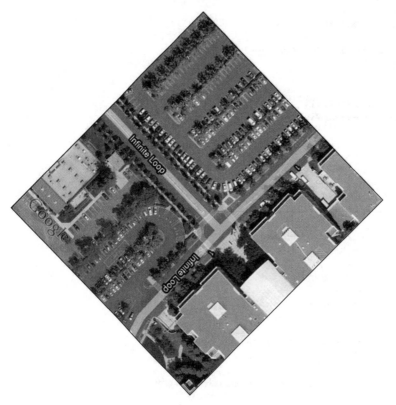

FIGURE 20-17

The trick is to embed the mapView within another View view and rotate it within the View. Hence, you added another View view (viewForMap) in the View window and set it to Clip Subviews. Essentially, all the views added to this View will not display beyond its boundary.

Instead of displaying the map in the original size, you needed to set it to a minimum of 459.67 x 459.67 pixels. This is the length of the diagonal of the viewable rectangle of the map. For simplicity, round it up to 500 x 500 pixels.

The mapView is then added to viewForMap, instead of self.view:

```
// [self.view addSubview:mapView];
[self.viewForMap addSubview:mapView];
```

Recall that the initial position of the `mapView` was (0, 130):

```
//---display the map in a region---
mapView = [[MKMapView alloc]
            initWithFrame:CGRectMake(0, 130, 320, 340)];
```

But it must now be changed to (−90, −85):

```
//---display the map in a region---
mapView = [[MKMapView alloc]
            initWithFrame:CGRectMake(-90, -85, 500,500)];
            //initWithFrame:CGRectMake(0, 130, 320, 340)];
```

Figure 20-18 shows how the new coordinate of (−90, −85) was derived. Remember that when you try to add a view to another view, the coordinate specified is always with respect to the view you are adding to. In this case, the reference point (0,0) is at `viewForMap`.

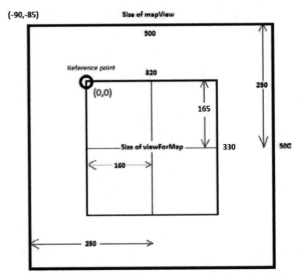

FIGURE 20-18

Finally, to rotate the map, you applied the `CGAffineTransformMakeRotation()` method to the `mapView`:

```
//---rotate the map---
mapView.transform = CGAffineTransformMakeRotation(-radians);
```

NOTE *In iOS 5, you can also use the new* `setUserTrackingMode:animated:` *method to automatically display a blue circle on the map showing the location of the user:*

```
[mapView setUserTrackingMode:MKUserTrackingModeFollowWithHeading
    animated:YES];
```

The `MKUserTrackingModeFollowWithHeading` constant causes the map to move with the user (see Figure 20-19) as well as rotate automatically based on the heading information.

FIGURE 20-19

Displaying Annotations

So far, you have used Core Location to report your current location and heading, and then Map Kit to display a map representing your location. A visual improvement you can make to the project is to add a pushpin to the map, representing your current location.

In the following Try It Out, you learn how to add annotations to the map in Map Kit. Annotations enable you to display pushpins on the map, denoting specific locations.

TRY IT OUT Displaying a Pushpin

1. Continuing with the LBS project, add a new Objective-C class file to the project (see Figure 20-20).

2. Name it **MyAnnotation.m**. Once it is added, you should see the `MyAnnotation.h` and `MyAnnotation.m` files under the project (see Figure 20-21).

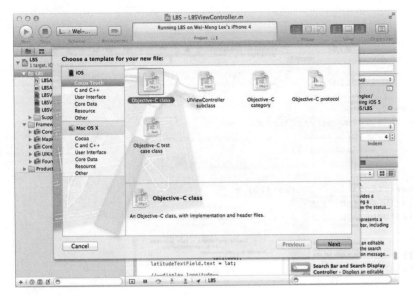

FIGURE 20-20

FIGURE 20-21

3. Populate the `MyAnnotation.h` file as follows:

```
#import <Foundation/Foundation.h>
#import <MapKit/MapKit.h>

@interface MyAnnotation : NSObject <MKAnnotation> {
    CLLocationCoordinate2D coordinate;
    NSString *title;
    NSString *subtitle;
}

@property (nonatomic, readonly) CLLocationCoordinate2D coordinate;
@property (nonatomic, readonly, copy) NSString *title;
@property (nonatomic, readonly, copy) NSString *subtitle;

-(id)initWithCoordinate:(CLLocationCoordinate2D) c
                  title:(NSString *) t
               subtitle:(NSString *) st;

@end
```

4. Populate the `MyAnnotation.m` file as follows:

```
#import "MyAnnotation.h"

@implementation MyAnnotation

@synthesize coordinate;
```

```
@synthesize title;
@synthesize subtitle;

- (id)init
{
    CLLocationCoordinate2D location;
    location.latitude = 0;
    location.longitude = 0;
    return [self initWithCoordinate:coordinate
                              title:nil
                           subtitle:nil];
}

-(id)initWithCoordinate:(CLLocationCoordinate2D) c
                  title:(NSString *) t
               subtitle:(NSString *) st {
    self = [super init];
    coordinate = c;
    title = [t retain];
    subtitle = [st retain];
    return self;
}

- (void) dealloc{
    [title release];
    [subtitle release];
    [super dealloc];
}

@end
```

5. In the `LBSViewController.h` file, add the following bold statements:

```
#import <UIKit/UIKit.h>
#import <CoreLocation/CoreLocation.h>
#import <MapKit/MapKit.h>

#import "MyAnnotation.h"

@interface LBSViewController : UIViewController
<CLLocationManagerDelegate, MKMapViewDelegate> {
    IBOutlet UITextField *accuracyTextField;
    IBOutlet UITextField *latitudeTextField;
    IBOutlet UITextField *longitudeTextField;
    CLLocationManager *lm;
    MKMapView *mapView;

    IBOutlet UIImageView *compass;
    IBOutlet UILabel *heading;
    IBOutlet UIView *viewForMap;

    MyAnnotation *annotation;
}

@property (retain, nonatomic) UITextField *accuracyTextField;
```

```
@property (retain, nonatomic) UITextField *latitudeTextField;
@property (retain, nonatomic) UITextField *longitudeTextField;

@property (nonatomic, retain) UIImageView *compass;
@property (nonatomic, retain) UILabel *heading;
@property (nonatomic, retain) UIView *viewForMap;

@end
```

6. In the `LBSViewController.m` file, add the following bold statements:

```
- (void) locationManager:(CLLocationManager *) manager
    didUpdateToLocation:(CLLocation *) newLocation
          fromLocation:(CLLocation *) oldLocation {

    //---display latitude---
    NSString *lat = [[NSString alloc] initWithFormat:@"%f",
                    newLocation.coordinate.latitude];
    latitudeTextField.text = lat;

    //---display longitude---
    NSString *lng = [[NSString alloc] initWithFormat:@"%f",
                    newLocation.coordinate.longitude];
    longitudeTextField.text = lng;

    //---display accuracy---
    NSString *acc = [[NSString alloc] initWithFormat:@"%f",
                    newLocation.horizontalAccuracy];
    accuracyTextField.text = acc;

    [acc release];
    [lat release];
    [lng release];

    //---update the map---
    MKCoordinateSpan span;
    span.latitudeDelta = .001;
    span.longitudeDelta = .001;

    MKCoordinateRegion region;
    region.center = newLocation.coordinate;
    region.span = span;
    [mapView setRegion:region animated:TRUE];

    //---display an annotation here---
    if (!annotation) {
        annotation = [[MyAnnotation alloc]
                    initWithCoordinate:newLocation.coordinate
                    title:@"You are here"
                    subtitle:[NSString
                            stringWithFormat:@"Lat: %@. Lng: %@",
                            latitudeTextField.text,
                            longitudeTextField.text]];
        [mapView addAnnotation:annotation];
```

```
        }
    }

    - (void)dealloc {
        [annotation release];
        [viewForMap release];
        [compass release];
        [heading release];
        [mapView release];
        [lm stopUpdatingLocation];
        [lm release];
        [latitudeTextField release];
        [longitudeTextField release];
        [accuracyTextField release];
        [super dealloc];
    }
```

FIGURE 20-22

7. Press Command-R to test the application on the iPhone Simulator.
    You'll see the pushpin inserted into the current position. When you tap
    on it, it displays the information in the annotation view as shown in
    Figure 20-22.

How It Works

You first created the `MyAnnotation` class, which inherits from the `MKAnnotation` base class. Within the
`MyAnnotation` class, you implemented several properties (including `coordinate`, which specifies the
center point of the annotation), in particular:

➤   `title` property — Returns the title to be displayed on the annotation

➤   `subtitle` property — Returns the subtitle to be displayed on the annotation

As you get a location of the device, you display an annotation to represent the current location:

```
    //---display an annotation here---
    if (!annotation) {
        annotation = [[MyAnnotation alloc]
                     initWithCoordinate:newLocation.coordinate
                     title:@"You are here"
                     subtitle:[NSString
                             stringWithFormat:@"Lat: %@. Lng: %@",
                             latitudeTextField.text,
                             longitudeTextField.text]];
        [mapView addAnnotation:annotation];
```

To remove the annotation from the map, use the `removeAnnotation:` method of the `MKMapView` object.

Reverse Geocoding

While knowing your location coordinates is useful, and displaying your location on the Google Maps is
cool, the capability to know your current address is even cooler! The process of finding your address
from a pair of latitude and longitude coordinates is known as *reverse geocoding*. The following

Try It Out shows how to obtain the address of a location given its latitude and longitude. You will do so via the API exposed by the Core Location framework.

TRY IT OUT Obtaining an Address from Latitude and Longitude

1. Continuing with the LBS project, add the following bold statements to the LBSViewController.h file:

```
#import <UIKit/UIKit.h>
#import <CoreLocation/CoreLocation.h>
#import <MapKit/MapKit.h>

#import "MyAnnotation.h"

@interface LBSViewController : UIViewController
<CLLocationManagerDelegate, MKMapViewDelegate> {
    IBOutlet UITextField *accuracyTextField;
    IBOutlet UITextField *latitudeTextField;
    IBOutlet UITextField *longitudeTextField;
    CLLocationManager *lm;
    MKMapView *mapView;

    IBOutlet UIImageView *compass;
    IBOutlet UILabel *heading;
    IBOutlet UIView *viewForMap;

    MyAnnotation *annotation;
    NSString *location;

    CLGeocoder *geocoder;
}

@property (retain, nonatomic) UITextField *accuracyTextField;
@property (retain, nonatomic) UITextField *latitudeTextField;
@property (retain, nonatomic) UITextField *longitudeTextField;

@property (nonatomic, retain) UIImageView *compass;
@property (nonatomic, retain) UILabel *heading;
@property (nonatomic, retain) UIView *viewForMap;

@end
```

2. In the LBSViewController.m file, add the following bold statements:

```
- (void) locationManager:(CLLocationManager *) manager
     didUpdateToLocation:(CLLocation *) newLocation
            fromLocation:(CLLocation *) oldLocation {

    //---display latitude---
    NSString *lat = [[NSString alloc] initWithFormat:@"%f",
                    newLocation.coordinate.latitude];
    latitudeTextField.text = lat;

    //---display longitude---
```

```
NSString *lng = [[NSString alloc] initWithFormat:@"%f",
                 newLocation.coordinate.longitude];
longitudeTextField.text = lng;

//---display accuracy---
NSString *acc = [[NSString alloc] initWithFormat:@"%f",
                 newLocation.horizontalAccuracy];
accuracyTextField.text = acc;

[acc release];
[lat release];
[lng release];

//---update the map---
MKCoordinateSpan span;
span.latitudeDelta = .001;
span.longitudeDelta = .001;

MKCoordinateRegion region;
region.center = newLocation.coordinate;
region.span = span;
[mapView setRegion:region animated:TRUE];

//---display an annotation here---
if (!annotation) {
    //---perform reverse geocoding---
    [geocoder reverseGeocodeLocation:newLocation
                completionHandler:^(NSArray *placemark, NSError *error){
        for (int i=0; i<=[placemark count] - 1; i++) {
            location =
                [NSString stringWithFormat:@"%@, %@",
                    ((CLPlacemark *) [placemark objectAtIndex:i]).locality,
                    ((CLPlacemark *) [placemark objectAtIndex:i]).country];
            UIAlertView *alert = [[UIAlertView alloc]
                initWithTitle:@"Your location"
                    message:location
                    delegate:self
                cancelButtonTitle:@"OK"
                otherButtonTitles:nil];
            [alert show];
            [alert release];
        }
    }];

    annotation = [[MyAnnotation alloc]
                    initWithCoordinate:newLocation.coordinate
                    title:@"You are here"
                    subtitle:[NSString
                            stringWithFormat:@"Lat: %f. Lng: %f",
                            newLocation.coordinate.latitude,
                            newLocation.coordinate.longitude]];

    [mapView addAnnotation:annotation];
}
```

```
    }

- (void)dealloc {
    [annotation release];
    [viewForMap release];
    [compass release];
    [heading release];
    [mapView release];
    [lm stopUpdatingLocation];
    [lm release];
    [latitudeTextField release];
    [longitudeTextField release];
    [accuracyTextField release];
    [super dealloc];
}
```

3. Press Command-R to test the application on the iPhone Simulator. Notice that when the address of the location is found, an alert is displayed (see Figure 20-23).

How It Works

FIGURE 20-23

To perform reverse geocoding, you use the CLGeocoder class:

```
CLGeocoder *geocoder;
```

The CLGeocoder class (located in the Core Location framework) is new in iOS 5 and replaces the older MKReverseGeocoder class (from the Map Kit framework), which has now been deprecated.

When a location is obtained (via the locationManager:didUpdateToLocation:fromLocation: event), you instantiate the CLGeocoder class by setting it to a location coordinate via the reverseGeocodeLocation:completionHandler: method:

```
//---display an annotation here---
if (!annotation) {
    //---perform reverse geocoding---
    [geocoder reverseGeocodeLocation:newLocation
                completionHandler:^(NSArray *placemark, NSError *error){
        for (int i=0; i<=[placemark count] - 1; i++) {
            location =
                [NSString stringWithFormat:@"%@, %@",
                    ((CLPlacemark *) [placemark objectAtIndex:i]).locality,
                    ((CLPlacemark *) [placemark objectAtIndex:i]).country];
            UIAlertView *alert = [[UIAlertView alloc]
                initWithTitle:@"Your location"
                      message:location
                     delegate:self
                cancelButtonTitle:@"OK"
                otherButtonTitles:nil];
            [alert show];
            [alert release];
        }
    }];
```

The CLGeocoder class works asynchronously, and will fire the CLGeocodeCompletionHandler block when an address has been found. The address(es) found are encapsulated in the placemark array, and here you simply printed out all the addresses using the alert view.

Displaying a Disclosure Button

When displaying an annotation on the map, it is customary to provide users with the option to select the annotation so that more details about the location can be shown. For example, the user may want to know the detailed address of the location, or you can provide routing information for the selected location. In Map Kit, you can add this option through a detail disclosure button. The following Try It Out shows how to display the disclosure button in an annotation.

TRY IT OUT   **Displaying a Disclosure Button**

1.   Continuing with the LBS project, add the following methods to the LBSViewController.m file:

```
- (MKAnnotationView *)mapView:(MKMapView *)aMapView
           viewForAnnotation:(id)ann {

    NSString *identifier = @"myPin";
    MKPinAnnotationView *pin = (MKPinAnnotationView *)
    [aMapView dequeueReusableAnnotationViewWithIdentifier:identifier];
    if (pin == nil) {
        pin = [[[MKPinAnnotationView alloc] initWithAnnotation:ann
                                            reuseIdentifier:identifier]
                 autorelease];
    } else {
        pin.annotation = ann;
    }

    //---display a disclosure button on the right---
    UIButton *myDetailButton =
    [UIButton buttonWithType:UIButtonTypeDetailDisclosure];
    myDetailButton.frame = CGRectMake(0, 0, 23, 23);
    myDetailButton.contentVerticalAlignment =
    UIControlContentVerticalAlignmentCenter;
    myDetailButton.contentHorizontalAlignment =
    UIControlContentHorizontalAlignmentCenter;

    [myDetailButton addTarget:self
                    action:@selector(checkButtonTapped:)
          forControlEvents:UIControlEventTouchUpInside];

    pin.rightCalloutAccessoryView = myDetailButton;
    pin.enabled = YES;
    pin.animatesDrop=TRUE;
    pin.canShowCallout=YES;

    return pin;
}

-(void) checkButtonTapped:(id) sender {
```

```
//---know which button was clicked;
// useful for multiple pins on the map---
// UIControl *btnClicked = sender;
UIAlertView *alert =
[[UIAlertView alloc] initWithTitle:@"Your Current Location"
                          message:location
                          delegate:self
                 cancelButtonTitle:@"OK"
                 otherButtonTitles:nil];
[alert show];
[alert release];
}
```

2. Press Command-R to test the application on the iPhone Simulator. The annotation view now displays a disclosure button to the right of it (see Figure 20-24). Clicking the button displays an alert view.

How It Works

What you did was override the mapView:viewForAnnotation: method (defined in the MKMapViewDelegate protocol), which is fired every time you add an annotation to the map.

Note the following block of code:

FIGURE 20-24

```
NSString *identifier = @"myPin";
MKPinAnnotationView *pin = (MKPinAnnotationView *)
[aMapView dequeueReusableAnnotationViewWithIdentifier:identifier];
if (pin == nil) {
    pin = [[[MKPinAnnotationView alloc] initWithAnnotation:ann
                                          reuseIdentifier:identifier]
          autorelease];
} else {
    pin.annotation = ann;
}
```

It tries to reuse any annotation objects that are currently not visible on the screen. Imagine you have 10,000 annotations on the map; maintaining MKPinAnnotationView objects in memory is not a feasible option (too much memory is used). Hence, this code tries to reuse MKPinAnnotationView objects that are currently not visible on the screen.

The following code block displays a disclosure button next to the annotation:

```
//---display a disclosure button on the right---
UIButton *myDetailButton =
[UIButton buttonWithType:UIButtonTypeDetailDisclosure];
myDetailButton.frame = CGRectMake(0, 0, 23, 23);
myDetailButton.contentVerticalAlignment =
UIControlContentVerticalAlignmentCenter;
myDetailButton.contentHorizontalAlignment =
UIControlContentHorizontalAlignmentCenter;

[myDetailButton addTarget:self
                   action:@selector(checkButtonTapped:)
```

```
                        forControlEvents:UIControlEventTouchUpInside];

        pin.rightCalloutAccessoryView = myDetailButton;
        pin.enabled = YES;
        pin.animatesDrop=TRUE;
        pin.canShowCallout=YES;
```

When the disclosure button is clicked, it fires the checkButtonTapped: method:

```
    -(void) checkButtonTapped:(id) sender {
        //---know which button was clicked;
        // useful for multiple pins on the map---
        // UIControl *btnClicked = sender;
        UIAlertView *alert =
        [[UIAlertView alloc] initWithTitle:@"Your Current Location"
                                   message:location
                                  delegate:self
                         cancelButtonTitle:@"OK"
                         otherButtonTitles:nil];
        [alert show];
        [alert release];
```

In this case, you simply displayed an Alert view. You can also display another View window to show more detailed information.

SUMMARY

This chapter explained how to use the Map Kit framework to display the Google Maps in your iPhone application. You also saw how to use the Core Location framework to help you obtain your location information. Combining the Map Kit and the Core Location frameworks enables you to create very compelling location-based services.

EXERCISES

1. Name the property of the MKMapView class that enables you to show your current location on the map.

2. Name the protocol that you need to implement in order to monitor changes in your map.

3. Name the method that you need to call to start updating your location.

4. Name the method that you need to call to start updating your heading.

5. Name the class responsible for reverse geocoding.

Answers to the exercises can be found in Appendix D.

▶ **WHAT YOU LEARNED IN THIS CHAPTER**

TOPIC	KEY CONCEPTS
Framework for displaying Google Maps	Map Kit
Framework for obtaining geographical location	Core Location
Class for displaying Google Maps	MKMapView
Showing current location on the map	showsUserLocation
Monitoring changes in the map	Implement the MKMapViewDelegate protocol.
Changing the zoom level of the map	Set the latitudeDelta and longitudeDelta properties of the map.
Monitoring changes in location	Implement the CLLocationManagerDelegate protocol.
Getting location updates	Call the startUpdatingLocation method.
Getting directional updates	Call the startUpdatingHeading method.
Rotating the map	Embed the MapView in another View and rotate the MapView.
Displaying annotations	Create a class that inherits from the MKAnnotation base class.

21

Programming Background Applications

WHAT YOU WILL LEARN IN THIS CHAPTER

➤ How background code execution works in your iPhone applications

➤ Monitoring application states

➤ How to detect and opt out of background execution

➤ How to track location information in the background

➤ Creating local notifications

One of the main features of iOS beginning with version 4 is its support for background applications. Unlike previous versions of the iPhone OS, iOS 4 (and later) does not automatically terminate your application when you press the Home button on your device. Instead, your application is put into a suspended state and all processing is paused. When you tap on the application icon again, the application resumes from its suspended state and continues execution. If your application should continue executing in the background, you need to modify it to inform the OS.

In this chapter, you will examine how background execution works and some of the limitations placed on your applications. In particular, you will learn how to modify the location application covered in Chapter 20 so that it will continue working even after the user has switched it to the background. Last but not least, you will learn about the local notification feature, which was introduced with iOS 4.

UNDERSTANDING BACKGROUND EXECUTION ON THE IOS

While iOS supports background code execution, you need to understand several things before you write your application:

➤ In order to support background code execution, all applications must be compiled against the latest iOS SDK. In other words, if you have downloaded an application from the App Store that is compiled using an older SDK (prior to 4.0), the application will still terminate when you press the Home button on your iOS 5 device.

➤ Background code execution is limited to three specific types of applications:

  ➤ **Audio** — Playing music in the background

  ➤ **Location** — Getting location data in the background

  ➤ **Voice Over IP (VOIP)** — Making phone calls through an Internet connection

➤ If an application does not meet any of the preceding three criteria, it will be suspended when the Home button is pressed.

➤ When an application switches to the background (regardless of whether it is allowed to execute in the background or not), you should always disconnect all network connections (with the exception of VOIP applications). Applications that have active network connections are automatically terminated by the OS when they enter background mode. For example, if your location-based application is transmitting location data to a remote server, you should disable the transmission when the application is switched to the background. While you can continue receiving location data, transmitting it over a network is prohibited when the application is in the background. In this scenario, you might want to log the location data to a database and resend it to the remote server when the application is in the foreground again.

Programming multitasking iOS applications can be a very complex task. The following sections touch on some of the basics to get you started quickly.

Examining the Different Application States

The iOS includes events that you can handle in your application delegate so that you can monitor your application's current state. The following Try It Out shows the various states that an application goes through.

TRY IT OUT Handling Application Event States

codefile States.zip available for download at Wrox.com

1. Using Xcode, create a Single View Application (iPhone) project and name it **States**. You will also use the project name as the Class Prefix and ensure that you have the Use Automatic Reference Counting option unchecked.

2. Add the following bold code to the `StatesAppDelegate.m` file:

```objc
#import "StatesAppDelegate.h"

#import "StatesViewController.h"

@implementation StatesAppDelegate

@synthesize window = _window;
@synthesize viewController = _viewController;

- (BOOL)application:(UIApplication *)application
    didFinishLaunchingWithOptions:(NSDictionary *)launchOptions
{
    NSLog(@"application:didFinishLaunchingWithOptions:");
    self.window = [[[UIWindow alloc] initWithFrame:[[UIScreen mainScreen] bounds]]
        autorelease];
    // Override point for customization after application launch.
    self.viewController = [[[StatesViewController alloc]
        initWithNibName:@"StatesViewController" bundle:nil] autorelease];
    self.window.rootViewController = self.viewController;
    [self.window makeKeyAndVisible];
    return YES;
}

- (void)applicationWillResignActive:(UIApplication *)application
{
    NSLog(@"applicationWillResignActive:");
    /*
     Sent when the application is about to move from active to inactive state.
This can occur for certain types of temporary interruptions (such as an
incoming phone call or SMS message) or when the user quits the application and
it begins the transition to the background state.
     Use this method to pause ongoing tasks, disable timers, and throttle down
OpenGL ES frame rates. Games should use this method to pause the game.
     */
}

- (void)applicationDidEnterBackground:(UIApplication *)application
{
    NSLog(@"applicationDidEnterBackground:");
    /*
     Use this method to release shared resources, save user data, invalidate
 timers, and store enough application state information to restore your
application to its current state in case it is terminated later.
     If your application supports background execution, this method is called
 instead of applicationWillTerminate: when the user quits.
     */
}

- (void)applicationWillEnterForeground:(UIApplication *)application
{
    NSLog(@"applicationWillEnterForeground:");
    /*
     Called as part of the transition from the background to the inactive state;
here you can undo many of the changes made on entering the background.
     */
```

```
    }

    - (void)applicationDidBecomeActive:(UIApplication *)application
    {
        NSLog(@"applicationDidBecomeActive:");
        /*
         Restart any tasks that were paused (or not yet started) while the
    application was inactive. If the application was previously in the background,
    optionally refresh the user interface.
         */
    }

    - (void)applicationWillTerminate:(UIApplication *)application
    {
        NSLog(@"applicationWillTerminate:");
        /*
         Called when the application is about to terminate.
         Save data if appropriate.
         See also applicationDidEnterBackground:.
         */
    }

    @end
```

3. In Xcode, press Command-Shift-C to display the output window.

4. Press Command-R to test the application on the iPhone Simulator.

5. Observe the output in the output window (see Figure 21-1).

FIGURE 21-1

6. On the iPhone Simulator, press the Home button to send the application to the background. Note the output in the output window again:

```
2011-08-16 19:38:04.253 States[2851:ef03] application:didFinishLaunchingWithOptions:
2011-08-16 19:38:04.257 States[2851:ef03] applicationDidBecomeActive:
2011-08-16 19:41:14.035 States[2851:ef03] applicationWillResignActive:
2011-08-16 19:41:14.036 States[2851:ef03] applicationDidEnterBackground:
```

7. In the Home screen of the iPhone Simulator, click the application icon to start the application again. Note the output in the output window:

```
2011-08-16 19:38:04.253 States[2851:ef03] application:didFinishLaunchingWithOptions:
2011-08-16 19:38:04.257 States[2851:ef03] applicationDidBecomeActive:
2011-08-16 19:41:14.035 States[2851:ef03] applicationWillResignActive:
2011-08-16 19:41:14.036 States[2851:ef03] applicationDidEnterBackground:
2011-08-16 19:42:11.173 States[2851:ef03] applicationWillEnterForeground:
2011-08-16 19:42:11.174 States[2851:ef03] applicationDidBecomeActive:
```

How It Works

This exercise demonstrates the various states that an application goes through when it is loaded and when it goes into background mode.

In general, you should save your application state in the `applicationDidEnterBackground:` event when the application goes into the background. When an application goes into the background, execution of the application is suspended.

When the application returns to the foreground, you should restore its state in the `applicationDidBecomeActive:` event.

Opting Out of Background Mode

Although the default behavior of all applications compiled using the iOS SDK is to support background mode, you can override this behavior by adding an entry to your application's `Info` `.plist` file. The following Try It Out demonstrates how.

TRY IT OUT Disabling Background Mode

1. Using the same project created in the previous section, select the `States-info.plist` file, right-click on any of the keys and select Show Raw Keys/Values. Then, add a new key to the file and label the key `UIApplicationExitsOnSuspend` (see Figure 21-2).

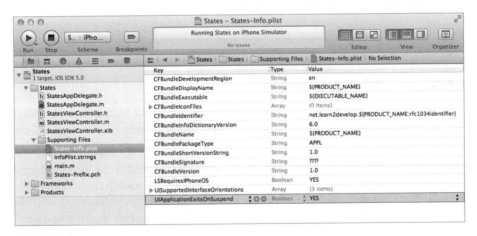

FIGURE 21-2

2. Set the value of this key to `YES`.

3. Press Command-R to test the application on the iPhone Simulator again. When the application has been loaded onto the Simulator, press the Home button. Note the output, as shown in Figure 21-3.

FIGURE 21-3

How It Works

This example demonstrates how to disable the background mode for your application. By enabling the UIApplicationExitsOnSuspend key in your application, the iOS automatically terminates your application when the Home button is pressed.

Detecting Multitasking Support

Because not all devices running the iOS support background applications, it is important that your applications have a way to detect this.

You can enable this via the following code snippet:

```
- (void)viewDidLoad
{
    UIDevice *device = [UIDevice currentDevice];
    bool backgroundSupported = NO;

    if ([device respondsToSelector:@selector(isMultitaskingSupported)])
        backgroundSupported = device.multitaskingSupported;

    if (backgroundSupported)
        NSLog(@"Supports multitasking");
    else {
        NSLog(@"Does not support multitasking");
    }
    [super viewDidLoad];
}
```

Tracking Locations in the Background

You have seen how an application behaves when it is suspended and how to disable multitasking for an application. This section looks at an example that demonstrates how an application can continue to run even when it is in the background.

One of the three types of applications permitted to run in the background is the location-based services application. In Chapter 20, you learn how to use the Core Location framework to obtain geographical data. The limitation with the example shown in that chapter is that as soon as the application goes into the background, your application can no longer receive location updates.

The following Try It Out demonstrates how to enable the application to continue receiving location updates even as it goes into the background.

TRY IT OUT   Tracking Locations in the Background

1.   Using the LBS project created in Chapter 20, select the LBS-Info.plist file and add a new key to it.

2.   Right-click on any of the keys and select Show Raw Keys/Values. Add the key named UIBackgroundModes (see Figure 21-4).

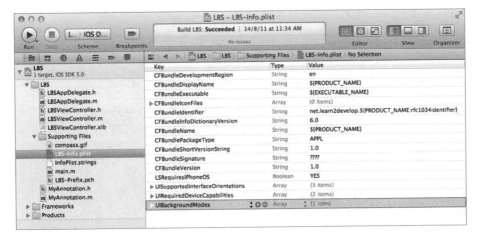

FIGURE 21-4

3. Expand the key and set its first value to `location` (see Figure 21-5).

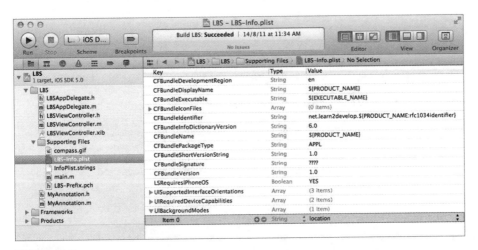

FIGURE 21-5

4. In the `LBSAppDelegate.m` file, add the following bold statements:

```
#import "LBSAppDelegate.h"

#import "LBSViewController.h"

@implementation LBSAppDelegate

@synthesize window = _window;
@synthesize viewController = _viewController;

- (BOOL)application:(UIApplication *)application
```

```
                didFinishLaunchingWithOptions:(NSDictionary *)launchOptions
{
    NSLog(@"application:didFinishLaunchingWithOptions:");
    self.window = [[[UIWindow alloc] initWithFrame:[[UIScreen mainScreen] bounds]]
        autorelease];
    // Override point for customization after application launch.
    self.viewController = [[[LBSViewController alloc]
        initWithNibName:@"LBSViewController" bundle:nil] autorelease];
    self.window.rootViewController = self.viewController;
    [self.window makeKeyAndVisible];
    return YES;
}


- (void)applicationWillResignActive:(UIApplication *)application
{
    NSLog(@"applicationWillResignActive:");
    /*
    Sent when the application is about to move from active to inactive state.
This can occur for certain types of temporary interruptions (such as an
incoming phone call or SMS message) or when the user quits the application and
it begins the transition to the background state.
    Use this method to pause ongoing tasks, disable timers, and throttle down OpenGL
ES frame rates. Games should use this method to pause the game.

    */
}


- (void)applicationDidEnterBackground:(UIApplication *)application
{
    NSLog(@"applicationDidEnterBackground:");
    /*
    Use this method to release shared resources, save user data, invalidate
timers, and store enough application state information to restore your
application to its current state in case it is terminated later.
    If your application supports background execution, this method is called
 instead of applicationWillTerminate: when the user quits.
    */
}


- (void)applicationWillEnterForeground:(UIApplication *)application
{
    NSLog(@"applicationWillEnterForeground:");
    /*
    Called as part of the transition from the background to the inactive state;
here you can undo many of the changes made on entering the background.
    */
}


- (void)applicationDidBecomeActive:(UIApplication *)application
{
    NSLog(@"applicationDidBecomeActive:");
    /*
    Restart any tasks that were paused (or not yet started) while the
application was inactive. If the application was previously in the background,
```

```
optionally refresh the user interface.
    */
}

- (void)applicationWillTerminate:(UIApplication *)application
{
    NSLog(@"applicationWillTerminate:");
    /*
    Called when the application is about to terminate.
    Save data if appropriate.
    See also applicationDidEnterBackground:.
    */
}

@end
```

5. In the `LBSViewController.m` file, add the following bold statements:

```
- (void) locationManager:(CLLocationManager *) manager
        didUpdateToLocation:(CLLocation *) newLocation
            fromLocation:(CLLocation *) oldLocation {

    //...
    //---display accuracy---
    NSString *acc = [[NSString alloc] initWithFormat:@"%f",
                        newLocation.horizontalAccuracy];
    accuracyTextField.text = acc;


    //---print out the lat and long---
    NSLog(@"%@|%@",latitudeTextField.text, longitudeTextField.text);

    [acc release];
    [lat release];
    [lng release];

    //---update the map---
    MKCoordinateSpan span;
    span.latitudeDelta = .001;
    span.longitudeDelta = .001;

    //...
}
```

6. Press Command-R to test the application on the iPhone Simulator. When the application has finished loading on the Simulator, press the Home button to send the application to the background. Select Debug ⇨ Location ⇨ Freeway Drive. Observe the output shown in the output window (press Command-Shift-C in Xcode):

```
2011-08-16 20:10:02.311 LBS[3322:11903]
    application:didFinishLaunchingWithOptions:
2011-08-16 20:10:02.327 LBS[3322:11903] applicationDidBecomeActive:
2011-08-16 20:10:06.868 LBS[3322:11903] applicationWillResignActive:
```

```
2011-08-16 20:10:06.869 LBS[3322:11903] applicationDidEnterBackground:
2011-08-16 20:10:12.655 LBS[3322:11903] 37.335275|-122.032547
2011-08-16 20:10:13.661 LBS[3322:11903] 37.335256|-122.032548
2011-08-16 20:10:14.655 LBS[3322:11903] 37.335236|-122.032549
2011-08-16 20:10:15.654 LBS[3322:11903] 37.335215|-122.032549
2011-08-16 20:10:16.655 LBS[3322:11903] 37.335196|-122.032550
2011-08-16 20:10:17.653 LBS[3322:11903] 37.335175|-122.032551
2011-08-16 20:10:18.650 LBS[3322:11903] 37.335151|-122.032553
2011-08-16 20:10:19.651 LBS[3322:11903] 37.335121|-122.032562
2011-08-16 20:10:20.683 LBS[3322:11903] 37.335072|-122.032604
```

How It Works

In order to enable your application to continue receiving location data even when it goes into the background, you need to set the UIBackgroundModes key in the Info.plist file to location. The UIBackgroundModes key is an array, and it can contain one or more of the following values:

➤   location

➤   audio

➤   voip

Note that no change to your code is required in order to enable your application to run in the background — you need only set the UIBackgroundModes key. The output shown in the window proves that even though the application has gone into the background, it continues to receive location data:

```
2011-08-16 20:10:06.868 LBS[3322:11903] applicationWillResignActive:
2011-08-16 20:10:06.869 LBS[3322:11903] applicationDidEnterBackground:
2011-08-16 20:10:12.655 LBS[3322:11903] 37.335275|-122.032547
2011-08-16 20:10:13.661 LBS[3322:11903] 37.335256|-122.032548
2011-08-16 20:10:14.655 LBS[3322:11903] 37.335236|-122.032549
```

Making Your Location Apps More Energy Efficient

The project that you modified in the previous section enables you to continuously track your location even though the application may be running in the background. While some scenarios require you to track all location changes, many do not. For example, your application may just need to track a point every few hundred meters. In this case, it is important to prevent the application from continuously tracking every single point, as this takes a heavy toll on the battery.

Instead of using the startUpdatingLocation method of the CLLocationManager class to receive location updates, you can use the startMonitoringSignificantLocationChanges method, like this:

```
- (void)viewDidLoad
{
    lm = [[CLLocationManager alloc] init];
    lm.delegate = self;
    lm.desiredAccuracy = kCLLocationAccuracyBest;

    //lm.distanceFilter = kCLDistanceFilterNone;
```

```
//[lm startUpdatingLocation];

[lm startMonitoringSignificantLocationChanges];

//---get the compass readings---
[lm startUpdatingHeading];

//...
[super viewDidLoad];
}
```

The `startMonitoringSignificantLocationChanges` method reports location data only when the device has moved a significant distance. Specifically, it reports location data only when it detects that the device has switched to another cell tower. This method works only with iPhones (and only iPhone 3GS, iPhone 4, and iPhone 4S; the older iPhone 3G does not support this feature). If you use this method to track location, the `distanceFilter` property is not needed. When a location update is received, it calls the same `locationManager:didUpdateToLocation:fromLocation:` method to report location data.

Using the `startMonitoringSignificantLocationChanges` method greatly reduces the power consumption of your device, as it does not use the power-intensive GPS radio. Note also that if you use this feature, there is no need to have the `UIBackgroundModes` key in the `Info.plist` file — the OS automatically wakes your application up from suspended mode to receive the location data.

If your application is terminated when a new location update event is received, it will automatically relaunch your application. To determine whether the application is restarted due to a change in location, you can check for the `UIApplicationLaunchOptionsLocationKey` key in the application's delegate's `application:didFinishLaunchingWithOptions:` event, like this:

```
- (BOOL)application:(UIApplication *)application
didFinishLaunchingWithOptions:(NSDictionary *)launchOptions
{
    NSLog(@"application:didFinishLaunchingWithOptions:");

    //---if application is restarted due to changes in location---
    if ([launchOptions
            objectForKey:UIApplicationLaunchOptionsLocationKey]) {

        UIAlertView *alert = [[UIAlertView alloc]
                        initWithTitle:@"LBS app restarted"
                        message:@"App restarted due to changes in location."
                        delegate:self
                        cancelButtonTitle:@"OK"
                        otherButtonTitles:nil];

        [alert show];
        [alert release];
    }

    self.window = [[[UIWindow alloc] initWithFrame:[[UIScreen mainScreen]
            bounds]] autorelease];
```

```
     // Override point for customization after application launch.
   self.viewController = [[[LBSViewController alloc]
initWithNibName:@"LBSViewController" bundle:nil] autorelease];
   self.window.rootViewController = self.viewController;
   [self.window makeKeyAndVisible];
   return YES;
}
```

Once the application is restarted, you should create another instance of the CLLocationManager class and start the monitoring again.

To stop monitoring for location changes, use the stopMonitoringSignificantLocationChanges method:

```
[lm stopMonitoringSignificantLocationChanges];
```

Note that you need to test the preceding using a real device as it has no effect on the iPhone Simulator.

LOCAL NOTIFICATION

In Chapter 19, you learn about the Apple Push Notification service (APNs), which enables an application to receive notifications even if it is no longer running on the device. Using the APNs, the provider of an application can continuously keep the user updated, by pushing messages directly to the user through Apple's Push server.

In addition to the APNs, the iPhone also supports another notification framework, *local notifications*. While the notifications for APNs are sent by the application provider, local notifications are scheduled by the application and delivered by the iOS on the same device. For example, suppose you are writing a to-do list application. At a specific time, your application will display notifications to the user, reminding them of some future tasks. This scenario is a perfect example of the use of local notifications. Another good use of a local notification is that of a location application. The user may be running your application in the background, and when the application detects that the user is in the vicinity of a certain location, it can display a notification.

The following example illustrates the building blocks that you need to have in place in order to create an application that uses local notifications.

TRY IT OUT Creating Local Notifications

codefile LocalNotification.zip available for download at Wrox.com

1. Using Xcode, create a new Single View Application (iPhone) project and name it **LocalNotification**. You need to use the project name (LocalNotification) as the Class Prefix and ensure that you have the Use Automatic Reference Counting option unchecked.

2. Select the LocalNotificationViewController.xib file to edit it in Interface Builder.

3. Populate the View window with the following views (see Figure 21-6):

➤ Label (name it **Enter notification message**)

➤ Text Field

➤ Two Round Rect Button (name them **Set** and **Cancel all notifications**)

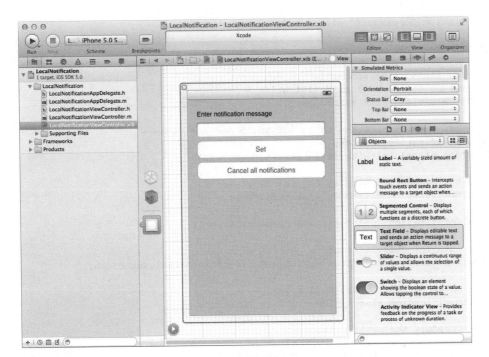

FIGURE 21-6

4. In the `LocalNotificationViewController.h` file, add the following bold statements:

```
#import <UIKit/UIKit.h>

@interface LocalNotificationViewController : UIViewController
{
    IBOutlet UITextField *message;
}

@property (nonatomic, retain) UITextField *message;

-(IBAction) btnSet:(id) sender;
-(IBAction) btnCancelAll:(id) sender;
@end
```

5. Back in Interface Builder, perform the following actions:

➤ Control-click the File's Owner item and drag and drop it over the Text Field. Select `message`.

➤ Control-click the Set button and drag and drop it over the File's Owner item. Select `btnSet:`.

➤   Control-click the Cancel All Notifications button and drag and drop it over the File's Owner item. Select `btnCancelAll:`.

6. In the `LocalNotificationViewController.m` file, add the following bold statements:

```
#import "LocalNotificationViewController.h"

@implementation LocalNotificationViewController

@synthesize message;

-(IBAction) btnSet:(id) sender {
    UILocalNotification *localNotification =
    [[UILocalNotification alloc] init];

    //---set the notification to go off in 10 seconds time---
    localNotification.fireDate =
    [[NSDate alloc] initWithTimeIntervalSinceNow:10];

    //---the message to display for the alert---
    localNotification.alertBody = message.text;

    localNotification.applicationIconBadgeNumber = 1;

    //---uses the default sound---
    localNotification.soundName = UILocalNotificationDefaultSoundName;

    //---title for the button to display---
    localNotification.alertAction = @"View Details";

    //---schedule the notification---
    [[UIApplication sharedApplication]
     scheduleLocalNotification:localNotification];

    [localNotification release];
}

-(IBAction) btnCancelAll:(id) sender {
    //---cancel all notifications---
    [[UIApplication sharedApplication] cancelAllLocalNotifications];
}

- (void)dealloc {
    [message release];
    [super dealloc];
}
```

7. In the `LocalNotificationAppDelegate.m` file, add the following bold statements:

```
#import "LocalNotificationAppDelegate.h"

#import "LocalNotificationViewController.h"

@implementation LocalNotificationAppDelegate

@synthesize window = _window;
```

```
@synthesize viewController = _viewController;

- (void)          application:(UIApplication *)application
didReceiveLocalNotification:(UILocalNotification *)notification {
    UIAlertView *alert = [[UIAlertView alloc]
        initWithTitle:@"Inside application:didReceiveLocalNotification:"
            message:notification.alertBody
            delegate:self
    cancelButtonTitle:@"OK"
    otherButtonTitles:nil];
    [alert show];
    [alert release];
}

- (BOOL)application:(UIApplication *)application
    didFinishLaunchingWithOptions:(NSDictionary *)launchOptions
{

    UILocalNotification *localNotification =
    [launchOptions objectForKey:
    UIApplicationLaunchOptionsLocalNotificationKey];

    if (localNotification) {
        UIAlertView *alert = [[UIAlertView alloc]
            initWithTitle:@"Inside application:didFinishLaunchingWithOptions:"
                message:localNotification.alertBody
                delegate:self
        cancelButtonTitle:@"OK"
        otherButtonTitles:nil];
        [alert show];
        [alert release];
    }

    self.window = [[[UIWindow alloc] initWithFrame:[[UIScreen mainScreen] bounds]]
        autorelease];
    // Override point for customization after application launch.
    self.viewController = [[[LocalNotificationViewController alloc]
        initWithNibName:@"LocalNotificationViewController" bundle:nil] autorelease];
    self.window.rootViewController = self.viewController;
    [self.window makeKeyAndVisible];
    return YES;

}
```

8. Press Command-R to test the application on the iPhone Simulator.

9. Enter the message **Time's up!** and click the Set button to set the local notification to fire in ten seconds (see Figure 21-7). Exit the application immediately by pressing the Home button. The application will go into the background.

10. Ten seconds later, the notification will appear (see Figure 21-8). If you click the View Details button, the application will return to the foreground. The alert view (see Figure 21-09) shows that the application:didReceiveLocalNotification: event in the application delegate was fired.

FIGURE 21-7

FIGURE 21-8

FIGURE 21-9

11. Stop the project in Xcode and then go to the iPhone Simulator and launch the project directly by clicking on the icon. Enter a notification message again and click the Set button again. This time, press the Home button to exit the application and then double-click the Home button and terminate the application so that it does not run in the background anymore.

12. Ten seconds later, the notification will appear again. If you click the View Details button, the application will return to the foreground. This time, the alert view shows that the `application:didFinishLaunchingWithOptions:` event in the application delegate was fired instead (see Figure 21-10).

How It Works

Creating a local notification using the `UILocalNotification` class is very straightforward:

```
UILocalNotification *localNotification =
[[UILocalNotification alloc] init];
```

FIGURE 21-10

Once you have obtained an instance of the `UILocalNotification` class, you need to configure the object with various information, such as the amount of time after which the notification will fire, the message to display, the badge number to display for your application icon, the sound to play, as well as the caption of the button to display:

```
//---set the notification to go off in 10 seconds time---
localNotification.fireDate =
```

```
[[NSDate alloc] initWithTimeIntervalSinceNow:10];

//---the message to display for the alert---
localNotification.alertBody = message.text;

localNotification.applicationIconBadgeNumber = 1;

//---uses the default sound---
localNotification.soundName = UILocalNotificationDefaultSoundName;

//---title for the button to display---
localNotification.alertAction = @"View Details";
```

In the preceding code, you use the `fireDate` property to set the local notification to fire in ten seconds. The `alertBody` property sets the message to display. The `applicationIconBadgeNumber` property displays a badge number next to the application's icon (this badge number is displayed when the local notification fires). The `soundName` property enables you to specify the filename of a sound resource that is bundled with your application. If you want to play the system's default sound, use the `UILocalNotificationDefaultSoundName` constant. Finally, the `alertAction` property enables you to set the button caption of the notification (see Figure 21-11).

FIGURE 21-11

To schedule a future local notification, use the `scheduleLocalNotification:` method of the `UIApplication` class:

```
//---schedule the notification---
[[UIApplication sharedApplication]
  scheduleLocalNotification:localNotification];
```

If you want to display the notification instantly, use the `presentLocalNotificationNow:` method instead:

```
//---display the notification now---
[[UIApplication sharedApplication]
  presentLocalNotificationNow:localNotification];
```

This is very useful for cases in which your application is executing in the background and you want to display a notification to draw the user's attention.

When the notification is displayed (it will be displayed only if the application is not in the foreground), the user has two options: Close the notification or view the application that generated the notification. When the user views the notification, the `application:didReceiveLocalNotification:` method in the application's delegate is called:

```
- (void)        application:(UIApplication *)application
didReceiveLocalNotification:(UILocalNotification *)notification {
    UIAlertView *alert = [[UIAlertView alloc]
                    initWithTitle:@"Inside
    application:didReceiveLocalNotification:"
                    message:notification.alertBody
```

```
                        delegate:self
                        cancelButtonTitle:@"OK"
                        otherButtonTitles:nil];

        [alert show];
        [alert release];
    }
```

Here, you can simply print out the details of the notification through the `notification` parameter.

Note that the `application:didReceiveLocalNotification:` method is also called when the application is running and the local notification is fired. In this case, the local notification will not appear.

If the application is not running when the local notification occurs, viewing the application will invoke the `application:didFinishLaunchingWithOptions:` method instead:

```
- (BOOL)          application:(UIApplication *)application
didFinishLaunchingWithOptions:(NSDictionary *)launchOptions
{

    UILocalNotification *localNotification =
    [launchOptions objectForKey:
     UIApplicationLaunchOptionsLocalNotificationKey];

    if (localNotification) {
        UIAlertView *alert = [[UIAlertView alloc]
            initWithTitle:@"Inside application:didFinishLaunchingWithOptions:"
                message:localNotification.alertBody
                delegate:self
        cancelButtonTitle:@"OK"
        otherButtonTitles:nil];
        [alert show];
        [alert release];
    }

    self.window = [[[UIWindow alloc] initWithFrame:[[UIScreen mainScreen]
    bounds]] autorelease];
    // Override point for customization after application launch.
    self.viewController = [[[LocalNotificationViewController alloc]
    initWithNibName:@"LocalNotificationViewController" bundle:nil] autorelease];
    self.window.rootViewController = self.viewController;
    [self.window makeKeyAndVisible];
    return YES;
}
```

To obtain more information about the notification, use the `launchOptions` parameter, by querying the details using the `UIApplicationLaunchOptionsLocalNotificationKey` constant.

To cancel all scheduled notifications, you can call the `cancelAllLocalNotifications` method of the `UIApplication` class:

```
        //---cancel all notifications---
        [[UIApplication sharedApplication] cancelAllLocalNotifications];
```

NOTIFYING OTHER OBJECTS USING THE NSNOTIFICATION CLASS

In this book, you have seen that all the delegate methods of objects are defined in the same class as the object. For example, one common class that you have seen is the UIAlertView class. When you have more than one button displayed in a UIAlertView object, you need to implement the alertView:clickedButtonAtIndex: method to handle the clicking of the buttons. This method can be defined with the same class it is used in (for example, in a View Controller class), or it can be declared separately in another class. However, if the method is defined in another class, how would you notify the View Controller when a button is clicked? This is the challenge: How do different classes communicate with one another? The following Try It Out shows you one way to do this using the NSNotification class.

TRY IT OUT Using Notifications

codefile Notifications.zip available for download at Wrox.com

1. Using Xcode, create a new Single View Application (iPhone) project and name it **Notifications**. You need to set the class prefix to the project name and ensure that you have the Use Automatic Reference Counting option unchecked.

2. Add a new Objective-C Class file to the project and name it **AlertViewDelegates.m**.

3. Add the following lines in bold to the AlertViewDelegates.h file:

```
#import <Foundation/Foundation.h>

@interface AlertViewDelegates : NSObject
<UIAlertViewDelegate>

@end
```

4. Add the following lines in bold to the AlertViewDelegates.m file:

```
#import "AlertViewDelegates.h"

@implementation AlertViewDelegates

- (id)init
{
    self = [super init];
    if (self) {
        // Initialization code here.
    }

    return self;
}

- (void)    alertView:(UIAlertView *)alertView
```

```
clickedButtonAtIndex:(NSInteger)buttonIndex {

    NSLog(@"Button %d was clicked.", buttonIndex);
    NSDictionary *dict =
        [[NSDictionary alloc] initWithObjectsAndKeys:
         [NSString stringWithFormat:@"%d", buttonIndex],
         @"buttonIndex", nil];

    //---send a notification to whoever is listening to tell
    // them that the user response has been handled---
    NSNotification *notification =
        [NSNotification notificationWithName:@"UserResponded"
                                     object:nil
                                   userInfo:dict] ;
    [[NSNotificationCenter defaultCenter] postNotification:notification];
    [dict release];
}

@end
```

5. Add the following lines in bold to the `NotificationsViewController.h` file:

```
#import <UIKit/UIKit.h>
#import "AlertViewDelegates.h"

@interface NotificationsViewController : UIViewController
{
    AlertViewDelegates *del;
}

@end
```

6. Add the following lines in bold to the `NotificationsViewController.m` file:

```
#import "NotificationsViewController.h"

@implementation NotificationsViewController

- (void)viewDidLoad
{
    del = [[AlertViewDelegates alloc] init];
    UIAlertView *alert = [[UIAlertView alloc] initWithTitle:@"Hello World"
                                                    message:@"Hello, Objective-C"
                                                   delegate:del
                                          cancelButtonTitle:@"OK"
                                          otherButtonTitles:@"Cancel", nil];
    [alert show];
    [alert release];

    //---notification to listen for the completion of user's response---
    [[NSNotificationCenter defaultCenter] addObserver:self
                                             selector:@selector(processNotification:)
                                                 name:@"UserResponded"
                                               object:nil];
```

```
    [super viewDidLoad];
}

//---called when there is a notification; a callback function---
-(void) processNotification:(NSNotification *) notification {
    NSDictionary *dict = [notification userInfo];
    NSLog(@"In processNotification:, Button clicked: %@", [dict
        objectForKey:@"buttonIndex"])
}

-(void) dealloc {
    [[NSNotificationCenter defaultCenter] removeObserver:self];
    [del release];
}
```

7. Press Command-R to run the application. Click either the OK button or the Cancel button (see Figure 21-12).

8. Observe the output in the output window, as shown in Figure 21-13.

```
Attaching to process 5140.
2011-07-06 21:46:54.730 Notifications[5140:ef03] Button 0 was clicked.
2011-07-06 21:46:54.732 Notifications[5140:ef03] In processNotification:,
Button clicked: 0
```

FIGURE 21-12   **FIGURE 21-13**

How It Works

You first create a class called `AlertViewDelegates` to contain all the methods that are related to the `UIAlertView` class. In particular, you implement the `alertView:clickedButtonAtIndex:` method:

```
- (void)    alertView:(UIAlertView *)alertView
clickedButtonAtIndex:(NSInteger)buttonIndex {

    NSLog(@"Button %d was clicked.", buttonIndex);
    NSDictionary *dict =
```

```
        [[NSDictionary alloc] initWithObjectsAndKeys:
         [NSString stringWithFormat:@"%d", buttonIndex],
         @"buttonIndex", nil];

    //---send a notification to whoever is listening to tell
    // them that the user response has been handled---
    NSNotification *notification =
        [NSNotification notificationWithName:@"UserResponded"
                                      object:nil
                                    userInfo:dict] ;
    [[NSNotificationCenter defaultCenter] postNotification:notification];
    [dict release];
}
```

Within this method, you create an NSDictionary object and use it to store the index of the button that was clicked. You then create a notification using the NSNotification class, and assign the dictionary object to this notification object. Essentially, you are broadcasting a notification to other objects listening for this notification, named UserResponded.

In the View Controller, you instantiate the AlertViewDelegates class and pass it as the delegate of the UIAlertView object:

```
    del = [[AlertViewDelegates alloc] init];
    UIAlertView *alert = [[UIAlertView alloc] initWithTitle:@"Hello World"
                                                    message:@"Hello, Objective-C"
                                                   delegate:del
                                            cancelButtonTitle:@"OK"
                                            otherButtonTitles:@"Cancel", nil];
    [alert show];
    [alert release];
```

You then listen for a notification named UserResponded:

```
    //---notification to listen for the completion of user's response---
    [[NSNotificationCenter defaultCenter] addObserver:self
                                             selector:@selector(processNotification:)
                                                 name:@"UserResponded"
                                               object:nil];
```

When a notification is received, the processNotification: method will be called:

```
    //---called when there is a notification; a callback function---
    -(void) processNotification:(NSNotification *) notification {
        NSDictionary *dict = [notification userInfo];
        NSLog(@"In processNotification:, Button clicked: %@", [dict
            objectForKey:@"buttonIndex"]);
    }
```

Here, you extract the NSDictionary object that is attached to the notification and print out the value of the button index.

Finally, in the `dealloc` method of your view controller, remember to stop listening for the notification:

```
-(void) dealloc {
    [[NSNotificationCenter defaultCenter] removeObserver:self];
    [del release];
}
```

SUMMARY

In this chapter, you have seen how background execution works and how you can utilize it to make your applications more useful. You have also seen the other types of notifications that you can utilize in your applications — scheduling local notifications though the operating system, and using the NSNotification class for notifying objects within your application.

Combining all the different concepts discussed in this chapter will enable you to write compelling iOS applications.

EXERCISES

1. Name the three types of applications that are allowed to execute in the background.

2. Which devices support multitasking?

3. For the CLLocationManager class, when should you use the startUpdatingLocation and startMonitoringSignificantLocationChanges methods? Why?

4. What is the difference between Apple Push Notification service and local notifications?

Answers to the exercises can be found in Appendix D.

▶ **WHAT YOU LEARNED IN THIS CHAPTER**

TOPIC	KEY CONCEPTS
Opting out of background execution	Use the `UIApplicationExitsOnSuspend` key.
Tracking locations in the background	Use the `UIBackgroundModes` key.
Monitoring significant location changes	Use the `startMonitoringSignificantLocationChanges` method.
Creating local notifications	Use the `UILocalNotification` class.
Scheduling a local notification	`[[UIApplication sharedApplication] scheduleLocalNotification:localNotification];`
Presenting a local notification	`[[UIApplication sharedApplication] presentLocalNotificationNow:localNotification];`
Notifying other objects when an event occurs	Use the `NSNotification` and `NSNotificationCenter` classes.

Testing on an Actual Device

Although the iOS Simulator is a very handy tool that enables you to test your iPhone/iPad applications without needing an actual device, nothing beats testing on a real device. This is especially true when you are ready to roll out your application to the world — you must ensure that it works correctly on real devices. In addition, if your application requires access to hardware features on an iPhone, iPod touch, or iPad, such as the accelerometer, gyroscope, and GPS, you need to test it on a real device — the iPhone Simulator is simply not adequate.

This appendix walks through the steps you need to take to test your applications on a real device, be it the iPhone, iPod touch, or iPad. In addition, you will also learn how to prepare your application for submission to the App Store, as well as how to distribute your application using the Ad Hoc distribution method.

SIGNING UP FOR THE IOS DEVELOPER PROGRAM

The first step toward testing your application on a real device is to sign up for the iOS Developer Program at http://developer.apple.com/programs/ios/. Two programs are available: Standard (Individual) and Enterprise. For most developers who want to release applications on the App Store, the Standard program, which costs $99, is sufficient. Check out http://developer.apple.com/programs/start/standard/ to learn more about the differences between the Standard and Enterprise programs.

If you just want to test your application on your actual iPhone/iPod touch, sign up for the Standard program.

OBTAINING THE UDID OF YOUR DEVICE

To test your application on your device, you need to prepare your Mac and your device. The following sections walk you through the necessary steps, from obtaining your certificate to deploying your application onto the device.

First, you need to obtain the 40-character identifier that uniquely identifies your device. This identifier is known as the UDID — Unique Device Identifier. Every device sold by Apple has a unique UDID. To do so, connect your device to your Mac and start Xcode. Choose Window ➪ Organizer to launch the Organizer application. Figure A-1 shows the Organizer application displaying the identifier of my iPad. Copy the identifier and save it somewhere; you will need it later.

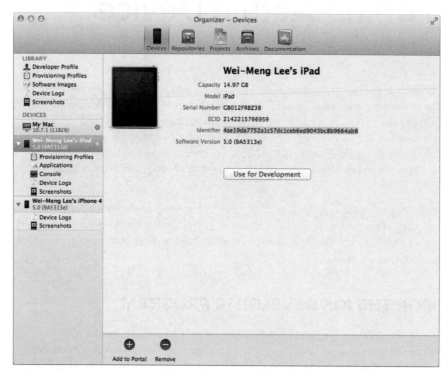

FIGURE A-1

If you are connecting your device to the Organizer for the first time, click the Use for Development button so that Organizer can prepare it for deployment. Essentially, you will be prompted to enter your credentials for login to the iPhone Dev Center (see Figure A-2). Once you have entered your username and password, Organizer will automatically register your device's UDID with the iOS Provisioning Portal.

If for some reason you are not prompted to enter your credentials, you can also manually register your device's UDID by right-clicking on the device name (see Figure A-3) and selecting Add Device to Provisioning Portal.

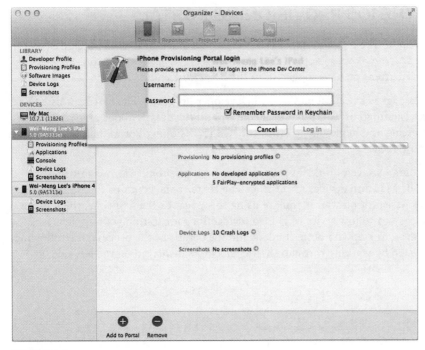

FIGURE A-2

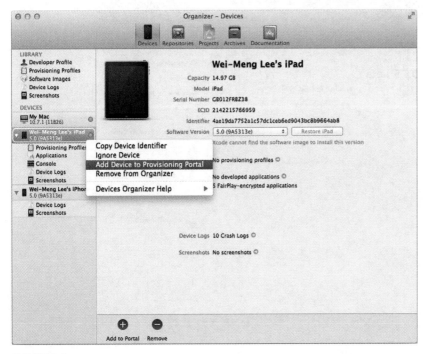

FIGURE A-3

LOGGING IN TO THE iOS PROVISIONING PORTAL

Once you have signed up for the iOS Developer Program, you can log in to the iOS Dev Center website located at `http://developer.apple.com/devcenter/ios/index.action`. Figure A-4 shows the page displayed after you have logged in to the iOS Dev Center.

On the right side of the page is a section named iOS Developer Program. The first item listed under this section is iOS Provisioning Portal. This portal contains all the details about preparing your Mac and devices for testing and deployment. Click the iOS Provisioning Portal item to display the window shown in Figure A-5.

The pane on the left contains several links to pages where you can submit various information required to prepare your Mac and devices for testing. The center pane contains the welcome message and a Launch Assistant button. If you are using this page for the first time, the Launch Assistant provides an easy-to-follow series of guided instructions for testing your applications on your devices. However, to help you better understand the details of the process, the following sections describe each step by walking through the various links displayed on the left side of the page.

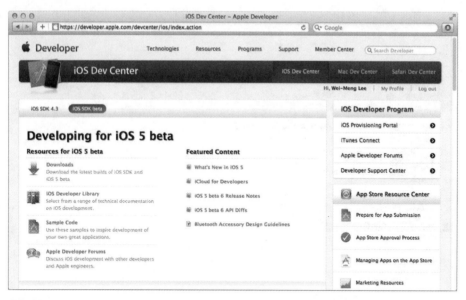

FIGURE A-4

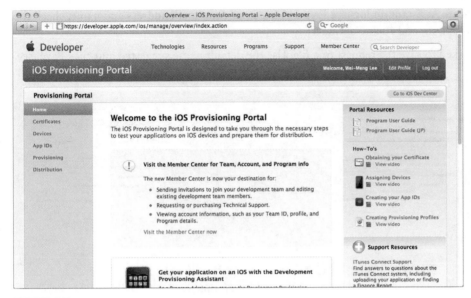

FIGURE A-5

GENERATING A CERTIFICATE

The first step toward testing your application on a real device is to obtain a digital certificate from Apple so that Xcode can use it to code-sign your application. Any applications that are run on your devices must be code-signed. For testing purposes, you need a *development certificate*. Once you are ready to distribute your application (such as through the App Store), you then need a *distribution certificate* (discussed later in this Appendix).

To request a development certificate from Apple, you must generate a certificate signing request (CSR). You can do this using the Keychain Access application located in the Applications/Utilities/ folder on your Mac.

In the Keychain Access application, choose Keychain Access ➪ Certificate Assistant, and select Request a Certificate From a Certificate Authority (see Figure A-6).

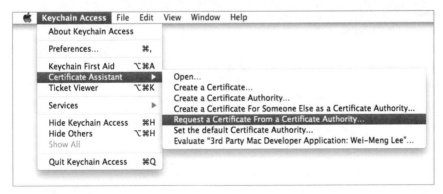

FIGURE A-6

In the Certificate Assistant dialog (see Figure A-7), enter your email address and name, check the Saved to disk option, and click Continue.

You will be asked to save the request to a file. Use the default name suggested and click Save (see Figure A-8).

FIGURE A-7

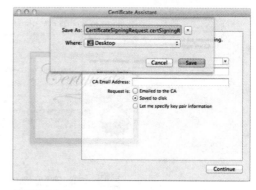

FIGURE A-8

On the iOS Provisioning Portal page, click the Certificates item displayed on the left (see Figure A-9). Four tabs are displayed on the right side of the page: Development, Distribution, History, and How To.

In the Development tab, click the Request Certificate button to request a development certificate from Apple. A detailed list of instructions will appear, telling you to generate a certificate request using the Keychain Access application (see Figure A-10). As you have already performed this step earlier in this Appendix, click the Choose file button to upload the certificate request file to Apple. After the file is selected, click Submit to send it to Apple.

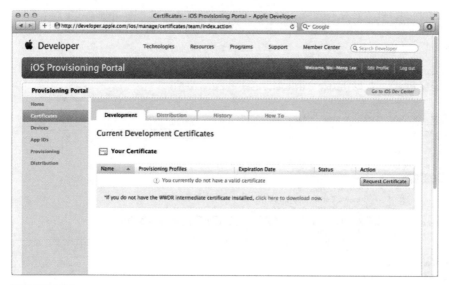

FIGURE A-9

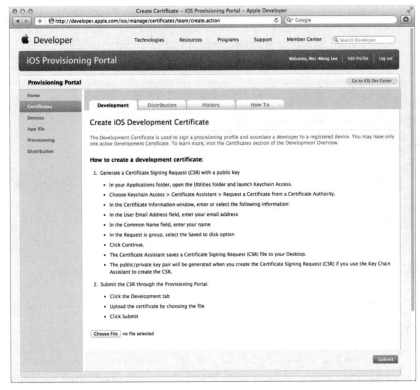

FIGURE A-10

The development certificate will now have a status of Pending Issuance. Simply refresh the page or click the Development tab once more and your development certificate should now be ready (see Figure A-11).

FIGURE A-11

Click the Download button to download the development certificate. When it is downloaded to your Mac, double-click the `developer_identity.cer` file. When prompted, click OK. The certificate will now be installed in the Keychain Access application, which you can verify (see Figure A-12).

FIGURE A-12

REGISTERING YOUR DEVICES

The next step is to register your devices with the iOS Provisioning Portal so that you can later associate them with the provisioning profiles (more on this shortly). As mentioned in the beginning of this appendix, when you connect your device to Organizer for the first time, Organizer will attempt to register your device with the iOS Provisioning Portal automatically. However, if you skipped that step, or you want to register additional devices manually, you need to register them manually.

Back on the iOS Provisioning Portal page, click the Devices item displayed on the left side of the page (see Figure A-13). On the right you will see options to both add devices and upload a list of devices to register.

FIGURE A-13

Click the Add Devices button to register one or more devices. Give your device a name and enter its Device ID (see Figure A-14). Recall that you obtained the Device ID (UDID) of your device earlier, in the "Obtaining the UDID of Your Device" section. To register additional devices, click the plus (+) button. Then click Submit.

 NOTE *For the Standard Program, you can register up to 100 devices for testing. All added devices count toward your 100-device limit, whether you use them or not. In other words, if you register five devices and then lose them in the bar, you can register only 95 more devices — the slots taken up by the other five devices cannot be recovered. You can reset the list only when you renew your membership annually.*

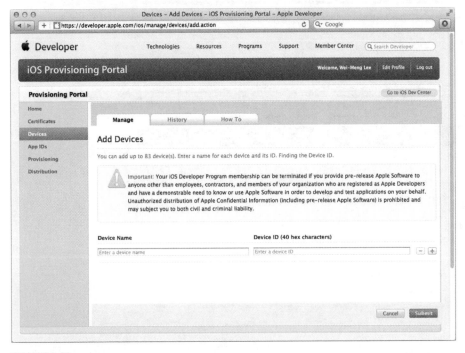

FIGURE A-14

CREATING AN APPLICATION ID

The next step of the process is to create an *Application ID (App ID)* that you use to identify your application. An App ID is a series of characters used to uniquely identify an application (or applications) on your iOS device. An App ID is represented in the following format: *<Bundle Seed ID>.<Bundle Identifier>*.

On the iOS Provisioning Portal page, click the App IDs item on the left (see Figure A-15). Click the New App ID button to create a new App ID. On a new page, you enter the details for the App ID (see Figure A-16).

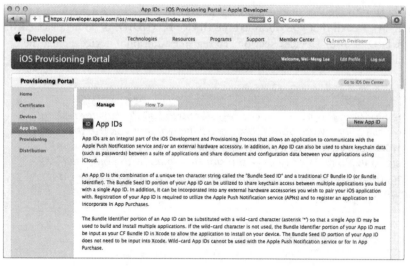

FIGURE A-15

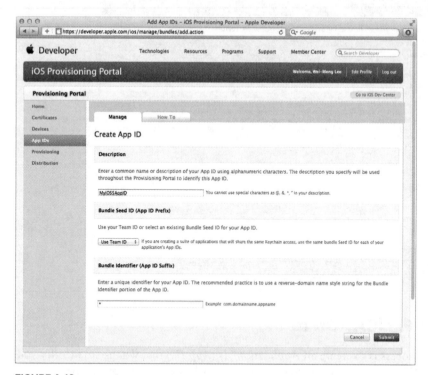

FIGURE A-16

Enter a description for the App ID you are creating. For this example, it is `MyiOS5AppID`. This name will be used to identify your App ID. Leave the Bundle Seed ID option as Use the Team ID. For the Bundle Identifier, you have two options:

➤ Give it a unique identifier, e.g., *com.yourcompany.appname*

➤ Use a wildcard character (*) as the trailing character, e.g., *com.yourcompany.**, or simply use *

Using the wildcard character enables you to use a single App ID for all your applications, whereas if you use a unique identifier for the Bundle Identifier, you will need a unique App ID for each application.

In general, it is easier to use the wildcard character, as you can use one App ID for all your applications. Here, I used the * for the Bundle Identifier. When you compile your application, this wildcard will be substituted with the Bundle Identifier specified in the info.plist file in your Xcode.

CREATING A PROVISIONING PROFILE

In order for your application to be able to execute on a device, the device must be provisioned with a file known as a *provisioning profile*. A provisioning profile contains one or more device IDs, and it must be installed on all the devices to which you want to deploy your applications.

On the iOS Provisioning Portal page, click the Provisioning item displayed on the left (see Figure A-17). Click the New Profile button to create a new provisioning profile.

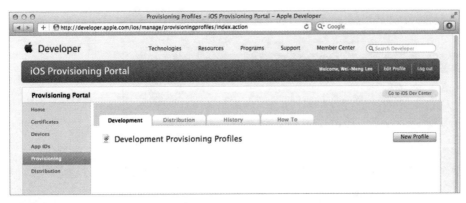

FIGURE A-17

Under the Development tab, shown in Figure A-18, provide a name for your provisioning profile, check the certificate name, select the App ID created in the previous section, and then check all the device names that you want to test on. Click Submit.

The provisioning profile that you have created will now be pending issuance, as shown in the Status field in Figure A-19.

Refresh the page or click the Development tab again and the provisioning profile should now be ready for download (see Figure A-20). Download the generated provisioning profile onto your Mac by clicking the Download button.

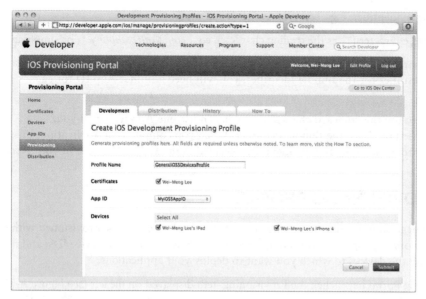

FIGURE A-18

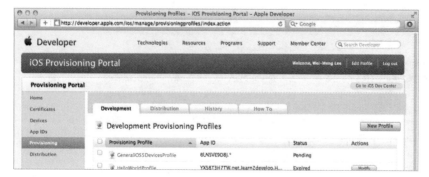

FIGURE A-19

FIGURE A-20

Drag and drop the downloaded provisioning profile onto the Xcode icon that is on the Dock (see Figure A-21). Alternatively, double-click the provisioning profile.

This installs the provisioning profile onto the Organizer application (part of Xcode). It also installs the provisioning profile onto your connected iPhone, iPod touch, or iPad device. To verify that the provisioning profile is indeed installed on your device, select the device that is currently connected to your Mac and view the Provisioning Profiles item (see Figure A-22).

FIGURE A-21

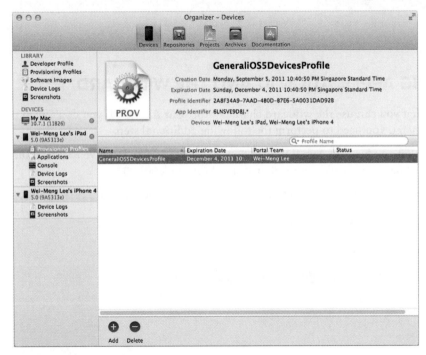

FIGURE A-22

 NOTE If you don't see the provisioning profile, simply disconnect your device and connect again. If, after reconnecting the device, the provisioning profile is not there, click the plus (+) button to manually add the provisioning profile to your device.

You are now almost ready to deploy your iPhone application onto your iPhone, iPod touch, or iPad. In Xcode, select the project name. Then, in the Build Settings page, go to the Code Signing Identity section. Under the `Debug/Any iOS SDK` key, select the `GeneraliOS5DeviceProfile` profile that you have just installed (see Figure A-23). Select the device to deploy to and then press Command-R.

The application should now be deployed onto the device.

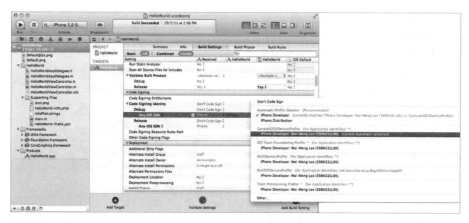

FIGURE A-23

UNDERSTANDING APPLICATION ID AND THE WILDCARD

Earlier, you learned that you can use the wildcard character for your App ID. If you don't want to use the wildcard character, you need to perform the following additional step.

Figure A-24 assumes that you have an App ID called `MyHelloWorldAppID`. Observe that its Bundle Identifier is `net.learn2develop.MyHelloWorld`, instead of the wildcard (*).

In Figure A-25, the provisioning profile `HelloWorldAppProfile` is associated with this App ID.

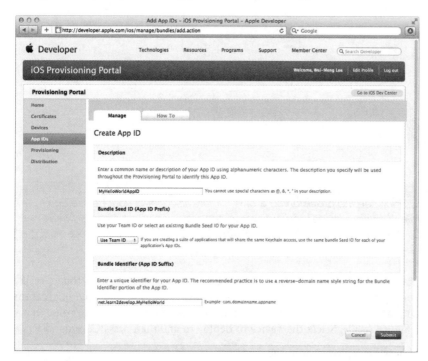

FIGURE A-24

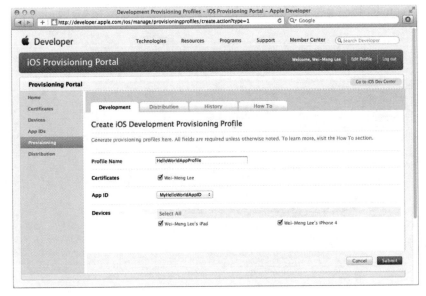

FIGURE A-25

If you were to install the `HelloWorldAppProfile` provisioning profile onto your device, you would have to modify the Bundle Identifier in your Xcode project to match the Bundle Identifier (`net.learn2 develop.MyHelloWorld`) specified in the `MyHelloWorldAppID` App ID. To do so, select the project name in Xcode and click the Info tab. Set the Bundle Identifier key to `net.learn2develop.MyHelloWorld` (see Figure A-26). This value must match the value that you have specified in your App ID.

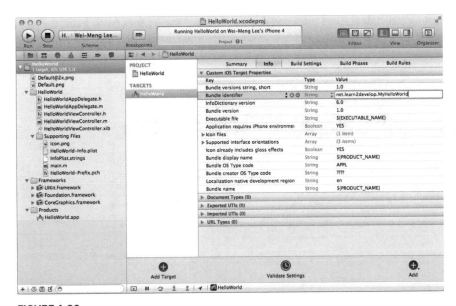

FIGURE A-26

In the Build Settings tab, under the Code Signing Identity section, select the `HelloWorldAppProfile` profile (see Figure A-27).

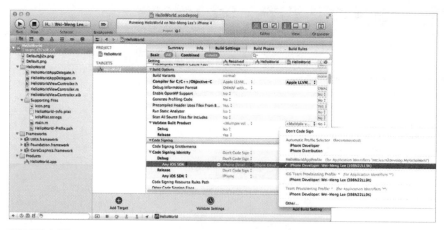

FIGURE A-27

You will now be able to deploy your application using this provisioning profile. In short, the Bundle Identifier in your project must match the one that you have specified in your App ID.

PREPARING FOR APP STORE SUBMISSION

Preparing for submission to the App Store is very similar to preparing your application for testing on your device. Instead of using a development certificate, you use a *distribution certificate*. Also, instead of using a development provisioning profile, you use a *distribution provisioning profile*.

To create a distribution certificate, repeat the same process outlined earlier for creating the development certificate. The distribution certificate is created in the Distribution tab (see Figure A-28).

FIGURE A-28

For the distribution provisioning profile, select Provisioning from the panel on the left, and then click the Distribution tab (see Figure A-29). Click the New Profile button to create a new distribution provisioning profile.

FIGURE A-29

You need to select the distribution method. In this case, select App Store, as shown in Figure A-30. (You would select Ad Hoc for ad hoc distribution, discussed in the next section), name the distribution provisioning profile, and select the App ID. Note that there is no need to select the devices because the application will be hosted on the App Store and available to all users (you need to select the devices if you choose the Ad Hoc distribution method). Here, the profile name is called `DLSDistributionProfile`.

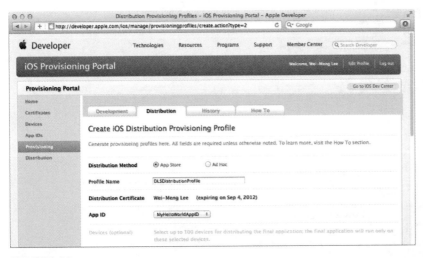

FIGURE A-30

Once the distribution provisioning profile is created, download it and install it in Xcode.

To prepare your application for submission, follow these steps:

1. Go to Xcode and set the `Release/Any iOS SDK` key to the `DLSDistributionProfile` profile (see Figure A-31).

2. In Xcode, select the Edit Scheme... item as shown in Figure A-32.

3. Select the Archive scheme and make sure you select the iOS Device destination (see Figure A-33). Click OK.

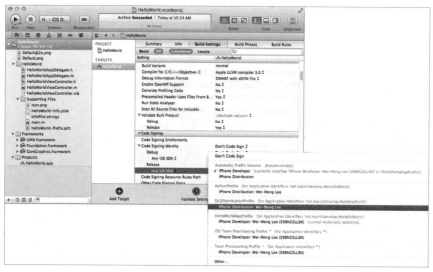

FIGURE A-31

FIGURE A-32

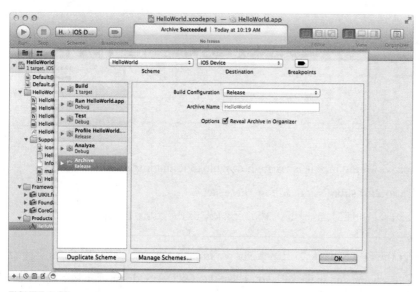

FIGURE A-33

4. Select Product ➪ Archive (see Figure A-34).

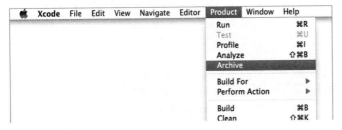

FIGURE A-34

The Organizer will now appear (see Figure A-35), and the HelloWorld executable is created. In this page, you can validate your application against the App Store, share the executable as an .ipa file, and submit the application to the App Store. Before you can validate or submit your application to the App Store, however, you need to create an entry in iTunes Connect. Once that is done, you can come back to the page and validate and then submit your application.

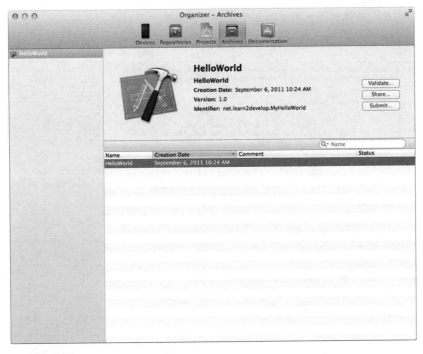

FIGURE A-35

For submission to the App Store, you use the iTunes Connect page shown earlier on the right side of the iOS Dev Center (refer to Figure A-4).

Inside iTunes Connect, you can find detailed instructions for submitting your application to the App Store (see Figure A-36). Click the Manage Your Applications link to create an entry for the application you are submitting and follow the steps. Once that is done, you can validate and submit your application to the App Store.

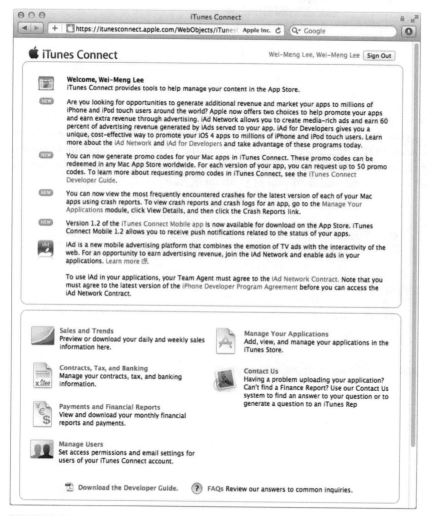

FIGURE A-36

USING AD HOC DISTRIBUTION

While distributing your application through the App Store enables you to distribute it to anyone with access to the App Store, you might want to limit the distribution of your application to a particular group of users. For example, you may be developing an application for your company's in-house use, in which case only the employees should install it. In such a case, you can use the Ad Hoc distribution method to distribute your application.

To use Ad Hoc distribution, execute the following steps:

1. You need to create an Ad Hoc distribution provisioning profile, as described in the previous section. The Ad Hoc distribution provisioning profile must contain the UDIDs of all the devices on which you want to install your application. Depending on the membership that you have enrolled in, there is a limit on how many devices you can install on (a maximum of 100 for the standard program).

2. Set the `Release/Any iOS SDK` key in your project to the Ad Hoc distribution provisioning profile.

3. Export the application as an `.ipa` file by clicking the Share button in Organizer (refer to Figure A-35).

4. Select the Identity of the `.ipa` file to the Ad Hoc distribution provisioning profile (see Figure A-37).

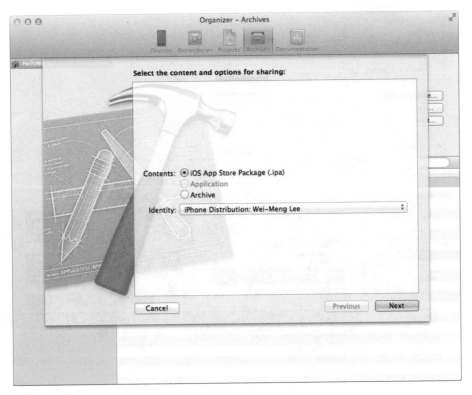

FIGURE A-37

5. Once the .ipa file is created, drag and drop it together with the Ad Hoc distribution provisioning profile onto the Library section in iTunes (see Figure A-38).

6. In iTunes, connect your iOS device. Under the Apps tab, check the Sync Apps check box (see Figure A-39). Ensure that the application you are deploying is also checked.

7. That's it! Click the Sync button and the application will be installed on the device.

FIGURE A-38

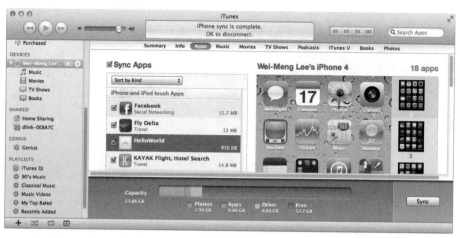

FIGURE A-39

B

Getting Around in Xcode

Xcode is the integrated development environment (IDE) that Apple uses for developing Mac OS X, iPhone, and iPad applications. It is a suite of applications that includes a set of compilers, documentation, and Interface Builder.

Using Xcode, you can build your iPhone and iPad applications from the comfort of an intelligent text editor, coupled with many different tools to help debug your applications. If you are new to Xcode, this appendix can serve as a useful guide to get you started quickly.

At the time of writing, the version of Xcode available is version 4.2. It is available as a free download from the Mac App Store.

LAUNCHING XCODE

The easiest way to launch Xcode is to type **Xcode** in the textbox of Spotlight. Alternatively, you can launch Xcode by navigating to the Developer/Applications/ folder and double-clicking the Xcode icon.

 NOTE For convenience, you can also drag the Xcode icon to the Dock so that in the future you can launch it directly from there.

Project Types Supported

Xcode supports the building of iPhone, iPad, and Mac OS X applications. When you create a new project in Xcode (which you do by choosing File ➪ New ➪ New Project . . .), the dialog shown in Figure B-1 appears.

As shown on the left, you can create two main project types: iOS and Mac OS X. Under the iOS category are the Application, Framework & Library, and Other items.

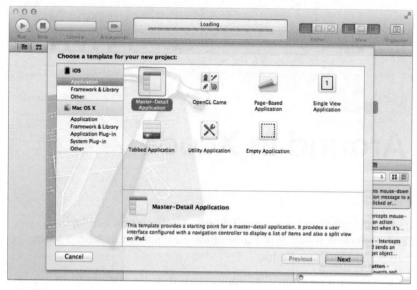

If you select the Application item, you will see all the different project types you can create:

➤ Master-Detail Application

➤ OpenGL Game

➤ Page-Based Application

➤ Single View Application

➤ Tabbed Application

➤ Utility Application

➤ Empty Application

Depending on the project type you select, you have the option to use either Core Data for storage, or Storyboard for transitioning of View windows.

NOTE *Core Data is part of the Cocoa API that was first introduced with the iPhone SDK 3.0. It is basically a framework for manipulating data without worrying about the details of storage and retrieval. Storyboard is a new feature in iOS 5 that helps you to manage the transitioning of View Controllers in your application. A discussion of Core Data and Storyboard is beyond the scope of this book.*

Select the project type you want to create and click the Next button. You will see the options for your project, as shown in Figure B-2.

FIGURE B-2

You will be asked to fill in several pieces of information for your project:

➤ **Product Name** — Name of your project

➤ **Company Identifier** — Use the reverse domain name of your organization for this.

➤ **Bundle Identifier** — Concatenation of the product name and company identifier

➤ **Class Prefix** — Name to be used to prefix all your project filenames. For example, if you set this to be the same as the product name, then all the files in your project will be prefixed with this name.

➤ **Device Family** — Select either iPhone, iPad, or Universal.

➤ **Additional options** — You can also enable the features for Storyboard, Automatic Reference Counting (ARC), and Unit Tests for your project.

 NOTE *All the projects in this book are created with ARC turned off.*

When the project is created, Xcode displays all the files that make up the project (see Figure B-3).

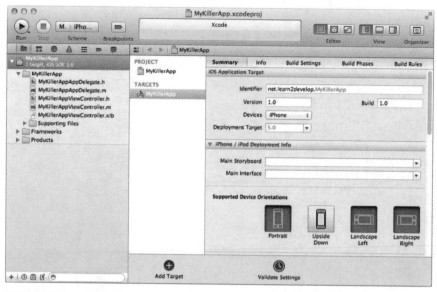

FIGURE B-3

To edit a code file, click the filename of a file to open the appropriate editor. For example, if you click an .h or .m file, the code editor in which you can edit your source code is displayed (see Figure B-4).

Click a .plist file, and the XML Property List editor launches (see Figure B-5).

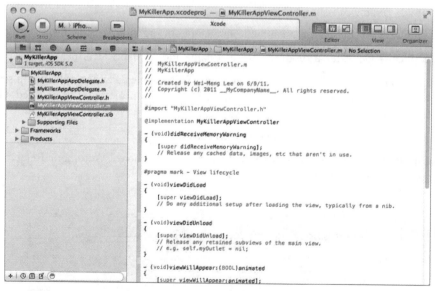

FIGURE B-4

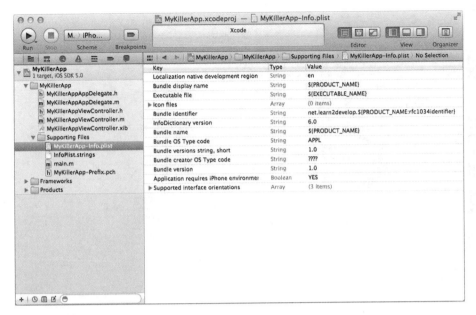

FIGURE B-5

Adding Frameworks

In iOS programming, you often need to add frameworks to your project in order to make use of certain functionalities in your application. Frameworks are basically class libraries providing specific functionalities. For example, if you need to play video within your application, you need to add the MediaPlayer framework to your project before you can use the specific classes for media playback.

To add a framework to your project, execute the following steps:

1. Double-click the project name in Xcode.

2. Select the Build Phases tab and click the "+" button displayed under the Link Binary With Libraries section (see Figure B-6).

3. Select the framework you need to use (see Figure B-7) to add it to the project and click Add.

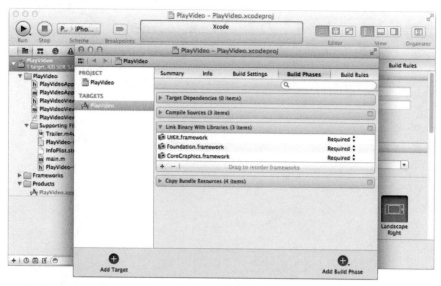

FIGURE B-6

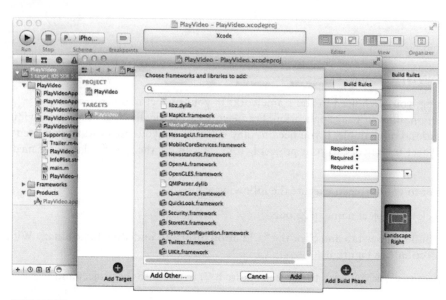

FIGURE B-7

The framework will now be added to the project. It is good practice to move the framework that you have just added into the Frameworks folder.

Code Sense

One of the most common features of a modern IDE is *code completion*, whereby the IDE automatically tries to complete the statement you are typing based on the current context. In Xcode, the code-completion feature is known as *Code Sense*. For example, if you type the letters uial in a method, such as the `viewDidLoad()` method, Code Sense automatically suggests the `UIAlertView` class, as shown in Figure B-8 (note that the suggested characters are displayed in gray). In addition, it displays a popup containing a list of matching method names.

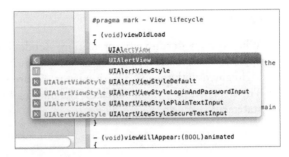

To accept the suggested word, simply press the Tab or Enter key, or Ctrl-/.

You can also invoke the Code Sense feature by pressing the Esc key. Xcode automatically

FIGURE B-8

recognizes the code you are typing and inserts the relevant parameters' placeholders. For example, if you invoke the methods of an object, Xcode inserts the placeholders of the various parameters. Figure B-9 shows an example of the placeholders inserted for the `UIAlertView` object after you type "i." To accept the placeholders for the various parameters, press the Tab key (you can also press the Enter key, or Ctrl-/). Press Ctrl-/ to move to each parameter placeholder, and then enter a value. Alternatively, click each placeholder and type over it.

FIGURE B-9

Running the Application

To execute an application, you first select the scheme to use. You also choose whether you want to test it on a real device or use the included iOS Simulator. You do so by selecting from the Scheme list (see Figure B-10).

To run the application, press Command-R, and Xcode builds and deploys the application onto the selected device or Simulator.

FIGURE B-10

DEBUGGING YOUR APPLICATIONS

Debugging your iOS applications is an essential part of your development effort. Xcode includes debugger utilities that help you trace and examine your code as you execute your application. The following sections describe some of the tips and tricks that you can employ when developing your iOS applications.

Errors

When you try to run your application, Xcode first tries to build the project before it can deploy the application onto the real device or Simulator. Any syntax errors that Xcode detects are immediately highlighted with the exclamation icons. Figure B-11 shows an Xcode-highlighted syntax error. The error within the code block is the missing brace symbol ([) for the [[UIAlertView alloc] statement.

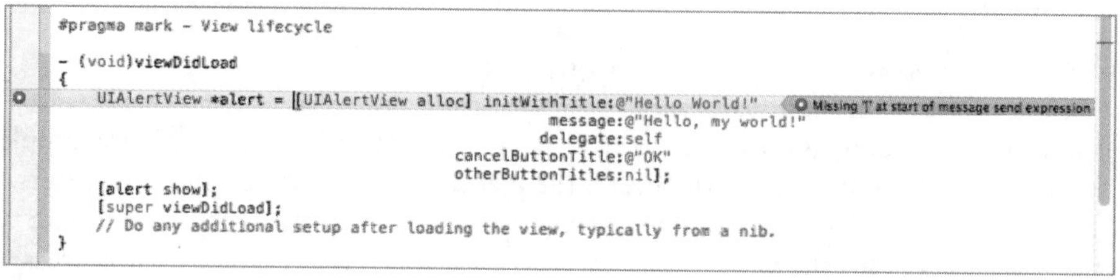

FIGURE B-11

You can also click the error icon to view the error and let Xcode suggest a fix (see Figure B-12).

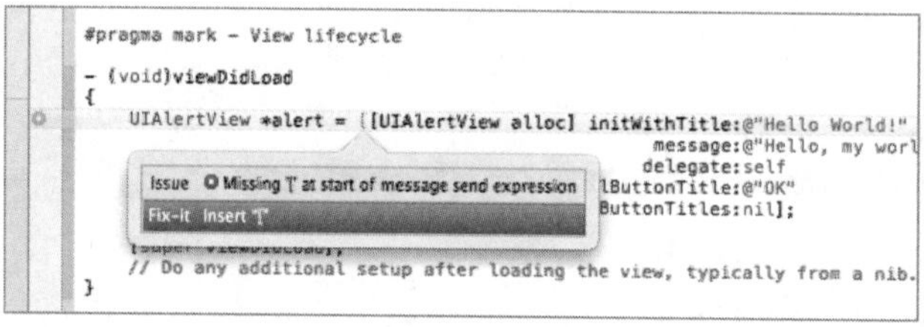

FIGURE B-12

Warnings

Because Objective-C is a case-sensitive language, a mistake often made by beginners is mixing up the capitalization for some of the method names. Consider the block of code shown in Figure B-13.

Can you spot the error? Syntactically, the statement is correct. However, one of the parameters appears with the wrong case: initwithTitle: was misspelled — it should be initWithTitle: (note the capital "W"). When you compile the program, Xcode will not flag this code as an error; instead, it issues a warning message (as shown in the figure).

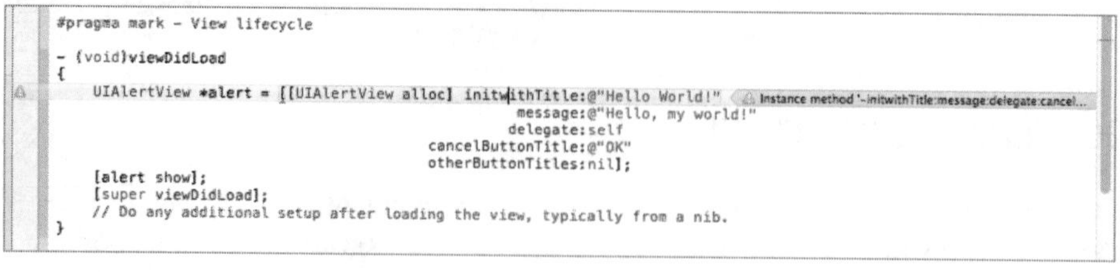

FIGURE B-13

Pay special attention to a warning message in Xcode, and verify that the method name is spelled correctly, including case. Failing to do so may result in a runtime exception.

When a runtime exception occurs, the best way to troubleshoot the error is to open the output window by pressing Shift-Command-C. The output window displays all the debugging information that is printed when Xcode debugs your application. This window usually contains the clue that helps you determine exactly what went wrong behind the scenes. Figure B-14 shows the content of the Debugger Console window when an exception occurs. To determine the cause of the crash, scroll to the bottom of the window and look for the section displayed in bold. In this case, note the reason stated — the problem is with the UIAlertView object.

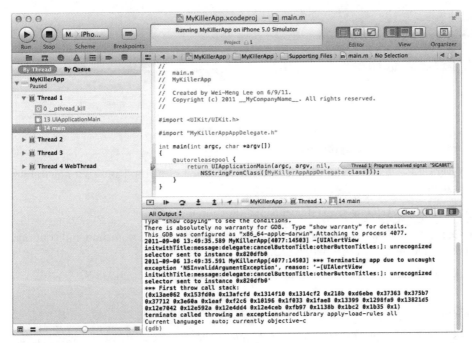

FIGURE B-14

Setting Breakpoints

Setting breakpoints in your code is helpful when debugging your application. Breakpoints enable you to execute your code line-by-line and examine the values of variables so you can check that they perform as expected.

```
- (void)viewDidDisappear:(BOOL)animated
{
    [super viewDidDisappear:animated];
}

- (BOOL)shouldAutorotateToInterfaceOrientation:(UIInterfaceOrientation)
    interfaceOrientation
{
    // Return YES for supported orientations
    return (interfaceOrientation != UIInterfaceOrientationPortraitUpsideDown);
}

@end
```

FIGURE B-15

In Xcode, you set a breakpoint by clicking the left column of the code editor — a breakpoint arrow will appear (see Figure B-15).

NOTE *You can toggle the state of a breakpoint by clicking it to enable or disable it. Breakpoints displayed in dark blue are enabled; those displayed in light blue are disabled. To remove a breakpoint, click on it and drag it out of its resting place. It will vanish in a puff of smoke.*

After you have set breakpoints in your application, press Command-R (just as you would to run your application) to debug it. The code will stop at your breakpoints.

When the application reaches the breakpoint you have set, Xcode indicates the current line of execution with a green arrow (see Figure B-16).

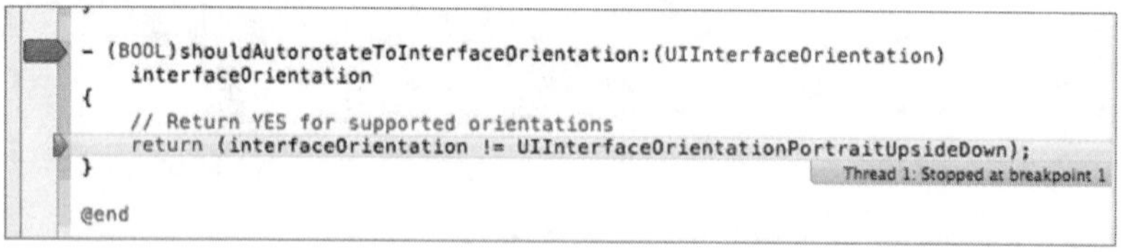

```
- (BOOL)shouldAutorotateToInterfaceOrientation:(UIInterfaceOrientation)
    interfaceOrientation
{
    // Return YES for supported orientations
    return (interfaceOrientation != UIInterfaceOrientationPortraitUpsideDown);
                                            Thread 1: Stopped at breakpoint 1
}

@end
```

FIGURE B-16

At this juncture, you can do several things:

➤ **Step Over (F6)** — Execute all the statements in a function or method and continue to the next statement.

➤ **Step Into (F7)** — Step into the statements in a function/method.

➤ **Step Out (F8)** — Finish executing all the statements in a function or method and continue to the next statement after the function call.

If you want to resume the execution of your application, press Option-Command-Y.

Using NSLog

In addition to setting breakpoints to trace the flow of your application, you can use the NSLog() macro to print debugging messages to the output window. Figure B-17 shows the output in the Output window (press Shift-Command-C to display it) when there is a change in orientation of the device/Simulator.

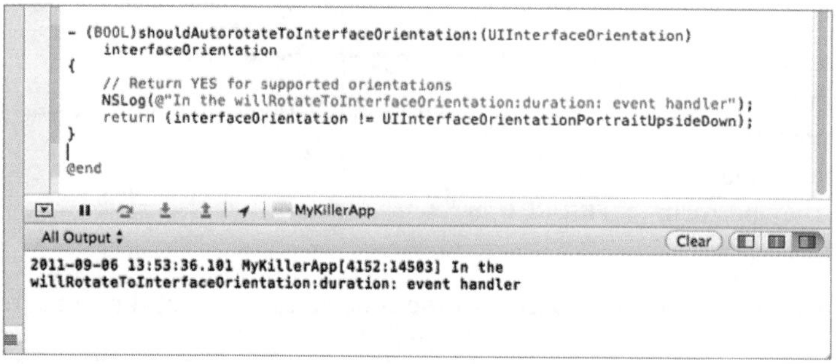

```
- (BOOL)shouldAutorotateToInterfaceOrientation:(UIInterfaceOrientation)
    interfaceOrientation
{
    // Return YES for supported orientations
    NSLog(@"In the willRotateToInterfaceOrientation:duration: event handler");
    return (interfaceOrientation != UIInterfaceOrientationPortraitUpsideDown);
}

@end
```

```
         ⏸  ↻  ⤓  ⤒  ✓ | MyKillerApp
All Output ⇕                                    ( Clear ) ▢ ▣ ▢
2011-09-06 13:53:36.101 MyKillerApp[4152:14503] In the
willRotateToInterfaceOrientation:duration: event handler
```

FIGURE B-17

Analyzing Your Code

A very useful feature of Xcode is its ability to analyze your code for potential memory leaks and logic faults. Beginning with Xcode 3.2, Apple has integrated the Clang Static Analyzer directly into Xcode. To use the Analyzer, press Option-Command-B. Figure B-18 (top) shows that Analyzer has detected a potential memory leak in the UIAlertView statement.

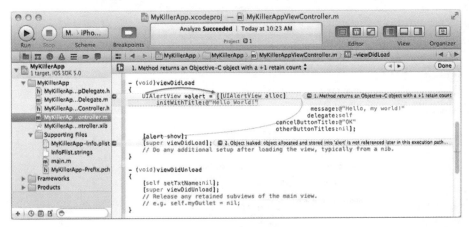

FIGURE B-18

Clicking on the blue arrow reveals the source of the potential leak. In this case, I have forgotten to release the alert object.

Documentation

During the course of your development, you often need to check the various methods, classes, and objects used in the iOS SDK. The best way to check them out is to refer to the documentation. Xcode enables you to quickly and easily browse the definitions of classes, properties, and methods.

To view the help documentation for an item, simply press the Option key. The cursor changes to cross-hairs. Double-click the item you want to check out, and a small window showing a summary of the selected item appears (see Figure B-19).

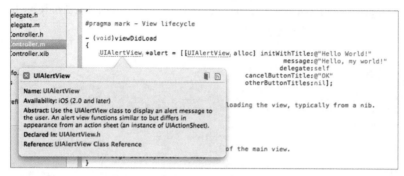

FIGURE B-19

Clicking the book icon (on the top-right corner of the help dialog) displays the full Developer Documentation window (see Figure B-20).

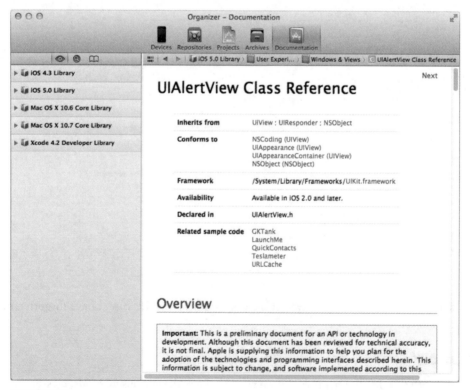

FIGURE B-20

INTERFACE BUILDER

Interface Builder is one of the tools included with the iOS SDK. It is a visual design aid that you can use to build the user interface of your iOS applications. Although it is not strictly required for the development of your iOS applications, Interface Builder plays an integral role in learning about iOS application development. This section covers some of the important features of Interface Builder.

.XIB WINDOW

In Xcode 4, Apple has integrated Interface Builder right into the Xcode IDE. You no longer need to launch Interface Builder as a separate application. To use Interface Builder, simply select any of the `.xib` files in your Xcode project. For example, if you have created a Single View Application project, there will be one `.xib` file in the project. Selecting it automatically launches Interface Builder.

When Interface Builder is launched, you should see something like Figure B-21.

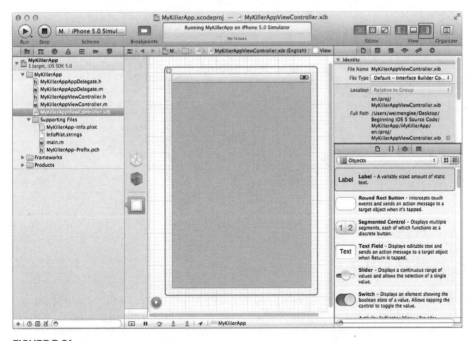

FIGURE B-21

Within this window are several items; and depending on what you have selected, you should see some of the following:

➤ File's Owner

➤ First Responder

➤ View, Table View, etc.

By default, the three items are displayed in icon mode; but you can also switch to display in document outline mode, where you can view some of the items in more detail. For example, Figure B-22 shows that when viewed in document outline mode, the View item displays a hierarchy of views contained within the View window.

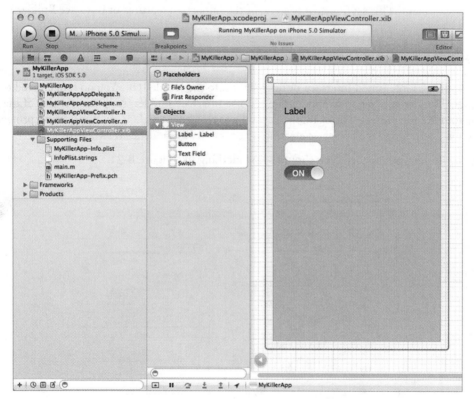

FIGURE B-22

DESIGNING THE VIEW

To design the user interface of your application, you typically select the .xib file to edit it using Interface Builder. To populate your View window with views, you drag and drop objects listed in the Library window (see the "Library" section for more information on the Library window). Figure B-23 shows some views being dropped and positioned onto the View window.

As you position a view on the View window, gridlines appear to guide you (see Figure B-24).

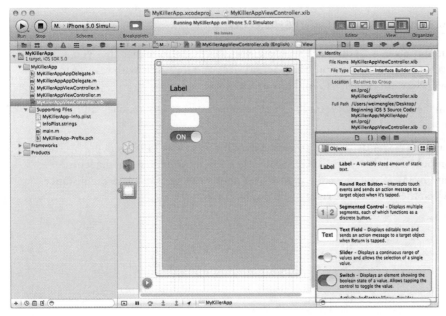

FIGURE B-23

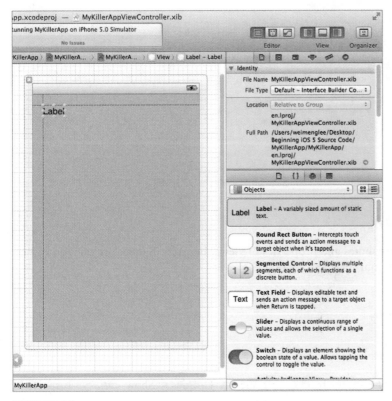

FIGURE B-24

INTERFACE BUILDER KEYBOARD SHORTCUTS

As you add more views to the View window, you will begin to realize that you are spending a lot of time figuring out their actual sizes and locations with respect to other views. Here are two tips to make your life easier:

➤ To make a copy of a view on the View window, simply Option-click and drag a view.

➤ If a view is currently selected, pressing the Option key and then moving the mouse over the view displays that view's size information (see the left of Figure B-25). If you move the mouse over another view, it displays the distance between the two (see the right of Figure B-25).

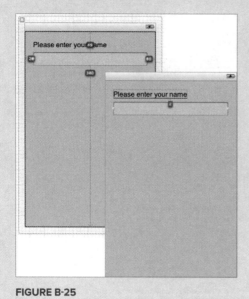

FIGURE B-25

INSPECTOR WINDOW

To customize the various attributes and properties of views, Interface Builder provides an Inspector window that is divided into four different windows:

➤ Attributes Inspector

➤ Connections Inspector

➤ Size Inspector

➤ Identity Inspector

You can invoke the Inspector window by choosing View ➪ Utilities ➪ Show *<utility>* Inspector.

The following sections discuss each of the Inspector windows in more detail.

Attributes Inspector Window

The Attributes Inspector window (see Figure B-26) is where you configure the attributes of views in Interface Builder. The window content is dynamic and varies according to what is selected in the View window.

To open the Attributes Inspector window, choose View ⇨ Utilities ⇨ Show Attributes Inspector.

Connections Inspector Window

The Connections Inspector window (see Figure B-27) is where you connect the outlets and actions of your views to the View Controller in Interface Builder. Its content is dynamic and varies according to what is selected in the View window.

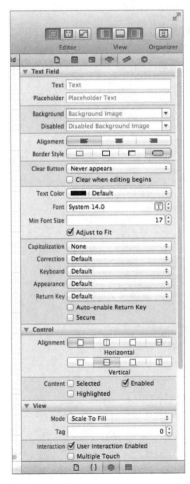

FIGURE B-26   **FIGURE B-27**

To open the Connections Inspector window, choose View ⇨ Utilities ⇨ Show Connections Inspector.

Size Inspector Window

The Size Inspector window (see Figure B-28) is where you configure the size and positioning of views in Interface Builder.

Open it by selecting View ⇨ Utilities ⇨ Show Size Inspector.

Identity Inspector Window

The Identity Inspector window (see Figure B-29) is where you configure the various properties of your selected view, such as the class controlling it.

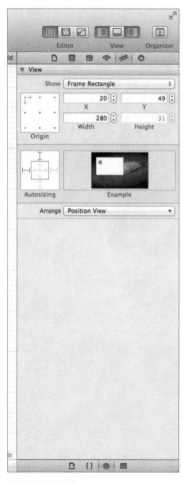

FIGURE B-28

FIGURE B-29

Open the Identity Inspector window by choosing View ⇨ Utilities ⇨ Show Identity Inspector.

LIBRARY

The Library (View ➪ Utilities ➪ Show Object Library) contains a set of views that you can use to build the user interface of your iOS application. Figure B-30 shows the Library's set of views in two different perspectives — List view and Icon view.

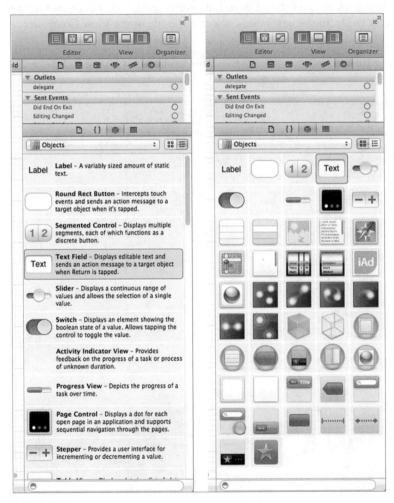

FIGURE B-30

OUTLETS AND ACTIONS

Outlets and actions are fundamental mechanisms in iOS programming through which your code can connect to the views in your user interface (UI). When you use outlets, your code can programmatically reference the views on your UI, with actions serving as event handlers that handle the different events fired by the various views.

Although you can write code to connect actions and outlets, Interface Builder simplifies the process by enabling you to use the drag-and-drop technique.

Creating Outlets and Actions

In Xcode 4, Interface Builder further simplifies the creation of outlets and actions. To create an action in Interface Builder, first click the Assistant Editor button to open another code editor pane next to the XIB file (see Figure B-31). In the new editor, select the .h file of the View Controller representing the XIB file.

Control-click the Round Rect Button and drag it onto the .h file as shown in Figure B-32.

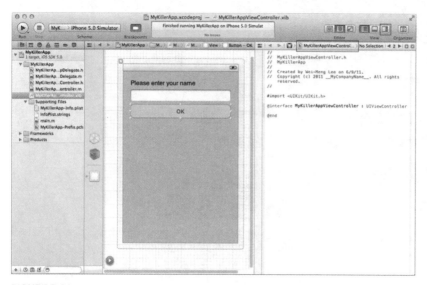

FIGURE B-31

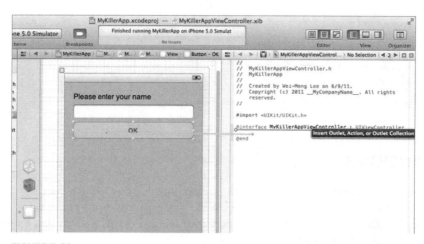

FIGURE B-32

You will be prompted to create either an outlet or an action. In this case, create an action as shown in Figure B-33 and then click the Connect button.

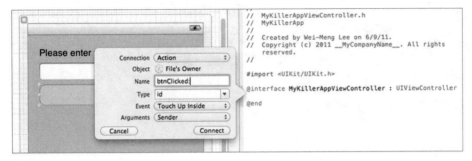

FIGURE B-33

Xcode will automatically create the declaration for the action in the .h file:

```
#import <UIKit/UIKit.h>

@interface MyKillerAppViewController : UIViewController
- (IBAction)btnClicked:(id)sender;

@end
```

Xcode will also create the method stub in the .m file:

```
- (IBAction)btnClicked:(id)sender {
}
```

To create an outlet, Control-click the TextField (as shown in Figure B-34) and drag it over the .h file.

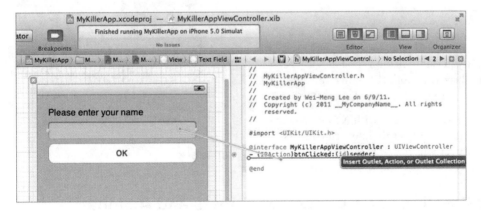

FIGURE B-34

Create the outlet as shown in Figure B-35 and then click the Connect button.

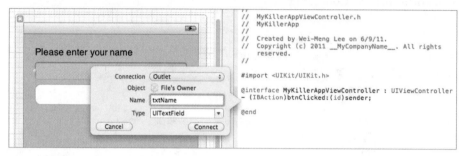

FIGURE B-35

The outlet will now be created in the .h file:

```
#import <UIKit/UIKit.h>

@interface MyKillerAppViewController : UIViewController
- (IBAction)btnClicked:(id)sender;

@property (retain, nonatomic) IBOutlet UITextField *txtName;

@end
```

In the .m file, Xcode will automatically add the @synthesize and release statements:

```
#import "MyKillerAppViewController.h"

@implementation MyKillerAppViewController
@synthesize txtName;

- (void)dealloc {
    [txtName release];
    [super dealloc];
}
```

Best of all, if you right-click on the File's Owner item, you will see that both the outlet and the action are connected automatically (see Figure B-36).

As you gain more experience with Xcode, you may find that it is much simpler to define the outlets and actions directly in the .h files of your View Controllers. The next section shows you how.

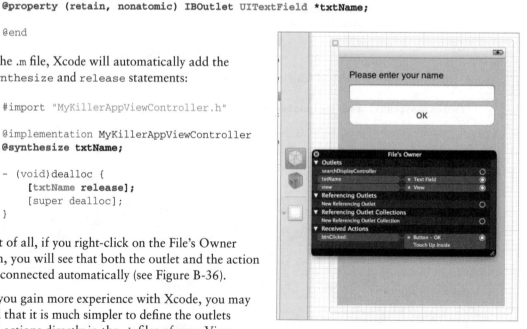

FIGURE B-36

Manually Creating and Connecting Outlets and Actions

The previous section showed how Interface Builder can help create actions and outlets for you automatically. However, you may wish to define the actions and outlets yourself and then link them up manually instead. The following sections discuss the two options you have for connecting the actions and outlets to the views.

It is assumed that you have already defined the outlet and action in the View Controller as follows:

```
#import <UIKit/UIKit.h>

@interface MyKillerAppViewController : UIViewController

- (IBAction)btnClicked:(id)sender;

@property (retain, nonatomic) IBOutlet UITextField *txtName;

@end
```

Method 1

To connect an outlet, Control-click and drag the File's Owner item to the view to which you want to connect (see Figure B-37).

When you release the mouse button, a list appears where you can select the correct outlet. When defining your outlets, remember that you can specify the type of view to which your outlet is referring. When you release the mouse button, Interface Builder lists only the outlets that match the type of view you have selected. For example, if you defined myOutlet1 as UIButton and you Control-click and drag the File's Owner item to a TextField on the View window, myOutlet1 does not appear in the list of outlets.

To connect an action, Control-click and drag the view to the File's Owner item in the .xib window (see Figure B-38).

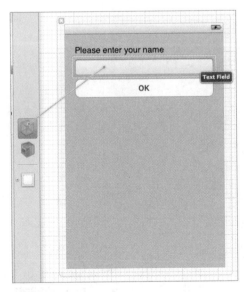

FIGURE B-37

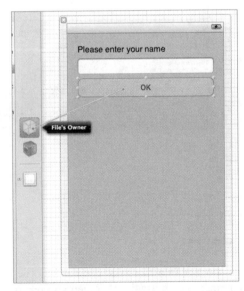

FIGURE B-38

When you release the mouse button, a list appears from which you can select the correct action.

When you have connected the outlets and actions, a good practice is to view all the connections in the File's Owner item by right-clicking it. Figure B-39 shows that the File's Owner item is connected to the Text Field view through the `txtName` outlet, and the Round Rect Button's `Touch Up Inside` event is connected to the `btnClicked:` action.

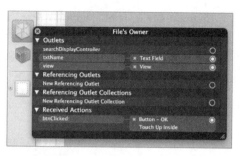

FIGURE B-39

How does the Button know that it is the `Touch Up Inside` event (and not other events) that should be connected to the `btnClicked:` action when you Control-click and drag the Button to the File's Owner item? The `Touch Up Inside` event is such a commonly used event that it is the default event selected when you perform a Control-click and drag action. What if you want to connect an event other than the default event? The next method shows you how.

Method 2

An alternative method for connecting an outlet is to right-click the File's Owner item and connect the outlet to the view directly (see Figure B-40).

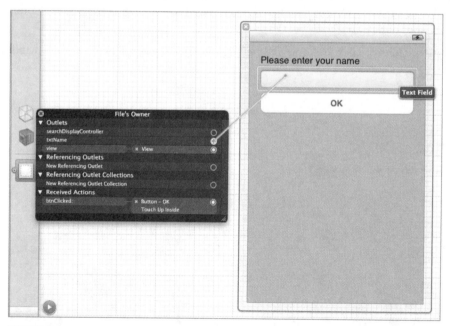

FIGURE B-40

To connect an action, you can connect the relevant action with the views to which you want to connect (see Figure B-41). When you release the mouse button, the list of available events appears, and you can select the one you want.

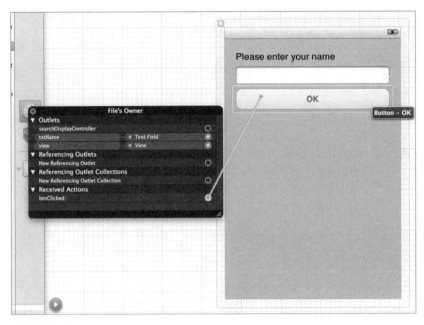

FIGURE B-41

Alternatively, you can right-click the view in question and connect the relevant events to the File's Owner item (see Figure B-42). When you release the mouse button, a list of your declared actions appears. Select the action to which you want to connect.

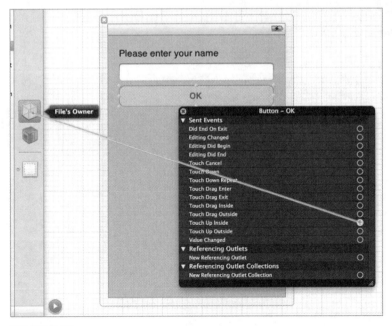

FIGURE B-42

As mentioned earlier, it is always good to right-click the File's Owner item after all the connections are made. One very common mistake that developers tend to make is changing the name of the actions or outlets after the connections are made. For example, suppose you now change the original outlet name from txtName to myTextField:

```
IBOutlet UITextField *myTextField;
```

Now, if you right-click the File's Owner item in Interface Builder, you will see a yellow triangle icon displayed on the right of the original connection (see Figure B-43). All broken connections in Interface Builder have the yellow triangle icon. To remedy this, click the "x" button to remove the connection and connect the appropriate outlet/action again.

FIGURE B-43

Crash Course in Objective-C

Objective-C is an object-oriented programming language used by Apple primarily for programming Mac OS X and iOS applications. It is an extension to the standard ANSI C language and hence it should be an easy language to pick up if you are already familiar with the C programming language. This appendix assumes that you already have some background in C programming and focuses on the object-oriented aspects of the language. If you are coming from a Java or .NET background, many of the concepts should be familiar to you; you just have to understand the syntax of Objective-C and, in particular, pay attention to the section on memory management.

Objective-C source code files are contained in two types of files:

➤ .h — header files

➤ .m — implementation files

FIGURE C-1

For the discussions that follow, assume that you have created a Single View Application project using Xcode named `LearningObjC` and added an empty `NSObject` class named `SomeClass` to your project (see Figure C-1).

DIRECTIVES

If you observe the content of the `SomeClass.h` file, you will notice that at the top of the file is an `#import` statement:

```
#import <Foundation/Foundation.h>

@interface SomeClass : NSObject {

}

@end
```

The `#import` statement is known as a *preprocessor directive*. In C and C++, you use the `#include` preprocessor directive to include a file's content with the current source. In Objective-C, you use the `#import` statement to do the same, except that the compiler ensures that the file is included at most only once. To import a header file from one of the frameworks, you specify the header filename using angle brackets (`<>`) in the `#import` statement. To import a header file from within your project, you use the " and " characters, as in the case of the `SomeClass.m` file:

```
#import "SomeClass.h"

@implementation SomeClass

@end
```

CLASSES

In Objective-C, you will spend a lot of time dealing with classes and objects. Hence, it is important to understand how classes are declared and defined in Objective-C.

@interface

To declare a class, you use the `@interface` compiler directive, like this:

```
@interface SomeClass : NSObject {

}
```

This is done in the header file (`.h`), and the class declaration contains no implementation. The preceding code declares a class named `SomeClass`, and this class inherits from the base class named `NSObject`.

> **NOTE** *While you typically put your code declaration in an* `.h` *file, you can also put it inside an* `.m` *if need be. This is usually done for small projects.*

> **NOTE** `NSObject` *is the root class of most Objective-C classes. It defines the basic interface of a class and contains methods common to all classes that inherit from it.* `NSObject` *also provides the standard memory management and initialization framework used by most objects in Objective-C, as well as reflection and type operations.*

In a typical View Controller class, the class inherits from the `UIViewController` class, such as in the following:

```
@interface HelloWorldViewController : UIViewController {

}
```

@implementation

To implement a class declared in the header file, you use the @implementation compiler directive, like this:

```
#import "SomeClass.h"

@implementation SomeClass

@end
```

This is done in a separate file from the header file. In Objective-C, you define your class in an .m file. Note that the class definition ends with the @end compiler directive.

> **NOTE** As mentioned earlier, you can also put your declaration inside an .m file. Hence, in your .m file you would then have both the @interface and @implementation directives.

@class

If your class references another class defined in another file, you need to import the header file of that file before you can use it. Consider the following example which defines two classes: SomeClass and AnotherClass. If you are using an instance of AnotherClass from within SomeClass, you need to import the AnotherClass.h file, as in the following code snippet:

```
//---SomeClass.h---
#import <Foundation/Foundation.h>
#import "AnotherClass.h"

@interface SomeClass : NSObject {
    //---an object from AnotherClass---
    AnotherClass *anotherClass;
}

@end

//---AnotherClass.h---
#import <Foundation/Foundation.h>

@interface AnotherClass : NSObject {

}

@end
```

However, if within AnotherClass you want to create an instance of SomeClass, you will not be able to simply import SomeClass.h in AnotherClass, like this:

```
//---SomeClass.h---
#import <Foundation/Foundation.h>
```

```
#import "AnotherClass.h"

@interface SomeClass : NSObject {
    //---an object from AnotherClass---
    AnotherClass *anotherClass;
}

@end

//---AnotherClass.h---
#import <Foundation/Foundation.h>
#import "SomeClass.h"        //---cannot simply import here---

@interface AnotherClass : NSObject {
    SomeClass *someClass;   //---using an instance of SomeClass---
}

@end
```

Doing so results in circular inclusion. To prevent that, Objective-C uses the @class compiler directive as a forward declaration to inform the compiler that the class you specified is a valid class. You usually use the @class compiler directive in the header file; and in the implementation file, you can use the @import compiler directive to tell the compiler more about the content of the class you are using.

Using the @class compiler directive, the program now looks like this:

```
//---SomeClass.h---
#import <Foundation/Foundation.h>

@class AnotherClass;    //---forward declaration---

@interface SomeClass : NSObject {
    //---an object from AnotherClass---
    AnotherClass *anotherClass;
}

@end


//---AnotherClass.h---
#import <Foundation/Foundation.h>

@class SomeClass;       //---forward declaration---

@interface AnotherClass : NSObject {
    SomeClass *someClass;   //---using an instance of SomeClass---
}

@end
```

NOTE *Another notable reason to use forward declaration where possible is that it reduces your compile times because the compiler does not need to traverse as many included header files and their includes, and so on.*

Class Instantiation

To create an instance of a class, you typically use the `alloc` keyword (more on this in the "Memory Management" section) to allocate memory for the object and then return it to a variable of the class type:

```
SomeClass *someClass = [SomeClass alloc];
```

In Objective-C, you need to prefix an object name with the * character when you declare an object. If you are declaring a variable of primitive type (such as `float`, `int`, `CGRect`, `NSInteger`, and so on), the * character is not required. Here are some examples:

```
CGRect frame;    //--CGRect is a structure--
int number;      //--int is a primitive type--
NSString *str;   //--NSString is a class
```

Besides specifying the returning class type, you can also use the `id` type, like this:

```
id someClass = [SomeClass alloc];
id str;
```

The `id` type means that the variable can refer to any type of object; hence, the * is implicitly implied.

Fields

Fields are the data members of objects. For example, the following code shows that `SomeClass` has three fields — `anotherClass`, `rate`, and `name`:

```
//---SomeClass.h---
#import <Foundation/Foundation.h>

@class AnotherClass;   //---forward declaration---

@interface SomeClass : NSObject {
    //---an object from AnotherClass---
    AnotherClass *anotherClass;
    float rate;
    NSString *name;
}

@end
```

Access Privileges

By default, the access privilege of all fields is `@protected`. However, the access privilege can also be `@public` or `@private`. The following list describes the various access privileges:

➤ `@private` — Visible only to the class that declares it

➤ `@public` — Visible to all classes

➤ `@protected` — Visible to the class that declares it and inheriting classes

Using the example shown in the previous section, if you now try to access the fields in `SomeClass` from another class, such as a View Controller, you will not be able to see them:

```
SomeClass *someClass = [SomeClass alloc];
someClass->rate = 5;                     //---rate is declared protected---
someClass->name = @"Wei-Meng Lee";  //---name is declared protected---
```

 NOTE Note that to access the fields in a class directly, you use the `->` operator.

To make the `rate` and `name` visible outside the class, modify the `SomeClass.h` file by adding the `@public` compiler directive:

```
//---SomeClass.h---
#import <Foundation/Foundation.h>

@class AnotherClass;    //---forward declaration---

@interface SomeClass : NSObject {
    //---an object from AnotherClass---
    AnotherClass *anotherClass;

@public
    float rate;

@public
    NSString *name;
}

@end
```

The following two statements would now be valid:

```
someClass->rate = 5;                     //--rate is now declared public--
someClass->name = @"Wei-Meng Lee";  //--name is now declared public--
```

Although you can access the fields directly, doing so goes against the design principles of object-oriented programming's rule of encapsulation. A better way is to encapsulate the two fields you want to expose in properties. Refer to the "Properties" section later in this appendix.

Methods

Methods are functions that are defined in a class. Objective-C supports two types of methods — *instance methods* and *class methods*.

Instance methods can be called only using an instance of the class; and they are prefixed with the minus sign (-) character.

Class methods can be invoked directly using the class name and do not need an instance of the class in order to work. Class methods are prefixed with the plus sign (+) character.

 NOTE *In some programming languages, such as C# and Java, class methods are commonly known as* static *methods.*

The following code sample shows `SomeClass` with three instance methods and one class method declared:

```
//---SomeClass.h---
#import <Foundation/Foundation.h>

@class AnotherClass;    //---forward declaration---

@interface SomeClass : NSObject {
    //---an object from AnotherClass---
    AnotherClass *anotherClass;
    float rate;
    NSString *name;
}

//---instance methods---
-(void) doSomething;
-(void) doSomething:(NSString *) str;
-(void) doSomething:(NSString *) str withAnotherPara:(float) value;

//---class method---
+(void) alsoDoSomething;

@end
```

The following shows the implementation of the methods that were declared in the header file:

```
#import "SomeClass.h"

@implementation SomeClass

-(void) doSomething {
    //---implementation here---
```

```
    }

    -(void) doSomething:(NSString *) str {
        //---implementation here---
    }

    -(void) doSomething:(NSString *) str withAnotherPara:(float) value {
        //---implementation here---
    }

    +(void) alsoDoSomething {
        //---implementation here---
    }

    @end
```

To invoke the three instance methods, you first need to create an instance of the class and then call them using the instance created:

```
        SomeClass *someClass = [SomeClass alloc];
        [someClass doSomething];
        [someClass doSomething:@"some text"];
        [someClass doSomething:@"some text" withAnotherPara:9.0f];
```

Class methods can be called directly using the class name, as the following shows:

```
        [SomeClass alsoDoSomething];
```

In general, you create instance methods when you need to perform some actions that are related to the particular instance of the class (that is, the object). For example, suppose you defined a class that represents the information of an employee. You may expose an instance method that enables you to calculate the overtime wage of an employee. In this case, you use an instance method because the calculation involves data specific to a particular employee object.

Class methods, on the other hand, are commonly used for defining helper methods. For example, you might have a class method called `GetOvertimeRate:` that returns the rate for working overtime. In a scenario in which all employees get the same rate for working overtime (assuming this is the case for your company), there is no need to create instance methods, and thus a class method will suffice.

The next section shows how to call methods with a varying number of parameters.

Message Sending (Calling Methods)

In Objective-C, you use the following syntax to call a method:

```
    [object method];
```

Strictly speaking, in Objective-C you do not call a method; rather, you send a message to an object. The message to be passed to an object is resolved during runtime and is not enforced at compile time. This is why the compiler does not stop you from running your program even though you may have misspelled the method name. It does warn you that the target object may not respond to your message, though, because the target object will simply ignore the message (and in most situations result in a runtime exception).

NOTE *For ease of understanding, I use the more conventional phrasing of "calling a method" to refer to Objective-C's message-sending mechanism.*

Using the example from the previous section, the doSomething method has no parameter:

```
-(void) doSomething {
    //---implementation here---
}
```

Therefore, you can call it like this:

```
[someClass doSomething];
```

If a method has one or more inputs, you call it using the following syntax:

```
[object method:input1];                           //---one input---
[object method:input1 andSecondInput:input2];     //---two inputs---
```

The interesting thing about Objective-C is the way you call a method with multiple inputs. Using the earlier example:

```
-(void) doSomething:(NSString *) str withAnotherPara:(float) value {
    //---implementation here---
}
```

The name of the preceding method is doSomething:withAnotherPara:. The first part of the method name, doSomething:, is called the label, and so is the second. Therefore, a method name in Objective-C is made up of one or more labels. Strictly speaking, the labels are optional. For example, the preceding method could be rewritten as follows:

```
-(void) :(NSString *) str :(float) value {
    //---implementation here---
}
```

To call the preceding method, I can use the following statement:

```
[someClass :@"some text" :9.0f];
```

This works because in Objective-C, arguments are passed according to positions. While this compiles, it is not recommended, because it makes your method ambiguous.

It is important to note the names of methods and to differentiate those with parameters from those without them. For example, doSomething refers to a method with no parameter, whereas doSomething: refers to a method with one parameter, and doSomething:withAnotherPara: refers to a method with two parameters. The presence or absence of colons in a method name dictates which method is invoked during runtime. This is important when passing method names as arguments, particularly when using the @selector notation (discussed in the "Selectors" section) to pass them to a delegate or notification event.

Method calls can also be nested, as the following example shows:

```
NSString *str = [[NSString alloc] initWithString:@"Hello World"];
```

Here, you first call the `alloc` class method of the `NSString` class and then call the `initWithString:` method of the returning result from the `alloc` method, which is of type `id`, a generic C type that Objective-C uses for an arbitrary object.

In general, you should not nest more than three levels because anything more than that makes the code difficult to read.

Properties

Properties enable you to expose the fields in your class so that you can control how values are set or returned. In the earlier example (in the "Access Privileges" section), you saw that you can directly access the fields of a class using the `->` operator. However, this is not the ideal way; ideally, you should expose your fields as properties.

Prior to Objective-C 2.0, programmers had to declare methods to make the fields accessible to other classes, like this:

```
//---SomeClass.h---
#import <Foundation/Foundation.h>

@class AnotherClass;   //---forward declaration---

@interface SomeClass : NSObject {
    //---an object from AnotherClass---
    AnotherClass *anotherClass;
    float rate;
    NSString *name;
}

//---expose the rate field---
-(float) rate;                        //---get the value of rate---
-(void) setRate:(float) value;        //---set the value of rate---

//---expose the name field---
-(NSString *) name;                   //---get the value of name---
-(void) setName:(NSString *) value;   //---set the value of name---

//---instance methods---
-(void) doSomething;
-(void) doSomething:(NSString *) str;
-(void) doSomething:(NSString *) str withAnotherPara:(float) value;

//---class method---
+(void) alsoDoSomething;

@end
```

These methods are known as *getters* and *setters* (or sometimes better known as *accessors* and *mutators*). The implementation of these methods may look like this:

```
#import "SomeClass.h"

@implementation SomeClass

-(float) rate {
    return rate;
}

-(void) setRate:(float) value {
    rate = value;
}

-(NSString *) name {
    return name;
}

-(void) setName:(NSString *) value {
    [value retain];
    [name release];
    name = value;
}

-(void) doSomething {
    //---implementation here---
}

-(void) doSomething:(NSString *) str {
    //---implementation here---
    NSLog(str);
}

-(void) doSomething:(NSString *) str withAnotherPara:(float) value {
    //---implementation here---
}

+(void) alsoDoSomething {
    //---implementation here---
}

@end
```

To set the value of these properties, you need to call the methods prefixed with the set keyword:

```
SomeClass *sc = [[SomeClass alloc] init];
[sc setRate:5.0f];
[sc setName:@"Wei-Meng Lee"];
```

Alternatively, you can use the dot notation introduced in Objective-C 2.0:

```
SomeClass *sc = [[SomeClass alloc] init];
sc.rate = 5.0f;
sc.name = @"Wei-Meng Lee";
```

To obtain the values of properties, you can either call the methods directly or use the dot notation in Objective-C 2.0:

```
NSLog([sc name]); //—call the method—
NSLog(sc.name);   //—dot notation
```

To make a property read-only, simply remove the method prefixed with the `set` keyword.

Notice that within the `setName:` method, you have various statements using the `retain` and `release` keywords. These keywords relate to memory management in Objective-C; you learn more about them in the "Memory Management" section, later in this appendix.

In Objective-C 2.0, you don't need to define getters and setters in order to expose fields as properties. You can do so via the `@property` and `@synthesize` compiler directives. Using the same example, you can use the `@property` directive to expose the `rate` and `name` fields as properties, like this:

```
//---SomeClass.h---
#import <Foundation/Foundation.h>

@class AnotherClass;    //---forward declaration---

@interface SomeClass : NSObject {
    //---an object from AnotherClass---
    AnotherClass *anotherClass;
    float rate;
    NSString *name;
}

@property float rate;
@property (retain, nonatomic) NSString *name;

//---instance methods---
-(void) doSomething;
-(void) doSomething:(NSString *) str;
-(void) doSomething:(NSString *) str withAnotherPara:(float) value;

//---class method---
+(void) alsoDoSomething;

@end
```

The first `@property` statement defines `rate` as a property. The second statement defines `name` as a property as well, but it also specifies the behavior of this property. In this case, it indicates the behavior as `retain` and `nonatomic`, which you learn more about in the section on memory management later in this appendix. In particular, `nonatomic` means that the property is not accessed in a thread-safe manner. This is OK if you are not writing multi-threaded applications. Most of the time, you will use the `retain` and `nonatomic` combination when declaring properties. The first property does not need the `retain` keyword, as it is a primitive type and not an object.

In the implementation file, rather than define the getter and setter methods, you can simply use the `@synthesize` keyword to get the compiler to automatically generate the getters and setters for you:

```
#import "SomeClass.h"

@implementation SomeClass

@synthesize rate, name;
```

As shown, you can combine several properties using a single @synthesize keyword. However, you can also separate them into individual statements:

```
@synthesize rate;
@synthesize name;
```

You can now use your properties as usual:

```
//---setting using setRate---
[sc setRate:5.0f];
[sc setName:@"Wei-Meng Lee"];

//---setting using dot notation---
sc.rate = 5;
sc.name = @"Wei-Meng Lee";

//---getting---
NSLog([sc name]); //---using the name method---
NSLog(sc.name);   //---dot notation---
```

To make a property read-only, use the readonly keyword. The following statement makes the name property read-only:

```
@property (retain, nonatomic, readonly) NSString *name;
```

Initializers

When you create an instance of a class, you often initialize it at the same time. For example, in the earlier example (in the "Class Instantiation" section), you had this statement:

```
SomeClass *sc = [[SomeClass alloc] init];
```

The alloc keyword allocates memory for the object; and when an object is returned, the init method is called on the object to initialize the object. Recall that in SomeClass, you do not define a method named init. So where does the init method come from? It is actually defined in the NSObject class, which is the base class of most classes in Objective-C. The init method is known as an initializer.

If you want to create additional initializers, you can define methods that begin with the init word (use of the init prefix is more of a norm than a hard-and-fast rule):

```
//---SomeClass.h---
#import <Foundation/Foundation.h>

@class AnotherClass;   //---forward declaration---

@interface SomeClass : NSObject {
```

```
        //---an object from AnotherClass---
        AnotherClass *anotherClass;
        float rate;
        NSString *name;
    }

    @property float rate;
    @property (retain, nonatomic) NSString *name;

    //---instance methods---
    -(void) doSomething;
    -(void) doSomething:(NSString *) str;
    -(void) doSomething:(NSString *) str withAnotherPara:(float) value;

    //---class method---
    +(void) alsoDoSomething;

    -(id)initWithName:(NSString *) n;
    -(id)initWithName:(NSString *) n andRate:(float) r;

    @end
```

The preceding example contains two additional initializers: initWithName: and
initWithName:andRate:. You can provide the implementations for the two initializers as follows:

```
    #import "SomeClass.h"

    @implementation SomeClass

    @synthesize rate, name;

    - (id)initWithName:(NSString *) n {
      return [self initWithName:n andRate:0.0f];
    }

    - (id)initWithName:(NSString *) n andRate:(float) r {
        if (self = [super init]) {
            self.name = n;
            self.rate = r;
        }
        return self;
    }

    //...
    //...
```

Note that in the initWithName:andRate: initializer implementation, you first call the init
initializer of the super (base) class so that its base class is properly initialized, which is necessary
before you can initialize the current class:

```
    - (id)initWithName:(NSString *) n andRate:(float) r {
      if (self = [super init]) {
          self.name = n;
```

```
            self.rate = r;
        }
        return self;
    }
```

The rule for defining an initializer is simple: If a class is initialized properly, it should return a reference to `self` (hence the `id` type). If it fails, it should return `nil`.

For the `initWithName:` initializer implementation, notice that it calls the `initWithName:andRate:` initializer:

```
- (id)initWithName:(NSString *) n {
    return [self initWithName:n andRate:0.0f];
}
```

In general, if you have multiple initializers, each with different parameters, you should chain them by ensuring that they all call a single initializer that performs the call to the super class's `init` initializer. In Objective-C, the initializer that performs the call to the super class's `init` initializer is called the *designated initializer.*

 NOTE *As a general guideline, the designated initializer should be the one with the greatest number of parameters.*

To use the initializers, you can now call them at the time of instantiation:

```
SomeClass *sc1 = [[SomeClass alloc] initWithName:@"Wei-Meng Lee"
                                         andRate:35];
SomeClass *sc2 = [[SomeClass alloc] initWithName:@"Wei-Meng Lee"];
```

MEMORY MANAGEMENT

Memory management in Objective-C programming (especially for iOS) is a very important topic that every iOS developer needs to be aware of. Like all other popular languages, Objective-C supports garbage collection, which helps to remove unused objects when they go out of scope and hence releases memory that can be reused. However, because of the severe overhead involved in implementing garbage collection, the iOS does not support garbage collection. This leaves you, the developer, to manually allocate and de-allocate the memory of objects when they are no longer needed.

This section discusses the various aspects of memory management on the iOS.

Reference Counting

To help you allocate and de-allocate memory for objects, the iOS uses a scheme known as *reference counting* to keep track of objects to determine whether they are still needed or can be disposed of. Reference counting basically uses a counter for each object; and as each object is created, the count increases by 1. When an object is released, the count decreases by 1. When the count reaches 0, the memory associated with the object is reclaimed by the OS.

In Objective-C, a few important keywords are associated with memory management. The following sections take a look at each of them.

NEW FEATURE: AUTOMATIC REFERENCE COUNTING

In iOS 5, Objective-C now supports a new feature known as *Automatic Reference Counting (ARC)*. Instead of needing you to keep track of each object's ownership, ARC enables the compiler to examine your code and automatically insert statements to release the objects at compile time. Using ARC:

➤ You no longer need to use the `retain`, `release`, `autorelease` keywords, and the `dealloc` method.

➤ You cannot use the `NSAutoreleasePool` object.

While ARC makes it easier for you to write applications without worrying about object memory management, a lot of third-party libraries still need to manually release objects. For this book, all the projects are created with ARC turned off. Moreover, it is important for you to understand the basics of how Objective-C manages the memory.

---

alloc

The `alloc` keyword allocates memory for an object that you are creating. You have seen it in almost all the exercises in this book. An example is as follows:

```
NSString *str = [[NSString alloc] initWithString:@"Hello"];
```

Here, you are creating an `NSString` object and instantiating it with a default string. When the object is created, the reference count of that object is 1. Because you are the one creating it, the object belongs to you, and it is your responsibility to release the memory when you are done with it.

 NOTE *See the "release" section for information on how to release an object.*

So how do you know when an object is owned, and by whom? Consider the following example:

```
NSString *str = [[NSString alloc] initWithString:@"Hello"];
NSString *str2 = str;
```

In this example, you use the `alloc` keyword for `str`, so you own `str`. Therefore, you need to release it when it's no longer needed. However, `str2` is simply pointing to `str`, so you do not own `str2`, meaning you need not release `str2` when you are done using it.

new

Besides using the `alloc` keyword to allocate memory for an object, you can also use the `new` keyword, like this:

```
NSString *str = [NSString new];
```

The `new` keyword is functionally equivalent to

```
NSString *str = [[NSString alloc] init];
```

As with the `alloc` keyword, using the `new` keyword makes you the owner of the object, so you need to release it when you are done with it.

retain

The `retain` keyword increases the reference count of an object by 1. Consider a previous example:

```
NSString *str = [[NSString alloc] initWithString:@"Hello"];
NSString *str2 = str;
```

Here, you do not own `str2` because you do not use the `alloc` keyword on the object. When `str` is released, the `str2` will no longer be valid.

To ensure that `str2` is available even if `str` is released, you need to use the `retain` keyword:

```
NSString *str = [[NSString alloc] initWithString:@"Hello"];
NSString *str2 = str;
[str2 retain];   //---str2 now also "owns" the object---
[str release];   //---str can now be released safely---
```

In the preceding case, the reference count for `str` is now 2. When you release `str`, `str2` will still be valid. When you are done with `str2`, you need to release it manually, like this:

```
[str2 release];   //---str2 can now be released when you are done with it---
```

 NOTE *As a general rule, if you own an object (using alloc or retain), you need to release it.*

release

When you are done with an object, you need to manually release it by using the `release` keyword:

```
NSString *str = [[NSString alloc] initWithString:@"Hello"];

//...do what you want with the object...

[str release];
```

When you use the `release` keyword on an object, it causes the reference count of that object to decrease by 1. When the reference count reaches 0, the memory used by the object is released.

One important aspect to keep in mind when using the `release` keyword is that you cannot release an object that is not owned by you. For example, consider the example used in the previous section:

```
NSString *str = [[NSString alloc] initWithString:@"Hello"];
NSString *str2 = str;
[str release];
[str2 release];   //---this is not OK as you do not own str2---
```

Attempting to release `str2` will result in a runtime error because you cannot release an object not owned by you. However, if you use the `retain` keyword to gain ownership of an object, you do need to use the `release` keyword:

```
NSString *str = [[NSString alloc] initWithString:@"Hello"];
NSString *str2 = str;
[str2 retain];
[str release];
[str2 release];   //---this is now OK as you now own str2---
```

Recall that earlier, in the section on properties, you defined the `setName:` method, where you set the value of the `name` field:

```
-(void) setName:(NSString *) value {
    [value retain];
    [name release];
    name = value;
}
```

Notice that you first had to retain the `value` object, followed by releasing the `name` object and then finally assigning the `value` object to `name`. Why do you need to do that as opposed to the following?

```
-(void) setName:(NSString *) value {
    name = value;
}
```

If you were using garbage collection, the preceding statement would be valid. However, because iOS does not support garbage collection, the preceding statement will cause the original object referenced by the `name` object to be lost, thereby causing a memory leak. To prevent that leak, you first retain the `value` object to indicate that you wish to gain ownership of it; then you release the original object referenced by `name`. Finally, assign `value` to `name`:

```
[value retain];
[name release];
name = value;
```

Convenience Method and Autorelease

So far, you learned that all objects created using the `alloc` or `new` keywords are owned by you. Consider the following case:

```
NSString *str = [NSString stringWithFormat:@"%d", 4];
```

In this statement, do you own the `str` object? The answer is no, you don't, because the object is created using one of the *convenience methods* — static methods that are used for allocating and initializing objects directly. In the preceding case, you create an object but you do not own it. Because you do not own it, you cannot release it manually. In fact, objects created using this method are known as *autorelease* objects. All autorelease objects are temporary objects and are added to an *autorelease pool*. When the current method exits, all the objects contained within it are released. Autorelease objects are useful for cases in which you simply want to use some temporary variables and do not want to burden yourself with allocations and de-allocations.

The key difference between an object created using the `alloc` (or new) keyword and one created using a convenience method is that of ownership, as the following example shows:

```
NSString *str1 = [[NSString alloc] initWithFormat:@"%d", 4];
[str1 release]; //—-this is ok because you own str1—-

NSString *str2 = [NSString stringWithFormat:@"%d", 4];
[str2 release]; //—-this is not ok because you don't own str2—-
//—-str2 will be removed automatically when the autorelease
// pool is activated—-
```

UNDERSTANDING REFERENCE COUNTING USING AN ANALOGY

When you think of memory management using reference counting, it is always good to use a real-life analogy to put things into perspective.

Imagine a room in the library that you can reserve for studying purposes. Initially, the room is empty and hence the lights are off. When you reserve the room, the librarian increases a counter to indicate the number of persons using the room. This is similar to creating an object using the `alloc` keyword.

When you leave the room, the librarian decreases the counter; and when the counter is 0, this means that the room is no longer being used and the lights can thus be switched off. This is similar to using the `release` keyword to release an object.

There may be times when you have booked the room and are the only person in it (hence, the counter is 1) until a friend of yours comes along. He may simply visit you and therefore not register with the librarian. Hence, the counter does not increase. Because he is just visiting you and hasn't booked the room, he has no rights to decide whether the lights should be switched off. This is similar to assigning an object to another variable without using the `alloc` keyword. In this case, if you leave the room (release), the lights will be switched off and your friend will have to leave.

Consider another situation in which you are using the room and another person also booked the room and shares it with you. In this case, the counter is now 2. If you leave the room, the counter goes down to 1, but the lights are still on because another person is in the room. This is similar to creating an object and assigning it to another variable that uses the `retain` keyword. In such a situation, the object is released only when both objects release it.

If you want to take ownership of an object when using a convenience method, you can do so using the `retain` keyword:

```
NSString *str2 = [[NSString stringWithFormat:@"%d", 4] retain];
```

To release the object, you can use either the `autorelease` or the `release` keyword. You learned earlier that the `release` keyword immediately decreases the reference count by 1 and that the object is immediately de-allocated from memory when the reference count reaches 0. In contrast, the `autorelease` keyword promises to decrease the reference count by 1 but not *immediately* — sometime later. It is like saying, "Well, I still need the object now, but later I can let it go." The following code makes it clear:

```
NSString *str = [[NSString stringWithFormat:@"%d", 4] retain];
[str autorelease];   //---you don't own it anymore; still available---
NSlog(str);          //---still accessible for now---
```

> **NOTE** After you have autoreleased an object, do not release it anymore.

Note that the statement

```
NSString *str2 = [NSString stringWithFormat:@"%d", 4];
```

has the same effect as

```
NSString *str2 = @"4";
```

Although autorelease objects seem to make your life simple by automatically releasing objects that are no longer needed, you have to be careful when using them. Consider the following example:

```
for (int i=0; i<=99999; i++){
    NSString *str = [NSString stringWithFormat:@"%d", i];
    //...
    //...
}
```

Here, you are creating an `NSString` object for each iteration of the loop. Because the objects are not released until the function exits, you may well run out of memory. One way to solve this dilemma is to use an autorelease pool, as discussed in the next section.

REFERENCE COUNTING: THE ANALOGY CONTINUES

Continuing with the analogy of the reserved room in the library, imagine that you are about to sign out with the librarian when you realize that you have left your books in the room. You tell the librarian that you are done with the room and want to sign out now, but because you left your books in the room, you tell the librarian not to switch off the lights yet so that you can go back to get them. Later, the librarian can switch off the lights at his or her own choosing. This is the behavior of autoreleased objects.

Autorelease Pools

All autorelease objects are temporary objects and are added to an *autorelease pool*. When the objects are no longer needed, all the objects contained within it are released. However, sometimes you want to control how the autorelease pool is emptied, rather than wait for it to be called by the OS. To do so, you can create an instance of the NSAutoreleasePool class, like this:

```
for (int i=0; i<=99999; i++){
    NSAutoreleasePool *pool = [[NSAutoreleasePool alloc] init];
    NSString *str1 = [NSString stringWithFormat:@"%d", i];
    NSString *str2 = [NSString stringWithFormat:@"%d", i];
    NSString *str3 = [NSString stringWithFormat:@"%d", i];
    //...
    //...
    [pool release];
}
```

In this example, for each iteration of the loop, an NSAutoreleasePool object is created, and all the autorelease objects created within the loop — str1, str2, and str3 — go into it. At the end of each iteration, the NSAutoreleasePool object is released so that all the objects contained within it are automatically released. This ensures that you have at most three autorelease objects in memory at any one time.

dealloc

You have learned that by using the alloc or new keyword, you own the object that you have created. You have also seen how to release the objects you own using the release or autorelease keyword. When is a good time for you to release them?

As a rule of thumb, you should release the objects as soon as you are done with them. Therefore, if you created an object in a method, you should release it before you exit the method. For properties, recall that you can use the @property compiler directive together with the retain keyword:

```
@property (retain, nonatomic) NSString *name;
```

Because the values of the property will be retained, it is important that you free it before you exit the application. A good place to do so is in the dealloc method of a class (such as a View Controller):

```
-(void) dealloc {
    [self.name release];    //---release the name property---
    [super dealloc];
}
```

The dealloc method of a class is fired whenever the reference count of its object reaches 0. Consider the following example:

```
SomeClass *sc1 = [[SomeClass alloc] initWithName:@"Wei-Meng Lee"
                                        andRate:35];
//...do something here…
[sc1 release];  //---reference count goes to 0; dealloc will be called---
```

The preceding example shows that when the reference count of sc1 reaches 0 (when the release statement is called), the dealloc method defined within the class will be called. If you don't define this method in the class, its implementation in the base class will be called.

Memory Management Tips

Memory management is a tricky issue in iOS programming. Although there are tools you can use to test for memory leaks, this section presents some simple things you can do to detect memory problems that might affect your application.

First, ensure that you implement the didReceiveMemoryWarning method in your View controller:

```
- (void)didReceiveMemoryWarning {
    // Releases the view if it doesn't have a superview.
    [super didReceiveMemoryWarning];
    //---insert code here to free unused objects---
    // Release any cached data, images, etc that aren't in use.
}
```

The didReceiveMemoryWarning method will be called whenever your iOS device runs out of memory. You should insert code in this method so that you can free resources/objects that you don't need.

In addition, you should also handle the applicationDidReceiveMemoryWarning: method in your application delegate:

```
- (void)applicationDidReceiveMemoryWarning:(UIApplication *)application {
    /*
    Free up as much memory as possible by purging cached
    data objects that can be recreated (or reloaded from
    disk) later.
    */
    //---insert code here to free unused objects---
}
```

In this method, you should stop all memory-intensive activities, such as audio and video playback. You should also remove all images cached in memory.

When dealing with arrays, remember to retain item(s) retrieved from an array:

```
NSMutableArray *array = [[NSMutableArray alloc] init];
[array addObject:@"Item 1"];
[array addObject:@"Item 2"];
[array addObject:@"Item 3"];

//---this is not safe as the object can be removed anytime---
//NSString *item = [array objectAtIndex:1];

//---do this instead---
NSString *item = [[array objectAtIndex:1] retain];
[array removeObjectAtIndex:1];

NSLog(@"item is %@", item);

[item release];
[array release];
```

When returning an alloc'ed object, remember to autorelease it:

```
-(NSString *) fullName {
    NSString *str = [[NSString alloc] initWithFormat:@"%@ %@",
                     firstName, lastName];
    //---remember to release str; else it will leak memory---
    [str autorelease];
    return str;
}
```

When setting an alloc'ed object to a property with a retain or copy, remember to autorelease it:

```
-(id) initWithFirstName:(NSString *) fName
         andLastName:(NSString *) lName
            andEmail:(NSString *) emailAddress {
    self = [super init];
    if (self) {
        self.firstName = fName;
        self.lastName = lName;

        if ([emailAddress length]==0) {
            //---this will result in a memory leak---
            // self.email = [[NSString alloc]
            //     initWithString:@"No email set"];

            //---do this instead---
            self.email =
            [[[NSString alloc] initWithString:@"No email set"]
             autorelease];
        } else {
            self.email = emailAddress;
        }
    }
    return self;
}
```

PROTOCOLS

In Objective-C, a *protocol* declares a programmatic interface that any class can choose to implement. A protocol declares a set of methods, and an adopting class may choose to implement one or more of its declared methods. The class that defines the protocol is expected to call the methods in the protocols that are implemented by the adopting class.

The easiest way to understand protocols is to examine the UIAlertView class. As you have experienced in the various chapters in this book, you can simply use the UIAlertView class by creating an instance of it and then calling its show method:

```
UIAlertView *alert = [[UIAlertView alloc]
                initWithTitle:@"Hello"
                      message:@"This is an alert view"
                     delegate:self
            cancelButtonTitle:@"OK"
            otherButtonTitles:nil];
[alert show];
```

The preceding code displays an alert view with one button — OK. Tapping the OK button automatically dismisses the alert view. If you want to display additional buttons, you can set the `otherButtonTitles:` parameter like this:

```
UIAlertView *alert = [[UIAlertView alloc]
                        initWithTitle:@"Hello"
                            message:@"This is an alert view"
                            delegate:self
                    cancelButtonTitle:@"OK"
                    otherButtonTitles:@"Option 1", @"Option 2", nil];
    [alert show];
```

The alert view now displays three buttons — OK, Option 1, and Option 2. How do you know which button was tapped by the user? You can determine that by handling the relevant method(s) that will be fired by the alert view when the buttons are clicked. This set of methods is defined by the `UIAlertViewDelegate` protocol, which defines the following methods:

➤ `alertView:clickedButtonAtIndex:`

➤ `willPresentAlertView:`

➤ `didPresentAlertView:`

➤ `alertView:willDismissWithButtonIndex:`

➤ `alertView:didDismissWithButtonIndex:`

➤ `alertViewCancel:`

If you want to implement any of the methods in the `UIAlertViewDelegate` protocol, you need to ensure that your class, in this case the View Controller, conforms to this protocol. A class conforms to a protocol using angle brackets (<>), like this:

```
@interface ObjCTestViewController : UIViewController
    <UIAlertViewDelegate> {  //---this class conforms to the
                             // UIAlertViewDelegate protocol---

}

@end
```

 NOTE To conform to more than one delegate, separate the protocols with commas, such as `<UIAlertViewDelegate, UITableViewDataSource>`.

After the class conforms to a protocol, you can implement the method in your class:

```
- (void)alertView:(UIAlertView *)alertView
clickedButtonAtIndex:(NSInteger)buttonIndex {

    NSLog([NSString stringWithFormat:@"%d", buttonIndex]);

}
```

Delegate

In Objective-C, a delegate is just an object that has been assigned by another object as the object responsible for handling events. Consider the case of the UIAlertView example shown previously:

```
UIAlertView *alert = [[UIAlertView alloc]
                     initWithTitle:@"Hello"
                           message:@"This is an alert view"
                          delegate:self
                 cancelButtonTitle:@"OK"
                 otherButtonTitles:@"Option 1", @"Option 2", nil];
[alert show];
```

The initializer of the UIAlertView class includes a parameter called the delegate. Setting this parameter to self means that the current object is responsible for handling all the events fired by this instance of the UIAlertView class. If you don't need to handle events fired by this instance, you can simply set it to nil:

```
UIAlertView *alert = [[UIAlertView alloc]
                     initWithTitle:@"Hello"
                           message:@"This is an alert view"
                          delegate:nil
                 cancelButtonTitle:@"OK"
                 otherButtonTitles:@"Option 1", @"Option 2", nil];
[alert show];
```

If you have multiple buttons on the alert view and want to know which button was tapped, you need to handle the method declared in the UIAlertViewDelegate protocol. You can either implement the method in the same class in which the UIAlertView class was instantiated (as shown in the previous section), or create a new class to implement the method, like this:

```
//---SomeClass.m---
@implementation SomeClass

- (void)    alertView:(UIAlertView *)alertView
clickedButtonAtIndex:(NSInteger)buttonIndex {

    NSLog([NSString stringWithFormat:@"%d", buttonIndex]);

}
@end
```

To ensure that the alert view knows where to look for the method, create an instance of SomeClass and then set it as the delegate:

```
SomeClass *myDelegate = [[SomeClass alloc] init];

UIAlertView *alert = [[UIAlertView alloc]
                     initWithTitle:@"Hello"
                           message:@"This is an alert view"
                          delegate:myDelegate;
                 cancelButtonTitle:@"OK"
                 otherButtonTitles:@"Option 1", @"Option 2", nil];
[alert show];
```

SELECTORS

In Objective-C, a selector refers to the name used to select a method to execute for an object. It is used to identify a method. You have seen the use of a selector in some of the chapters in this book. Here is one of them:

```
//---create a Button view---
CGRect frame = CGRectMake(10, 50, 300, 50);
UIButton *button = [UIButton buttonWithType:UIButtonTypeRoundedRect];
button.frame = frame;
[button setTitle:@"Click Me, Please!"
        forState:UIControlStateNormal];
button.backgroundColor = [UIColor clearColor];
[button addTarget:self
        action:@selector(buttonClicked:)
  forControlEvents:UIControlEventTouchUpInside];
```

The preceding code shows that you are dynamically creating a `UIButton` object. In order to handle the event (for example, the `Touch Up Inside` event) raised by the button, you need to call the `addTarget:action:forControlEvents:` method of the `UIButton` class:

```
[button addTarget:self
        action:@selector(buttonClicked:)
  forControlEvents:UIControlEventTouchUpInside];
```

The `action:` parameter takes an argument of type `SEL` (selector). In the preceding code, you pass in the name of the method that you have defined — `buttonClicked:` — which is defined within the class:

```
-(IBAction) buttonClicked: (id) sender {
    //...
}
```

Alternatively, you can create an object of type `SEL` and then instantiate it by using the `NSSelectorFromString` function (which takes a string containing the method name):

```
NSString *nameOfMethod = @"buttonClicked:";
SEL methodName = NSSelectorFromString(nameOfMethod);
```

The call to the `addTarget:action:forControlEvents:` method now looks like this:

```
[button addTarget:self
        action:methodName
  forControlEvents:UIControlEventTouchUpInside];
```

 NOTE When naming a selector, be sure to specify the full name of the method. For example, if a method name has one or more parameters, you need to add a ":" in the sector, such as the following:

```
NSString *nameOfMethod = @"someMethod:withPara1:andPara2:";
```

NOTE *Because Objective-C is an extension of C, it is common to see C functions interspersed throughout your Objective-C application. C functions use parentheses () to pass in arguments for parameters.*

CATEGORIES

A category in Objective-C enables you to add methods to an existing class without the need to subclass it. You can also use a category to override the implementation of an existing class.

NOTE *In some languages (such as C#), a category is known as an extension method.*

For example, imagine you want to test whether a string contains a valid e-mail address. You can add an `isEmail` method to the `NSString` class so that you can call the `isEmail` method on any `NSString` instance, like this:

```
NSString *email = @"weimenglee@gmail.com";
if ([email isEmail]) {
    //...
}
```

To do so, simply create a new class file and code it as follows:

```
//---Utils.h---
#import <Foundation/Foundation.h>

//---NSString is the class you are extending---
@interface NSString (Utilities)

//---the method you are adding to the NSString class---
-(BOOL) isEmail;

@end
```

Basically, it looks the same as declaring a new class except that it does not inherit from any other class. The `stringUtils` is a name that identifies the category you are adding, and you can use any name you want.

Next, you need to implement the method(s) you are adding:

```
//---Utils.m---
#import "Utils.h"

@implementation NSString (Utilities)

- (BOOL) isEmail {
```

```
NSString *emailRegEx =
@"(?:[a-z0-9!#$%\\&'*+/=?\\^_`{|}~-]+(?:\\.[a-z0-9!#$%\\&'*+/=?\\^_`{|}"
@"~-]+)*|\"(?:[\\x01-\\x08\\x0b\\x0c\\x0e-\\x1f\\x21\\x23-\\x5b\\x5d-\\"
@"x7f]|\\\\[\\x01-\\x09\\x0b\\x0c\\x0e-\\x7f])*\")@(?:(?:[a-z0-9](?:[a-"
@"z0-9-]*[a-z0-9])?\\.)+[a-z0-9](?:[a-z0-9-]*[a-z0-9])?|\\[(?:(?:25[0-5"
@"]|2[0-4][0-9]|[01]?[0-9][0-9]?)\\.){3}(?:25[0-5]|2[0-4][0-9]|[01]?[0-"
@"9][0-9]?|[a-z0-9-]*[a-z0-9]:(?:[\\x01-\\x08\\x0b\\x0c\\x0e-\\x1f\\x21"
@"-\\x5a\\x53-\\x7f]|\\\\[\\x01-\\x09\\x0b\\x0c\\x0e-\\x7f])+)\\])";

NSPredicate *regExPredicate = [NSPredicate
                    predicateWithFormat:@"SELF MATCHES %@",
                    emailRegEx];

return [regExPredicate evaluateWithObject:self];
}

@end
```

> **NOTE** The code for validating an e-mail address using a regular expression is adapted from http://cocoawithlove.com/2009/06/verifying-that-string-is-email-address.html.

You can then test for the validity of an e-mail address using the newly added method:

```
NSString *email = @"weimenglee@gmail.com";
if ([email isEmail])
    NSLog(@"Valid email");
else
    NSLog(@"Invalid email");
```

Answers to Exercises

This appendix provides the solutions for the end-of-chapter exercises located in Chapters 2–21 (there are no exercises in Chapter 1).

CHAPTER 2 EXERCISE SOLUTIONS

Answer to Question 1

The minimum image size you should design is 57 × 57 pixels (or 114 × 114 pixels for high resolution). It is OK to design a larger image because the iPhone automatically resizes it for you. In general, try to design a larger image because doing so prepares your application for the newer devices that Apple may roll out.

Answer to Question 2

The easiest way to add a launch image is to add an image named `Default.png` to your Xcode project. This image must be sized 480 × 320 pixels (or 960 × 640 pixels for high resolution).

Answer to Question 3

This ensures that the image is always copied into the project folder. If not, Xcode only makes a reference to the image; it is not physically in the project folder.

CHAPTER 3 EXERCISE SOLUTIONS

Answer to Question 1

In the .h file:

```
#import <UIKit/UIKit.h>

@interface OutletsAndActionsViewController : UIViewController
{
    //---declaring the outlet---
    IBOutlet UITextField *txtName;
}

//---expose the outlet as a property---
@property (nonatomic, retain) UITextField *txtName;

@end
```

In the .m file:

```
#import "OutletsAndActionsViewController.h"

@implementation OutletsAndActionsViewController

//---synthesize the property---
@synthesize txtName;

- (void)dealloc {
    //---release the outlet---
    [txtName release];
    [super dealloc];
}
```

Answer to Question 2

In the .h file:

```
#import <UIKit/UIKit.h>

@interface OutletsAndActionsViewController : UIViewController
{
    //---declaring the outlet---
    IBOutlet UITextField *txtName;
}

//---expose the outlet as a property---
@property (nonatomic, retain) UITextField *txtName;

//---declaring the action---
-(IBAction) btnClicked:(id) sender;

@end
```

In the .m file:

```
@implementation OutletsAndActionsViewController

-(IBAction) btnClicked:(id) sender {
    //---action implementation here---
}
```

Answer to Question 3

Use the alert view when you simply want to notify the user when something happens. Use an action sheet when the user needs to make a selection, usually from a set of options.

Answer to Question 4

```
//---create a Button view---
frame = CGRectMake(10, 70, 300, 50);
UIButton *button = [UIButton buttonWithType:UIButtonTypeRoundedRect];
button.frame = frame;
[button setTitle:@"Click Me, Please!" forState:UIControlStateNormal];
button.backgroundColor = [UIColor clearColor];
button.tag = 2000;
[button addTarget:self
           action:@selector(buttonClicked:)
 forControlEvents:UIControlEventTouchUpInside];
```

CHAPTER 4 EXERCISE SOLUTIONS

Answer to Question 1

```
mySecondViewController = [[MySecondViewController alloc]
                          initWithNibName:@"MySecondViewController"
                                   bundle:nil];
```

Answer to Question 2

```
- (void)viewDidLoad {
    //---create a CGRect for the positioning---
    CGRect frame = CGRectMake(20, 10, 280, 50);

    //---create a Label view---
    label = [[[UILabel alloc] initWithFrame:frame] autorelease];
    label.textAlignment = UITextAlignmentCenter;
    label.font = [UIFont fontWithName:@"Verdana" size:20];
    label.text = @"This is a label";

    //---create a Button view---
    frame = CGRectMake(20, 60, 280, 50);
    button = [UIButton buttonWithType:UIButtonTypeRoundedRect];
```

```
        button.frame = frame;
        [button setTitle:@"OK" forState:UIControlStateNormal];
        button.backgroundColor = [UIColor clearColor];

        //---add the views to the View window---
        [self.view addSubview:label];
        [self.view addSubview:button];
        [super viewDidLoad];
    }
```

Answer to Question 3

```
        //---add the action handler and set current class as target---
        [button addTarget:self
                   action:@selector(buttonClicked:)
         forControlEvents:UIControlEventTouchUpInside];

        ...
        ...

-(IBAction) buttonClicked: (id) sender{
    //--add implementation here--
}
```

Answer to Question 4

In the `HelloWorldViewController.m` file, add the following code:

```
-(IBAction) buttonClicked: (id) sender{
    UIAlertView *alert =
        [[UIAlertView alloc] initWithTitle:@"Button Clicked!"
                                   message:@"Button was clicked!"
                                  delegate:self
                         cancelButtonTitle:@"OK"
                         otherButtonTitles:nil];
    [alert show];
    [alert release];
}
```

CHAPTER 5 EXERCISE SOLUTIONS

Answer to Question 1

To detect the platform on which your application is running, use the `UI_USER_INTERFACE_IDIOM()` function.

Answer to Question 2

The different values for the Targeted Device Family setting are iPhone, iPad, and iPhone/iPad.

CHAPTER 6 EXERCISE SOLUTIONS

Answer to Question 1

First, handle the `Did End on Exit` event (or implement the `textFieldShouldReturn:` method in the View Controller). Then call the `resignFirstResponder` method of the `UITextField` outlet to release its first-responder status.

Answer to Question 2

Register for the notifications `UIKeyboardDidShowNotification` and `UIKeyboardDidHideNotification`.

Answer to Question 3

```
NSDictionary* info = [notification userInfo];

//---obtain the size of the keyboard---
NSValue *aValue = [info objectForKey:UIKeyboardFrameEndUserInfoKey];
CGRect keyboardRect =
    [self.view convertRect:[aValue CGRectValue] fromView:nil];

NSLog(@"%f", keyboardRect.size.height);
```

Answer to Question 4

Use the `UIScrollView` to contain views so that the user can scroll through them. Then, set the new size of the scroll view:

```
- (void)viewDidLoad {
    //---set this to the screen size---
    scrollView.frame = CGRectMake(0, 0, 320, 460);

    //---set this to the final size of the scroll view---
    [scrollView setContentSize:CGSizeMake(320, 713)];

    [super viewDidLoad];
}
```

CHAPTER 7 EXERCISE SOLUTIONS

Answer to Question 1

```
- (BOOL)shouldAutorotateToInterfaceOrientation:
(UIInterfaceOrientation)interfaceOrientation {
    // Return YES for supported orientations
    return (interfaceOrientation ==
            UIInterfaceOrientationLandscapeRight ||
        interfaceOrientation ==
            UIInterfaceOrientationLandscapeLeft);
}
```

Answer to Question 2

The `frame` property defines the rectangle occupied by the view, with respect to its superview (the view that contains it). Using the `frame` property enables you to set the positioning and size of a view. Besides using the `frame` property, you can also use the `center` property, which sets the center of the view, also with respect to its superview. You usually use the `center` property when you are performing some animation and just want to change the position of a view.

CHAPTER 8 EXERCISE SOLUTIONS

Answer to Question 1

The two protocols are `UITableViewDataSource` and `UITableViewDelegate`.

The `UITableViewDataSource` protocol contains events that you can implement to populate the Table view with the various items.

The `UITableViewDelegate` protocol contains events that you can implement to handle the selection of rows in a Table view.

Answer to Question 2

To add an index list to your Table view, you need to implement the `sectionIndexTitlesForTableView:` method.

Answer to Question 3

The three disclosure and checkmark accessories are as follows:

➤ `UITableViewCellAccessoryDetailDisclosureButton`

➤ `UITableViewCellAccessoryCheckmark`

➤ `UITableViewCellAccessoryDisclosureIndicator`

The `UITableViewCellAccessoryDetailDisclosureButton` image handles a user's tap event. The event name is `tableView:accessoryButtonTappedForRowWithIndexPath:`.

CHAPTER 9 EXERCISE SOLUTIONS

Answer to Question 1

To retrieve the values for preferences settings, you use the `objectForKey:` method. To save the values for preferences settings, you use the `setObject:forKey:` method.

Answer to Question 2

You can either remove the application from the device or Simulator, or you can remove the file ending with *application_name*.`plist` in the application folder within the Simulator.

CHAPTER 10 EXERCISE SOLUTIONS

Answer to Question 1

The three folders are Documents, Library, and tmp. Developers can use the Documents folder to store application-related data. Files saved in the Documents folder are backed up by iTunes. The Library folder stores application-specific settings, such as those used by the `NSUserDefaults` class, as well as snapshots of the application's screen. The tmp folder can be used to store temporary data that will not be backed up by iTunes.

Answer to Question 2

The `NSDictionary` class creates a dictionary object whose items are immutable; that is, after it is populated, you can no longer add items to it. The `NSMutableDictionary` class, conversely, creates a mutable dictionary object that allows items to be added to it after it is loaded.

Answer to Question 3

Location of the Documents folder on a real device:

```
/private/var/mobile/Applications/<application_id>/Documents/
```

Location of the tmp folder on a real device:

```
/private/var/mobile/Applications/<application_id>/tmp/
```

Answer to Question 4

The class is `UIDocumentInteractionController`.

Answer to Question 5

The key is `UIFileSharingEnabled`.

Answer to Question 6

The key is `CFBundleDocumentTypes`.

CHAPTER 11 EXERCISE SOLUTIONS

Answer to Question 1

The `sqlite3_exec()` function is actually a wrapper for the three functions `sqlite3_prepare()`; `sqlite3_step()`; and `sqlite3_finalize()`. For nonquery SQL statements (such as for creating tables, inserting rows, and so on), it is always better to use the `sqlite3_exec()` function.

Answer to Question 2

To obtain a C-style string from an NSString object, use the UTF8String method from the NSString class.

Answer to Question 3

```
-(void) getAllRowsFromTableNamed: (NSString *) tableName {
    //---retrieve rows---
    NSString *qsql = [NSString stringWithFormat:@"SELECT * FROM %@",
                        tableName];

    sqlite3_stmt *statement;
    if (sqlite3_prepare_v2( db, [qsql UTF8String], -1,
        &statement, nil) == SQLITE_OK) {
        while (sqlite3_step(statement) == SQLITE_ROW) {
            char *field1 = (char *) sqlite3_column_text(statement, 0);
            NSString *field1Str =
                [[NSString alloc] initWithUTF8String: field1];

            char *field2 = (char *) sqlite3_column_text(statement, 1);
            NSString *field2Str =
                [[NSString alloc] initWithUTF8String: field2];

            NSString *str = [[NSString alloc] initWithFormat:@"%@ - %@",
                                field1Str, field2Str];
            NSLog(@"%@", str);

            [field1Str release];
            [field2Str release];
            [str release];
        }

        //---deletes the compiled statement from memory---
        sqlite3_finalize(statement);
    }
}
```

CHAPTER 12 EXERCISE SOLUTIONS

Answer to Question 1

The method is URLForUbiquityContainerIdentifier:.

Answer to Question 2

The advantage is that all the files stored in the Documents folder are exposed in the Settings ⇨ iCloud ⇨ Storage & Backup ⇨ Manage Storage page. You can manage the files directly using this page.

Answer to Question 3

Storing key-value data on iCloud ensures that application-specific data can be accessed by the application running on different devices. This enables users to enjoy a consistent, synchronized experience no matter where they access your application.

CHAPTER 13 EXERCISE SOLUTIONS

Answer to Question 1

The three affine transformations are translation, rotation, and scaling.

Answer to Question 2

The only way to pause the `NSTimer` object is to call its invalidate method. To resume it, you have to create a new `NSTimer` object.

Answer to Question 3

The `animatingWithDuration:animations:` method of the `UIView` class enables you to enclose a block of code that causes visual changes to your views, such that the changes in visual appearance will be animated, and not appear choppily.

Answer to Question 4

You can play a video using the `MPMoviePlayerController` class.

CHAPTER 14 EXERCISE SOLUTIONS

Answer to Question 1

For invoking Safari:

```
@"http://www.apple.com"
```

For invoking Mail:

```
@"mailto:?to=weimenglee@gmail.com&subject=Hello&body=Content of email"
```

For invoking SMS:

```
@"sms:96924065"
```

For invoking Phone:

```
@"tel:1234567890"
```

Answer to Question 2

The class name is `UIImagePickerController`.

Answer to Question 3

The class name is `MFMailComposeViewController`.

Answer to Question 4

The class name is `MFMessageComposeViewController`.

CHAPTER 15 EXERCISE SOLUTIONS

Answer to Question 1

The class is `CMMotionManager`.

Answer to Question 2

The three events are as follows:

- ➤ `motionBegan:`
- ➤ `motionEnded:`
- ➤ `motionCancelled:`

CHAPTER 16 EXERCISE SOLUTIONS

Answer to Question 1

The four ways are SOAP 1.1/1.2, HTTP GET, HTTP POST, and JSON.

Answer to Question 2

The three key events are as follows:

- ➤ `connection:didReceiveResponse:`
- ➤ `connection:didReceiveData:`
- ➤ `connectionDidFinishLoading:`

Answer to Question 3

The `NSXmlParser` class fires off the following events as it parses the content of an XML document:

- ➤ `parser:didStartElement:namespaceURI:qualifiedName:attributes:`
- ➤ `parser:foundCharacters:`
- ➤ `parser:didEndElement:namespaceURI:qualifiedName:`

Answer to Question 4

The class is `TWTweetComposeViewController`.

CHAPTER 17 EXERCISE SOLUTIONS

Answer to Question 1

The class is `GKPeerPickerController`.

Answer to Question 2

The class is `GKSession`.

Answer to Question 3

Call the `startVoiceChatWithParticipantID:error:` method from the `GKVoiceChatService` class.

Answer to Question 4

On the initiator, call the `voiceChatService:sendData:toParticipantID:` method defined in the `GKVoiceChatClient` protocol.

On the receiver, call the `receivedData:fromParticipantID:` method defined in the `GKVoiceChatClient` protocol.

CHAPTER 18 EXERCISE SOLUTIONS

Answer to Question 1

The class is `NSNetService`.

Answer to Question 2

The class is `NSNetServiceBrowser`.

Answer to Question 3

The method name is `netServiceBrowser:didFindService:moreComing:`.

Answer to Question 4

The method name is `netServiceBrowser:didRemoveService:moreComing:`.

CHAPTER 19 EXERCISE SOLUTIONS

Answer to Question 1

The two certificates are the development certificate and the SSL certificate for the provider application.

Answer to Question 2

This ensures that you have the private and public key pair of the certificate.

Answer to Question 3

The method is `registerForRemoteNotificationTypes:`.

Answer to Question 4

The device token is used to uniquely identify the device of the recipient of the push notification, and is needed by the APNs server.

Answer to Question 5

The event is `application:didReceiveRemoteNotification:`.

CHAPTER 20 EXERCISE SOLUTIONS

Answer to Question 1

The property is `showsUserLocation`.

Answer to Question 2

The protocol is `MKMapViewDelegate`.

Answer to Question 3

The method is `startUpdatingLocation`.

Answer to Question 4

The method is `startUpdatingHeading`.

Answer to Question 5

The class is `CLGeocoder`.

CHAPTER 21 EXERCISE SOLUTIONS

Answer to Question 1

The three types of applications are audio, location, and VOIP.

Answer to Question 2

At the time of writing, multi-tasking is supported only on iPod touch (third generation), iPhone 3GS, and iPhone 4.

Answer to Question 3

You use the `startUpdatingLocation` method to keep track of changes in location coordinates (using a combination of GPS, cell tower triangulation, and WiFi triangulation), while the `startMonitoringSignificantLocationChanges` method monitors for significant location changes (using cell tower triangulation) and notifies you only when the cell tower changes.

Answer to Question 4

Apple Push Notification service is a mobile service provided by Apple. It uses push technology to forward notification messages to the iPhone/iPod touch/iPad through a constantly connected IP connection. To use this service, an application provider must send a message to Apple's server, which in turn sends a notification to the application on the user's device.

Local notification, conversely, is a messaging service that can be used locally on the device. Applications running on an iPhone/iPod touch/iPad can schedule notifications to be fired at a scheduled time.

INDEX

V

Z